Study Guide Plus

Gwendolyn E. Nyden
Oakton Community College

Sinikka Dixon
Canadian University College

Sociology

A Down-to-Earth Approach

Fourth Canadian Edition

James M. Henslin
Southern Illinois University

Dan Glenday
Brock University

Ann Duffy
Brock University

Norene Pupo
York University

Toronto

ISBN 0-205-46012-7

Acquisitions Editor: Patty Riediger
Sponsoring Editor: Carolin Sweig
Developmental Editor: Joel Gladstone
Production Editor: Richard di Santo
Copy Editor: Emmanuelle Dauplay
Production Manager: Wendy Moran

4 5   11 10 09 08

Printed and bound in Canada.

TABLE OF CONTENTS

INTRODUCTION

Welcome to Sociology! You are about to embark on a fascinating journey in which you will discover all sorts of new and interesting information about yourself and the world around you. This study guide has been prepared to accompany *Sociology: A Down-to-Earth Approach,* Fourth Canadian Edition, by James M. Henslin, Dan Glenday, Ann Duffy, and Norene Pupo.

The study guide includes the following:

- A **Chapter Summary** that summarizes the main ideas found in the chapter.
- A set of **Learning Objectives** that provides statements concerning the main ideas of the chapter. If you want to check your responses, refer back to the page numbers listed with each question.
- A **Chapter Outline** that provides a point-by-point overview of the theories and substantive topics of the chapter.
- A listing of **Key Terms to Define** that contains all of the **sociological concepts** that are introduced within the chapter.
- A listing of **Key People** that includes some of the major sociologists whose work is discussed within the chapter. In some cases, these are early sociologists who contributed insights in theory and research to the discipline; in other cases, they are contemporary sociologists who are currently doing research and developing theory on the subject.
- A **Self-Test** that provides you with an opportunity to see how much of the information you have retained. Each Self-Test includes **multiple choice, true/false, fill-in**, **matching,** and **essay** questions.
- A section titled **Down-to-Earth Sociology** in a box that asks questions about the material you have read so that you can relate it to your own life and the world with which you are familiar. Remember: There is not necessarily a right or wrong answer for these; rather, they are designed to get your opinion, based on your understanding of the facts you have read.
- An **Answer Key** that provides answers for all of the questions in the Self-Test. Check your answers against this; if you got the question wrong, refer back to the pages in the textbook and read those again.

The study guide is intended to be used together with the text to maximize your mastery of the material. Here are some suggestions for making the best use of the resources in both the text and the study guide:

- Before reading each chapter, **refer to the Chapter Summary and Learning Objectives** that are found in the **Study Guide**. The Chapter Summary will provide you with a capsule statement of what the chapter is about, and the **Learning Objectives** will tell you how you should be focusing your attention. Then read the textbook.

- Rather than plunging headlong into the chapter, **take a few minutes and orient yourself**. Start with the chapter title. This tells you what broad area of sociology will be discussed. Keep the title in mind as you read through the chapter and try to create a mental picture of how the various parts of the chapter fit together within this broad area.
- **Approach each chapter one section at a time.** Use the section headings to pose questions that you can ask yourself when you finish reading the section. As you finish a section, go back to the **Learning Objectives in the Study Guide** and try to answer the statement(s) that apply. If you can provide an answer, then proceed to the next section; if you can't, go back to the textbook and review the section you've just read.
- **Remember to read the boxed texts;** these pertain to the material in the body of the textbook and are included to give you insights into Canadian society as well as societies around the world. They are designed to bring sociology alive for you.

Once you feel you have achieved some familiarity with the material, go back to the study guide and follow these steps:

- **Check the list of Key Terms to Define.** Try and define each word and think of an example. Then check the definitions that are provided within each chapter of the **Study Guide** to see if you are correct. If you need help thinking of an example, refer back to the textbook chapter.
- **Check the list of Key People.** See how many you know and whether or not you can identify their contribution to sociology. If you can't, go back to the textbook and locate them within the chapter. (A quick way to do this is to refer to the **Index** at the back of the textbook, and then go directly to the page listed.)
- **Take the Self-Test.** Mark those questions that you got wrong, and go back to the text to find the correct answer. Then a few days later try them again to see if you've now mastered the material. Use the self-test to review the material just before a test.

We hope you have found the preceding tips useful. If you begin to incorporate some of them into your regular study routines, attend class regularly, take good notes on material covered in class, read each chapter (ideally before the material is presented in class and then review the chapter as you are going over the material in class), and use the resources in the Study Guide, you should finish the semester with good grades and a better understanding not only of the discipline of sociology, but of yourself and your social world. We hope that you will enjoy your adventure and find that this subject opens new vistas of understanding to you. **Good luck!**

Gwen Nyden, Ph.D.

Oakton Community College
Des Plaines, Illinois

Sinikka Dixon, Ph.D.

Canadian University College
Lacombe, Alberta

CHAPTER 1
THE SOCIOLOGICAL PERSPECTIVE

CHAPTER SUMMARY

- The sociological perspective stresses the social contexts in which people live and examines how these contexts influence their lives.

- Sociology is the scientific study of society and human behaviour and, as such, is one of the social sciences that study human relationships, in contrast to the natural sciences which attempt to understand the world of nature.

- Although it is difficult to state precisely when it began, sociology emerged during the upheavals of the Industrial Revolution. Early sociologists such as Auguste Comte, Karl Marx, Emile Durkheim, and Max Weber focused on how the sweeping social changes brought about by the Industrial Revolution affected human behaviour.

- Sociologists agree on the ideal of objectivity, but disagree concerning the proper purposes and uses of sociology. Some believe its purpose should be only to advance understanding of human behaviour; others, that its goal should be to reform harmful social arrangements.

- Weber believed that sociologists must try to see the world from another's perspective in order to understand their behaviour (*Verstehen*); Durkheim stressed the importance of uncovering the objective social conditions that influence behaviour (social facts).

- In the early years of sociology, only a few wealthy women received an advanced education. Harriet Martineau was an Englishwoman who wrote about social life in Great Britain and the United States and published a book entitled *Society in America*.

- In North America, departments of sociology began to be established at the end of the nineteenth century. In the early years, the contributions of women and minorities were largely ignored.

- A theory is a general statement about how sets of facts are related to one another. Because no one theory encompasses all of reality, the major theoretical perspectives that sociologists use are: (1) symbolic interactionism, concentrating on the meanings that underlie people's lives, usually focuses on the micro level; (2) functional analysis, stressing that society is made up of various parts which, when working properly, contribute to the stability of society, focuses on the macro level; (3) conflict theory, emphasizing social inequalities and seeing the basis of social life as a competitive struggle to gain control over scarce resources, also focuses on the macro level; (4) feminist theories, which examine the social, historical, and cultural aspects of gender and gender relations, focusing on both the micro- and macro- levels; (5) postmodernism, focusing on language and culture on the macro-level and describing the socially constructed postmodern individual on the micro-level; (6) an emergent queer theory, focusing on individual sexual identities on the micro-level; and (7) critical race theory, focusing on discrimination and the law on the macro-level.

- Pure sociology is research whose only purpose is to make discoveries, while applied sociology is the application of sociology to solve social problems in a variety of settings from the workplace to the family.

LEARNING OBJECTIVES

As you read Chapter 1, use these learning objectives to organize your notes. After completing your reading, briefly state an answer to each of the objectives, and review the text pages in parentheses.

1. Explain the sociological perspective and discuss the contribution that it makes to our understanding of human behaviour, including the growing global context of our lives. (2-3)
2. Define sociology and compare it with the other social sciences. (3-5)
3. Discuss how and why sociology emerged as a science in the middle of the nineteenth century in Europe. (6-7)
4. Explain each of the following sociologists' contributions to the development of sociology: Auguste Comte, Karl Marx, Emile Durkheim, and Max Weber. (7-10)
5. State the key issues in the debate about the proper role of values in sociology. (10-11)
6. Explain what Max Weber meant by *Verstehen* and Emile Durkheim by social facts and how these two can fit together. (11)
7. Explain the absence of women in the early years of sociology. (11-12)
8. Trace the development of sociology in Canada and the United States from its origins in the late nineteenth century to its present-day perspectives. (12-14)
9. Identify the contributions that each of the following made to the development of sociology in North America: Leon Gérin, Carl Dawson, Harold Innis, Dorothy Smith, Margrit Eichler, Albion Small, Jane Addams, W.E.B. Du Bois, Talcott Parsons, Robert Merton, C. Wright Mills. (12-14)
10. Explain the chief differences in the major theoretical perspectives: symbolic interactionism, functional analysis, conflict theory, feminist theories, postmodernism, and the two emergent theories, queer theory and critical race theory. (15-19)
11. Compare micro-level and macro-level analysis and state which level of analysis is utilized by each of the major theoretical perspectives. (15, 19-20)
12. Describe the three phases of sociology and note the differences in pure, applied, and clinical sociology. (20-21)

CHAPTER OUTLINE

I. **The Sociological Perspective**
   A. This perspective is important because it provides a different way of looking at familiar worlds. It allows us to gain a new vision of social life.
   B. This perspective stresses the broader social context of behaviour by looking at individuals' social location—employment, income, education, gender, age, and race—and by considering external influences—people's experiences—which are internalized and become part of a person's thinking and motivations. We are able to see the links between what people do and the social settings that shape their behaviour.
   C. This perspective enables us to analyze and understand both the forces that contribute to the emergence and growth of the global village and our unique experiences in our own smaller corners of this village.

II.   **Sociology and the Other Sciences**
   A. Sociology is defined as "the scientific study of society and human behaviour."
      1. Science is the systematic methods used to obtain knowledge and the knowledge obtained by those methods.
      2. Science can be divided into the natural sciences and the social sciences.
   B. The natural sciences attempt to comprehend, explain, and predict events in our natural environment.
   C. Social sciences attempt to objectively study the social world. Like the natural sciences, the social sciences are divided into specialized fields based on their subject matter.
      1. Political science focuses on politics or government.
      2. Economics analyzes the production, distribution, and allocation of the material goods and services of a society.
      3. Anthropology attempts to understand culture (a people's total way of life) by focusing primarily on preliterate people.
      4. Psychology concentrates on processes that occur within the individual.
      5. Sociology is the study of human social behaviour, especially the investigation of the origins, classifications, institutions, and development of human society on a global level.

III.   **The Development of Sociology**
   A. Sociology developed in the middle of the nineteenth century when European social observers began to use scientific methods to test their ideas. Three factors led to its development:
      1. the social upheaval in Europe as a result of the Industrial Revolution and the political revolutions in America and France;
      2. the development of imperialism—as the Europeans conquered other nations, they came in contact with different cultures and began to ask why cultures varied; and
      3. the success of the natural sciences, which created a desire to apply scientific methods in order to find answers for the questions being raised about the social world as well.
   B. Auguste Comte coined the term "sociology" and suggested the use of positivism—applying the scientific approach to the social world—but he did not utilize this approach himself.
   C. Karl Marx, founder of the conflict perspective, believed that class conflict—the struggle between the proletariat and the bourgeoisie—was the key to human history.
   D. Emile Durkheim played an important role in the development of sociology.
      1. One of his primary goals was to get sociology recognized as a separate academic discipline.
      2. He was interested in understanding the social factors that influence individual behaviour; he studied suicide rates among different groups and concluded that social integration, the degree to which people are tied to their social group, was a key social factor in suicide. He further classified suicide as three different types—egoistic, altruistic, and anomic suicide.

   3. Durkheim's third concern was that social research be practical; sociologists should not only diagnose the causes of social problems but should also develop solutions for them.

E. Max Weber defined religion as a central force in social change (i.e., Protestantism encourages greater economic development and was the central factor in the rise of capitalism in some countries).

IV.   The Role of Values in Social Research

A. Max Weber advocated that sociological research should be value free—personal values or biases should not influence social research—and objective—totally neutral.

   1. Sociologists agree that objectivity is a proper goal but acknowledge that no one can escape values entirely.
   2. Replication—repeating a study to see if the same results are found—is one means to avoid the distortions that values can cause.

B. The proper purposes and uses of sociology are argued among sociologists.

   1. Some take the position that the proper role of sociology is to advance understanding of social life, while others believe that it is the responsibility of sociologists to explore harmful social arrangements of society.
   2. Some feel that the knowledge gained by social research belongs to the scientific community and the world, to be used by anyone for any purpose, while others feel that the knowledge should be used to reform society.

V.   *Verstehen* and Social Facts

A. Weber argued that sociologists should use *Verstehen* ("to grasp by insight") in order to see beyond the social facts to the meanings that people attach to their own behaviour.

B. Durkheim believed that social facts, patterns of behaviour that characterize a social group, reflect some underlying condition of society and should be used to interpret other social facts.

C. Social facts and *Verstehen* fit together because they reinforce each other; sociologists use *Verstehen* in order to interpret social facts.

VI.   Sexism in Early Sociology

A. In the early years of sociology, the field was dominated by men because rigidly defined social roles and the realities of economic life prevented most women from pursuing an education.

   1. Women were supposed to devote themselves to the four K's—*Kirche, Kuchen, Kinder, und Kleider* (church, cooking, children, and clothes).
   2. At the same time, a few women from wealthy families managed to get an education; a few even studied sociology although sexism in the universities stopped them from earning advanced degrees, becoming professors, or having their research recognized.

B. Harriet Martineau studied social life in both Great Britain and the United States, publishing *Society in America* decades before Durkheim and Weber were even born. While her original research has been largely ignored by the discipline, she is known for her translations of Comte's ideas into English.

VII. **Sociology in Canada and the United States**
  A. Sociology in Canada was influenced by both the British and American traditions. The first program in sociology in Canada was at McGill University (1922).
    1. American sociologists at the University of Chicago influenced the development of sociology at McGill, under the direction of Carl Dawson.
    2. The other predominant approach to the development of sociology in Canada was the British tradition, which influenced sociology at the University of Toronto.
    3. At the University of Toronto, Harold Innis and Samuel Clark studied the economic history of Canada and illustrated the ways in which Canada developed as a distinct economy and society.
    4. Contemporary feminist scholars such as Margrit Eichler and Dorothy Smith are widely recognized for their work in nonsexist research methods and studies of feminist theory.
  B. The first departments of sociology in the U.S. were at the University of Kansas (1889) and the University of Chicago (1892);
    1. Albion Small, founder of the Department of Sociology at the University of Chicago, also established the *American Journal of Sociology*.
    2. Other early sociologists from the University of Chicago were Robert E. Park, Ernest Burgess, and George Herbert Mead.
  C. The situation of women in North America was similar to that of European women and their contributions to sociology met a similar fate. Denied a role in the universities, many turned to social activism, working with the poor and regarded as social workers.
    1. Jane Addams is an example; she founded Hull House, a settlement house for the poor, and worked to bridge the gap between the powerful and the powerless.
    2. She invited sociologists from nearby University of Chicago to visit.
    3. She is the only sociologist to have won the Nobel Peace Prize, being awarded this in 1931.
  D. African American professionals also faced problems.
    1. W.E.B. Du Bois conducted extensive research on race relations in the U.S., publishing a book a year on this subject between 1896 and 1914.
    2. Despite his accomplishments he encountered prejudice and discrimination in his professional and personal life, helping to found the National Association for the Advancement of Colored People (NAACP).
    3. Until recently, his contributions to sociology were overlooked.
  E. Many early North American sociologists combined the role of sociologist with that of social reformer. For example, University of Chicago sociologists Park and Burgess studied many urban problems and offered suggestions on how to alleviate them.

F. In the 1940s, as sociologists became more concerned with establishing sociology as an academic discipline, the emphasis shifted from social reform to social theory.
1. Talcott Parsons developed abstract models of society to show how the parts of society harmoniously work together.
2. Countering this development was C. Wright Mills, who urged sociologists to get back to social reform.
3. Robert K. Merton stressed the development of middle-range theories— explanations of human behaviour that go beyond the particular observation or research but avoid sweeping generalizations that attempt to explain everything.
G. Sociology in North America today is not dominated by any one theoretical orientation or single concern.
1. Social activism remains an option.
2. Sociologists are employed in teaching, the government, the private sector in management and planning positions, and in a number of other fields.

VIII. Theoretical Perspectives in Sociology

A. Theory is a general statement about how some parts of the world fit together and how they work; it is an explanation of how two or more facts are related to one another. Sociologists use different theoretical perspectives to understand social behaviour.
B. Symbolic interactionism views symbols, things to which we attach meaning, as the basis of social life.
1. Through the use of symbols people are able to define relationships to others, to coordinate actions with others, making social life possible, and to develop a sense of self.
2. A symbolic interactionist studying divorce would focus on the changing meaning of marriage, family, and work and how they have contributed to the increase in the rate of divorce in our society.
C. The central idea of functional analysis is that society is a whole unit, made up of interrelated parts that work together.
1. To understand society, we must look at both structure, how the parts of society fit together to make up the whole, and function, how each part contributes to society.
2. Robert Merton used the term function to refer to the beneficial consequences of people's actions to keep society stable and dysfunction to refer to consequences that undermine stability. Functions can be either manifest (actions that are intended) or latent (unintended consequences).
3. In trying to explain divorce, a functionalist would look at how industrialization and urbanization both contributed to the changing function of marriage and the family.
D. According to conflict theory, society is viewed as composed of groups competing for scarce resources.
1. Karl Marx focused on struggles between the bourgeoisie, the small group of capitalists who own the means of production, and the proletariat, the masses of workers exploited by the capitalists.

      2.   Contemporary conflict theorists have expanded this perspective to include conflict in all relations of power and authority.

      3.   Divorce is seen as the outcome of the shifting balance of power within a family; as women have gained power and try to address inequalities in their relationships, men resist.

E. Feminist theories study the social, historical, and cultural aspects of gender and gender relations.

      1.   Marxist–Feminist theories relate gender inequalities in society to economic inequities, specifically the property relations of capitalism.

      2.   Liberal Feminists claim that legal restraints and customs are at the root of the subservience of women in society.

      3.   Non-Marxist Feminist theories focus on the ways in which women are oppressed by patriarchy, a system of power, dominance, hierarchy, and competition.

F. Postmodernism emphasizes the complex patterns of social and cultural difference in contemporary societies.

      1.   Postmodernism views present-day society as a cultural collage where people can live in their own cultural and social spaces.

      2.   Jean Baudrillard studies the ways in which symbols have become detached, or autonomous, from the real world.

G. The perspectives differ in their level of analysis. Functionalists and conflict theorists provide macro-level analysis because they examine the large-scale patterns of society. Symbolic interactionists carry out micro-level analysis because they focus on the small-scale patterns of social life.

H. Each perspective provides a different and often sharply contrasting picture of the world. However, sociologists often use several perspectives because no one theory or level of analysis encompasses all of reality.

I. Queer theory, an emergent theory, has become associated with gay and lesbian studies—a recent academic achievement spanning the social sciences and humanities. Queer theory deliberately challenges all notions of a fixed identity. Therefore, instead of viewing sex, gender, and desire as a continuum, queer theory smashes these links.

J. Critical race theory is linked to the development of African-American legal thought in the post-civil rights era. Today it takes in the disciplines of anthropology, sociology, history, philosophy, and political science.

IX.   Applied and Clinical Sociology

A. Sociologists Paul Lazarsfeld and Jeffrey Reitz divide sociology into three phases.

      1.   In the first phase the primary concern of sociologists was making the world a better place.

      2.   During the second phase sociologists sought to establish sociology as a respected field of knowledge.

      3.   In the third (current) phase there has been an attempt to merge sociological knowledge and practical work.

B. Applied sociology is the attempt to blend sociological knowledge and practical results. It refers to the use of sociology to solve problems. Applied sociologists recommend practical changes to solve problems.

    C. Clinical sociologists become directly involved in bringing about social change through work in various social settings.

    D. In the future, it is likely that applied sociology will grow, as more departments of sociology offer courses, specialties, and even internships in applied sociology.

KEY TERMS

After reading the chapter, review the definitions for each of the key terms listed below.

applied sociology: the use of sociology to solve problems—from the micro-level of family relationships to the macro-level of crime and pollution

authority: power that people consider legitimate

bourgeoisie: Karl Marx's term for capitalists; those who own the means to produce wealth

class conflict: Marx's term for the struggle between the proletariat and the bourgeoisie

conflict theory: a theoretical framework in which society is viewed as composed of groups competing for scarce resources

critical race theory: a focus on discrimination and the law on the macro-level

feminist theories: theories that examine the social, historical, and cultural aspects of gender and gender relations from Marxist, Liberal, and Non-Marxist perspective

functional analysis: a theoretical framework in which society is viewed as composed of various parts, each with a function that, when fulfilled, contributes to society's equilibrium; also known as functionalism and structural functionalism

macro-level analysis: an examination of large-scale patterns of society

micro-level analysis: an examination of small-scale patterns of society

middle-range theories: explanations of human behaviour that go beyond a particular observation or research but avoid sweeping generalizations that attempt to account for everything

natural sciences: the intellectual and academic disciplines designed to comprehend, explain, and predict events in our natural environment

nonverbal interaction: communication without words through gestures, space, silence, and so on

objectivity: total neutrality

positivism: the application of the scientific approach to the social world

postmodernism: a theoretical perspective that emphasizes the complex patterns of social and cultural difference in contemporary societies

proletariat: Marx's term for the exploited class, the mass of workers who do not own the means of production

pure or basic sociology: sociological research whose only purpose is to make discoveries about life in human groups, not to make changes in those groups

queer theory: a focus on individual sexual identity on the micro-level

replication: repeating a study in order to check the findings of a previous study

science: the application of systematic methods to obtain knowledge and the knowledge obtained by those methods

scientific method: the use of objective, systematic observations to test theories

social facts: Durkheim's term for the patterns of behaviour that characterize a social group

social integration: the degree to which people feel a part of social groups

social interaction: what people do when they are in one another's presence

social location: the group memberships that people have because of their location in history and society

social sciences: the intellectual and academic disciplines designed to understand the social world objectively by means of controlled and repeated observations

society: a term used by sociologists to refer to a group of people who share a culture and a territory

sociological perspective: an approach to understanding human behaviour by placing it within its broader social context

sociology: the scientific study of society and human behaviour

subjective meanings: the meanings that people give to their own behaviour

symbolic interactionists: theorists who view symbols—things to which we attach meaning—as the basis of social life

theory: a general statement about how some parts of the world fit together and how they work; an explanation of how two or more facts are related to one another

value free: the view that a sociologist's personal values or biases should not influence social research

Verstehen: a German word used by Weber that is perhaps best understood as "to have insight into someone's situation"

KEY PEOPLE

The following are key people in the development of sociology.

Jane Addams: Addams was the founder of Hull House—a settlement house in the immigrant community of Chicago. She invited sociologists from nearby University of Chicago to visit. In 1931 she was a winner of the Nobel Peace Prize.

Jean Baudrillard: Baudrillard is a postmodern theorist who argues that symbols have become autonomous from the real world in contemporary society.

Auguste Comte: Comte is often credited with being the founder of sociology because he was the first to suggest that the scientific method be applied to the study of the social world.

Lewis Coser: Coser pointed out that conflict is likely to develop among people in close relationships because they are connected by a network of responsibilities, power and rewards.

Ralf Dahrendorf: Dahrendorf's work is associated with the conflict perspective; he suggested that conflict is inherent in all relations that have authority.

Carl Dawson: Dawson led the development of Canada's first sociology program at McGill University. Dawson used the University of Chicago sociology program to develop sociology at McGill.

W.E.B. Du Bois: Du Bois was the first African-American to earn a doctorate at Harvard University. For most of his career he taught sociology at Atlanta University. He was concerned about social injustice, wrote about race relations, and was one of the founders of the National Association for the Advancement of Colored People.

Emile Durkheim: Durkheim was responsible for getting sociology recognized as a separate discipline. He was interested in studying how individual behaviour is shaped by social forces and in finding remedies for social ills. He stressed that sociologists should use social facts—patterns of behaviour that reflect some underlying condition of society.

Harold Innis: Innis was the head of the Department of Political Economy at the University of Toronto, where there was no independent department of sociology until the 1960s. Innis created the model of economic development known as the staples theory of international trade to explain Canada's economic history.

Paul Lazarsfeld: Along with **Jeffrey Reitz**, Lazarsfeld divided the development of sociology into three stages: (1) an initial period in which sociologists were engaged in social reform; (2) a period in which sociologists worked to have sociology established as a respected field of knowledge; and (3) the contemporary period in which sociologists are trying to merge sociological knowledge with practical work.

Harriet Martineau: An Englishwoman who studied British and U.S. social life and published *Society in America* decades before either Durkheim or Weber was born.

Karl Marx: Marx believed that social development grew out of conflict between social classes; under capitalism, this conflict was between the *bourgeoisie*—those who own the means to produce wealth—and the *proletariat*—the mass of workers. His work is associated with the conflict perspective.

George Herbert Mead: Mead was one of the founders of symbolic interactionism, a major theoretical perspective in sociology.

Robert Merton: Merton encouraged the development of middle-range theories—explanations that tie together research findings but avoid sweeping generalizations that try to account for everything. Merton contributed the terms *manifest* and *latent functions* and *dysfunctions* to the functionalist perspective.

C. Wright Mills: Mills suggested that external influences—or a person's experiences—become part of his or her thinking and motivations and explain social behaviour.

Talcott Parsons: Parsons' work dominated sociology in the 1940s-1950s. He developed abstract models of how the parts of society harmoniously work together.

John Porter: Porter was one of the leading sociologists during post-World War II period in Canada.

Albion Small: Small was the founder of the sociology department at the University of Chicago and the *American Journal of Sociology*.

Dorothy Smith: Smith is a Canadian feminist sociologist who is best known for her studies of feminist theory, in particular her work on the sociology of the "everyday world" of people's lives.

Max Weber: Weber's most important contribution to sociology was his study of the relationship between the emergence of the Protestant belief system and the rise of capitalism. He believed that sociologists should not allow their personal values to affect their social research; objectivity should become the hallmark of sociology. He argued that sociologists should use *Verstehen*—those subjective meanings that people give to their behaviour.

SELF-TEST

After completing this self-test, check your answers against the Answer Key at the back of this Study Guide and against the text on the page(s) indicated in parentheses.

MULTIPLE CHOICE QUESTIONS

1. An approach to understanding human behaviour by placing it within its broader social context is known as: (3)
   a. social location.
   b. the sociological perspective.
   c. common sense.
   d. generalization.

2. Using systematic methods to study and explain the social and natural worlds is the intent of: (3)
   a. arm-chair philosophers.
   b. scientists.
   c. methodologists.
   d. religious leaders.

3. Sociology is the scientific study of: (3)
   a. the production and distribution of the material goods and services of a society.
   b. preliterate cultures.
   c. society and human behaviour.
   d. mental processes that occur within the individual.

4. The application of the scientific method to the social world is known as: (7)
   a. ethnomethodology.
   b. sociobiology.
   c. natural science.
   d. positivism.

5. Interested in the twin problems of social order and social change, this individual was responsible for giving the name "sociology" to this emerging social science. (7)
   a. Auguste Comte
   b. Herbert Spencer
   c. Emile Durkheim
   d. Max Weber

6. According to Karl Marx, the controlling class of capitalists exploits the: (8)
   a. bourgeoisie.
   b. proletariat.
   c. masses.
   d. peasants.

7. According to Emile Durkheim, suicide rates can be explained by: (8)
   a. social factors.
   b. common sense.
   c. the oppression of the proletariat by the bourgeoisie.
   d. the survival of the fittest.

8. Regarding the uses of sociology, those who say that understanding is sociology's proper goal take the position that: (10)
   a. the knowledge gained by social research belongs to the scientific community and to the world.
   b. sociology should explore harmful social arrangements.
   c. sociologists should use their studies to alleviate human suffering.
   d. sociology should make society a better place.

9. Max Weber theorized that _____ led to the development of capitalism. (10)
   a. ownership of property
   b. political reforms
   c. Protestantism
   d. slavery

10. Replication: (10)
    a. helps researchers overcome distortions that values can cause.
    b. makes it possible to see how results compare when a study is repeated.
    c. involves the repetition of a study by other researchers.
    d. All of the above

11. Social facts and *Verstehen*: (11)
    a. have no relationship to each other.
    b. have been disproved.
    c. go hand-in-hand.
    d. were both concepts developed by Durkheim.

12. In the nineteenth century, it was unlikely that women would become sociology professors because: (11)
    a. they were more interested in fields of study like English and foreign languages.
    b. sexism in the universities stopped them from obtaining advanced degrees.
    c. they had no training in scientific methods.
    d. they were not interested in social inquiry or social reform.

13. Sociology in Canada is the story of the "two solitudes," where Quebec sociology: (12)
    a. was influenced by the sociology of the French sociologist Frederic LePlay.
    b. focused on the rural family in Quebec.
    c. concentrated on the microcosm of the individual and family.
    d. all of the above.

14. Which is true of sociology in English-speaking Canada? (12)
    a.   It was influenced by the British tradition.
    b.   It was influenced by the U.S. tradition.
    c.   Canada's first major program in Sociology began in 1922 at McGill University.
    d.   All of the above.

15. The model of economic development known as the staples theory of international trade: (12)
    a.   was particularly useful when studying the development of Canada as a distinct economy and society.
    b.   was created by Everett Hughes.
    c.   was developed by Carl Dawson.
    d.   was introduced by Frederic LePlay.

16. By the early 1970s, if not earlier, (13)
    a.   there was a large influx of American-trained sociologists in universities across Canada.
    b.   there was a lack of interest in developing a distinctively Canadian sociology.
    c.   U.S. theories, practices, and academics dominated in Canadian departments of sociology.
    d.   all of the above.

17. Which of the following North American sociologists wrote extensively on race relations, experienced prejudice and discrimination personally and professionally, and helped to found the NAACP? (13-14)
    a.   C. Wright Mills
    b.   Talcott Parsons
    c.   W.E.B. Du Bois
    d.   Jane Addams

18. The theoretical perspective that views society as composed of symbols that we use to establish meaning, develop our views of the world, and communicate with one another is: (16-17)
    a.   functionalism.
    b.   symbolic interactionism.
    c.   dramaturgical theory.
    d.   conflict theory.

19. The _____ perspective focuses on the symbolic meaning attached to social relationships to understand the social world. (16-17)
    a.   conflict
    b.   functional
    c.   symbolic interaction
    d.   exchange

20. According to Robert Merton, if an action is intended to help some part of the system, it is a: (16)
    a. manifest function.
    b. latent function.
    c. dysfunction.
    d. latent dysfunction.

21. Conflict theory was first asserted by: (17)
    a. Karl Marx.
    b. Emile Durkheim.
    c. Ralf Dahrendorf.
    d. Auguste Comte.

22. Contemporary conflict theorists such as Dahrendorf attribute conflict in society to: (17)
    a. the changing meanings associated with social equality.
    b. relations of authority in all layers of society.
    c. social changes that have weakened the family unit.
    d. the increasing division of labour associated with postindustrial capitalism.

23. _____feminist theories claim that legal restraints and customs are at the root of the subservience of women in society. (17)
    a. Non-Marxist
    b. Marxist
    c. Liberal
    d. Positivist

24. Postmodernism emphasizes the following characteristic of contemporary societies: (18)
    a. they are structured by inequalities based on gender.
    b. they are characterized by cultural and sexual diversity.
    c. they are divided into interrelated parts that all work together.
    d. they are based on the principles of reason and science.

25. All of the following are true regarding the symbolic interactionist perspective, *except*: (15-16)
    a. this perspective tends to focus on macro-level analysis.
    b. this perspective tends to focus on micro-level analysis.
    c. this perspective looks at social interaction.
    d. this perspective focuses on communications—both talk and nonverbal interactions.

26. In studying the homeless, functionalists would focus on: (19)
    a. what the homeless say and what they do.
    b. how changes in parts of the society are related to homelessness
    c. the micro-level inequalities in society
    d. their nonverbal interaction

27. According to your text, which theoretical perspective is best for studying human behaviour? (20)
   a. The functionalist perspective
   b. The symbolic interactionist perspective
   c. The conflict perspective
   d. A combination of all of the above, by putting the contribution of each perspective and level of analysis together

28. Research that makes discoveries about life in human groups rather than about making changes in those groups is: (20-21)
   a. pure or basic sociology.
   b. applied sociology.
   c. clinical sociology.
   d. none of the above.

29. Efforts to blend sociological knowledge and practical results are known as: (21)
   a. political sociology.
   b. basic sociology.
   c. applied sociology.
   d. pure sociology.

30. Out of an initial concern for improving society—from seeking abstract knowledge to seeking ways to apply their findings—many Sociology departments today offer courses in: (21)
   a. gender and workplace issues.
   b. criminology and family violence.
   c. co-ops and internships.
   d. one or more of the above.

TRUE-FALSE QUESTIONS

T F   1. The sociological perspective helps us to understand that people's social experiences underlie what they feel and what they do. (3)

T F   2. Social location is where people are located in a particular society in terms of things like jobs, income, education, and ethnicity. (3)

T F   3. Sociologists believe that internal mechanisms are very important in explaining an individual's thinking and motivations. (3)

T F   4. Political scientists study the ways in which people govern themselves. (4)

T F   5. Anthropology focuses on preliterate peoples. (4)

T F   6. Unlike political scientists and economists, sociologists do not concentrate on a single social institution. (5)

T F   7. Unlike psychologists, sociologists stress factors external to the individual to determine what influences people. (5)

T F   8. Sociology is a relatively recent discipline. It emerged about the middle of the nineteenth century when European social observers began to use scientific methods to test their ideas. (6)

T F   9. The success of the natural sciences was an impetus for the development of sociology. (7)

T F   10. Historically, the success of the natural sciences led to the search for answers to the social world as well. (7)

T F   11. Durkheim sought recognition for sociology as a separate academic discipline and succeeded when he received the first academic appointment in sociology in France in 1887. (8)

T F   12. Karl Marx thought that a classless society eventually would exist. (8)

T F   13. According to Durkheim, social integration is the degree to which people are tied to their social group. (8)

T F   14. The ideas of Max Weber and Karl Marx are almost identical. (8,10)

T F   15. Durkheim's study of suicide is still quoted because of its scientific rigour and excellent theoretical interpretations. (9)

T F   16. According to Weber, subjective meanings are important in understanding human behaviour. (11)

T F   17. To Durkheim, social facts are patterns of behaviour that characterize a social group. (11)

T F   18. Harriet Martineau published *Society in America*, an insightful examination of U.S. life before Durkheim and Weber were born. (12)

T F   19 W.E.B. du Bois founded the National Association for the Advancement of Colored People in the U.S.A. but was buried in Ghana, West Africa. (14)

T F   20. Besides the five major theoretical perspectives within the discipline of sociology, there are no new emergent theories. (15)

T F   21. Symbolic interactionists analyze how our behaviours depend on how we define ourselves and others. (16)

T F   22. The central idea of functional analysis is that conflict is especially likely to develop among people in close relationships. (16-17)

T F   23. Ralf Dahrendorf sees conflict as inherent in all relations that have authority. (17)

T F   24. The three feminist theories—Marxist-Feminist, Liberal Feminist, and Non-Marxist Feminist—have no common elements. (18)

T F   25. Postmodernism as a theory of present-day society recognizes diversity where modernity pushes sameness. (18)

T F   26. Queer theory deliberately challenges all notions of a fixed identity. (19)

T F   27 Since the 1970s U.S. sociology has not been dominated by any one theoretical orientation or by any single concern. (14)

FILL-IN QUESTIONS

1. People's group memberships because of their location in history and society are known as _____. (3)

2. The _____ are the intellectual and academic disciplines designed to comprehend, explain, and predict the events in our natural environment. On the other hand, the _____ examine human relationships. (4)

3. The use of objective systematic observation to test theories is _____. (7)

4. _____ was Karl Marx's term for the struggle between the proletariat and the bourgeoisie. (8)

5. Durkheim used the term _____ to refer to the degree to which people feel a part of social groups. (8)

6. _____ is the view that a sociologist's personal values or biases should not influence social research, while _____ is total neutrality. (10)

7. The meanings that people attach to their own behaviour are called _____. (11)

8. Durkheim used the term _____ to refer to patterns of behaviour that characterize a social group. (11)

9. A _____ is a general statement about how some parts of the world fit together and how they work. (15)

10. The theoretical perspective in which society is viewed as composed of symbols that people use to establish meaning, develop their views of the world, and communicate with one another is _____. (16)

11. _____ analysis is a theoretical framework in which society is viewed as composed of various parts, each with a function that contributes to society's equilibrium. (16)

12. Power that people consider legitimate is known as _____. (17)

13. _____ stresses that the exploitation of women includes their objectification into roles that serve men's interests. (17)

14. _____ analysis examines large-scale patterns of society, while _____ analysis examines small-scale patterns of society. (19)

15. _____ sociology makes discoveries about life in human groups, not to make changes in those groups; _____ sociology is the use of sociology to solve problems. (21)

16. _____ and _____ are two emergent theories. The former owes much to developments in feminist and postmodern scholarship, while the latter is a more distinctly U.S.-based multidisciplinary theory. (22)

MATCH THESE SOCIAL SCIENTISTS WITH THEIR CONTRIBUTIONS

1.	Auguste Comte	a.	*was an early African American sociologist*
2.	Karl Marx	b.	*proposed the use of positivism*
3.	C. Wright Mills	c.	*stressed social facts*
4.	Emile Durkheim	d.	*believed religion was a central force in social change*
5.	Harriet Martineau	e.	*believed the key to human history was class struggle*
6.	Robert Merton	f.	*encouraged the use of the sociological perspective*
7.	W.E.B. Du Bois	g.	*published Society in America and translated Comte's work into English*
8.	Max Weber	h.	*stressed the need for middle-range theories*
9.	Ralf Dahrendorf	i.	*was a conflict theorist*
10.	Carl Dawson	j.	*Canada's first major program began in 1927 at McGill University under his leadership*

ESSAY QUESTIONS

1. Explain what the sociological perspective encompasses and then, using that perspective, discuss the forces that shaped the discipline of sociology.
2. The textbook notes that *Verstehen* and social facts go hand in hand; explain how this is so. Assume that you have been asked to carry out research to find out more about why growing numbers of women and children are homeless and what particular problems they face. Discuss how you could you use both *Verstehen* and social facts in your study.
3. Explain each of the theoretical perspectives that are used in sociology and discuss how they can be used in research.
4. Explain what is meant by levels of analysis and give examples of theoretical perspectives on both levels.

"DOWN-TO-EARTH SOCIOLOGY"

1. Were you surprised to learn that all of the common sense notions in the quiz on page 6 were not true? Can you think of other common sense ideas that may or may not be true?
2. In the debate over the purposes and uses of sociological research, what is your position? Do you think sociologists should only advance our understanding of social life or is it their responsibility to explore harmful social arrangements and try to alleviate human suffering?
3. Reflecting on the introduction to sociological perspectives that was presented in this chapter, does your view on social life fit most closely with the symbolic interactionist, functionalist, conflict, feminist, or postmodern perspective? Why?

CHAPTER 2
WHAT DO SOCIOLOGISTS DO?

CHAPTER SUMMARY

- The case of Meredith McKie illustrates the nature of social problems and how they are researched.
- Sociologists conduct research about almost every area of human behaviour. The choice of research topics depends on the sociologists' interests, the availability of subjects, the appropriateness of methods, and ethical considerations.
- Sociological research is needed to test common sense ideas because not all common sense ideas are true.
- Sociologists use six basic research methods: surveys, participant observations, qualitative interviews, secondary analysis, documents, and unobtrusive measures. The choice of the research method depends on the research questions to be asked and the sampling methods need to fit the research.
- Typically, eight basic steps are included in scientific research: (1) selecting a topic, (2) defining the problem, (3) reviewing the literature, (4) formulating a hypothesis, (5) choosing a research method, (6) collecting the data, (7) analyzing the results, and (8) sharing the results. By random sampling researchers attempt to compensate for lack of experimentation. Major characteristics of the various methods are explained.
- Table 2.2 is included to illustrate how published results are often displayed.
- Ethics are of concern to sociologists, who are committed to openness, honesty, truth, and protecting subjects.
- Research and theory must work together because without theory research is of little value, and if theory is unconnected to research it is unlikely to represent the way life really is. Real-life situations often force sociologists to conduct research in less than ideal circumstances, but even such research stimulates both the development of theory and the need for more research.
-

LEARNING OBJECTIVES

As you read Chapter 2, use these learning objectives to organize your notes. After completing your reading, briefly state an answer to each of the objectives, and review the text pages in parentheses.

1. Explain why common sense is an inadequate source of knowledge. (25)
2. List and describe each of the six research methods, noting the major advantages and disadvantages of each. (26-30)
3. Enumerate the four primary factors involved in a researcher's choice of method. (30)
4. Differentiate between quantitative techniques and qualitative techniques. (30)
5. Identify the eight steps in a research model. (33-35)
6. Describe how sociologists go about selecting a topic for their research. (33)
7. Describe the process of formulating the research question. Define the following terms: hypothesis, operational definition, validity, reliability, and replication. Explain the role each plays in the research process. (34-35)

8. Describe the major ethical issues involved in sociological research; demonstrate these issues by using the Brajuha, Scarce, and Humphreys research as examples. (35-38)
9. Discuss how research and theory work together. Note reasons why much research must be conducted under less than ideal circumstances, bearing in mind that systematic research methods together with the application of social theory take us beyond common sense. (38-39)

CHAPTER OUTLINE

I.   **What Is a Valid Sociological Topic?**
    A. Sociologists research just about every area of human behaviour.
    B. Sociologists study social interaction; no human behaviour is ineligible for research, whether it is routine or unusual, respectable or reprehensible.

II.   **Common Sense and the Need for Sociological Research**
    A. Common sense cannot be relied on as a source of knowledge because it is highly limited and its insights often are incorrect.
    B. To move beyond common sense and understand what is really going on, it is necessary to do sociological research.

III. **Six Research Methods**
    A. Surveys involve collecting data on a research topic by having people answer a series of questions.
        1. The first step is to determine a population, the target group to be studied, and selecting a sample, individuals from within the target population who are intended to represent the population to be studied.
        2. In a random sample everyone in the target population has the same chance of being included in the study.
        3. The respondents (people who respond to a survey) must be allowed to express their own ideas so that the findings will not be biased.
        4. The questionnaires can be administered either by asking respondents to complete the survey themselves (self-administered questionnaires) or by directly questioning respondents (interviews).
        5. In designing a questionnaire, the researcher must consider the effects that interviewers have on respondents that lead to biased answers (interview bias), and whether to make the questions structured (closed-ended questions in which the answers are provided) or unstructured (open-ended questions which people answer in their own words).
        6. It is important to establish rapport—a feeling of trust between researchers and subjects.
    B. In participant observation, the researcher participates in a research setting while observing what is happening in that setting.
        1. Personal characteristics of the researcher—such as gender, age, race, personality, and even height and weight—are very important in this type of research.

2. Generalizability—the extent to which the findings from one group (or sample) can be generalized or applied to other groups (or populations)—is a problem in participant observation studies.

C. A qualitative interview, or structured conversation, is used to gather in-depth information from one or more participants. The interviewer is a participant in this conversation, but records it on tape and asks most of the questions.
   1. Qualitative interviews are used to obtain detailed, descriptive information, and can be used, in conjunction with other methods, to construct sociological explanations.
   2. Feminist researchers have attempted to develop a distinctive feminist methodology that uses qualitative interviews to allow women to "tell their own stories."

D. Secondary analysis—analysis of data already collected by other researchers—is used when resources are limited and/or existing data are an excellent source of information. To avoid many of the pitfalls of secondary analysis, such as reliability and validity of the data, many researchers in Canada use Statistics Canada data bases.

E. Documents—written sources—may be obtained from many sources, including books, newspapers, police reports, and records kept by various organizations.

F. Unobtrusive measures are the process of observing social behaviour of people who do not know they are being studied.

G. Deciding which method to use involves four primary factors:
   1. resources; the researcher must match the method to both time and money available.
   2. access to subjects; the sample may be physically inaccessible to the researcher, thereby influencing the choice of methods.
   3. purpose of the research; the researcher will choose the method that will be most suitable for obtaining answers to the questions posed.
   4. the researcher's background or training; those trained in use of quantitative research methods (emphasis is placed on precise measurement, the use of statistics and numbers) are likely to choose surveys, while those trained in use of qualitative research methods (emphasis is placed on describing and interpreting people's behaviour) lean toward participant observation.

IV. A Research Model

A. Selecting a topic is guided by sociological curiosity, interest in a particular topic, research funding from governmental or private source, and pressing social issues.

B. Defining the problem involves specifying exactly what the researcher wants to learn about the topic.

C. Reviewing the literature uncovers existing knowledge about the problem, helps to narrow down the problem, and provides ideas about what questions to ask.

D. Formulating a hypothesis involves stating the expected relationship between variables, based on a theory. Hypotheses need operational definitions—precise ways to measure the variables.

E. Choosing a research method is influenced by the research topic.

F. Collecting the data involves concerns over validity, the extent to which operational definitions measure what was intended, and reliability, the extent to which data produce consistent results. Inadequate operational definitions and sampling hurt reliability.

G. Analyzing the results involves the use of either qualitative or quantitative techniques to analyze data. Computers have become powerful tools in data analysis because they reduce large amounts of data to basic patterns, take the drudgery out of analyzing data, allows the researcher to use a variety of statistical tests, and give the researcher more time to interpret the results.

H. Sharing the results by writing a report and publishing the results makes the findings available for replication.

V. **Ethics in Sociological Research**

A. Ethics are of fundamental concern to sociologists when it comes to doing research.

B. Ethical considerations include being open, honest, and truthful, not harming the subject in the course of conducting the research, protecting the anonymity of the research subjects, and researchers not misrepresenting themselves to the research subjects.

C. The Brajuha and Scarce research demonstrates the lengths sociologists will go to in order to protect the anonymity of research subjects, while the Humphreys research illustrates questionable research ethics.

VI. **How Research and Theory Work Together**

A. Sociologists combine research and theory in different ways. Theory is used to interpret data (i.e., functionalism, symbolic interaction, conflict theory, feminist theories, and postmodernism provide frameworks for interpreting research findings) and to generate research. Research helps to generate theory.

B. Social researchers must operate under less than ideal circumstances because of real-life situations. Researchers must often settle for something that falls short of the ideal.

    1.   Sociology needs more imaginative, and sometimes daring, research conducted in an imperfect world under less than ideal conditions.

    2.   Research takes people beyond common sense and allows them to penetrate surface realities so they can better understand social life.

KEY TERMS

After studying the chapter, review the definition for each of the following terms.

closed-ended questions: questions followed by a list of possible answers to be selected by the respondent

dependent variable: a factor that is changed by an independent variable (the effect or outcome variable)

documents: in its narrow sense, written sources that provide data; in its extended sense, archival material of any sort, including photographs, movies and so on

generalizability: the extent to which the findings from one group (or sample) can be generalized or applied to other groups (or populations)

hypothesis: a statement of the expected relationship between variables according to predictions from a theory

independent variable: a factor that causes a change in another variable, called the dependent variable

interview: direct questioning of respondents

operational definition: the way in which a variable in a hypothesis is measured

participant observation (or fieldwork): research in which the researcher *participates* in a research setting while *observing* what is happening in that setting

population: the target group to be studied

qualitative or field interview, commonly referred to as **structured conversation:** a research method used to gather in-depth information from one or more participants through a structured conversation that is tape recorded

qualitative research method: research in which the emphasis is placed on observing, describing, and interpreting people's behaviour

quantitative research method: research in which the emphasis is placed on precise measurement, the use of statistics and numbers

questionnaires: a list of questions to be asked

random sample: a sample in which everyone in the target population has the same chance of being included in the study

rapport: a feeling of trust between researchers and subjects

reliability: the extent to which data produce consistent results

replication: repeating a study in order to test its findings

research method (or research design): one of seven procedures sociologists use to collect data: surveys, participant observation, qualitative interviews, secondary analysis, documents, unobtrusive measures, and experiments

respondents: people who respond to a survey, either in interviews or in self-administered questionnaires

sample: the individuals intended to represent the population to be studied

secondary analysis: the analysis of data already collected by other researchers

self-administered questionnaire: questionnaire filled out by respondents

structured interviews: interviews that use closed-ended questions

survey: the collection of data by having people answer a series of questions

unobtrusive measures: the various ways of observing people who do not know they are being studied

validity: the extent to which an operational definition measures what was intended

variable: a factor or concept thought to be significant for human behaviour, which varies from one case to another

KEY PEOPLE

Review the major theoretical contributions or findings of these people.

Mario Brajuha: During an investigation into a restaurant fire, officials subpoenaed notes taken by this sociologist in connection with his participant observation research on restaurant work. He was threatened with jail.

Laud Humphreys: This sociologist carried out doctoral research on homosexual activity, but ran into problems when he misrepresented himself to his research subjects. Although he earned his doctorate degree, he was fired from his position because of his questionable ethics.

Elton Mayo: Mayo is famous for his research at the Western Electric Company Hawthorne plant during the 1920s. He found that workers' productivity changed in directions that had not been originally hypothesized. He concluded that workers adjusted their productivity because they knew they were being observed. This phenomenon came to be known as the *Hawthorne effect*.

C. Wright Mills: Mills argued that research without theory is of little value, simply a collection of unrelated "facts," and theory that is unconnected to research is abstract and empty, unlikely to represent the way life really is.

Rik Scarce: Scarce was a graduate student doing research on animal rights groups when there was a break-in and vandalism in one of his university's research labs. He became famous because he refused to turn over research information that he had collected to authorities investigating the crime. He was imprisoned for 159 days on contempt charges.

Diana Scully and Joseph Marolla: These two sociologists interviewed convicted rapists in prison and found that rapists are not sick or overwhelmed by uncontrollable urges, but rather men who have learned to view rape as appropriate in various circumstances.

SELF-TEST

After completing this self-test, check your answers against the Answer Key at the back of this Study Guide and against the text on page(s) indicated in parentheses.

MULTIPLE CHOICE QUESTIONS

1. A researcher interested in doing a macro-level study would choose _____ as a topic. (25)
   a. waiting in public places
   b. multinational corporations
   c. interactions between people on street corners
   d. meat packers at work

2. Sociologists believe that research is necessary because: (25)
   a. common sense notions may be misleading.
   b. they want to move beyond guesswork.
   c. researchers want to know what really is going on.
   d. all of the above

3. Which of the following is *not* a research design? (26)
   a. ethnocentrism
   b. surveys
   c. participant observation
   d. qualitative interviews

4. A random sample is defined as: (26-27)
    a. whoever happens to walk by.
    b. the total population.
    c. a sample drawn from the population so that everyone has the same chance of being selected.
    d. a snowball sample.

5. Which of the following may be called "loading the dice"? (27)
    a. choose a biased sample
    b. ask biased questions
    c. discard undesirable results
    d. all of the above

6. A large number of people can be sampled at relatively low cost by (27)
    a. participant observation.
    b. self-administered questionnaires.
    c. interviews.
    d. structured interviews.

7. The primary advantage of structured interviews is that (27)
    a. they are slower to administer.
    b. they make it harder for answers to be coded.
    c. the answers listed on the questionnaire may not include all the respondent's opinions.
    d. None of the above

8. In doing participant observation research, which of the following personal characteristics of the researcher can affect their findings? (28)
    a. sex
    b. age
    c. race
    d. All of the above

9. Why might a researcher "load the dice" in designing a research project? (27)
    a. The researcher doesn't know any better.
    b. The researcher may have a vested interest in the outcome of the research.
    c. Research must be objective if it is to be scientific.
    d. If the researchers produce the right finding, more funding will come their way

10. A qualitative interview, commonly referred to as a structured conversation, is the research method in which: (29)
    a. the interviewer and the interviewee should see themselves as participants in a conversation.
    b. the interviewer is asking most of the questions.
    c. conversation is tape recorded.
    d. all of the above

11. The analysis of data already collected by other researchers is referred to as: (29)
    a. surveying the literature.
    b. use of documents.
    c. secondary analysis.
    d. replication.

12. Which of the following are documents that provide useful information for investigating social life? (29-30)
    a. newspapers and videos
    b. diaries and photos
    c. bank records and police reports
    d. all of the above

13. To study patterns of alcohol consumption in different neighbourhoods, you decide to go through the recycling bins and count the beer cans, wine and liquor bottles. You would be using: (30)
    a. participant observation
    b. experimental methods
    c. unobtrusive methods
    d. qualitative methods

14. When deciding which method to use, sociologists consider (30)
    a. the purpose of the research.
    b. sources of potential funding.
    c. access to subjects.
    d. all of the above

15. Sociologists trained in quantitative research methods emphasize (30)
    a. measurements, numbers, and statistics
    b. observation and description
    c. lean toward participant observation
    d. are likely to use qualitative interviews

16. _____ steps are involved in scientific research. (33)
    a. Four
    b. Six
    c. Eight
    d. Ten

17. The change in behaviour that occurs when subjects know they are being studied is: (31)
    a. the Hawthorne effect.
    b. the Humphreys effect.
    c. the unobtrusive effect.
    d. the obtrusive effect.

18. Surveys are more likely to be used by researchers trained in: (30)
    a. social psychology.
    b. ethnomethodology.
    c. quantitative research methods.
    d. qualitative research methods.

19. Marketing researchers attempt to find out: (30)
    a. what customers think they want.
    b. how customers select and use products.
    c. what images they hold of a product or service.
    d. all of the above

20. Which of the following is *not* one of the reasons why researchers review the literature? (33)
    a. To help them to narrow down the problem by pinpointing particular areas to examine
    b. To get ideas about how to do their own research
    c. To find out whether or not the topic is controversial
    d. To determine whether or not the problem has been answered already

21. A relationship between or among variables is predicted: (34)
    a. by a hypothesis.
    b. by use of operational definitions.
    c. when the researcher selects the topic to be studied.
    d. when the researcher is analyzing the results.

22. Reliability refers to: (34)
    a. the extent to which operational definitions measure what they are intended to measure.
    b. the extent to which data produce consistent results from one study to the next.
    c. the integrity of the researcher .
    d. the ways in which the variables in a hypothesis are measured.

23. In analyzing data gathered by participant observation, a researcher is likely to choose: (35)
    a. computer analysis.
    b. quantitative analysis.
    c. qualitative analysis.
    d. statistical analysis.

24. Replication: (35)
    a. is the extent to which operational definitions measure what was intended.
    b. is the examination of a source to identify its themes.
    c. is the repetition of research by others in order to test its findings.
    d. is copying the work of some other researcher.

25. Research ethics require: (35)
    a. openness.
    b. that a researcher not falsify results or plagiarize someone else's work.
    c. that research subjects should not be harmed by the research.
    d. All of the above

TRUE-FALSE QUESTIONS

T F   1.   Race relations is an acceptable topic for sociological research. (25)
T F   2.   Research generally confirms common sense. (25-26)
T F   3.   One of the first steps in conducting survey research is to determine a population. (26)
T F   4.   In survey research, it is undesirable for respondents to express their own ideas. (25)
T F   5.   The wording of questionnaires can affect research results. (27)
T F   6.   Structured interviews always use closed-ended questions. (27)
T F   7.   The researcher's personal characteristics are extremely important in participant observation. (28)
T F   8.   Feminist methodologists attempt to replicate the objective, scientific method in their research. (29)
T F   9.   Secondary analysis and use of documents mean the same thing in terms of research methods. (29)
T F   10. Plagiarism is stealing someone else's work. (35)
T F   11. It is generally considered unethical for researchers to misrepresent themselves. (35)
T F   12. Validity is the extent to which different studies come up with similar results. (35)
T F   13. Quantitative research methods emphasize precise measurement, the use of statistics and numbers. (30)
T F   14. After selecting a topic, the next step in the research model is defining the problem. (33)
T F   15. An operational definition refers to the precise ways in which researchers measure their variables. (34)
T F   16. In general, researchers give higher priority to reliability than validity. (34)
T F   17. Reliability is the extent to which data produce consistent results. (35)
T F   18. Computers are valuable to research sociologists because they can store a great deal of information very efficiently. (35)
T F   19. Sharing the results is the final step in the research model. (35)
T F   20. Reviewing the literature is the most important step in the research process if sociologists are to distinguish themselves from newspaper and TV reporters. (33)

FILL-IN QUESTIONS

1. The six research methods are: (1) _____, (2) _____, (3)_____, (4) _____, (5) _____, (6)_____. (26)
2. A(n) _____ allows a large number of people to be sampled at a relatively low cost. (27)
3. Closed-ended questions are used in _____. (27)
4. _____ is a feeling of trust between researchers and subjects. (28)
5. _____ is a form of research where the researcher spends a great deal of time with the people he or she is studying. (28)
6. Generalizability is one of the major problems in _____. (28)
7. A hypothesis predicts a relationship between or among _____. (34)
8. _____ is the extent to which operational definitions measure what they are intended to measure. (34)
9. Research in which the emphasis is placed on precise measurement, the use of statistics and numbers is _____. (30)
10. Research in which the emphasis is placed on describing and interpreting people's behaviour is _____. (30)
11. A factor or concept thought to be significant for human behaviour, which varies from one case to another, is a(n) _____. (34)
12. Hypotheses need _____, which are precise ways to measure variables. (34)
13. _____ is the extent to which data produce consistent results. (35)
14. Research _____ require openness, honesty, and truth. (35)
15. Research and _____ are interdependent, and sociologists combine them in their work. (38)
16. Hypotheses need _____ to measure their variables. (34)

MATCH THESE CONCEPTS WITH THEIR DEFINITIONS

___	1. Hawthorne effect	a.	*the observations of people who are unaware of being watched*
___	2. population	b.	*behaviour change due to subject's awareness of being studied*
___	3. sample	c.	*the interviewer effect on respondents that leads to biased answers*
___	4. interview bias	d.	*a factor that is changed by an independent variable*
___	5. secondary analysis	e.	*written sources*
___	6. documents	f.	*the target group to be studied*
___	7. independent variable	g.	*the analysis of data already collected by other researchers*
___	8. dependent variable	h.	*the individuals intended to represent the population to be studied*
___	9. unobtrusive measures	i.	*a factor that causes a change in another variable*

ESSAY QUESTIONS

1. Choose a topic and explain how you would go through the different steps in the research model.
2. Discuss some of the things that can go wrong in the process of doing research and provide suggestions on how to overcome such problems.
3. Explain why ethical guidelines are necessary in social science research.
4. Describe the Hawthorne effect—what did it reveal about the research process itself?

"DOWN-TO-EARTH SOCIOLOGY"

1. If you were to pursue a career in sociology, what research topics would you find interesting? What methods would you use?
2. Can you give examples similar to those in your text where researchers have loaded the dice (27) to enhance the qualities of a product or a political candidate?
3. Have you ever changed your appearance or behaviour because you knew you were being observed or studied? Was your change an example of the Hawthorne effect (31)?
4. After reading about how some sociologists use their training and knowledge to do marketing research (32), do you see this as a legitimate area of research for them? How does it relate to the ethical concerns of the profession? The need to be objective?
5. Were you surprised by the findings on homelessness reported on pages 32-33? How did the reaction to the research reflect the political nature of the problem? Why do you think the homeless advocates were upset by the outcome of the research?
6. The author provides examples of three different research projects that involved some ethical considerations. In each of these cases, did you agree or disagree with the position taken by the researcher? How would you have reacted in the same situation? (37)
7. Why do you think that sociologists like Scully and Marolla (38) pursue certain research topics even when it requires them to work under less than ideal conditions?

CHAPTER 3
CULTURE

CHAPTER SUMMARY

- Culture is universal; all human groups create a design for living that includes both material and nonmaterial culture. Ideal culture, a group's ideal norms and values, exists alongside its real culture, the actual behaviour which often falls short of the cultural ideals.
- Culture's significance is profound; it touches almost every aspect of who and what we are. Culture becomes the lens through which we perceive and evaluate what is going on around us. As a consequence we tend to become ethnocentric, to use our own culture as the yardstick for judging others.
- To counter our tendency to use our own culture as a standard to judge other cultures, we can practice cultural relativism by trying to understand a culture on its own terms.
- Symbols are the basis of culture; these components of nonmaterial culture include gestures, language, values, norms, sanctions, folkways and mores. Language is essential for culture because it facilitates our having shared understandings that form the essence of social life. It makes it possible to engage in goal orientated behaviour; it allows us to move beyond the present, sharing with others our past experiences and our future plans. According to the Sapir-Whorf hypothesis, language not only expresses our thinking and perceptions but actually shapes them.
- All groups have values and norms and use positive and negative sanctions to show approval or disapproval of those who do or don't follow the norms.
- A subculture is a group whose values and behaviours set it apart from the general culture; a counterculture holds values that stand in opposition to the mainstream culture.
- Although Canada is a pluralistic society made up of many groups, each with its own set of values, certain core values dominate. Some values cluster together to form a larger whole. Core values that contradict one another indicate areas of social tension and are likely points of social change. For over twenty years (since 1983) Maclean's magazine has polled Canadians on a wide variety of topics; there is evidence of a move to more liberal moral values for most Canadians.
- Based on Goodall's research, it seems that on a rudimentary level, animal culture exists.
- However, no animals have language in the sociological sense of the term.
- With today's technology in travel and communications, cultural diffusion is occurring rapidly, resulting in cultural levelling, a process in which cultures become similar to one another along some dimensions.

LEARNING OBJECTIVES

As you read Chapter 3, use these learning objectives to organize your notes. After completing your reading, briefly state an answer to each of the objectives, and review the text pages in parentheses.

1. Define culture and explain its material and nonmaterial components. (42)
2. Explain why ethnocentrism is a natural tendency and why this orientation towards your own and other cultures can lead to culture shock. (43)
3. State what cultural relativism is and discuss why it is a worthwhile goal even though it presents challenges to us. (43-44)

4. Discuss the components of symbolic culture. (44-48)
5. Identify the different ways in which language makes human life possible. (45-47)
6. Define the following terms: values, norms, sanctions, folkways, mores, and taboos. (48)
7. Compare and contrast dominant culture, subcultures, and countercultures. (48-49)
8. List the examples of values in Canadian society as identified by *The National Magazine/Maclean's* poll. (49-51)
9. Explain what is meant by *value clusters* and *value contradictions*. (51-52)
10. Discuss why core values do not change without meeting strong resistance. (53)
11. Explain the difference between "ideal" and "real" cultures. (53)
12. Define cultural universals and state whether, in actuality, they exist or not. (54)
13. Answer the question, "Do animals have culture?" (54-55)
14. State what technology is and explain its sociological significance. (55)
15. Define cultural lag and explain its role in relationship to cultural change. (55)
16. Discuss the link between technology, cultural diffusion, and cultural levelling. (56-57)

CHAPTER OUTLINE

I.   **What is Culture?**
    A. Culture is defined as the language, beliefs, values, norms, behaviours, and even material objects passed from one generation to the next.
        1. Material culture is things such as jewellery, art, buildings, weapons, machines, clothing, hairstyles, etc.
        2. Nonmaterial culture is a group's ways of thinking (beliefs, values, and assumptions) and common patterns of behaviour (language, gestures, and other forms of interaction). We come into this world without language, without values and morality.
    B. Culture provides a taken-for-granted orientation to life.
        1. Culture becomes the lens through which we perceive and evaluate things around us. We assume that our own culture is normal or natural; in fact, it is not natural, but rather is learned.
        2. It provides implicit instructions that tell us what we ought to do and a moral imperative that defines what we think is right and wrong.
        3. Coming into contact with a radically different culture produces "culture shock," challenging our basic assumptions.
        4. A consequence of internalizing culture is ethnocentrism, using our own culture (and assuming it to be good, right, and superior) to judge other cultures. It is functional when it creates in-group solidarity, but can be dysfunctional if it leads to harmful discrimination.
        5. Additionally the relationships between men and women, and women and women vary greatly from culture to culture.
    C. Cultural relativism consists of trying to appreciate other groups' ways of life in the context in which they exist, without judging them as superior or inferior to our own.
        1. Cultural relativism is an attempt to refocus our cultural lens and thereby appreciate other ways of life, rather than simply asserting "our way is the right way."
        2. Robert Edgerton argues that those cultural practices that result in exploitation should be judged morally inferior to those that enhance people's lives.

II. **Components of Symbolic Culture**
  A. Sociologists sometimes refer to nonmaterial culture as symbolic culture.
    1. A central component of culture is the symbols—something to which people attach meaning—that people use to communicate.
    2. Symbols include gestures, language, values, norms, sanctions, folkways, and mores.
  B. Gestures, using one's body to communicate with others, are shorthand means of communication.
    1. Gestures are used by people in every culture, although the gestures and the meanings differ; confusion or offense can result because of misunderstandings over the meaning of a gesture or misuse of a gesture.
    2. There is disagreement over whether there are any universal gestures.
  C. Language consists of a system of symbols that can be put together in an infinite number of ways in order to communicate abstract thought. Each word is a symbol to which a culture attaches a particular meaning. It is important because it is the primary means of communication between people.
    1. It allows human experiences to be cumulative; each generation builds on the body of significant experiences that is passed on to it by the previous generation, thus freeing people to move beyond immediate experiences. It extends time back into the past and forward into the future, enabling us to share with others both past experiences as well as future plans. It expands connections beyond our immediate, face-to-face groups.
    2. Words are the embodiment of experiences distilled and codified into a readily exchangeable form, intelligible to people who have learned that language
    3. It allows people to engage in complex, shared, goal-directed behaviour.
    4. The Sapir-Whorf hypothesis states that our thinking and perception are not only expressed by language but are actually shaped by language. This is because we are taught not only words but also a particular way of thinking and perceiving. Rather than objects and events forcing themselves onto our consciousness, our very language determines our consciousness.
  D. Culture includes values, norms, and sanctions.
    1. Values are the standards by which people define good and bad, beautiful and ugly. Every group develops both values and expectations regarding the right way to reflect them.
    2. Norms are the expectations or rules of behaviour that develop out of a group's values.
    3. Sanctions are the positive or negative reactions to the way in which people follow norms. Positive sanctions (a money reward, a prize, a smile, or even a handshake) are expressions of approval; negative sanctions (a fine, a frown, or harsh words) denote disapproval for breaking a norm.
  E. Norms vary in terms of their importance to a culture.
    1. Folkways are norms that are not strictly enforced, such as passing on the left side of the sidewalk. They may result in a person getting a dirty look.
    2. Mores are norms that are believed to be essential to core values and we insist on conformity. A person who steals, rapes, and kills has violated some of society's most important mores.

3. Norms that one group considers to be folkways another group may view as mores. A male walking down the street with the upper half of his body uncovered may be violating a folkway; a female doing the same thing may be violating accepted mores.
4. Taboos are norms so strongly ingrained that even the thought of them is greeted with revulsion. Eating human flesh and having sex with one's parents are examples of such behaviour.

F. Subcultures and countercultures are often found within a broader culture.
1. Subcultures are groups whose values and related behaviours are so distinct that they set their members off from the dominant culture. Each subculture is a world within the larger world of the dominant culture, and has a distinctive way of looking at life, but remains compatible with the dominant culture.
2. Countercultures are groups whose values set their members in opposition to the dominant culture. Countercultures are usually associated with negative behaviour, although some are not. Countercultures are often perceived as a threat by the dominant culture because they challenge the culture's values; for this reason the dominant culture will move against a particular counterculture in order to affirm its own core values.

III. Values in Canadian Society

A. Identifying core values in Canadian society is difficult because it is a pluralistic society with many different religious, racial, ethnic, and special interest groups.
1. On many social and political issues, Canadians display liberal moral values. Liberal values are even more strongly expressed in the province of Quebec.
2. Sociologist John Porter remarked that Canadians, unlike Americans, lack a unifying ideology. Canadians, however, are preoccupied with who we are as a nation.

B. Some values conflict with each other. There cannot be full expressions of democracy, equality, racism, and sexism at the same time. These are value contradictions and, as society changes, some values are challenged and undergo modification.

C. Values are not independent units; value clusters are made up of related core values that come together to form a larger whole. A cluster that is emerging within Canadian society—in response to fundamental changes in the society—is one made up of the values of leisure, self-fulfillment, physical fitness, and youngness.

D. Core values do not change without meeting strong resistance.

E. Values and their supporting beliefs may emerge in relation to our social circumstances. In recent years, Canadians have developed a genuine and long-term concern for the environment because we now recognize our dependence on our natural resources.

F. Ideal culture refers to the ideal values and norms of a people. What people actually do usually falls short of this ideal, and sociologists refer to the norms and values that people actually follow as real culture.

IV. Cultural Universals

A. Anthropologist George Murdock concluded that all human groups have certain cultural universals: customs about courtship, cooking, marriage, funerals, games, laws, music, myths, incest taboos, and toilet training are present in all cultures.

B. Even so, the specific customs differ from one group to another: by way of example, there is no universal form of the family, no universal way of disposing of the dead, and even the methods of toilet training differ from one culture to another.

V.   Animals and Culture

A. The basic sociological question is this: are there any behaviours that animals learn, and then pass on to others?

    1. Anthropologist Jane Goodall discovered that chimpanzees made and used a form of simple tool (a blade of grass, stripped of its leaves and licked on one end) that they would stick into a nest of termites and then pull out, enabling them to eat the termites. This conduct on the part of the chimpanzees was a form of animal culture: learned, shared behaviour among animals.

    2. On a rudimentary level, animal culture exists. Although this principle has been established, we do not yet know the particulars.
To the extent that some animals teach their young certain behaviours, they have culture. Social scientists think of language as more complex than mere sounds. They view language as symbols that can be infinitely strung together to communicate abstract thought. No animals, however, have language in the sociological sense of that term

VI.   Technology in the Global Village

A. In its simplest sense, technology can be equated with tools. In its broadest sense, technology also includes the skills or procedures necessary to make and to use those tools.

    1. The emerging technologies of an era that make a major impact on human life are referred to as new technologies. The printing press and the computer are both examples of new technologies.

    2. The sociological significance of technology is that it sets the framework for the nonmaterial culture, influencing the way people think and how they relate to one another.

B. Not all parts of culture change at the same pace; cultural lag was Ogburn's term for situations where the material culture changes first and the nonmaterial culture lags behind.

C. Although for most of human history cultures had little contact with one another, there has always been some contact with other groups, resulting in groups learning from one another.

    1. This transmission of cultural characteristics is cultural diffusion; it is more likely to produce changes in material culture than the nonmaterial culture.

    2. Cultural diffusion occurs more rapidly today, given the technology.

    3. Travel and communication unite the world to such an extent that there almost is no "other side of the world." Where travel to Africa was so unusual for a few hardy people, today hundreds of thousands make the trip every year. Another example, Japan, no longer a purely Eastern culture, has adapted Western economic production, forms of dress, music, and so on. This leads to cultural levelling—cultures become similar to one another.

KEY TERMS

After studying the chapter, review the definition for each of the following terms.

animal culture: learned, shared behaviour among animals

counterculture: a group whose values, beliefs, and related behaviours place its members in opposition to the values of the broader culture

cultural diffusion: the spread of cultural characteristics from one group to another

cultural lag: William Ogburn's term for a situation in which nonmaterial culture lags behind changes in the material culture

cultural levelling: the process by which cultures become similar to one another, and especially by which Western industrial culture is imported and diffused into developing nations

cultural relativism: understanding a people in the framework of its own culture

cultural universal: a value, norm, or other cultural trait that is found in every group

culture: the language, beliefs, values, norms, behaviours, and even material objects that are passed from one generation to the next

ethnocentrism: the use of one's own culture as a yardstick for judging the ways of other individuals or societies, generally leading to a negative evaluation of their values, norms, and behaviours

folkways: norms that are not strictly enforced

gestures: the ways in which people use their bodies to communicate with one another

ideal culture: the ideal values and norms of a people, the goals held out for them

language: a system of symbols that can be combined in an infinite number of ways and can represent not only objects but also abstract thought

material culture: the material objects that distinguish a group of people, such as their art, buildings, weapons, utensils, machines, hairstyles, clothing, and jewellery

mores: norms that are strictly enforced because they are thought essential to core values

negative sanction: an expression of disapproval for breaking a norm, ranging from a mild, informal reaction such as a frown to a formal prison sentence or an execution

new technology: the emerging technologies of an era that have a significant impact on social life

nonmaterial culture: a group's ways of thinking (including its beliefs, values, and other assumptions about the world) and doing (its common patterns of behaviour, including language and other forms of interaction)

norms: the expectations, or rules of behaviour, that develop out of values

pluralistic society: a society made up of many different groups

positive sanction: a reward given for following norms, ranging from a smile to a prize

real culture: the norms and values that people actually follow

sanctions: expressions of approval or disapproval given to people for upholding or violating norms

Sapir-Whorf hypothesis: Edward Sapir and Benjamin Whorf's theory that language itself creates ways of thinking and perceiving

social construction of technology: the view (opposed to *technological determinism*) that culture (people's values and special interests) shapes the use and development of technology

subculture: the values and related behaviours of a group that distinguish its members from the larger culture; a world within a world

symbol: something to which people attach meaning and then use to communicate with others

symbolic culture: another term for nonmaterial culture

taboo: a norm so strong that it brings revulsion if it is violated

technological determinism: the view that technology determines culture, that technology takes on a life of its own and forces human behaviour to follow

technology: in its narrow sense, tools: its broader sense includes the skills or procedures necessary to make and use those tools

tool: an object that is created or modified for a specific purpose

value clusters: a series of interrelated values that together form a larger whole

value contradictions: values that conflict with one another; to follow the one means to come into conflict with the other

values: the standards by which people define what is desirable or undesirable, good or bad, beautiful or ugly

KEY PEOPLE

Review the major theoretical contributions or findings of these people.

Reginald Bibby: Bibby studied the tendency towards Americanization in Canadian life.

Charles Darwin: Darwin studied the principles upon which natural selection occurred.

Robert Edgerton: Edgerton attacks the concept of cultural relativism, suggesting that because some cultures endanger their people's health, happiness, or survival, there should be a scale to evaluate cultures on their "quality of life."

Jane Goodall: Goodall studied the behaviour of chimpanzees and discovered that they not only communicate using gestures, hoots, and facial expressions, but they also use tools.

Marshall McLuhan: An optimist about technology, McLuhan tried to understand the impact of electronic media on people's ideas, values, and way of life.

George Murdock: Murdock was an anthropologist who sought to determine cultural values, norms, or traits universally across the globe.

William Ogburn: Ogburn coined the term "cultural lag."

John Porter: Porter saw Canadians as lacking a unifying ideology; we are not brought up with a set of beliefs and values that tell us who we are and what we should strive for in order to make our lives meaningful and fulfilling.

Edward Sapir and Benjamin Whorf: These two anthropologists argued that language not only reflects thoughts and perceptions, but that it actually shapes the way a people think and perceive the world.

William Sumner: Sumner developed the concept of ethnocentrism.

SELF-TEST

After completing this self-test, check your answers against the Answer Key at the back of this Study Guide and against the text on page(s) indicated in parentheses.

MULTIPLE CHOICE QUESTIONS

1. Which of the following characteristics are indicative of culture? (42)
    a. language
    b. beliefs and values
    c. norms and behaviours
    d. all of the above

2. Which of the following is *not* part of material culture? (42)
    a. weapons and machines
    b. eating utensils
    c. jewellery, hairstyles, and clothing
    d. language

3. In the textbook the author, James Henslin, describes his reaction to life in Morocco. Which of the following best describes what he was feeling? (43)
    a. cultural diffusion
    b. cultural levelling
    c. cultural relativism
    d. cultural shock

4. Which of these statements regarding culture is *not* true? (42-43)
    a. Culture provides a fundamental basis for decision making.
    b. By internalizing a culture, people learn ideas of right and wrong.
    c. The effects of our own culture are always clear to us.
    d. At birth, people do not possess culture.

5. A Canadian thinks citizens of another country are barbarians if they like to attend bullfights. Which of the following concepts best describes this reaction? (43)
    a. cultural shock
    b. cultural relativism
    c. ethnocentrism
    d. ethnomethodology

6. Symbols are the basis of culture and include: (44)
    a. gestures.
    b. language.
    c. values and norms.
    d. all of the above

7. Which of the following provides transmission of a social or shared past and planning for a future (46-47)
    a. grunts
    b. gestures
    c. language
    d. feelings

8. As Inuit children learn their language, they learn distinctions between types of snowfalls in a way that is not apparent to non-Inuit children. Which of the following perspectives is reflected in this example? (47)
    a. sociobiology
    b. the Davis-Moore theory
    c. the Sapir-Whorf hypothesis
    d. the Linguistic perspective

9. Your mother has prepared your lunch package and you run out of the door without saying "thank you." Which of the following cultural components have you violated? (48)
    a. taboos
    b. mores
    c. folkways
    d. sanctions

10. Which of the following statements about mores is correct? (48)
    a. Mores are essential to our core values and require conformity.
    b. Mores are norms that are not strictly enforced.
    c. Mores state that a person should not try to pass you on the left side of the sidewalk.
    d. Mores have been lost in contemporary society.

11. Subcultures: (48-49)
    a. are a world within the larger world of the dominant culture.
    b. are groups whose values and norms place them in opposition to mainstream culture.
    c. exclude occupational groups.
    d. exclude ethnic groups.

12. Sociologists consider heavy metal adherents who glorify Satanism, cruelty, and sexism to be an example of: (49)
    a. ethnocentrists.
    b. perverted people.
    c. a counterculture.
    d. a universal culture.

13. Canadian society is made up of many different groups. Which of the following terms would a sociologist use to describe this type of society? (49-50)
    a.   a melting pot
    b.   a pluralistic society
    c.   a conflicted society
    d.   a counterculture

14. Based on one of the latest polls (2003) which of the following statements concerning Canadian core values is *not* correct? (50)
    a.   a move to more liberal values of most Canadians
    b.   An emerging cluster of core values includes leisure, self-fulfillment, physical fitness, and youth, and more acceptance of homosexual relations regardless of age group.
    c.   They change over time.
    d.   A lack of endorsement for a woman's right to a legal abortion if her health is in danger.

15. Which is true of the Native People's position in Canada? (51-52)
    a.   Their present status as Canadians has been enshrined in the Indian Act of 1876.
    b.   Their adverse social, psychological, and economic conditions serve to heighten susceptibility to illness and poor health.
    c.   1973 Native leaders reclaimed their right to educate their children through their culture.
    d.   all of the above

16. Which of the following appear to be emerging as core values in a value cluster in Canada and the United States? (53)
    a.   leisure
    b.   self-fulfillment
    c.   physical fitness and youth
    d.   all of the above

17. A Maclean's (2004) survey shows that _____ of Canadians describe Canadians and Americans as "essentially the same." (53)
    a.   8% in 1999, 7% in 2002, 12% in 2004
    b.   44% in 1999, 34% in 2002, 32% in 2004
    c.   23% in 1999, 29% in 2002, 23% in 2004
    d.   24% in 1999, 28% in 2002, 31% in 2004

18. Which of the following is a conclusion drawn from studies of animal culture? (54-55)
    a.   Animals do not have culture.
    b.   We can't say if animals have culture or not if we cannot communicate with them.
    c.   On a rudimentary level, animal culture exists, but researchers are still studying to learn more about it.
    d.   Animals not only have culture but also have an extensive capacity for language.

19. There are computer tests that outperform physicians in diagnosing and prescribing treatment, yet most of us still visit doctors and rely on their judgment. What does this situation reflect? (55)
    a. resistance to new technologies
    b. cultural diffusion
    c. the social construction of technology
    d. cultural lag

20. Today bagels, woks, and hammocks are all a part of Canadian culture. The adoption of these objects illustrates which of the following processes or concepts? (56)
    a. cultural levelling
    b. nonmaterial culture
    c. cultural diffusion
    d. cultural universals

TRUE-FALSE QUESTIONS

T F   1. Culture becomes the lens through which we perceive and evaluate what is going on around us. (42)
T F   2. A tendency to use our own group's values as the yardstick for judging others is ethnocentrism. (43)
T F   3. We can practice cultural relativism by trying to understand a culture in its own terms. (43)
T F   4. Anthropologist Robert Edgerton, a critic of cultural relativism, asks why we should consider cultures that endanger their people's health and happiness morally equivalent to cultures that do not. (44)
T F   5. Online communication has developed no way to communicate humour, disappointment, or other indicators of mood or attitude. (45)
T F   6. Language allows culture to develop by freeing people to move beyond their immediate experiences. (45)
T F   7. Sanctions are positive or negative reactions to the ways people follow norms. (48)
T F   8. Although there are universal human activities, there is no universally accepted way of doing any of them. (54)
T F   9. All motorcycle enthusiasts belong to a counterculture. (49)
T F   10. There are no statistically significant differences between Quebec and the rest of the country on matters of parenting, sex and teens. (46)
T F   11. A large majority of Quebecois support more funding for Canadian military than the rest of Canada. (50-51)
T F   12. The majority of Canadians are embracing the changing moral values of tolerance and respect for other ways of life and cultures. (53)
T F   13. John Porter remarked that Canadians, unlike Americans, lack a unifying ideology. (53)
T F   14. Concern for the environment has always been a core value in Canadian society. (52-53)

T F   15.   Core values do not change without meeting strong resistance. (53)
T F   16.   Stimulated by Goodall's research, scientists began trying to determine the extent of animal culture, and now believe that on a rudimentary level animal culture exists. (55)
T F   17.   Central to a group's material culture is its technology. (55)
T F   18.   Technology influences the way people think and how they relate to one another. (55)
T F   19.   Cultural leveling is slowly occurring around the world. (57)
T F   20.   According to William Ogburn, a group's nonmaterial culture usually changes first, with the material culture lagging behind. (55)

FILL-IN QUESTIONS

1. Objects such as art, buildings, weapons, utensils, machines, hairstyles, clothing, and jewellery, which distinguish a group of people, are known as _____; their ways of thinking and doing are _____. (42)
2. A _____ is something to which people attach meaning and then use to communicate with others. (44)
3. _____ is a system of symbols that can be combined in an infinite number of ways and can represent not only objects but also abstract thought. (45)
4. _____ are ideas of what is desirable in life. (48)
5. The expectations or rules of behaviour that develop out of values are referred to as _____. (48)
6. A _____ is a norm so strongly ingrained that even the thought of its violation is greeted with revulsion. (48)
7. _____ are a series of interrelated values that together form a larger whole. (51)
8. _____ may not exist because even though there are universal human activities, there is no universally accepted way of doing any of them. (53-54)
9. Studies of chimpanzees indicate that they were able to make and use _____; they actually modified objects and used them for specific purposes. (54)
10. In its broader sense, _____ includes the skills or procedures necessary to make and use tools. (55)
11. Both the printing press and the computer represent _____ because they had a significant impact on society following their introduction. (55)
12. The idea that technology is the single greatest force in shaping our lives is central to the point of view called _____. (56)
13. William Ogburn used the term _____ to reflect the condition in which not all parts of a culture change at the same pace. (55)
14. The spread of cultural characteristics from one group to another is _____. (56)
15. When Western industrial culture is imported and diffused into developing nations, the process is called _____. (57)

MATCH THESE SOCIAL SCIENTISTS WITH THEIR CONTRIBUTIONS

__1.   Edward Sapir and Benjamin Whorf
__2.   John Porter
__3.   George Murdock
__4.   Jane Goodall

__5.   Robert Edgerton
__6.   William Sumner

__7.   Marshall McLuhan
__8.   William Ogburn

a.   *studied animal culture*
b.   *introduced the concept of cultural lag*
c.   *looked for cultural universals*
d.   *remarked that Canadians lack a unifying ideology*
e.   *coined the term "global village"*
f.   *stated that language shapes perceptions of reality*
h.   *criticized aspects of cultural relativism*
g.   *developed the concept of ethnocentrism*

ESSAY QUESTIONS

1. Explain cultural relativism and discuss both the advantages and disadvantages of practicing it.
2. Consider the differences between Quebec and the rest of Canada on matters of parenting, sex, and teens.
3. Evaluate what is gained and what is lost as technology advances in society.

"DOWN-TO-EARTH SOCIOLOGY"

1. What is your evaluation of the "Americanization of Canadian values?" (53)
2. With which side of the technology debate would you place yourself (Global Village or Big Brother?) (56). Are we able to control technology or does it control us?

CHAPTER 4
SOCIALIZATION

CHAPTER SUMMARY

- In the nineteenth and early twentieth century, many researchers believed that human behaviour was innate. This debate about the roots of human behaviour is still with us. There is considerable scientific evidence that society and social experience intersect with biological potentiality to make us human.
- Recent animal research, indicating the ability of pygmy chimpanzees to use language, has blurred the lines between humans and other animals. Add to this the growing documentation of abusive mothers and fathers, and we are faced with a profound issue—what does it mean to be a human being and how do we differ from other animals?
- Charles H. Cooley, George H. Mead, and Sigmund Freud provide insights into the social development of human beings. The work of Cooley and Mead demonstrates that the self is created through our interactions with others. Freud defined the personality in terms of the id, ego, and superego; personality developed as the inborn desires (id) clashed with social constraints (superego).
- The process by which we learn the ways of society is called socialization. Smoking cigarettes provides a useful example of the power and complexity of socialization.
- Socialization influences not only *how* we express our emotions, but *what* emotions we feel.
- Gender socialization is a primary means of controlling human behaviour, and a society's ideals of sex-linked behaviours are reinforced by its social institutions, such as family, and mass media
- Social institutions, organizations, groups, and individual people all influence our self-concept, emotions, attitudes, and behaviours.
- Socialization, which begins at birth, continues throughout the life course; at each stage the individual must adjust to a new set of social expectations. Most Canadians will be learning how to fit into the workplace which may involve anticipatory socialization, learning to play a role before entering it. We may also face situations in which we undergo resocialization, learning new norms, values, attitudes, and behaviours to match the new situation. The harshest of these is a total institution that strips the person of his or her personal identity kit.
- The life course is not experienced by all in the same ways, however; our socialization experiences are shaped by social and historical location.

LEARNING OBJECTIVES

As you read Chapter 4, use these learning objectives to organize your notes. After completing your reading, briefly state an answer to each of the objectives, and review the text pages in parentheses.

1. Discuss the basic assumptions about human nature and the degree to which animals have culture. (61)
2. Define socialization. (61)
3. Explain the theories of social development by Charles H. Cooley and George H. Mead. (62-63)

4. Review Freud's theory of personality development and note what sociologists appreciate about this theory as well as their criticisms of it. (63-64)
5. Discuss what the example of smoking tells us about processes of socialization. (64-65)
6. Describe ways in which gender socialization by the family channels human behaviour. (65-66)
7. Identify the ways in which cultural stereotypes of the sexes are perpetuated in the mass media and how peer groups use media images to construct ideas about gender appropriate behaviour. (66-69)
8. List and describe the influence of each agent of socialization on individuals. (69-73)
9. Define the term resocialization and discuss the process of resocialization that takes place within total institutions. (74-75)
10. Discuss socialization through the life course by summarizing each of the stages. (75-79)
11. Explain the important outcome of ongoing socialization—interpersonal trust, and the influence of historical and social location on the interactive process of socialization. (79-81)

CHAPTER OUTLINE

I.   **Social Experience or Genetic Predisposition?**
    A. In the nineteenth and early twentieth century many researchers believed that human behaviour was innate, but this thinking was challenged by early sociology.
    B. Research on children raised in orphanages, and cases like Genie's, the 13 1/2-year-old who had been kept locked in a small room for years, demonstrate the importance of early interaction for human development.
    C. Language is the key to human behaviour. This language system may take various forms—spoken, written, or, as with the American Sign Language, signed. This key experience is powerfully portrayed in the story of Helen Keller. Deaf, blind, and mute, as a child, Helen was seemingly trapped in her own world, until her teacher opened the world of communication for her.
    D. Babies do not "naturally" develop into human adults; although their bodies grow, human interaction is required for them to acquire the traits we consider normal for human beings.

II.   **The Social Development of the Self, Mind, and Emotions**
    A. Socialization is the process by which we learn the ways of our society.
    B. Charles H. Cooley (1864-1929) concluded that human development is socially created—that our sense of self develops from interaction with others. He coined the term "looking-glass self" to describe this process.
        1. According to Cooley, this process contains three steps: (1) we imagine how we look to others; (2) we interpret others' reactions (how they evaluate us); and (3) we develop a self-concept.
        2. A favourable reflection in the "social mirror" leads to a positive self-concept, while a negative reflection leads to a negative self-concept.
        3. Even if we misjudge others' reactions, the misjudgments become part of our self-concept.
        4. This development process is an ongoing, lifelong process.

C. George H. Mead (1863-1931) agreed with Cooley, but added that play is critical to the development of a self. In play, we learn to take the role of others: to understand and anticipate how others feel and think.
   1. Mead concluded that children are first able to take only the role of significant others (parents or siblings, for example); as the self develops, children internalize the expectations of other people, and eventually the entire group. Mead referred to the norms, values, attitudes, and expectations of people "in general" as the generalized other.
   2. According to Mead, the development of the self goes through stages: (1) imitation (children initially can only mimic the gestures and words of others); (2) play (beginning at age three, children play the roles of specific people, such as a firefighter or the Lone Ranger); and (3) games (in the first years of school, children become involved in organized team games and must learn the role of each member of the team).
   3. He distinguished the "I" from the "me" in development of the self: the "I" component is the subjective, active, spontaneous, creative part of the social self (for instance, "I shoved him"), while the "me" component is the objective part—attitudes internalized from interactions with others (for instance, "He shoved me").
D. Prominent Canadian sociologist Marlene Mackie uses Mead's three stages of "learning to take the role of the other," to explain how we learn our gender roles. While there may be generally similar gender socialization processes at work, gender socialization intersects in complicated ways with sexual orientation, social class, race, (dis)ability, and age.
E. Sigmund Freud (1856-1939) believed that personality consists of three elements—the id, ego, and superego.
   1. The id, inherited drives for self-gratification, demands fulfillment of basic needs such as attention, safety, food, and sex.
   2. The ego balances between the needs of the id and the demands of society.
   3. The superego, the social conscience we have internalized from social groups, gives us feelings of guilt or shame when we break rules, and feelings of pride and self-satisfaction when we follow them.
   4. Sociologists object to Freud's view that inborn and unconscious motivations are the primary reasons for human behaviour, for this view denies the central tenet of sociology: that social factors shape people's behaviours.
F. Smoking cigarettes provides a useful example of the power and complexity of socialization, seen in "The Social Creation of Teen Smokers."
G. Most socialization is meant to turn us into conforming members of society. We do some things and not others as a result of socialization. When we contemplate an action, we know the emotion (good or bad) that would result; thus, society sets up controls on our behaviour. Western males are socialized to express less emotion than are females, but in recent years they have been allowed to more openly express emotions, even in the military.

III.   Socialization Into Gender

A. By expecting different behaviours from people because they are male or female, society nudges boys and girls in separate directions. This foundation of contrasting attitudes and behaviours is so thorough that, as adults, most of us simply take gendered behaviour for granted. Often, we automatically act, think, and even feel emotions according to the guidelines laid down by our culture as appropriate for our sex.

B. Parents begin the process but much of this gender socialization is not intentional; rather, it is part of the taken-for-granted reality in which families unconsciously reflect and perpetuate societal beliefs and values. For example, the researchers found that parents of daughters tended to evaluate their children as lower in science interest and ability than parents of sons—even when not reflected in science grades at school.

C. The mass media also create and reinforce cultural expectations of gender.

    1. Although advertising uses a mix of gender images, it continues to perpetuate stereotypes by portraying males as more dominant and rugged and females as more sexy and submissive. In prime-time commercials women continue to be underrepresented.

    2. On prime-time TV, male characters outnumber females two to one and are more likely to be portrayed in higher-status positions.

    3. Male and female stereotypes may be changing. Research into popular situations comedies on TV found that male characters are expressing themselves emotionally and more frequently than females. Perhaps the most dramatic shift in the portrayal of girls and women on TV and film has been in horror and related genre. Males are much more likely than females to play video games; we have no studies of how these games affect their players' ideas of gender.

    4. Sociologist Melissa Milkie concluded that males used media images to discover who they were and what was expected of them as males.

IV.   Agents of Socialization

A. Our experiences in the family have a lifelong impact on us, laying down a basic sense of self, motivation, values, and beliefs.

B. Religion plays a major role in the socialization of many Canadians, even though we live in an increasingly secular period of Canadian history.

C. Increases in maternal employment and child care are global patterns, and day care has become a significant agent of socialization.

    1. Researchers have found that the effects of day care depend on the child's background and the quality of the care provided.

    2. Overall, the research findings suggest that children from stable homes receive no clear benefit or detriment from day care, and children in poverty and from dysfunctional families benefit from it.

D. Schools serve many manifest (intended) functions for society, including teaching skills and values thought to be appropriate. Schools also have several latent (unintended) functions.

    1. School children are placed outside the direct control of friends/relatives and exposed to new values and ways of looking at the world.

      2. Schools also have a hidden curriculum: values not explicitly taught but inherent in school activities.

  E. One of the most significant aspects of education is that it exposes children to peer groups. A peer group is a group of persons of roughly the same age who are linked by common interests. Next to the family, peer groups are the most powerful socializing force in society.

  F. Sports are also powerful socializing agents; children are taught not only physical skills but also values. Researchers have examined the role of sports in gender socialization.

  G. The workplace is a major agent of socialization for adults; from jobs, we learn not only skills but also a perspective on the world. We may engage in anticipatory socialization, learning to play a role before actually entering it, and enabling us to gradually identify with the role.

V.   Resocialization

  A. Resocialization refers to the process of learning new norms, values, attitudes and behaviours. Resocialization in its most common form occurs each time we learn something contrary to our previous experiences. Resocialization can be intense, involving the learning of a fundamentally different way of life, such as Alcoholics Anonymous.

  B. Erving Goffman coined the term total institution to refer to a place in which people are cut off from the rest of society and are under almost total control of agents of the institution, e.g. boot camps and prisons.

      1. A person entering the institution is greeted with a degradation ceremony through which his or her current identity is stripped away and replaced (e.g., fingerprinting, shaving the head, banning personal items, and being forced to strip and wear a uniform).

      2. Total institutions are quite effective as a result of isolating people from outside influences and information; supervising their activities; suppressing previous roles, statuses, and norms, and replacing them with new rules and values; and controlling rewards and punishments.

VI.   Socialization Through the Life Course

  A. Socialization occurs throughout a person's entire lifetime and can be broken up into different stages.

  B. Childhood (birth to 12): In earlier times, children were seen as miniature adults, who served an apprenticeship. To keep them in line, they were beaten and subjected to psychological torture. The current view is that children are tender and innocent, needing more adult care, comfort, and protection.

  C. Adolescence (13-17): Economic changes resulting from the Industrial Revolution brought about material surpluses that allowed millions of teenagers to remain outside the labour force, while at the same time the demand for education increased. A gap was created between childhood and adulthood; the term adolescence was coined to indicate this new stage in life. In particular, music, television, movies, and computer technology have served to frame this stage.

  D. Young Adulthood (18-29): Historian Kenneth Keniston noted that industrialized societies add a period of prolonged youth to the life course, in which postadolescents postpone adult responsibilities. Increasing numbers opt for intermediate steps, such as common law relationships. Also, more and more young Canadians are continuing to live with their parents or move out and then back in.

E. The Middle Years (30-65): This can be separated into two periods.
1. Early Middle Years: People are surer of themselves and their goals in life than before, but severe jolts such as divorce or being fired can occur. For Canadian women, it can be a trying period due to trying to "have it all"—job, family, and everything.
2. Later Middle Years: A different view of life—trying to evaluate the past and to come to terms with what lies ahead—emerges. Individuals may feel they are not likely to get much farther in life, while health and mortality become concerns. However, for most people it is the most comfortable period in their entire lives.

F. Older years (66 and beyond): This can also be separated into two periods.
1. The Early Older Years: For those in good health, being over 65, it is often experienced not as old age, but as an extension of the middle years, especially if they continue to work or be active in rewarding social activities.
2. The Later Older Years: There is no precise beginning point to this last stage, but may come around age threshold 75-85. For most, this stage is marked by growing frailty and illness, and eventually death.

G. The social significance of the life course is how it is shaped by social factors—the time period in which the person is born and lives his or her life as well as social location, the individual's social class, gender and race.

H. One of the most important outcomes of ongoing socialization is a sense of trust and belonging in the group, community, organization, or society, seen as dramatically accentuated by the experiences of "September 11."

KEY TERMS

After studying the chapter, review the definition for each of the following terms.

agents of socialization: people or groups that affect our self-concept, attitudes or orientations towards life

anticipatory socialization: because one anticipates a future role, one learns part of it now

degradation ceremony: a term coined by Harold Garfinkel to describe an attempt to remake the self by stripping away an individual's self-identity and stamping a new identity in its place

ego: Freud's term for a balancing force between the id and the demands of society

gender roles: the behaviours and attitudes considered appropriate because one is male or female

gender socialization: the ways in which society sets children onto different courses in life because they are male or female

generalized other: the norms, values, attitudes, and expectations of people "in general"; the child's ability to take the role of the generalized other is a significant step in the development of a self

id: Freud's term for the individual's inborn basic drives

latent function: the unintended consequences of people's actions that help to keep a social system in equilibrium

life course: the sequence of events that we experience as we journey from birth to death

looking-glass self: a term coined by Charles Horton Cooley to refer to the process by which our self develops through internalizing others' reactions to us

manifest functions: the intended consequences of people's actions designed to help some part of the social system

mass media: forms of communication, such as radio, newspapers, and television, directed to huge audiences

peer group: a group of individuals roughly the same age and linked by common interests

personal identity kit: items people use to decorate their bodies

resocialization: process of learning new norms, values, attitudes, and behaviours

self: the uniquely human capacity of being able to see ourselves "from the outside"; the picture we gain of how others see us

significant other: an individual who significantly influences someone else's life

social environment: the entire human environment, including direct contact with others

socialization: the process by which people learn the characteristics of their group—the attitudes, values, and actions thought appropriate for them

superego: Freud's term for the conscience, the internalized norms and values of our social groups

taking the role of the other: putting oneself in someone else's shoes; understanding how someone else feels and thinks and thus anticipating how that person will act

total institution: a place in which people are cut off from the rest of society and are almost totally controlled by the officials who run the place

KEY PEOPLE

Review the major theoretical contributions or findings of these people.

David Baxter: a Canadian demographer, argues that daycare children are more likely to be "cookie-sharing kids" than self-centred individualists.

Charles H. Cooley: Cooley studied the development of the self, coining the term "the looking-glass self."

Sigmund Freud: Freud developed a theory of personality development that took into consideration inborn drives (id), the internalized norms and values of one's society (superego), and the individual's ability to balance the two competing forces (ego).

Erving Goffman: Goffman studied the process of resocialization within total institutions.

Susan MacDaniel: writes on possible emergent schisms between younger and older women caused by greater opportunities for education for the younger women.

Mary and James Maxwell: The Maxwells studied socialization processes in a private school.

George Herbert Mead: Mead emphasized the importance of play in the development of the self, noting that children learn to take on the role of the other and eventually learn to perceive themselves as others do.

Melissa Milkie: This sociologist studied how adolescent boys use media images to discover who they are as males.

SELF-TEST

After completing this self-test, check your answers against the Answer Key at the back of this Study Guide and against the text on page(s) indicated in parentheses.

MULTIPLE CHOICE QUESTIONS

1. Which is true of the relationship between social experience and genetic predisposition? (61)
   a. In the nineteenth and early twentieth century many researchers believed that human behaviour was innate.
   b. The debate about the roots of human behaviour is not settled.
   c. Modern sociology has been an exploration of how social forces and the social environment shape human experience.
   d. all of the above

2. What conclusions can be drawn from the experience of Helen Keller? (61)
   a. Language is not a key to human behaviour.
   b. Language system comes only in one form.
   c. Humans, like animals, have instincts that take the place of language.
   d. Without language, people have no mechanism for developing thought and self-awareness.

3. What conclusions does the textbook suggest can be drawn from the case of Genie? (61)
   a. Mental retardation is biological.
   b. Early physical contact does little to change the intelligence levels of children.
   c. If bonding and learning to communicate with others does not occur prior to age 13, the biological window of opportunity may close.
   d. Linguistic acquisition in the teenage years is fundamental to development into adulthood.

4. Which of the following statements about the looking-glass self is *incorrect*? (62)
   a. The development of self is an ongoing, lifelong process.
   b. We move beyond the looking-glass self as we mature.
   c. The process of the looking-glass self applies to old age.
   d. The self is always in process.

5. According to Mead's theory, at what stage do children pretend to take the roles of specific people? (62-63)
   a. imitation
   b. game
   c. play
   d. generalized other

6. To George Mead, what is the "I"? (80)
   a. It is the self as subject.
   b. It is the self as object.
   c. It is the same as the id.
   d. It represents the passive robot aspect of human behaviour.

7. According to analysts, childhood socialization may have long-term influence on which of the following? (70)
   a. educational aspirations
   b. self-esteem
   c. personality traits
   d. all of the above

8. Researchers in Britain report that smoking imagery in films and youth style magazines was experienced by first year university students as (70)
   a. positive.
   b. sickly.
   c. depressed.
   d. anti-social.

9. What is the term Freud used to describe the balancing force between the inborn drives for self-gratification and the demands of society? (63)
   a. id
   b. superego
   c. ego
   d. libido

10. .In Freud's scheme, the superego represents (64)
    a. culture within us.
    b. the norms and values we have internalized from our social groups.
    c. the moral component of the personality.
    d. All of the above.

11. What is the significance of the example of smoking for our understanding of socialization? (64-65)
    a. Young people around the world feel the same pressures to smoke.
    b. It illustrates that the pressures from our social environment influence our behaviour.
    c. For the most part, smoking results in biological pressures.
    d. Smoking tells us very little about socialization.

12. According to this chapter, socialization is significant because: (62)
    a. it allows us to overcome innate biological instincts.
    b. it ensures that we abide by the rules of society.
    c. it shapes our fundamental sense of self.
    d. it helps us learn appropriate male and female roles.

13. What do we call the ways in which society sets children onto different courses for life purely because they are male or female? (65)

a. sex socialization
b. gender socialization
c. masculinization and feminization
d. brainwashing

14. What is true of sport as a socialization agent? (73)
    a. Everyone recognizes that sports teach not only physical skills but also values.
    b. Sports play little or no role in gender socialization.
    c. Sports are unrelated to construction of masculinities.
    d. Social class has no effect on children's involvement in sports.

15. Which of the following statements reflects the findings of research by Melissa Milkie? (72)
    a. Young males actively used media images to help them understand what was expected of them as males in our society.
    b. Young males avoided talking about male images in television and movies because they wanted to avoid being labelled a "weenie."
    c. Young females are passive consumers of media images, rather than active ones.
    d. Young males were very similar to young females in how they used media images as role models for "cool" behaviour.

16. What term does Erving Goffman use to define the family? (70)
    a. a total institution
    b. a backstage setting
    c. a socialization depot
    d. a primary agent of socialization

17. Religion plays a significant role in the socialization of many Canadians by (70)
    a. influencing reality
    b. becoming a key component in deciding right from wrong
    c. belonging to the church family
    d. All of the above

18. Which of the following statements summarizes the research findings on the impact that day care has on preschool children? (71)
    a. Regardless of the quality, day care benefits children.
    b. Children from poor and dysfunctional families do not benefit from day care, while children from stable families do.
    c. Children from poor and dysfunctional families benefit from quality day care.
    d. It is not the quality of the day care, but the quality of home life that makes the difference.

19. What is it that teachers are doing when they use stories and examples to teach math and English grammar that contain lessons in gender inequality? (71)
    a. following the formal curriculum
    b. teaching the hidden curriculum
    c. fulfilling a manifest function of education
    d. satisfying a latent function of education

20. Which of the following may be factors encouraged by peer groups? (72)
    a. success at school
    b. "girl gangs"
    c. female adolescent dress code pressure
    d. all of the above

21. Under which of the following conditions is resocialization likely to occur? (74)
    a. when we take a new job
    b. if we become members of Alcoholics Anonymous
    c. when we are sent to military boot camp
    d. all of the above would involve resocialization

22. Which of the following statements about total institutions is *incorrect*? (74)
    a. They suppress preexisting statuses, so that the inmates will learn that previous roles mean nothing and that the only thing that counts is their current role.
    b. They are not very effective in stripping away people's personal freedom.
    c. They are isolated, with barriers to keep inmates in and keep outsiders from interfering.
    d. They suppress the norms of the "outside world," replacing them with their own values, rules and interpretations.

23. What is it that historians have concluded about childhood? (75)
    a. It has always existed as a special time in a child's life.
    b. It was not as harsh in the past as it is today.
    c. It didn't exist in the past, as we know it; children were viewed as miniature adults.
    d. It was longer in the past because children stayed home until they were married.

24. Which of the following best describes the "sandwich generation"? (79)
    a. women who are in the early middle years, caring for young children
    b. grandparents who find themselves saddled with the care of grandchildren while their adult children are employed in the workforce
    c. older people who are caught between the world of retirement and their impending death
    d. people in their later middle years who are caught between caring for their own children and their aging parents

TRUE-FALSE QUESTIONS

T F   1.   In order for human interaction to occur, there needs to be a shared use of symbols. (61)

T F   2.   We routinely believe that human mothers will act in a way which, at least does not harm their children. (60)

T F   3.   Question of what it means to be human and where human nature is located remains as troubling as ever. (60)

T F   4.   George H. Mead introduced the concept of the generalized other to sociology. (62)

T F   5.   Recent research, such as with the pygmy chimpanzee, has blurred the lines between humans and other animals as far as existence of animal culture is concerned. (60)

T F   6.   According to Freud, the ego is the balancing force between the id and the demands of society that suppress it. (63)

T F   7.   Since smoking results from a biological addiction, socialization has very little to do with it. (64)

T F   8.   Socialization is important because it shapes what we desire, who we love, and how we experience sadness. (65)

T F   9.   Because social groups do not see boys and girls as fundamentally different from one another, they do not encourage them to develop different aspirations in life. (65)

T F 10. Advertisements continue to perpetuate gender stereotypes by portraying males as more dominant and rugged, and females as more sexy and submissive. (66)

T F 11. Homeless boys and girls rely heavily on their peers as a source of community. (72)

T F 12. The benefits of day care depend on the quality of the day care. (71)

T F 13. A latent function of education is the transmission of knowledge and skills needed in society. (71)

T F 14. Next to the family, the peer group is the most powerful socializing force in society. (72)

T F 15. Resocialization always requires learning a radically different perspective. (74)

T F 16. Total institutions are very effective in stripping away people's personal freedom. (74)

T F 17. Adolescence is a social creation in industrialized societies. (77-78)

T F 18. Early middle years pose a special challenge for Canadian women who believe that they can be super workers, super wives and super mums at the same time. (75-79)

T F 19. Industrialization brought with it a delay in the onset of old age. (79)

T F 20. Sociologists consider the stages of the life course to be a universal process; that is, all people experience these stages in the same way. (75-79)

FILL-IN QUESTIONS

1. Sociologists are interested in studying how the _____ influence(s) human experience. (61)

2. _____ is the process by which people learn the characteristics of their group— the attitudes, values, and actions thought appropriate for them. (61)

3. Charles H. Cooley coined the term _____ to describe the process by which a sense of self develops. (62)

4. _____ is the term Mead used to describe someone, such as a parent and/or a sibling, who plays a major role in our social development. (62)

5. According to George Herbert Mead, the development of the self through role-taking goes through three stages: (1) _____ ; (2) _____; and (3) _____. (62-63)

6. The idea that personality consists of the id, ego, and superego was developed by _____. (63-64)

7. We refer to the behaviours and attitudes which are considered appropriate for females and males as _____. (65)

8. Television, music, and advertising are all types of _____ which reinforce society's expectations of gender. (66-69)

9. _____ include the family, school, religion, peers, mass media, and workplace. (69)

10. Transmitting skills of reading, writing, and arithmetic is part of the _____ of education. (71)

11. The _____ refers to values that may not be taught explicitly, but nevertheless form an inherent part of a school's "message." (71)

12. _____ are made up of individuals the same age linked by common interests. (72)

13. The mental rehearsal for some future activity, or learning to play a role before actually entering it, is referred to as _____. (73)

14. Resocialization generally takes place in _____ such as boot camps, prisons, and concentration camps. (74)

15. _____ refers to the attempt to remake the self by stripping away an individual's self-identity and stamping a new identity in its place. (74)

MATCH THESE SOCIAL SCIENTISTS WITH THEIR CONTRIBUTIONS

___ 1. Erving Goffman

___ 2. George Herbert Mead

___ 3. Charles H. Cooley

___ 4. Sigmund Freud

___ 5. Melissa Milkie

___ 6. Susan MacDaniel

___ 7. David Baxter

a. *coined the term "looking-glass self"*

b. *studied the impact of media messages on adolescent males*

c. *coined the term "generalized other"*

d. *studied total institutions*

e. *asserted that human behaviour is based on unconscious drives*

f. *a Canadian demographer, argues that day care children are more likely to be "cookie-sharing kids" than self-centred individualists*

g. *possible schisms between younger/older women*

ESSAY QUESTIONS

1. Explain what is necessary in order for us to develop into full human beings.
2. Why do sociologists argue that socialization is a process and not a product?
3. How do ads play a role in creating and sustaining our societal views of gender?

"DOWN-TO-EARTH SOCIOLOGY"

1. On prime-time television, male characters outnumber female two to one. What impact will this have on the early development of most Canadians in whose lives television plays a prominent part? (67)
2. Peer groups tend to reinforce gender norms rewarding boys for athletic ability and girls physical appearance. Research also shows that boys use media images to discover who they are as males. (72)
3. Think of the many agents of socialization and evaluate the impact they have made on your life thus far, at whatever stage in the life course you are right now.

CHAPTER 5
SOCIAL STRUCTURE AND SOCIAL INTERACTION

CHAPTER SUMMARY

- There are two levels of sociological analysis; macrosociology investigates the large-scale features of social structure, while microsociology focuses on social interaction. Functional and conflict theorists tend to use a macrosociological approach.

- With their focus on face-to-face interaction, symbolic interactionism, queer theory, and feminism that emphasizes the social construction of gender are examples of microsociology. Postmodernism can be viewed as a recent example of both macrosociology and microsociology.

- The term social structure refers to a society's framework, which forms an envelope around us and sets limits on our behaviour. Social structure is also gendered.

- Social institutions are the organized and standard means that a society develops to meet its basic needs. Functionalists view social institutions as established ways of meeting universal group needs; however, conflict theorists see social institutions as the primary means by which the elite maintains its privileged position.

- Most sociologists agree that the mass media can be considered a social institution and research on it can contribute to our better understanding of contemporary society.

- Over time, social structure undergoes changes—sometimes very dramatic—as illustrated by Durkheim's concepts of mechanical and organic solidarity, and Tönnies' constructs of *Gemeinschaft* and *Gesellschaft* at the macro-level of society.

- An individual's location in the social structure affects his or her perceptions, attitudes, and behaviours. Culture, social class, social status, roles, groups, and institutions are the major components of the social structure.

- Groups are the essence of life in society. By standing between the individual and the larger society, groups help to prevent anomie. An essential feature of a group is that its members have something in common and that they believe what they have in common makes a difference. Society is the largest and most complex group that sociologists study.

- The following types of groups exist within society: primary groups, secondary groups, in-groups and out-groups, reference groups, and social networks. Changed technology has given birth to a new type of group—the electronic community.

- Group dynamics concern the ways in which individuals affect groups and the ways in which groups affect individuals. Group size is a significant aspect of group dynamics. Leaders can be either instrumental (task-oriented) or expressive (socioemotional); both are essential for the functioning of the group.

- The Asch experiment demonstrates the influence of peer groups over their members, while the Milgram experiment shows how powerfully people are influenced by authority. Groupthink may lead to overconfidence, illusions of invincibility, and blindness to risks.

- In contrast to functionalist and conflict theorists, who as macrosociologists focus on the "big picture," symbolic interactionists tend to be microsociologists who look at social interaction in everyday life. They examine how people look at things and how that, in turn, affects their behaviour.

- Stereotypes, assumptions we make about others based on their visible characteristics, guide our behaviour toward them; they, in turn, are influenced to behave in ways that reinforce our stereotypes.
- Symbolic interactionists note that each of us is surrounded by a "personal bubble" that we carefully protect. The size of the bubble varies from one culture to another. North Americans have four different "distance zones": intimate, personal, social, and public.
- The dramaturgical analysis provided by Erving Goffman analyzes everyday life in terms of the stage. At the core of this approach is the analysis of the impressions we attempt to make on others by using sign-vehicles (setting, appearance, and manner), teamwork, and face-saving behaviour.
- Ethnomethodologists try to uncover our background assumptions that provide us with basic ideas about the way life is. The social construction of reality refers to how we each create a view, or understanding, of how our world is.
- Both macrosociology and microsociology are needed to understand human behaviour because we must grasp both social structure and social interaction.

LEARNING OBJECTIVES

As you read Chapter 5, use these learning objectives to organize your notes. After completing your reading, briefly state an answer to each of the objectives, and review the text pages in parentheses.

1. Differentiate between macrosociology and microsociology and indicate which is most likely to be used by functionalists, conflict theorists, queer and feminist theorists, and symbolic interactionists. Post modernism can be viewed as a recent example of both macrosociology and microsociology. (83)
2. Discuss social structure and explain why a person's location in this structure affects his or her perceptions, attitudes, and behaviours. (83-84)
3. Explain what social institutions are, identify the social institutions common to all industrialized societies, and summarize the basic features of each. (84-86)
4. Compare and contrast functionalist feminist and conflict perspectives of society. (86)
5. Use Durkheim's concepts of mechanical and organic solidarity and Tönnies' typologies of *Gemeinschaft* and *Gesellschaft* to explain what holds societies together, and discuss their continuing relevance. (87-88)
6. Define the following concepts: culture, social class, social status, roles, and groups. (88-93)
7. Explain why groups are so important to individuals and to societies. (91)
8. Distinguish between a group, an aggregate, and a category. (91)
9. Define each of the following: primary groups, secondary groups, in-groups and out-groups, reference groups, and social networks. (91-94)
10. Identify the changes that have contributed to the emergence of the electronic community. (94-95)
11. Explain the concept of group dynamics and indicate how group size affects interaction. (95)
12. Describe the two types of leaders in groups. (95)
13. Discuss the impact of peer pressure on conformity by analyzing the Asch experiment. (96)
14. Explain the following about the Milgram experiment: purpose of study, how it was conducted, conclusions reached, and why the methodology was questioned. (97)
15. Discuss groupthink, explain how it can be dangerous for a society, and identify how this can be prevented. (96)

16. State the key assumptions of the symbolic interaction perspective regarding social life. (98)
17. Explain how stereotypes influence people's behaviour. (98)
18. Explain the concepts of personal space and touching and discuss how they are used differently in different cultures. (98-99)
19. Outline the key components of the dramaturgical view of everyday life and discuss how we manage our impression using sign-vehicles, teamwork, and face-saving behaviour. (100-102)
20. Describe the essence of postmodernism. (102-103)
21. Explain what "the social construction of reality" means and how this is related to the Thomas theorem. (103-104)
22. Indicate why macrosociology and microsociology are both needed to understand social life. (104)

CHAPTER OUTLINE

I.   **Levels of Sociological Analysis**
      A. Macrosociology places the focus on large-scale features of social structure. It investigates large-scale social forces and the effects they have on entire societies and the groups within them. It is utilized by functionalist and conflict theorists.
      B. Microsociology places the emphasis on social interaction and language, or what people do when they come together and how they communicate with each other. Symbolic interactionism, queer theory and feminism that emphasize the social construction of gender are examples. Postmodernism can be viewed as both macrosociology and microsociology..

II.   **The Macrosociological Perspective: Social Structure**
      A. Social structure is defined as the patterned relationships between people that persist over time. Behaviours and attitudes are determined by our location in the social structure. Components of social structure are culture, social class, social status, roles, groups, and institutions.
      B. Social institutions are the organized means that each society develops to meet its basic neeeds.
         1. The family, religion, law, politics, economics, education, science, medicine, and the military all are social institutions.
         2. Social institutions are sociologically significant because they set limits and provide guidelines for our behaviour.
      C. The mass media is an emerging social institution; it influences our attitudes toward social issues, other people, and even our self-concept. Of interest is who controls the mass media. Functionalists would say that the mass media represent the varied interests of the many groups that make up the nation, while conflict theorists would see that the interests of the political elite are represented.
      D. The functionalists and conflict theorists differ in how they see social institutions.
         1. Functionalists view social institutions as established ways of meeting universal group needs, including replacing members; socializing new members; producing and distributing goods and services; preserving order; and providing a sense of purpose.

   2. Conflict theorists look at social institutions as the primary means by which the elite maintains its privileged position.
   3. The main point recent feminist perspectives have stressed about gender inequality is that gender also is an element of social structure, not simply a characteristic of individuals.
E. Changes in social structure occur as a result of changes in culture, globalization, shifts in social classes and racial and ethnic groups, and so forth.
F. Many sociologists have tried to find an answer to the question of what holds society together.
   1. Social cohesion is the degree to which members of a society feel united by shared values and other social bonds.
   2. Emile Durkheim used mechanical solidarity and organic solidarity to explain what holds society together. Mechanical solidarity is a collective consciousness that people experience as a result of performing the same or similar tasks, while organic solidarity is a collective consciousness based on the interdependence brought about by the division of labour—how people divide up tasks.
   3. Ferdinand Tönnies analyzed how intimate community (*Gemeinschaft*) was being replaced by impersonal associations (*Gesellschaft*). *Gemeinschaft* is a society in which life is intimate; a community in which everyone knows everyone else and people share a sense of togetherness. *Gesellschaft* is a society dominated by impersonal relationships, individual accomplishments, and self-interest.
   4. These concepts are still relevant today, helping us to understand contemporary events such as the rise of Islamic fundamentalism.
G. Culture refers to a group's language, beliefs, values, behaviours, and gestures. It includes the material objects used by a group. It determines what kind of people we will become.
H. Social class is based on income, education, and occupational prestige. Large numbers of people who have similar amounts of income and education and who work at jobs that are roughly comparable in prestige make up a social class.
I. Social status refers to the positions that an individual occupies.
   1. Status set refers to all the statuses or positions that an individual occupies.
   2. Ascribed statuses are positions an individual either inherits at birth or receives involuntarily later in life. Achieved statuses are positions that are earned, accomplished, or involve at least some effort or activity on the individual's part.
   3. Status symbols are signs that identify a status.
   4. A master status—such as being male or female—cuts across the other statuses that an individual occupies. Status inconsistency is a contradiction or mismatch between statuses.
J. Roles are the behaviours, obligations, and privileges attached to a status. The individual occupies a status, but plays a role. Roles are an essential component of culture because they lay out what is expected of people, and as individuals perform their roles, those roles mesh together to form the society.

III.   Social Groups and Societies

A. Groups are the essence of life in society; the groups to which we belong help to determine our goals and values, how we feel about ourselves, and even how we feel about life itself.

B. An essential element of a social group is that its members have something in common and that they believe what they have in common makes a difference.

C. Society, which consists of people who share a culture and a territory, is the largest and most complex group that sociologists study.

IV.   Groups Within Society

A. Groups are viewed as a buffer between individuals and society.

1. Durkheim believed that small groups serve as a sort of lifeline that helps to prevent anomie.

2. Sociologists distinguish aggregates and categories from groups. An aggregate is made up of individuals who temporarily share the same physical space but do not have a sense of belonging together; a category is a collection of people who have similar characteristics. Unlike groups, the individuals who make up aggregates or categories do not interact with one another or take one another into account.

B. Sociologist Charles H. Cooley used the term "primary group" to refer to groups characterized by cooperative, intimate, long-term, face-to-face relationships.

1. The primary group becomes part of the individual's identity and the lens through which to view life.

2. Primary groups are essential to an individual's emotional well-being, since humans have an intense need for associations that provide feelings of self-esteem.

3. Some primary groups can be dysfunctional. Examples are families whose members quarrel and humiliate one another and gangs that purposely set themselves against society.

C. Secondary groups are larger, relatively temporary, more anonymous, formal, and impersonal than are primary groups, and are based on some interest or activity.

1. Members are likely to interact on the basis of specific roles, such as president, manager, worker, or student.

2. Although contemporary society could not function without secondary groups, such groups fail to satisfy deep human needs for intimate association.

3. To meet this need friendship cliques tend to form at school or work. These groups serve as a buffer between the individual and the needs of the larger secondary group.

D. Groups toward which individuals feel loyalty are called in-groups, while those toward which they feel antagonisms are called out-groups.

1. The division is significant sociologically because in-groups provide a sense of identification or belonging and exert a high degree of control over their members.

2. In-groups also foster ethnocentrism, encouraging members to judge their own accomplishments and characteristics as superior. Sociologist Robert K. Merton observed how this creates a double standard: the traits of an in-group are seen as virtues, while the same traits in an out-group are viewed as vices.

     3. Dividing the world into "us" and "them" can sometimes lead to acts directed against the out-groups.

  E. Reference groups are the groups we use as standards to evaluate ourselves, whether or not we actually belong to those groups.

     1. The yardsticks provided by reference groups operate as a form of social control.

     2. Having two reference groups that clearly conflict with each other can lead to internal turmoil.

  F. Social networks consist of people linked by various social ties.

     1. Think of a social network as ties that expand outward from yourself, gradually encompassing more and more people.

     2. Stanley Milgram did an experiment that demonstrated how small our social world really is; he found that social networks are so interrelated that almost everyone in the U.S. is connected by just five links.

     3. The term "networking" refers to the conscious use or even cultivation of contacts that people think will be helpful to them, for instance, by joining and belonging to clubs. Many networks are hard to break into; such as the "old boy" network, which keeps jobs moving in the direction of male friends and acquaintances.

  G. In the 1990s, due to technology, an entirely new type of human group made its appearance—the electronic community.

     1. Through the Internet, people around the world interact with one another in news groups.

     2. While most news groups are only an interesting, new way of communicating, some meet our definition of a group, because the people who use them have established relationships and think of themselves as belonging together.

     3. It is likely we are seeing a new form of social intimacy emerging. It is increasingly common to know friends or family members who have met on the web and formed long term relationships, even marriages.

V.   Group Dynamics

  A. How individuals affect groups and groups affect individuals is known as group dynamics.

     1. The study of group dynamics focuses on group size, leadership, conformity, and decision making.

     2. Sociologists recognize a small group as one that is small enough for everyone in it to interact directly with all the other members.

  B. As sociologist Georg Simmel (1858-1918) noted, the size of the group is significant for its dynamics.

     1. He used the term dyad for the smallest possible group, which consists of two people. A love affair is an example; if one member loses interest the dyad collapses.

     2. A triad is a group of three persons—a married couple with a first child, for example. Triads basically are stronger than dyads, but still potentially unstable. It is not uncommon for two members to feel stronger bonds with one another leaving the third member feeling hurt and excluded.

3. As more members are added to a group, its intensity decreases and its stability increases. To see why, look at Figure 5.2. As groups grow they tend to develop a more formal structure and more specialized roles to accomplish their goals. This structure enables groups to survive over time.

C. A leader may be defined as someone who influences the behaviour of others.

   1. There are two types of group leaders. Instrumental (task-oriented) leaders are those who try to keep the group moving toward its goals, reminding the members of what they are trying to accomplish. Expressive (socioemotional) leaders are those who are less likely to be recognized as leaders but help with the group's morale. Both types of leadership are essential: the one to keep the group on track, the other to increase harmony and minimize conflict.

   2. In general, sociologists do not think that people are "born" to be leaders. Rather, they find that people with certain characteristics are more likely to become leaders—those who represent the group's values, are seen as capable of leading the group out of crisis, are more talkative, express determination and self-confidence, are taller or are judged better looking.

   3. Lloyd Howells and Selwyn Becker discovered that the direction of interactions in a group had an impact on who became group leaders.

D. A study by Dr. Solomon Asch indicates that people are strongly influenced by peer pressure. Asch was interested in seeing whether individuals would resist the temptation to change a correct response to an incorrect response because of peer pressure.

   1. Asch held cards up in front of small groups of people and asked them which sets of cards matched; one at a time, they were supposed to respond aloud. All but one of the group members were confederates, having been told in advance by the researcher how to answer the question.

   2. After two trials in which everyone answered correctly, the confederates intentionally answered incorrectly, as they had been previously instructed to do.

   3. Of the fifty people tested, 33 percent ended up giving the incorrect answers of the rest of the group at least half of the time, even though they knew the answers were wrong; only 25 percent always gave the right answer despite the peer pressure.

E. Dr. Stanley Milgram sought to determine why otherwise "good people" apparently participated in the Nazis' slaughter of Jews and others.

   1. He conducted experiments in which one person (the "teacher") was instructed to administer an electric shock to the other person (the "learner") for each wrong answer given to certain questions, and to increase the voltage of the shock after each wrong answer.

   2. In fact, the "learner" was playing a role, intentionally giving wrong answers but only pretending to be receiving an electrical shock.

   3. Since a person in apparent authority (scientist, white coat, university laboratory) continually stated that the experiment had to go on, most of the "teachers" gave in to that authority and continued to administer the "shocks" even when they appeared to produce extreme pain.

   4. The scientific community was disturbed not only by Milgram's findings but also by his methods. Associations of social researchers accordingly adopted

codes of ethics to require that subjects be informed of the nature and purpose of social research, and almost all deception was banned.

F. Sociologist Irving Janis coined the word "groupthink" to refer to situations in which a group of people think alike and any suggestion of alternatives becomes a sign of disloyalty. Even moral judgments are put aside for the perceived welfare of the group.
1. The Asch and Milgram experiments demonstrate how groupthink can develop.
2. Groupthink can be prevented by giving free rein to diverse opinions and widest possible circulation to freely conducted social research.

VI.   The Microsociological Perspective: Social Interaction in Everyday Life

A. The microsociological approach places emphasis on face-to-face social interaction, or what people do when they are in the presence of one another.
B. Symbolic interactionists are interested in the symbols that people use to define their worlds, how people look at things, and how that affects their behaviour. Included within this perspective are studies of stereotypes, personal space and touching.
1. Stereotypes are used in everyday life. First impressions are shaped by the assumptions one person makes about another person's sex, race, age, and physical appearance. Such assumptions affect one's ideas about the person and how one acts toward that person. Stereotypes tend to bring out the very kinds of behaviour that fit the stereotype.
2. Personal space refers to the physical space that surrounds us and that we claim as our own. The amount of personal space people prefer varies from one culture to another.
3. Anthropologist Edward Hall found that North Americans use four different distance zones: (1) Intimate distance—about 45 centimetres from the body—for lovemaking, wrestling, comforting and protecting. (2) Personal distance—from 45 centimetres – 120 centimetres—for friends, acquaintances, and ordinary conversations. (3) Social distance—from 1 to 3.5 metres —for impersonal or formal relationships such as job interviews. (4) Public distance—beyond 3.5 metres—for even more formal relationships such as separating dignitaries and public speakers from the general public.
4. From our culture we learn rules about touching. Both the frequency and the meaning of touching vary from one culture to the next. Men and women react differently to being touched.
C. Dramaturgy is an analysis of how we present ourselves in everyday life.
1. Dramaturgy is the name given to an approach pioneered by Erving Goffman analyzing social life in terms of drama or the stage.
2. According to Goffman, socialization prepares people for learning to perform on the stage of everyday life. Front stage is where performances are given (wherever lines are delivered). Back stage is where people rest from their performances, discuss their presentations, and plan future performances.
3. Role performance is the particular emphasis or interpretation that an individual gives a role, the person's "style." Role conflict occurs when the expectations attached to one role are incompatible with the expectations of another role—in other words, conflict between roles. Role strain refers to conflicts that someone feels within a role.

4. Impression management is the person's efforts to manage the impressions that others receive of her or him.

5. Three types of sign-vehicles are used to communicate information about the self: (1) social setting—where the action unfolds, which includes scenery (furnishings used to communicate messages); (2) appearance—how a person looks when he or she plays his or her role, and this includes props which decorate the person; and (3) manner—the attitudes demonstrated as an individual plays her or his roles.

6. Teamwork, when two or more players work together to make sure a performance goes off as planned, shows that we are adept players.

7. When a performance doesn't come off, we engage in face-saving behaviour—ignoring flaws in someone's performance.

D. The social construction of reality refers to what people define as real because or their background assumptions and life experiences.

1. Symbolic interactionists believe that people define their own reality and then live within those definitions.

2. The Thomas theorem (by sociologist W. I. Thomas) states, "If people define situations as real, they are real in their consequences."

VII. The Need for Both Macrosociology and Microsociology

A. To understand human behaviour, it is necessary to grasp both social structure (macrosociology) and social interaction (microsociology).

B. Both are necessary for us to understand social life fully because each in its own way adds to our knowledge of human experience.

KEY TERMS

After studying the chapter, review the definitions of the following terms.

achieved statuses: positions that are earned, accomplished, or involve at least some effort or activity on the individual's part

aggregate: individuals who temporarily share the same physical space but do not see themselves as belonging together

appearance: how an individual looks when playing a role

ascribed statuses: positions an individual either inherits at birth or receives involuntarily later in life

back stage: where people rest from their performances, discuss their presentations, and plan future performances

background assumptions: deeply embedded common understandings, or basic rules, concerning our view of the world and how people ought to act

category: people who have similar characteristics

clique: clusters of people within a larger group who choose to interact with one another; an internal faction

coalition: the alignment of some members of a group against others

definition of the situation: the way we look at matters in life; the way we define reality or some particular situation

division of labour: the splitting of a group's or a society's tasks into specialties

dramaturgy: the name given to an approach, pioneered by Erving Goffman, analyzing social life in terms of drama or the stage; also called dramaturgical analysis

dyad: the smallest possible group, consisting of two persons

electronic community: individuals who more or less regularly interact with one another on the Internet

"electronic primary group": individuals who regularly interact with one another on the Internet, who see themselves as a group. and who develop close ties with one another

expressive leader: an individual who increases harmony and minimizes conflict in a group; also known as a socioemotional leader

face-saving behaviour: techniques used to salvage a performance that is going sour

front stage: where performances are given

functional requisites: the major tasks that a society must fulfill if it is to survive

Gemeinschaft: a type of society in which life is intimate; a community in which everyone knows everyone else and people share a sense of togetherness

Gesellschaft: a type of society dominated by impersonal relationships, individual accomplishments, and self-interests

group: defined differently by various sociologists, but in a general sense, people who have something in common and who believe that what they have in common is significant; also called a social group

group dynamics: the ways in which individuals affect groups and the ways in which groups affect individuals

groupthink: Irving Janis's term for a narrowing of thought by a group of people, leading to the perception that there is only one correct answer, in which the suggestion of alternatives becomes a sign of disloyalty

impression management: the term used by Erving Goffman to describe people's efforts to control the impressions that others receive of them

in-groups: groups toward which one feels loyalty

instrumental leader: an individual who tries to keep the group moving toward its goals; also known as a task-oriented leader

leader: someone who influences the behaviour of others

macrosociology: analysis of social life focusing on broad features or social structure, such as social class and the relationships of groups to one another; an approach usually used by functionalist and conflict theorists

manner: the attitudes that people show as they play their roles

master status: a status that cuts across the other statuses that an individual occupies

mechanical solidarity: a shared consciousness that people experience as a result of performing the same or similar tasks

microsociology: analysis of social life focusing on social interaction; an approach usually used by symbolic interactionist

networking: the process of consciously using or cultivating networks for some gain

organic solidarity: solidarity based on the interdependence brought about by the division of labour

out-groups: groups toward which one feels antagonism

postmodernism: analysis of contemporary social life where the use of images to convey meaning replaces social reality

primary group: a group characterized by intimate, long-term, face-to-face association and cooperation

reference group: Herbert Hyman's term for the groups we use as standards to evaluate ourselves

role: the behaviours, obligations, and privileges attached to a status

role performance: the ways in which someone performs a role within the limits that the role provides; showing a particular "style" or "personality"

secondary group: compared with a primary group, a larger, relatively temporary, more anonymous, formal, and impersonal group based on some interest or activity, whose members are likely to interact on the basis of specific roles

sign-vehicles: the term used by Goffman to refer to how people use social setting, appearance, and manner to communicate information about the self

small group: a group small enough for everyone to interact directly with all the other members

social class: a large number of people with similar amounts of income and education who work at jobs that are roughly comparable in prestige

social cohesion: the degree to which members of a group or society feel united by shared values and other social bonds

social construction of reality: the process by which people use their background assumptions and life experiences to define what is real for them

social institutions: the organized, usual, or standard ways by which society meets its basic needs

social interaction: what people do when they are in the presence of one another

social network: the social ties radiating outward from the self that link people together

social setting: the place where the action of everyday life unfolds

social structure: the framework that surrounds us, consisting of the relationship of people and groups to one another which give direction to and set limits on behaviour

society: people who share a culture and a territory

status: the position that someone occupies in society or a social group

status inconsistency (or discrepancy): a contradiction or mismatch between statuses

status set: all of the statuses or positions that an individual occupies

status symbols: items used to identify a status

stereotype: assumptions of what people are like, based on previous associations with them or with people who have similar characteristics, or based on information, whether true or false

teamwork: the collaboration of two or more persons interested in the success of a performance to manage impressions jointly

Thomas theorem: William I. Thomas's classic formulation of the definition of the situation: "If people define situations as real, they are real in their consequences."

triad: a group of three persons

KEY PEOPLE

Review the major theoretical contributions or findings of these people.

Solomon Asch: Asch is famous for his research on conformity to group pressure.

William Chambliss: Chambliss used macro- and microsociology to study high school gangs and found that social structure and interaction explained the patterns of behaviour in these groups.

Charles H. Cooley: It was Cooley who noted the central role of primary groups in the development of one's sense of self.

Emile Durkheim: Durkheim identified mechanical and organic solidarity as the keys to social cohesion. Durkheim also viewed the small group as a buffer between the individual and society, helping to prevent anomie.

Erving Goffman: Goffman developed dramaturgy, the perspective within symbolic interactionism that views social life as a drama on the stage.

Edward Hall: This anthropologist found that personal space varied from one culture to another and that North Americans use four different "distance zones."

Lloyd Howells and Selwyn Becker: These social psychologists found that factors such as location within a group underlie people's choices of leaders.

Irving Janis: Janis coined the term "groupthink" to refer to the tunnel vision that a group of people sometimes develops.

Robert K. Merton: Merton observed that the traits of in-groups become viewed as virtues, while those same traits in out-groups are seen as vices.

Joshua Meyrowitz: This sociologist stresses that the media should not be considered as passable channels of information, but rather, they shape our lives.

Stanley Milgram: Milgram's research has contributed greatly to sociological knowledge of group life. He did research on social networks as well as individual conformity to group pressure.

Georg Simmel: This early sociologist was one of the first to note the significance of group size; he used the terms dyad and triad to describe small groups.

Mark Snyder: Snyder carried out research in order to test whether or not stereotypes are self-fulfilling; he found that subjects were influenced to behave in a particular way based on their stereotypes.

W. I. Thomas: This sociologist was known for his statement, "If people define situations as real, they are real in their consequences."

Ferdinand Tönnies: Tönnies analyzed different types of societies that existed before and after industrialization. He used the terms *Gemeinschaft* and *Gesellschaft* to describe the two types of societies.

SELF-TEST

After completing this self-test, check your answers against the Answer Key at the back of this Study Guide and against the text on page(s) indicated in parentheses.

MULTIPLE CHOICE QUESTIONS

1. Which of the following statements applies to microsociology? (83)
    a. It focuses on social interaction.
    b. It investigates large-scale social forces.
    c. It focuses on broad features of social structure.
    d. It is used by functionalists and conflict theorists.

2. Which level of analysis do sociologists use to study social class and group structure? (83-84)
    a. dramaturgy
    b. ethnomethodology
    c. macrosociology
    d. microsociology

3. You want to study how homeless mothers care for their children. Which would you use? (83)
    a. macrosociology
    b. microsociology
    c. functionalism
    d. conflict perspective

4. The term social structure refers to: (83-84)
    a. the framework of society.
    b. the patterns of society.
    c. relationships between individuals or groups within a society.
    d. all of the above.

5. Of what are religion, politics, education, and the military all examples? (85)
    a. involuntary groups
    b. voluntary associations
    c. social institutions
    d. social fixtures

6. What term do sociologists use to describe activities such as the replacement of members and the socialization of new members of a society? (86)
    a. functional necessities
    b. functional requisites
    c. functional prerequisites
    d. dysfunctional prerequisites

7. Which perspective states that social institutions are controlled by an elite that uses them to its own advantage? (86)
   a. functionalist
   b. conflict
   c. symbolic interactionist
   d. dramaturgy

8. Which of the following would be found in a society characterized by organic solidarity? (87-88)
   a. a highly specialized division of labour
   b. members who are interdependent on one another
   c. a high degree of impersonal relationships
   d. all of the above

9. What type of society is it where everyone knows everyone else, people conform because they are very sensitive to the opinions of others and want to avoid being gossiped about, and people draw comfort from being part of an intimate group? (88)
   a. *Gemeinschaft*
   b. *Gesellschaft*
   c. mechanical society
   d. organic society

10. Which of the following refers to the position that an individual holds in a social group? (89)
    a. social class
    b. social status
    c. social role
    d. social location

11. A person is simultaneously a daughter, a lawyer, a wife, and a mother. All together, what are these? (89)
    a. social status
    b. social class
    c. status position
    d. status set

12. Which of the following describes an individual's race, sex, and inherited social class? (90)
    a. ascribed statuses
    b. achieved statuses
    c. status inconsistencies
    d. status incongruities

13. Wedding rings, military uniforms, and clerical collars are all examples of what? (90)
    a. social stigma
    b. social class
    c. status symbols
    d. achieved statuses

14. Which of the following statements regarding status symbols is incorrect? (90)

a. Status symbols are signs that identify a status.
b. Status symbols often are used to show that people have "made it."
c. Status symbols are always positive signs or people would not wear them.
d. Status symbols are used by people to announce their statuses to others.

15. What is a master status? (90)
a. It is always an ascribed status.
b. It is a status that cuts across the other statuses that a person holds.
c. It can be fairly easily changed.
d. It is a status that identifies high ranking members of a society.

16. Under what conditions is status inconsistency most likely to occur? (90)
a. when a contradiction or mismatch between statuses exists
b. when we know what to expect of other people
c. when a person wears too many status symbols at once
d. when a society has few clearly defined master statuses

17. What do we call the behaviours, obligations, and privileges attached to statuses? (91)
a. status sets
b. master statuses
c. status differentiations
d. roles

18. How does thinking of your high school hockey team give you a clearer picture of social structure? (89)
a. Each position in the team is a status.
b. For each of the statuses, there is a role.
c. Each of the status positions has particular expectations attached to it.
d. all of the above

19. The essential feature of a _____ is that its members have something in common and they believe that what they have in common makes a difference. (91)
a. assembly
b. aggregate
c. category
d. group

20. A _____ consist of people who have similar characteristics. (91)
a. group
b. aggregate
c. category
d. society

21. According to Emile Durkheim, what is the value of small groups? (91)
    a. They promote diversity.
    b. They generate change.
    c. They prevent anomie.
    d. They encourage conformity.

22. According to Cooley, _____ are essential to our emotional well-being and he calls them the "springs of life." (92)
    a. primary groups
    b. secondary groups
    c. therapy groups
    d. interpersonal groups

23. Secondary groups: (92)
    a. have members who are likely to interact on the basis of specific roles.
    b. are characteristic of industrial societies.
    c. are essential to the functioning of contemporary societies.
    d. all of the above

24. Attacks against immigrants or a national anti-immigration policy is an example of: (93)
    a. homophobia.
    b. arachnophobia.
    c. agoraphobia.
    d. xenophobia.

25. Why are reference groups important? (93)
    a. They meet our intense need for face-to-face interaction.
    b. They are an efficient way in which to achieve goals or complete tasks.
    c. They provide us with standards we use to evaluate ourselves.
    d. They are groups towards which we feel an intense sense of loyalty.

26. What term describes the social ties radiating out from the self, linking people together? (93)
    a. social networks
    b. reference groups
    c. cliques
    d. inner-circles

27. Sociologists refer to the conscious use or cultivation of networks for some gain as: (93)
    a. networking.
    b. group dynamics.
    c. social climbing.
    d. being a user.

28. Dyads: (95)
    a. are the most intense or intimate of human groups.
    b. require continuing active participation and commitment of both members.
    c. are the most unstable of social groups.
    d. all of the above

29. Personal space might be a research topic for a sociologist using which type of perspective? (98)
    a. macro-level analysis
    b. functional analysis
    c. symbolic interactionism
    d. the conflict perspective

30. According to Goffman, where do we go when we want to retreat and let our hair down? (100)
    a. front stage
    b. back stage
    c. inside the drama
    d. outside the drama

31. Although our statuses usually fit together fairly well, sometimes a mismatch occurs, such as a 14-year old university student. This is known as a (90)
    a. status inconsistency.
    b. role performance.
    c. role demands.
    d. role conflict.

32. The largest and most complex group that sociologists study is (91)
    a. society.
    b. dyad.
    c. triad.
    d. primary group.

33. To communicate information about the self, we use three types of sign vehicles: (102)
    a. social setting, teamwork, manner
    b. social setting, appearance, manner
    c. gender roles, teamwork, manner
    d. social setting, gender roles, teamwork

34. When a performance does not come off quite right, it may require (102)
    a. face-saving behaviour.
    b. teamwork.
    c. role performance.
    d. sign-vehicles.

35. Within which sociological perspective would you place the Thomas theorem? (104)
    a. functionalism
    b. conflict theory
    c. symbolic interactionism
    d. exchange theory

TRUE-FALSE QUESTIONS

T F   1.   Social structure has little impact on the typical individual. (83)

T F   2.   Sociologists have identified five basic social institutions in contemporary societies. (84)

T F   3.   Most sociologists agree that the mass media can be considered a social institution. (86)

T F   4.   According to Emile Durkheim, as societies increase in size, their division of labour becomes more specialized and a new form of solidarity he called organic solidarity emerges. (87-88)

T F   5.   *Gemeinschaft* society is characterized by impersonal, short-term relationships. (88)

T F   6.   The differences in behaviour and attitudes are not due to biology, but to people's location in the social structure. (84)

T F   7.   To sociologists, the terms "social class" and "social status" mean the same thing. (89)

T F   8.   Being a student is an example of an achieved status. (90)

T F   9.   The purpose of status symbols is to tell the world that you've made it to a particular place in society. (90)

T F   10.   Being male or female is not considered a master status. (90)

T F   11.   You occupy a status, but you play a role. (91)

T F   12.   The groups to which we belong have no impact on how we feel about ourselves. (91)

T F   13.   Society is the largest and most complex group that sociologists study. (91)

T F   14.   Anomie is most likely to occur in the absence of ties to primary groups. (91)

T F   15.   Members of primary groups are likely to interact with each other on the basis of specific roles. (92)

T F   16.   Robert Merton observed that traits of our in-groups tend to be viewed as virtues, while those same traits are seen as vices when found among members of out-groups. (92)

T F   17   Reference groups are the groups we use as standards to evaluate ourselves. (93)

T F   18.   Research by Stanley Milgram demonstrates how small our social world really is. (93)

T F   19.   Networking refers to the conscious use or even cultivation of networks. (93)

T F   20.   Dyads are more intimate and stable than triads. (95)

T F   21.   As a small group grows larger, its intensity decreases and its stability increases. (95)

T F   22.   The Asch experiment used fake shocks to demonstrate that people would do anything for authority figures. (96)

T F   23.   We have a tendency to make assumptions about a person based on his or her visible features; these stereotypes may affect how we act toward that person. (98)

T F   24.   The amount of personal space people prefer varies from one culture to another. (98)

T F   25.   Researchers have found that lower-status individuals tend to touch more, because touching is a way of claiming more status. (99)

T F   26.   According to Erving Goffman, back stages are where we can let our hair down. (100)

T F   27.   The same setting can serve as both a back and a front stage. (100)

T F   28.   Most advertising and television programs that focus on weight are directed at women. (101)

T F   29.   A face-saving technique in which people give the impression that they are unaware of a flaw in someone's performance is known as impression management. (102)

T F   30.   To understand social life adequately, we need both microsociology and macrosociology.. (102)

FILL-IN QUESTIONS

1.   _____ investigates such things as social class and how groups are related to one another. (83)

2.   The level of sociological analysis used by symbolic interactionists and postmodernists is _____. (83)

3.   The _____ perspective states that societies must replace their members, teach new members, produce and distribute goods and services, preserve order, and provide a sense of purpose. (86)

4.   A society's basic needs, which are required in order to guarantee survival, are called _____. (86)

5.   Durkheim referred to a collective consciousness that people experience due to performing the same or similar tasks as _____. (87)

6.   _____ is all of the statuses or positions that an individual occupies. (89)

7.   A social position that a person assumes voluntarily is _____. (90)

8.   _____ are signs used to identify a status. (90)

9.   Groups in which people are assigned membership rather than choosing to join are _____. (91)

10. The term _____ is used to describe individuals who temporarily share the same physical space but do not see themselves as belonging together. (91)

11. A _____ group is characterized by relatively temporary, more anonymous, formal, and impersonal relationships. (92)

12. _____ provide a sense of identification or belonging while producing feelings of antagonism towards _____. (92)

13. The groups we use as standards to evaluate ourselves are _____. (93)

14. Individuals who interact with one another on the Internet, whether on a regular basis or not, are known as a(n) _____. (94)

15. The smallest possible group is a(n) _____. (95)

16. Someone who influences the behaviour of others is a(n) _____. (95)

17. An individual who tries to keep the group moving toward its goals is a(n) _____ leader. An individual who increases harmony and minimizes conflict is a(n) _____ leader. (95)

18. The events in the United States called 9/11 are an example of _____. (96)

19. _____ is a narrowing of thought by a group of people, which results in overconfidence and tunnel vision. (96)

20. _____ focuses on face-to-face social interactions. (98)

21. Erving Goffman believed that in order to communicate information about the self, individuals use three types of _____. (102)

22. Goffman called the sign-vehicle that refers to the attitudes that we demonstrate as we play our roles _____. (102)

23. For _____, television and electronic media are the two primary "socializing" agents. (103)
24. What people define as real because of their background assumptions and life experiences is the _____. (103)
25. The _____ states, "If people define situations as real, they are real in their consequences." (104)

MATCH THESE SOCIAL SCIENTISTS WITH THEIR CONTRIBUTIONS

__1.   Emile Durkheim
__2.   Ferdinand Tönnies
__3.   Edward Hall
__4.   Erving Goffman
__5.   W. I. Thomas
__6.   Irving Janis
__7.   Georg Simmel
__8.   Emile Durkheim
__9.   Stanley Milgram
__10.   Solomon Asch
__11.   Charles H. Cooley
__12.   Robert K. Merton
__13.   Mark Snyder

a.   *described* Gemeinschaft *and* Gesellschaft *societies*
b.   *wrote about mechanical and organic solidarity*
c.   *analyzed everyday life in terms of dramaturgy*
d.   *studied the concept of personal space*
e.   *wrote a theorem about the nature of social reality*
f.   *primary groups*
g.   *obedience to authority*
h.   *dyads*
i.   *studied how stereotypes influence behaviour*
j.   *small groups and anomie*
k.   *groupthink*
l.   *conformity to peer pressure*
m.   *in-group prejudice leads to double standard*

ESSAY QUESTIONS

1. Choose a research topic and discuss how you approach this topic using both macrosociological and microsociological approaches.
2. Describe Tonnies term *Gemeinschaft* as an ideal type of construct. Then, describe the community you have experienced that most closely resembles this type.
3. Discuss the benefits and drawbacks to in-groups and out-groups.
4. Assume that you have been asked to give a presentation to your sociology class on Goffman's dramaturgy approach. Describe what information you would want to include in such a presentation.

"DOWN-TO-EARTH SOCIOLOGY"

1. Can you identify the social structure of some group to which you belong? What conclusions can you draw about the importance of social structure?
2. Are you a member of an electronic community like the ones described on page 94? If you are, how would you describe your relationships with others within your particular community? Do you find yourself in closer, more personal relationships with your electronic friends than those you see every day? Why do you think that is? If you have never participated in an electronic community, why not?
3. After reading about the Milgram experiments on page 97, consider how you would have reacted if you had been selected to participate. Under what conditions would you have carried out the orders? Under what conditions would you have disobeyed? Did the fact that Milgram was able to discover an important aspect of human behaviour justify the methods which he used?
4. After reading on pages 100-101 about the mass media and the presentation of the body in everyday life, think about your own sense of your body. How do you see yourself? How do you think others see you? To what degree do you think that your views reflect cultural expectations? Do you think that our cultural standards concerning body image are tougher on women than men?
5. After reading this chapter, try and analyze the statuses, roles, and so on in your own life.
6. What reference groups have you used in anticipatory socialization?

CHAPTER 6
SOCIAL INEQUALITY: GLOBAL AND NATIONAL PERSPECTIVES

CHAPTER SUMMARY

- Social stratification is a system in which people are divided into layers according to their relative power, property, and prestige. The nations of the world, as well as people within a nation, are stratified into groups based on relative power, prestige, and property. Social stratification affects our life chances—from material possessions to the age at which we die. Every society stratifies its members in some form.

- Four major systems of social stratification include (1) slavery—owning other people; (2) caste—lifelong status determined by birth; (3) clan—status depends on lineage; and (4) class—based on possession of money or material possessions. Class systems are characteristic of industrialized societies.

- Early sociologists disagreed about the meaning of social class in industrialized nations. Karl Marx argued that a person's relationship to the means of production was the only factor determining social class. Max Weber argued that three elements—property, prestige, and power—dictate an individual's standing in society.

- Most sociologists have adopted Weber's definition of social class as a large group of people who rank closely to one another in terms of wealth, power, and prestige. Social class can be measured in three different ways: subjective method, reputational method, and objective method. Most sociologists prefer the objective method.

- The three criteria for measuring social class are wealth, consisting of property and income; power, consisting of the ability to carry out one's will despite the resistance of others; and prestige, consisting of the regard or respect accorded an individual or social position. Most people are status consistent, meaning that they rank high or low on all three dimensions of social class. People who rank high on some dimensions and low on others are status inconsistent. According to Lenski, the frustration of status inconsistency tends to produce political radicalism.

- Various arguments have been developed to explain the universal presence of stratification. Kingsley Davis and Wilbert Moore argued that society must offer rewards in order to assure that important social positions are filled by the most competent people.

- To maintain stratification within a nation, the ruling class controls ideas and information, depends on social networks, and relies on force.

- The classification of nations into most industrialized, industrializing, and least industrialized is helpful, pointing to gross differences among them, but adding a fourth category of the oil-rich, non-industrialized nations is more accurate.

- Four theories explaining the origins of global stratification are imperialism and colonialism, world system theory, dependency theory, and the culture of poverty. International stratification is maintained through neocolonialism, the ongoing dominance of the Least Industrialized Nations by the Most Industrialized nations, and multinational corporations which operate across national boundaries. The new technology gives advantage to the world's Most Industrialized nations.

- Sociologists use two models to portray the social class structure. Erik Wright developed a four-class model based on the ideas of Karl Marx. Dennis Gilbert and Joseph Kahl developed a six-class model based on the ideas of Max Weber.
- Social class leaves no aspect of life untouched. Class membership affects life chances, physical and mental health, family life, politics, religion, education, and contact with crime and the criminal justice system.
- In studying the mobility of individuals within society, sociologists look at intergenerational mobility, individual changes in social class from one generation to the next; exchange mobility, the movement of large numbers of people from one class to another; structural mobility, the social and economic changes that affect the social class position of large numbers of people; and the impact of new technology.
- Poverty is unequally distributed across Canada. While poverty is related to geography, however, the greatest predictors of poverty are race/ethnicity, education, and the sex of the person who heads the family. Sociologists generally focus on structural factors, such as employment opportunities, in explaining poverty, sifting facts from myths.
- The Horatio Alger myth encourages people to strive to get ahead, and blames failures on individual shortcomings.

LEARNING OBJECTIVES

As you read Chapter 6, use these learning objectives to organize your notes. After completing your reading, briefly state an answer to each of the objectives, and review the text pages in parentheses.

1. Define social stratification and explain why it is of sociological significance. (109)
2. Describe the characteristics of slavery and note the uses of slavery in the New World. (110)
3. Identify the features of caste systems. Give examples of different ones. (110-111)
4. List the characteristics of a class system and contrast its features with those of other systems of stratification. (111)
5. Identify the basic assumptions of Karl Marx regarding what determines social class. (111-112)
6. Explain why Max Weber was critical of Marx's perspective, and summarize Weber's views regarding social class position. (112-113)
7. Compare the three ways of measuring social class. (114)
8. Outline and explain the components of social class. (114-119)
9. Define status inconsistency and discuss the consequences for individual behaviour. (119)
10. State the basic assumptions of functionalists like Davis and Moore, and present Tumin's criticisms of this viewpoint. (119-120)
11. Explain the mechanisms by which the elite maintains stratification. (121)
12. Describe the major characteristics of the three worlds of development, name the regions that fit in each category, and summarize some of the problems presented by this classification. (122-124)
13. Outline the major theories of how the world's nations became stratified and explain how global stratification has been maintained. (124-125)
14. Explain Erik Wright's updated model of Marx's class theory. (127-128)
15. Discuss Gilbert and Kahl's updated model of Weber's perspective. (128)
16. Examine the consequences of social class for new technology, physical and mental health, family life, education, religion, politics, and the criminal justice system. (130)

17. Discuss the patterns of social mobility within Canada and note the role that technology has played in terms of mobility, both upward and downward. (132-133)
18. Indicate how the poverty line is drawn and state the major characteristics of the poor in Canada. (134-135)
19. Assess individual versus structural explanations of poverty. (136-141)
20. Identify the social functions of the Horatio Alger myth. (141-142)

CHAPTER OUTLINE

I.   What is Social Stratification?
        A. Social stratification is a system in which large groups of people are divided into layers according to their relative power, property, and prestige.
        B. Stratification exists within a society and among nations and affects our life chances and our orientations to life.

II.   **Systems of Social Stratification**
        A. Slavery is a form of social stratification in which some people own other people.
            1. Initially, slavery was based on debt, punishment for violation of the law, or defeat in battle.
            2. Slavery could be temporary or permanent and was not necessarily passed on to one's children. Typically, slaves owned no property and had no power; however, this was not universally true.
            3. The first form of slavery in the New World was indentured service—a contractual system in which someone voluntarily sold his or her services for a specified period of time; at the end of that time the individual was freed.
            4. Given the shortage of indentured servants, American colonists first tried to enslave Indians and then turned to Africans, who were being brought to North and South America by the British, Dutch, English, Portuguese, and Spanish.
        B. In a caste system, status is determined by birth and is lifelong.
            1. Ascribed status is the basis of a caste system. Societies with this form of stratification try to make certain that boundaries between castes remain firm by practicing endogamy (marriage within their own group) and developing rules about ritual pollution—teaching that contact with inferior castes contaminates the superior caste.
            2. Although abolished by the Indian government in 1949, the caste system remains part of everyday life in India, as it has for almost three thousand years. This system is based on religion and is made up of four main castes, or *varnas*, which are subdivided into thousands of specialized subcastes or *jati*. The lowest caste is considered to be "untouchable," and ablutions—washing rituals—are required to restore purity for those contaminated by individuals from this group. India's caste system is finally breaking down because of industrialization and urbanization.
        C. Clan systems used to be common in agricultural societies. Each individual is linked to a large network of relatives. A clan system is one in which the individual's status depends on lineage linking him or her to an extended network of relatives.
            1. Although clan membership is determined by birth and is lifelong, interclan marriage is permitted and is sometimes used to forge alliances between clans.

2. Industrialization and urbanization are making clans more fluid, even replacing them by social classes.

D. A class system is a form of social stratification based primarily on the possession of money or material possessions.

1. Initial social class position is based on that of one's parents (ascribed status).

2. With relatively fluid boundaries, a class system allows for social mobility—movement up or down the social class ladder—based on achieved status.

III. What Determines Social Class?

A. According to Karl Marx, social class is determined by one's relationship to the means of production—the tools, factories, land, and investment capital used to produce wealth.

1. The bourgeoisie (capitalists) own the means of production; the proletariat (workers) are the people who work for those who own the means of production.

2. As capital becomes more concentrated, the two classes will become increasingly more hostile to one another.

3. Class consciousness—awareness of a common identity based on position in the means of production—will develop; it is the essential basis of the unity of workers, according to Marx.

4. Marx believed that the workers would revolt against the capitalists, take control of the means of production, and usher in a classless society. However, the workers' unity and revolution are held back by false consciousness—the mistaken identification of workers with the interests of capitalists.

B. Unlike Marx, Max Weber did not believe that property was the sole basis of a person's position in the stratification system, but rather that property, prestige, and power determine social class.

1. Property is an essential element; however, powerful people, like managers of corporations, control the means of production although they do not own them.

2. Prestige may be derived from ownership of property; however, it also may be based on other factors such as athletic skills.

3. Power is the ability to control others, even over their objections.

C. Social class can be defined as a large group of people who rank close to each other in wealth, power, and prestige.

D. There are three ways of measuring social class.

1. The subjective method consists of asking people what their own social class is; however, most people give the wrong answer.

2. The reputation method consists of asking people what class other people belong to, based on their reputations. It generally is useful only in smaller cities, where people know each other's reputations.

3. The objective method consists of ranking people according to objective criteria such as wealth, power, and prestige. Most sociologists use the objective method.

IV.   The Components of Social Class

A. Wealth consists of property (what we own) and income (money we receive). Wealth and income are not always the same—a person may own much property yet have little income, or vice versa. Usually, however, wealth and income go together.

   1. Ownership of property (real estate, stocks and bonds, etc.) is not distributed evenly; 80% of all corporate stocks and bonds are owned by fewer than 1000 individuals. These "super-rich" make up less than 2% of the Canadian population.

   2. Currently, the wealthiest 50 percent of the Canadian population own 94 percent of all national wealth, and the poorest 50 percent is left with only 6 percent.

   3. The average family income of Canadian families in 2000, shows the highest decile with $185,070 and the lowest decile with $10,341. The most affluent group in Canadian society is the executive officers (CEOs) of the largest corporations. Canada's top ten CEOs each took home over $10 million in 1997.

B. Power is the ability to carry out your will despite resistance. Power is concentrated in the hands of a few—the "power elite"—who share the same ideologies and values, belong to the same clubs, and reinforce each other's world view. No major decision in government is made without their approval.

C. Prestige is the respect or regard people give to various occupations and accomplishments.

   1. Occupations are the primary source of prestige, although some people gain prestige through inventions, feats, or doing good to others. Occupations with the highest prestige pay more, require more education, entail more abstract thought, and offer greater autonomy.

   2. For prestige to be valuable, people must acknowledge it. The elite traditionally has made rules to emphasize its higher status.

   3. Status symbols, which vary according to social class, are ways of displaying prestige. They may include designer label clothing, expensive cars, and prestigious addresses.

D. Status inconsistency is the term used to describe the situation of people who have a mixture of high and low rankings in the three components of social class (wealth, power, and prestige).

   1. Most people are status consistent—they rank at the same level in all three components. People who are status inconsistent want others to act toward them on the basis of their highest status, but others tend to judge them on the basis of their lowest status.

   2. Sociologist Gerhard Lenski determined that people suffering the frustrations of status inconsistency are more likely to be radical and approve political action aimed against higher status groups.

V. Why Is Social Stratification Universal?

    A. According to the functionalist view expressed by Kingsley Davis and Wilbert Moore, stratification is inevitable.

        1. Society must make certain that its important positions are filled; to guarantee that the more important positions are filled by the more qualified people, society must offer them greater rewards.

        2. Davis and Moore argued that society offers greater rewards for its more responsible, demanding, and accountable positions.

    B. Melvin Tumin was the first to present a number of criticisms to the Davis and Moore thesis.

        1. He asked how the importance of a position is measured (e.g., "Is a surgeon really more important to society than a garbage collector?"). Rewards can not be used to measure the importance of a job; there must be some independent measure of importance.

        2. He noted that if stratification worked as Davis and Moore describe it, society would be a meritocracy—a form of social stratification in which all positions are awarded on the basis of merit—but it does not work this way (e.g., the best predictor of college entrance is family income, not ability).

        3. He also argued that money and fringe benefits are not the only reasons people take jobs.

        4. Finally, he noted that stratification is dysfunctional to many people, thus not functional.

    C. Conflict theorists stress that conflict, not function, is the basis of social stratification.

        1. Every society has only limited resources to go around, and in every society groups struggle with one another for those resources.

        2. Whenever a group gains power, it uses that power to extract what it can from the groups beneath it. The dominant group takes control of the social institutions, using them to keep other groups weak and to preserve the best resources for itself. Ruling classes develop an ideology to justify people's relative positions.

        3. Modern conflict theorists such as C. Wright Mills, Ralf Dahrendorf, and Randall Collins stress that conflict between capitalists and workers is not the only important conflict in contemporary society, but rather, that groups within the same class compete for scarce resources, resulting in conflict between many groups (e.g., young vs. old; women vs. men).

VI. How Do Elites Maintain Social Inequality?

    A. Social stratification is maintained within a nation by elites who control ideas and information, maintain social networks, and use force.

    B. The control of ideas and information can be remarkably more effective than the use of brute force and is used by elites everywhere to maintain their positions of power—whether in dictatorships or in democracies.

    C. Social networks are also critical in maintaining social stratification because they supply valuable information and tend to perpetuate social inequality.

    D. Technology, especially monitoring devices, helps the elite maintain its position.

  E. Underlying the maintenance of stratification is control of social institutions—the legal establishment, the police, and the military.

VII. Global Stratification: Three Worlds of Development

  A. Until recently, a simple model was used, consisting of the First World (industrialized, capitalistic nations), Second World (communist nations), and Third World (any nations that didn't fit the other categories). A more neutral way is to use terms related to a nation's level of industrialization: "Most Industrialized," "Industrializing," and "Least Industrialized."

  B. Classifying the nations of the world into these three categories creates certain problems.

    1. How much industrialization does a nation need in order to be classified as most industrialized?

    2. Does the fact that some nations have become "postindustrial" mean that a separate classification needs to be created?

    3. While the oil-rich nations of the world are immensely wealthy, they are not industrialized. How are they classified? Table 6.7 shows an alternative Model of Global Stratification.

VIII. How the World's Nations Become Stratified

  A. The explanation of how the world became stratified focuses on how European nations exploited weaker nations.

    1. Imperialism (the pursuit of unlimited geographic expansion) was practiced by European powers over the centuries. Industrialized nations needed consumers elsewhere; through conquests, markets expanded and businessmen gained access to new markets and raw materials. Nations that industrialized first got ahead of the rest of the world and became the most powerful.

    2. Colonization occurred when industrialized nations made colonies of weaker nations and exploited their labour/natural resources. European nations tended to focus on Africa, while the U.S. concentrated on Central and South America.

  B. According to world system theory as espoused by Immanuel Wallerstein, countries are politically and economically tied together.

    1. There are four groups of interconnected nations: (1) core nations, where capitalism first developed; (2) semi-periphery (Mediterranean area), highly dependent on trade with core nations; (3) periphery (eastern Europe), mainly limited to selling cash crops to core nations, with limited economic development; (4) external area (most of Africa/Asia) left out of growth of capitalism, with few economic ties to core nations.

    2. A capitalist world economy (capitalist dominance) results from relentless expansion: even external area nations are drawn into the commercial web.

    3. Globalization (the extensive interconnections among nations resulting from the expansion of capitalism) has speeded up because of new forms of communication and transportation. The consequence is that no nation is able to live in isolation.

  C. Dependence theory attributes the Least Industrialized nations' low economic development to dominance by the Most Industrialized nations. The Most Industrialized nations turned the Least Industrialized nations into their plantations and mines, taking whatever they needed; many of the Least Industrialized nations thus specialized in a single cash crop.

    D. John Kenneth Galbraith argued that some nations remained poor because they were crippled by a culture of poverty, a way of life based on traditional values and religious beliefs that perpetuated poverty from one generation to the next and kept some of the Least Industrialized nations from developing.

    E. Most sociologists find imperialism, world system, and dependency theory explanations preferable to the culture of poverty theory because the last places the blame on the victim, but each theory only partially explains global stratification.

IX.   Maintaining Global Stratification

    A. Neocolonialism is the economic and political dominance of the Least Industrialized nations by the Most Industrialized nations. Michael Harrington assets that the Most Industrialized nations control the Least Industrialized nations because they control markets, sets prices, etc. The Most Industrialized nations move hazardous industries to the Least Industrialized nations. The Most Industrialized nations sell weapons and manufactured goods to the Least Industrialized nations, preventing them from developing their own industrial capacity.

    B. Multinational corporations contribute to exploitation of the Least Industrialized nations.

        1. Some exploit the Least Industrialized nations directly by controlling national and local politics, running them as a fiefdom.

        2. The Most Industrialized nations are primary beneficiaries of profits made in the Least Industrialized nations.

        3. They often work closely with the elite of the Least Industrialized nations, many times in informal partnerships that are mutually beneficial.

        4. In some situations, multinational corporations may bring prosperity to the Least Industrialized nations because new factories provide salaries and opportunities which otherwise would not exist for workers in those countries.

    C. The new technology favours the Most Industrialized nations, enabling them to maintain their global domination.

        1. The profits of multinational corporations can be invested in developing and acquiring the latest technology, thereby generating even greater profits.

        2. Many of the Least Industrialized nations do not have the resources to invest in new technology, creating an even gap between the levels of industrialization globally.

X.   Applying Sociological Models of Social Class

    A. How many classes exist in industrial society is a matter of debate, but there are two main models, one that builds on Marx and the other on Weber.

    B. Sociologist Erik Wright realized that not everyone falls into Marx's two broad classes (capitalists and workers, which were based upon a person's relationship to the means of production). For instance, although executives, managers, and supervisors would fall into Marx's category of workers, they act more like capitalists.

        1. Wright resolved this problem by regarding some people as simultaneously members of more than one class, which he called contradictory class locations.

    2. Wright identified four classes: capitalists (owners of large enterprises); petty bourgeoisie (owners of small businesses); managers (employees, but who have authority over others); and workers.

C. Using the model originally developed by Weber, sociologists Dennis Gilbert and Joseph Kahl created a model to describe class structure in the U.S. and other capitalist countries.

    1. The capitalist class (1.1 percent of the population) is composed of investors, heirs, and a few executives; it is divided into "old" money and "new" money. The children of "new" money move into the old money class by attending the right schools and marrying "old" money.

    2. The upper-middle class is composed of professionals and upper managers, almost all of whom have attended college or university and frequently have postgraduate degrees.

    3. The lower-middle class is composed of lower managers, craftspeople and foremen. They have at least a high school education.

    4. The upper- and lower-middle class constitute 26.5 percent of the population.

    5. The working class is composed of factory workers and low-paid white-collar workers. Most have high school education.

    6. The working poor is composed of relatively unskilled blue-collar and white-collar workers, and those with temporary and seasonal jobs. If they graduated from high school, they probably did not do well in school.

    7. The working class and working poor constitute 63.7 percent of the population.

    8. The lower class and underclass (8.7 percent of the population) is concentrated in the inner cities and has little connection with the job market. Welfare is their main support.

D. The homeless are so far down the class structure that their position must be considered even lower than the underclass. They are the "fallout" of industrialization, especially the postindustrial developments that have contributed to a decline in the demand for unskilled labour.

XI. Consequences of Social Class

A. The new technology does not affect social classes in the same way.

    1. The higher one is on the social class ladder, the more likely they are to benefit from technology. For the capitalist class, the new technology is a means to extensive, worldwide profits.

    2. The upper-middle class also benefit because the new technology enables them to achieve in their chosen professions, and their education prepares them to take a leading role in managing in the new global system.

    3. Below these top two classes, technology creates much more uncertainty, with uncertainty increasing as you move down the ladder. Those at the bottom have few technological skills.

B. The lower a person's social class, the more likely that person is to die at an earlier age than people in higher classes; this is true at all ages. As well, mental health is worse for the lower classes because of stresses associated with their class position.

C. Social class also plays a role in family life.
  1. Children of the capitalist class are under great pressure to select the right mate in order to assure the continuity of the family line. Parents in this social class play a large role in mate selection.
  2. Marriages are more likely to fail in the lower social classes; the children of the poor thus are more likely to live in single-parent households.
  3. Child rearing varies by class, with each class raising its children with attitudes and behaviours suited to the kinds of occupations they will eventually hold. Lower class families teach children to defer to authority, as is required in their jobs. Higher class families encourage freedom, creativity, and self-expression, as is found in their jobs.
D. Education levels increase as one moves up the social class ladder. The change occurs not only in terms of the amount of education you obtain, but also in terms of the type of education, with the capitalist class bypassing public schools in favour of exclusive private schools, where its children are trained to take a commanding role in society.
E. All aspects of religious orientation follow class lines. Social classes tend to cluster around different denominations. Lower classes are attracted to spontaneous worship services and louder music, while higher classes prefer more restrained worship services.
F. Political views and involvement are influenced by social class. However, there is no class majority supporting any one party.
  1. The rich and the poor take divergent political paths, with people in lower social classes more likely to vote New Democrat, while those in higher classes vote Progressive Conservative; the parties are seen as promoting different class interests.
  2. People in working classes are more likely to be liberal on economic issues and more conservative on social issues.
  3. Political participation is not equal: the higher classes are more likely to vote and get involved in politics than those in lower social classes.
G. The criminal justice system is not blind to class: members of lower classes are more likely to be arrested, are more likely to be on probation, parole, or in jail, and more crimes occur in lower class neighbourhoods.

XII. Social Mobility

A. There are three basic types of social mobility: intergenerational, structural, and exchange.
  1. Intergenerational mobility is the change that family members make in their social class from one generation to the next. As a result of individual effort, a person can rise from one level to another; in the event of individual failure, the reverse can be true.
  2. Structural mobility involves social changes that affect large numbers of people. By way of example, when computers were invented, many opportunities opened up for people to switch from blue-collar to white-collar work. While individual effort played a role, the major reason for the change in position was structural.

      3. Exchange mobility is movement of people up and down the social class system, where, on balance, the system remains the same. The term refers to general, overall movement of large numbers of people that leaves the class system basically untouched.

  B. Women have been largely ignored in studies of occupational mobility. Studies of social mobility among men indicate that about one-half of sons have moved beyond their fathers; about one-third have stayed at the same level; and about one-sixth have fallen down the ladder.

      1. With the large numbers of women now working for pay, studies of their mobility patterns have appeared.

      2. One study indicated that women that did move up were encouraged by their parents to postpone marriage and get an education.

  C. There is a complex interrelationship between gender, race, and class.

  D. Technology is responsible for much of the uncertainty and downward mobility of Canadian workers. Computers and instantaneous communications enable companies to relocate production worldwide, locating in areas with lower paid, non-unionized work forces.

XIII. Poverty

  A. Statistics Canada uses the Low-Income Cut-Off (LICO) to identify the poverty line. The LICO assumes that poor families are those whose income requires them to spend more than 54.7 percent of their gross income on food, clothing, and shelter.

  B. Poverty is not evenly distributed across Canada. The greatest predictors of whether Canadians are poor are race/ethnicity, education, and sex of the person who heads the family.

      1. Reflecting differences in the local economies, poverty rates in Canada between1993 and 1998, at least 21 percent of visible minority Canadians experienced low income, compared with only 7 percent of other Canadians.

      2. Almost half (44 percent) of all Canadian Aboriginals and 60 percent of Aboriginal children are reported to be living below the LICOs.

      3. The chances of being poor decrease as the amount of education increases. However, many heads of poor families have education beyond high school.

      4. The sex of the person who heads a family is another major predictor of whether or not a family is poor. Most poor families are headed by women. They are several times more likely to be poor than families headed by two parents. The major causes of this phenomenon, called the feminization of poverty, are divorce, births to unwed mothers, and the lower wages paid to women.

      5. As women age, the poverty rate for unattached women 65 and older was 45.6 percent in 2001, while for comparative men it was 32.8 percent.

  C. In 1998, there were over 1 353 000 million children living below the LICOs in Canada.

XIV. **The Dynamics of Poverty**
  A. In the 1960s Michael Harrington and Oscar Lewis suggested that the poor get trapped in a "culture of poverty" as a result of having values and behaviours that make them "fundamentally different" from others.
     1. National statistics indicate that most poverty is short, lasting one year or less.
     2. Since the number of people who live in poverty remains fairly constant, this means that as many people move into poverty as move out of it.
  B. In trying to explain poverty, the choice is between focusing on individual explanations or on social structural explanations.
     1. Sociologists look to such factors as inequalities in education, access to learning job skills, racial, ethnic, age, and gender discrimination, and large-scale economic change to explain the patterns of poverty in society.
     2. The other explanation is individualistic, focusing on the characteristics of individuals that are assumed to contribute to their poverty.
     3. Recent welfare reforms across Canada have dramatically cut back on income supports for those facing economic stress.
  C. Because the poor don't see the future as different from the past, they find it difficult to defer gratification—give up things now for the sake of greater gains in the future.
  D. Real-life examples of people from humble origins who climbed far up the social ladder encourage the widely held belief that anyone has a chance of getting ahead.
     1. The Horatio Alger myth obviously is a statistical impossibility. Despite this, functionalists would stress that this belief is functional for society because it encourages people to compete for higher positions, while placing the blame for failure squarely on the individual.
     2. As Marx and Weber both noted, social class affects our ideas of life and our proper place in society. At the same time, the dominant ideology often blinds us to these effects in our own lives.
  E. Global warning regarding consequences of poverty.

KEY TERMS

After studying the chapter, review the definition for each of the following terms.

bourgeoisie: Karl Marx's term for the people who own the means of production

capitalist world economy: the dominance of capitalism in the world along with the international interdependence that capitalism has created

caste system: a form of social stratification in which one's status is determined by birth and is lifelong

clan: an extended network of relatives

clan system: a form of social stratification in which individuals receive their social standing through belonging to an extended network of relatives

class consciousness: Karl Marx's term for awareness of a common identity based on one's position in the means of production

class system: a form of social stratification based primarily on the possession of money or material possessions

colonization: the process by which one nation takes over another nation, usually for the purpose of exploiting its labour and natural resources

contradictory class location: Erik Wright's term for a position in the class structure that generates contradictory interests

culture of poverty: a culture that perpetuates poverty from one generation to the next

deferred gratification: forgoing something in the present in the hope of achieving greater gains in the future

dependency theory: the belief that lack of industrial development in the Least Industrialized nations is caused by the industrialized nations dominating the world economy

divine right of kings: the idea that the king's authority comes directly from God

downward social mobility: movement down the social class ladder

endogamy: marriage within one's own group

exchange mobility: about the same numbers of people moving up and down the social class ladder, such that, on balance, the social class system shows little change

false consciousness: Karl Marx's term to refer to workers identifying with the interests of capitalists

feminization of poverty: women are at greater risk for poverty than men

globalization: the extensive interconnections among world nations due to the expansion of capitalism

ideology: beliefs about the way things ought to be that justify social arrangements

imperialism: a nation's attempt to create an empire; its pursuit of unlimited geographical expansion

indentured service: a contractual system in which someone sells his or her body (services) for a specified period of time in an arrangement very close to slavery, except that it is voluntarily entered into

intergenerational mobility: the change that family members make in social class from one generation to the next

means of production: the tools, factories, land, and investment capital used to produce wealth

meritocracy: a form of social stratification in which all positions are awarded on the basis of merit

multinational corporations: companies that operate across many national boundaries; also called transnational corporations

neocolonialism: the economic and political dominance of the Least Industrialized nations by the Most Industrialized nations

objective method (of measuring social class): a system in which people are ranked according to objective criteria such as their wealth, power, and prestige

power: the ability to get your way in spite of the desires of other people

power elite: C. Wright Mills's term for the top people in Canadian corporations, military, and politics who make the nation's major decisions

prestige: respect or regard

proletariat: Karl Marx's term for the people who work for those who own the means of production

reputational method (of measuring social class): a system in which people who are familiar with the reputations of others are asked to identify their social class

slavery: a form of social stratification in which some people own other people

social class: according to Weber, a large group of people who rank close to one another in wealth, power, and prestige; according to Marx, one of two groups: capitalists who own the means of production and workers who sell their labour

social mobility: movement up or down the social class ladder

social stratification: the division of large numbers of people into layers according to their relative power, property, and prestige; applies both to nations and to people within a nation, society, or other group

status: social ranking

status consistency: ranking high or low on all three dimensions of social class

status inconsistency (or status discrepancy): a condition in which a person ranks high on some dimensions of social class and low on others

structural mobility: movement up or down the social class ladder that is attributable to changes in the structure of society, not to individual efforts

subjective method (of measuring social class): a system in which people are asked to state the social class to which they belong

underclass: a small group of people for whom poverty persists year after year and across generations

upward social mobility: movement up the social class ladder

wealth: property and income

world system: economic and political connections that tie the world's countries together

KEY PEOPLE

Review the major theoretical contributions or findings of these people.

Wallace Clement: Clement studied the distribution of wealth and power in Canada.

Kingsley Davis and Wilbert Moore: These functionalists developed a theory of stratification that suggests inequality is universal because it helps societies survive by motivating the most qualified members of society to strive to fill the most important social positions.

William Domhoff: Drawing upon the work of C. Wright Mills, Domhoff analyzed the workings of the ruling class.

John Kenneth Galbraith: This economist argued that the Least Industrialized nations remain poor because their own culture holds them back.

Dennis Gilbert and Joseph Kahl: These sociologists developed a more contemporary stratification model based on Max Weber's work.

Ray Gold: In research on status inconsistency, Gold studied tenant reactions to janitors who earned more than they did. He found that the tenants acted "snooty" to the janitors, and the janitors took pleasure in knowing the intimate details of the tenants' lives.

Michael Harrington: Harrington saw that colonialism has been replaced by neocolonialism.

Melvin Kohn: Kohn studied social class differences in child-rearing patterns.

Gerhard Lenski: Lenski noted that everyone wants to maximize their status, but that others often judge them on the basis of their lowest status despite the individual's efforts to be judged on the basis of his highest status.

Elliot Liebow: writes on the links and consequences between poverty and gratification

Karl Marx: Marx concluded that social class depended exclusively on the means of production; an individual's social class was determined by whether or not he owned the means of production.

C. Wright Mills: Mills used the term power elite to describe the top decision-makers in the nation.

John Porter: Porter demonstrated the ways in which wealth and power are concentrated in Canada.

Melvin Tumin: Tumin was the first to offer a criticism of the functionalist view on stratification.

Immanuel Wallerstein: This historian proposed a world system theory to explain global stratification.

W. Lloyd Warner: Warner did a classic study of stratification using the reputational method.

Max Weber: Weber argued that social class was based on three components—class, status, and power.

Erik Wright: Wright proposed an updated version of Marx's theory of stratification.

SELF-TEST

After completing this self-test, check your answers against the Answer Key at the back of this Study Guide and against the text on page(s) indicated in parentheses.

MULTIPLE CHOICE QUESTIONS

1. What is the division of large numbers of people into layers according to their relative power, property, and prestige? (109)
    a. social distinction
    b. social stratification
    c. social distance
    d. social diversification

2. What is a form of social stratification in which some people own other people? (110)
    a. a caste system
    b. slavery
    c. a class system
    d. apartheid

3. In which stratification system are individuals linked into a large network of relatives? (111)
    a. clan system
    b. caste system
    c. slavery system
    d. class system

4. Which of the following characterizes class systems? (111)
    a. It allows for the possibility of social mobility.
    b. It denies geographic mobility.
    c. Distribution of social standings belonging to an extended network of relatives.
    d. Fixed boundaries between layers of the stratification system.

5. According to Marx, on what single factor does social class depend? (111)
    a. wealth, power, and prestige
    b. the means of production
    c. where one is born in the social stratification system
    d. what a person achieves during his or her lifetime

6. According to Max Weber, what determines social class? (112)
    a. one's property, prestige, and power
    b. one's relationship to the means of production
    c. one's tasks and how important they are to society
    d. one's political power

7. Which of the ways of measuring social class asks people to identify their own social class? (114)
    a. objective
    b. reputational
    c. subjective
    d. individualistic

8. With which social class do the vast majority of Canadians identify? (114)
    a. upper
    b. middle
    c. working
    d. lower

9. On what is the objective method of measuring social class based? (114)
    a. asking people who are familiar with the reputations of others to judge their social class
    b. ranking people according to criteria such as wealth, power, and prestige
    c. asking people to define their own social class
    d. none of the above

10. According to Paul Samuelson, if an income pyramid were made out of a child's blocks, where would most people be? (115)
    a. near the top of the pyramid
    b. near the middle of the pyramid
    c. near the bottom of the pyramid
    d. none of the above

11. Which of the statements regarding jobs that have the most prestige is not true? (118)
    a. They pay more.
    b. They require more education.
    c. They require less abstract thought.
    d. They offer greater autonomy.

12. Mills coined the term _____ to refer to those who make the big decisions in society? (117)
    a. the decision elite
    b. the power elite
    c. the power corps
    d. the power brokers

13. Which of these statements is consistent with the functionalist view of stratification? (119-120)
    a. Stratification is dysfunctional for society.
    b. Stratification is the outcome of conflict between different social classes.
    c. Stratification will disappear in societies that are characterized by a meritocracy.
    d. Stratification is an inevitable feature of social organization.

14. Which of these is *not* one of Tumin's criticisms of the functionalist theory of stratification? (120)
    a. The importance of a social position cannot be measured by the rewards it carries.
    b. The functionalists ignore the impact of family background.
    c. Stratification is not functional for everyone.
    d. The functionalists focus too much on status and power and not enough on income.

15. A form of social stratification in which positions are awarded based on merit is called a(n): (120)
    a. meritocratic system.
    b. egalitarian system.
    c. socialistic system .
    d. democratic system.

16. According to conflict theorists, the basis of social stratification is: (120)
    a. functional necessity in society.
    b. conflict over limited resources.
    c. ascribed statuses.
    d. the way in which individuals perceive their social class position.

17. The majority of the world's population lives in the _____ nations. (122)
    a. most Industrialized
    b. industrializing
    c. least Industrialized
    d. old-rich

18. Why is it difficult to know how to classify some nations into a global system of stratification? (122-124)
    a. It is difficult because the dividing line between levels—Most Industrialized, Industrializing, and Least Industrialized—are soft.
    b. Some nations have moved beyond industrialization.
    c. Some nations have not yet industrialized but are still extremely wealthy.
    d. All of the above reflect problems with classifying nations into a global system.
19. What are some facts about the plight of poor children in the world? (123)

a. In Brazil children swarm over garbage dumps in search of food.
b. In Brazil owners of garbage dumps hire armed guards to keep people out.
c. Every year the Brazilian police and death squads murder 2000 children.
d. all of the above.

20. According to world system theory, all of the following are groups of interconnected nations, except: (125)
a. core nations.
b. nations around the Mediterranean, the semiperiphery
c. western European nations, the periphery.
d. the external area composed of nations that include most of Africa and Asia

21. The culture of poverty theory was used to analyze global stratification by: (126)
a. Immanuel Wallerstein.
b. Max Weber.
c. John Kenneth Galbraith.
d. Karl Marx.

22. Neocolonialism refers to: (126)
a. recent efforts by the Most Industrialized nations to colonize Least Industrialized nations.
b. the economic policies of the Most Industrialized nations that are designed to control the markets of the Least Industrialized nations.
c. programs like the Peace Corps that attempt to teach residents of the Least Industrialized countries the skills necessary to survive in an industrial society.
d. the economic policy of the Least Industrialized nations in which they hold the Most Industrialized nations hostage by controlling access to national resources like oil.

23. Multinational corporations: (126)
a. are companies that operate across many national boundaries.
b. always exploit the Least Industrialized nations directly.
c. benefit the Least Industrialized nations as much as the Most Industrialized nations.
d. All of the above

24. How did Erik Wright update Marx's class categories in response to criticisms that they were too broad? (127)
a. He divided each of the two classes into three sub-classes, making six classes in all.
b. He created an open scale in which people place themselves into classes.
c. He recommended listing people's different associations and then classifying them on the basis of their most important one.
d. He recognized that some people can be members of more than one class at the same time and created four categories, yet maintaining the primary distinction between the employer and worked.

25. Based on the Canadian Social Class Ladder (by Gilbert and Kahl), which of the following statements is correct? (128)
    a. On each lower rung you find more wealth.
    b. The super-rich who occupy the top rung is so wealthy that its members are worth more than the entire bottom 90 percent of the nation.
    c. Lower class and underclass make up the highest percentage of the population.
    d. Working class and working poor are the smallest class.

26. What is true of the benefits from new technology? (130)
    a. Working class is ill prepared for the changes ushered in by new technology.
    b. The higher one goes up the social ladder, the more technology is a benefit.
    c. New technology transforms the workplace, eliminating jobs and outdated skills.
    d. all of the above

27. Sociologist Melvin Kohn finds significant class differences in parenting; lower class parents are concerned that their children be (131-132)
    a. creative.
    b. independent.
    c. conformists.
    d. all of the above

28. Social class plays a significant role in education: which class tends to bypass public schools entirely, in favour of exclusive private schools? (132)
    a. capitalist
    b. upper-middle
    c. middle
    d. all of the above

29. Members of the _____ class are more likely to be robbed, burglarized, or murdered. (132)
    a. upper
    b. middle
    c. lower
    d. none of the above

30. In terms of social mobility, a homeless person whose father was a physician has experienced: (132-133)
    a. exchange mobility.
    b. structural mobility.
    c. upward mobility.
    d. downward mobility.

31. Which of the following facts is true of social mobility studies? (133)
    a. Sociologists used to focus only on the social mobility of men.
    b. Major studies of intergenerational mobility concluded that half of sons stayed at the level of their fathers.
    c. Now with the majority of women working for pay, they are still excluded from social mobility studies.
    d. none of the above

32. Currently, the wealthiest _____ percent of the Canadian population own _____ percent of the national wealth (134)
    a.   50, 94
    b.   20, 50
    c.   10, 10
    d.   50, 50

33. In exploring myths about the poor, which of the following is not true? (135)
    a.   Although many poor people are employed, their jobs pay so poorly that one income does not lift them above the low-income cut offs.
    b.   Only 36 percent of poor children are living in mother-headed families.
    c.   The majority of poor Canadians are living off welfare.
    d.   In 2001, the poverty rate for two parent families with one earner was 28 percent.

34. Which factors are the important predictors of poverty? (136-137)
    a.   race/ethnicity
    b.   education
    c.   sex of person who heads the family
    d.   all of the above

35. Canadians who are born with or acquire disability are likely to: (137)
    a.   experience economic difficulties.
    b.   experience discrimination in hiring.
    c.   receive inadequate disability benefits.
    d.   all of the above

TRUE-FALSE QUESTIONS

T F   1.   Social stratification refers only to individuals. (109)
T F   2.   Throughout history, slavery has always been based on racism . (110)
T F   3.   Indentured service represents a fuzzy line between contract and slavery and was practiced in the New World (110)
T F   4.   A caste system is a form of social stratification in which individual status is determined by birth and is lifelong. (110)
T F   5.   A class system is based primarily on money or material possessions. (111)
T F   6.   According to Karl Marx, the means of production is the only factor in determining social class. (111)
T F   7.   According to Max Weber, class standing is a combination of power, prestige, and property. (112)
T F   8.   The reputation method of measuring social class involves asking people to define their own social class. (114)
T F   9.   Recent immigrants are often members of the working poor. (129)
T F   10. The total net worth of all Canadian households is estimated at about $3 trillion, most of it in real estate, corporate stocks, bonds and business assets. (114)
T F   11. The homeless are the "fallout" of our developing post-industrial economy; in another era they would have had plenty of work. (130)

T F   12.   Each year, *Canadian Business* ranks Canada's wealthiest people, and all of them sit atop corporate empires. (117)

T F   13.   According to conflict theorists, the oppressed often support laws even when the laws operate against their own interests. (121)

T F   14.   The idea of the divine right of kings is an example of how the ruling elite used ideas to maintain stratification. (121)

T F   15.   To maintain their position of power, elites also try to control information. (122)

T F   16.   Capitalism's relentless expansion has given birth to a capitalist world economy, dominated by the most industrialized nations.(125)

T F   17.   Most industrialized nations rejected imperialism as a strategy for expanding their economic markets and gaining access to cheap raw materials. (125)

T F   18.   Western imperialism and colonization shaped the least industrialized nations. (125)

T F   19.   Dependency theory stresses how the least industrialized nations grew dependent on the most industrialized nations. (125)

T F   20.   The extensive movement of capital and ideas between the nations of the world by the expansion of capitalism is called globalization. (125)

T F   21.   Of all the social classes, the upper middle is the one most shaped by education. (129)

T F   22.   The underclass is concentrated in the inner city and has little or no connection with the job market. (129)

T F   23.   For the capitalist class, the new technology is a dream come true: global profits through global integration. (130)

T F   24.   Social class affects a person's chances of living and dying. (131)

T F   25.   Marriages of the poor are more likely to fail and their children to group up in broken homes. (131)

T F   26.   Members of the lower classes are more likely to be on probation, on parole, or in jail than members of the upper classes. (132)

T F   27.   Structural mobility refers to social and economic changes that caused huge shifts in the occupational structure that opened so many doors that it became taken for granted that children could surpass their parents. (133)

T F   28.   Exchange mobility leaves the class system basically untouched. (133)

T F   29.   In the Liebow (1967) study of African American street-corner men, their practice of immediate gratification was not the cause of their poverty, but its consequence. (141)

T F   30.   As Marx and Weber pointed out, social class penetrates our consciousness, shaping our ideas of life and our proper place in society (142)

FILL-IN QUESTIONS

1. _____ is a system in which people are divided into layers according to their relative power, property, and prestige. (109)

2. A form of social stratification in which some people own other people is _____. (110)

3. A(n) _____ system is a form of social stratification in which individual status is determined by birth and is lifelong. (110)

4. Sociologists refer to movement up or down the social class ladder as _____. (132)
5. According to Marx, the tools, factories, land, and investment capital used to produce wealth is _____. (111)
6. According to Marx, the awareness of a common identity based on one's position in the means of production is _____. (112)
7. According to Max Weber, the three dimensions of social class are (1)_____; (2)_____; and (3)_____. (114-118)
8. Most sociologists use the _____ method of measuring social class in which people are ranked according to objective criteria such as wealth, power, and prestige. (114)
9. Property and income together make up an individual's _____. (114)
10. According to C. Wright Mills, the _____ makes the big decisions in society. (117)
11. A _____ is a form of social stratification in which all positions are awarded on the basis of merit. (120)
12. The _____ is the idea that the king's authority comes directly from God. (121)
13. _____ is the process in which one nation takes over another nation, usually for the purpose of exploiting its labour and natural resources. (125)
14. _____ is the extensive interconnections among world nations resulting from the expansion of capitalism. (125)
15. _____ is a way of life that perpetuates poverty from one generation to the next. (126)
16. _____ refers to the economic and political dominance of the Least Industrialized nations by the Most Industrialized Nations. (126)
17. Companies that operate across many national boundaries are _____. (126)
18. Erik Wright referred to a position in the class structure that generates inconsistent interests as _____. (127)
19. According to Gilbert and Kahl, the capitalist class can be divided into two groups: (1) _____ and (2) _____. (128-129)
20. _____ is movement up the social class ladder. (132)
21. An official measure of poverty is referred to as the _____; it is a calculation based on a ratio of gross income to family spending on food, clothing, and shelter. (134)
22. _____ is a trend whereby most poor families in Canada are headed by women. (137)
23. Sociologists focus on _____ as the source of poverty. (140-141)
24. The greatest predictor of whether Canadians are poor is not geography , but race/ethnicity, _____ , age and the _____ of the head of the family. (136)
25. Forgoing something in the present in hope of achieving greater gains in the future is _____. (141)

MATCH THESE SOCIAL SCIENTISTS WITH THEIR CONTRIBUTIONS

___1. Karl Marx   a. *world system theory*
___2. Kingsley Davis & Wilbert Moore   b. *criticism of functional view of stratification*
___3. Immanuel Wallerstein   c. *stressed culture of poverty*
___4. Michael Harrington   d. *false consciousness*
___5. John Kenneth Galbraith   e. *functionalist view of stratification*
___6. Max Weber   f. *neocolonialism*

___7.   Melvin Tumin   g.   *class based on property, prestige, and*
                                                       power

___8.   Gerhard Lenski   h.   *power elite*
___9.   C. Wright Mills   i.   *social class patterns of child rearing*
___10.   Erik Wright   j.   *status inconsistency*
___11.   Gilbert & Kahl   k.   *updated Marx's model*
___12.   W. Lloyd Warner   l.   *pioneered the reputational model*
___13.   Melvin Kohn   m.   *updated Weber's model*

ESSAY QUESTIONS

1. Compare Marx's theory of stratification with Weber's theory.
2. Assume that you carry out a study of social class. Review the different ways that social class can be measured and select the one that would be most appropriate for your study. Explain your selection.
3. Consider why ideology is a more effective way of maintaining stratification than brute force.
4. Of what use is a division of the poor into deserving and undeserving? Would we let some people starve because they "brought poverty upon themselves"? Would we let the children go hungry because their parents are unmarried, uneducated and unskilled? (139)
5. Describe which groups are a greatest risk of poverty and then suggest ways in which poverty can be reduced by targeting these populations.

"DOWN-TO-EARTH SOCIOLOGY"

1. Why do you think the income per person is so much higher in highly industrialized nations than in the least industrialized nations? Does money just "go a lot farther" in less industrialized nations or do people in these countries have much lower standards of living than people in highly industrialized nations? Could you live on $3.600 a year?
2. Study the figure on page 115 and then explain the consistency of income distribution across the years to someone who is unfamiliar with Canadian society.
3. What was your reaction after reading about children in the least industrialized nations who are growing up in poverty? (123) How does the image of life in the slums compare with your image of the lives of Canada's poor? Do you think that people in highly industrialized nations should do anything about this situation? If yes, what?
4. Which myths about the poor that are listed on page 135 reflect your own ideas about poverty? Did the facts help you in understanding the realities of poverty?
5. After reading "Children in Poverty" (138), is child poverty a concern only for the poor or is it everyone's concern? What should be done to relieve the problem?
6. Do you often distinguish the deserving poor from the undeserving poor? Why do you think we do this? What are the social characteristics of both groups? What are the social conditions that contribute to their poverty? What can be done about it?

CHAPTER 7
INEQUALITIES OF GENDER

CHAPTER SUMMARY

- Gender stratification refers to unequal access to power, property, and prestige on the basis of sex. Each society establishes a structure that, on the basis of sex and gender, opens and closes access to privileges. Gender inequality is especially significant because it cuts across all aspects of social life. Sex refers to biological distinctions between males and females; gender refers to behaviours and attitudes thought to be socially acceptable for males and females. In the "nature versus nurture" debate, almost all sociologists take the side of nurture. In recent years the door to biology has opened somewhat.

- George Murdock found a pattern of sex-typed activities among premodern societies, with greater prestige given to those activities performed by males. From Murdock's cross-cultural survey we can conclude that nothing about biology requires men and women to be assigned different work.

- Patriarchy or male dominance does appear to be universal. The dominant theory to explain the status of women as a minority group focuses on the physical limitations imposed by childbirth.

- Although feminist movements have battled to eliminate some of the most blatant forms of gender discrimination, there are still many areas of inequality. More females than males now attend college, but both generally end up in gender-biased academic fields although there are some signs of change today. Two indicators of gender inequality in everyday life are the general devaluation of femininity and the male dominance of conversation.

- In the workplace women's problems include gender segregation, unequal pay, obstacles to occupational mobility, and sexual harassment.

- Traditional gender patterns still exist in regard to violent behaviour. Female circumcision is a special case of violence against women.

- Women in Canada have the numerical capacity to take over politics and transform society, but continue to encounter obstacles to their full participation as elected officials.

- As females come to play a larger role in decision-making processes of Canadian social institutions, stereotypes will be broken, and new role models arise. It is possible that a new concept of the human personality—one that allows males and females to pursue their individual interests unfettered by gender—might occur.

LEARNING OBJECTIVES

As you read Chapter 7, use these learning objectives to organize your notes. After completing your reading, briefly state an answer to each of the objectives, and review the text pages in parentheses.

1. Define gender stratification and differentiate between sex and gender. (146)
2. Discuss the continuing controversy regarding the biological and cultural factors that come into play in creating gender differences in societies. (147)
3. Summarize findings of research studies that suggest biology does play a role in gender behaviour. (146-148)
4. Describe the global nature of male dominance. (148-149)

5. Discuss the dominant theories about the origins of discrimination against women. (150-152)
6. Describe the major factors that contributed to the two "waves" of feminism in Canada and note how successful this movement has been up to this point in time. (152-153)
7. Discuss ways in which educational systems may perpetuate gender inequality. (153-154)
8. Describe how gender inequality is expressed in everyday life. (154-155)
9. Explain gender relations in the workplace, including the pay gap, the glass ceiling, the "mommy track," and sexual harassment. (155-160)
10. Explain what the authors mean when they say gender violence is a "one-way street." (161-162)
11. Explain why women historically have not taken over politics and transformed Canadian life. (163-164)
12. Describe what the future looks like in terms of gender relations in Canada. (164-166)

CHAPTER OUTLINE

I. **Issues of Sex and Gender**
    A. Gender stratification refers to men's and women's unequal access to power, prestige, and property.
    B. Sex and gender reflect different bases.
        1. Sex is biological characteristics distinguishing males and females—primary sex organs (organs related to reproduction) and secondary sex organs (physical distinctions not related to reproduction).
        2. Gender is a social characteristic that varies from one society to another and refers to what the group considers proper for its males and females. The sociological significance of gender is that it is the means by which society controls its members; it sorts us, on the basis of sex, into different life experiences.
    C. Some researchers argue that biological factors (two X chromosomes in females, one X and one Y in males) result in differences in conduct, with men being more aggressive and domineering and women being more comforting and nurturing.
    D. The dominant sociological position is represented by the symbolic interactionists, who stress that people in every society determine what physical differences mean to them: males and females take the positions that society assigns to them.
    E. Alice Rossi suggested that women are better prepared biologically for "mothering" than are men: nature provides biological predispositions which are overlaid with culture.
    F. Real-life cases provide support for the argument that men's and women's behaviour is influenced by both culture and biology.
        1. A medical accident led to a young boy being reassigned to the female sex. Reared as a female, the child behaved like a girl; however, by adolescence she was unhappy and having a difficult time adjusting to being a female.

II. **Gender Inequality in Global Perspective**
   A. Historian and feminist Gerda Lerner has concluded that women as a group have never held decision-making power over men as a group. This was true even in the earliest known societies, in which there was much less gender discrimination.
   B. George Murdock, who surveyed 324 premodern societies, found activities to be sex-typed in all of them, although activities considered female in one society may be male in another. There is nothing about anatomy that requires this.
   C. Universally, greater prestige is given male activities regardless of what they are. If caring for cattle is men's work, it carries high prestige; if it is women's work, it has less prestige.
   D. Globally, gender discrimination occurs in the areas of education, politics, and paid employment. A global human rights issue is violence against women

III. **Gender Inequality in Theoretical Perspective**
   A. Around the world, gender is the primary division between people. Because society sets up barriers to deny women equal access, they are referred to as a minority even though they outnumber men.
   B. Although the origin of patriarchy (male dominance) is unknown, the dominant theory assumes that patriarchy is universal and that biology along with social factors plays a role in male dominance.
      1. In early societies, life was short and many children needed to be born in order for the group to survive. Consequently, women were pregnant or nursing young children for much of their adult lives. As a result of these biologically driven activities, women were limited in terms of alternatives and assumed tasks associated with the home and child care.
      2. Men took over tasks requiring greater strength and longer absences, such as hunting animals. This enabled men to make contact with other tribes, trade with those other groups, and wage war and gain prestige by returning home with prisoners of war or with large animals to feed the tribe; little prestige was given to women's more routine tasks.
   C. The answer as to the accuracy of this theory is buried in human history, and there is no way of testing either this one or others suggested by Marvin Harris, Frederick Engels, or Gerda Lerner. Whatever the origin, male dominance continues into the present.

IV. **Gender Inequality in Canada**
   A. A society's culture and institutions both justify and maintain its customary forms of gender inequality.
   B. Until this century, Canadian women did not have the right to vote, hold property, testify in court, or serve on a jury; if a woman worked outside the home, she handed the wages she earned over to her father or husband.
      1. Males did not willingly surrender their privileges; rather, greater political rights for women resulted from a prolonged and bitter struggle waged by a first wave of feminists in the nineteenth and early twentieth centuries.
      2. A second wave of feminism began in the 1960s. As more women gained an education and began to work outside the home, they compared their wages and working conditions to those of men. As awareness of gender inequalities grew,

protest and struggle emerged. The goals of this second wave of feminism are broad, from changing work roles to changing policies on violence against women.

   3. Both waves of feminism were characterized by two branches—one conservative and the other liberal—each of which has had different goals and different tactics.

   4. While women enjoy more rights today, gender inequality still exists.

C. Despite evidence of educational gains made by women—more females than males are enrolled in Canadian universities and females earn 59 percent of all bachelor's and first professional degrees—some traditional male-female distinctions persist.

   1. At university males and females are channelled into different fields. According to Statistics Canada (2004), men earn over 75 percent bachelor degrees in engineering and 67 percent in mathematics and physical sciences, while women are awarded 73 percent of bachelor degrees in health professions and occupations, over 71 percent in education and 68 percent in fine arts.

   2. Because gender socialization gives men and women different orientations in life, they enter higher education with gender-linked aspirations. Therefore, the proportion of females decreases in graduate school.

   3. There is gender stratification in both the rank and pay within higher educational institutions. Women are less likely to be in the higher ranks of academia, and at all levels are paid less than their male counterparts.

   4. Changes are occurring. The proportion of women earning professional degrees has increased sharply.

D. Patterns of gender discrimination continue to exist in everyday life.

   1. Females' capacities, interests, attitudes, and contributions are not taken as seriously as those of males. For example, the worst insult that can be thrown at a male is that he is a sissy, or they he does things like a girl.

   2. Patterns of conversation reflect inequalities between men and women. Men are more likely than women to interrupt a conversation and to control a change in topics.

V.   Gender Relations in the Workplace

A. Men continue to earn more than women in the Canadian work force, although the gap is closing.

   1. At all levels of educational achievement women earn less than men.

   2. The gender gap in wages is pervasive. In 1999 women were paid an average of 80 cents for every dollar their male counterparts earned.

   3. Research by Fuller and Schoenberger found that upon entry to a career, women averaged lower pay than men, even when they have more qualifications than their male counterparts; five years after graduation from college, the pay gap was even wider than it was upon entering the job market.

   4. A 1993 *Financial Post* survey found that less than 2 percent of all CEOs are women.

B. The "glass ceiling" describes an invisible barrier that women face in trying to reach the executive suites.

   1. Researchers find that women are not in the positions like marketing, sales, and production—positions from which top executives are recruited. Rather they

are in human resources and public relations; their work is not appreciated to the same degree because it does not bring in profits.

2. Much of the blame for this situation rests with the male corporate culture. Those in power look for potential leaders who have the same characteristics as themselves; they steer white males into the "pipeline" for promotions and women and minorities into other positions.

3. Another explanation for the situation is that women lack mentors; male executives are reluctant to mentor them because they fear the gossip and sexual harassment charges if they get too close to female subordinates, or because they see women as weak.

4. There are cracks in the glass ceiling as women learn to play by "men's rules" and develop a style with which men feel comfortable.

5. Men who go into nontraditional fields do not encounter a glass ceiling; rather they find a "glass escalator"—they move up more quickly than female co-workers.

C. Since most wives spend more time and take greater responsibility in caring for the children, it has been suggested that corporations offer women a choice of two parallel career paths.

1. The "fast track" (may require 60 or 70 hours of work per week, unexpected out-of-town meetings, etc.); or the "mommy track" (stresses both career and family).

2. Critics suggest that the mommy track would encourage women to be satisfied with lower aspirations and fewer promotions, it would perpetuate or increase the executive pay gap, and it would confirm stereotypes about female executives.

3. Critics suggest that a better way than the mommy track is for husbands to share responsibility at home and for firms to provide day care.

D. Until the 1970s, women did not draw a connection between unwanted sexual advances on the job and their subordinate positions at work.

1. As women began to discuss the problem, they named it (sexual harassment) and came to see such unwanted sexual advances by men in powerful positions as a structural problem. The change in perception resulted from reinterpreting women's experiences—giving them a name.

2. As more women have moved into positions of power, sexual harassment has not been exclusively a woman's problem, although male victims are less frequent than female victims and are less likely to find sympathy for their situation.

VI. Gender and Violence

A. Most victims of violence are females.

1. Women are more likely than men to experience assault from an intimate male partner, while men are more likely to be assaulted by a stranger. In both Canada and the United States, convicted rapists are almost exclusively young males.

2. Date rape—sexual assault in which the assailant is acquainted with the victim—is not an isolated event and is most likely to occur between couples who have known each other for about a year.

3. Males are more likely than females to commit murder and be the victim of murder.
4. Other forms of violence against women include battering, spousal abuse, incest and female circumcision.

B. Feminists use symbolic interactionism to understand violence against women. They stress that Canadian culture promotes violence by males. It teaches men to associate power, dominance, strength, virility, and superiority with masculinity. Men use violence to try and maintain a higher status.

C. To solve violence we must first break the link between violence and masculinity.

VII. Gender and Change

A. Despite the gains Canadian women have made in recent elections, they continue to be underrepresented in political office, especially in higher office. Reasons for this include:
   1. Women are still underrepresented in law and business, the careers from which most politicians are drawn.
   2. Women do not see themselves as a voting bloc who needs political action to overcome discrimination.
   3. Women still find the roles of mother and politician incompatible.
   4. Males seldom incorporate women into the centres of decision making or present them as viable candidates.
   5. Trends in the 1990s indicate that women will participate in political life in far greater numbers than in the past.

B. Canadian women are developing a notable presence in professional, amateur, and school-sponsored sports of all types, at all levels.
   1. Women's sports continue to be under funded, however, and are often marginalized.
   2. Images of lean, muscular bodies and competitive spirits conflict with dominant conceptions of femininity and motherhood.
   3. Despite these obstacles, women's participation in organized sports is increasing.

C. As women have challenged gendered norms, men have begun to adapt.
   1. More men are working outside the home and undertaking unpaid housekeeping duties.
   2. Awareness of men's concerns over body image has been raised in recent studies.
   3. The men's cosmetic industry has experienced a boom in recent years and men's clothing lines have grown.

VIII. Glimpsing the Future—With Hope

A. As women play a fuller role in the decision-making processes, further structural obstacles to women's participation in society will give way.

B. As gender stereotypes are abandoned, both males and females will be free to feel and express their needs and emotions, something that present arrangements deny them.

KEY TERMS

After studying the chapter, review the definition for each of the following terms.

agency: the ways in which women are responding positively to change their circumstances.

feminism: the philosophy that men and women should be politically, economically, and socially equal, and organized activity on behalf of this principle

gender: the social characteristics that a society considers proper for its males and females; masculinity or femininity

gender inequality: males' and females' unequal access to power, prestige, and property on the basis of sex

matriarchies: a society in which women dominate men

minority group: a group that is discriminated against on the basis of its members' physical or cultural characteristics

patriarchy: a society in which men dominate women

sex: biological characteristics that distinguish females and males, consisting of primary and secondary sex characteristics

sex-typing: the association of behaviours with one sex or the other

sexual harassment: the abuse of one's position of authority to force unwanted sexual demands on someone

KEY PEOPLE

Review the major theoretical contributions or findings of these people.

Janet Chafetz: Chafetz studied the second wave of feminism in the 1960s, noting that as large numbers of women began to work in the economy, they began to compare their working conditions with those of men.

Frederick Engels: Engels argued that male dominance developed with the origin of private property.

Cynthia Fuchs: Epstein: Epstein is a proponent of the view that differences between males' and females' behaviour is solely the result of social factors such as socialization and social control.

Douglas Foley: This sociologist's study of sports lends support to the view that things feminine are generally devalued.

Rex Fuller and Richard Schoenberger: These economists examined the starting salaries of business majors and found that women averaged 11 percent lower pay than men right out of college, and that the gap grew to 14 percent after five years in the work force.

Steven Goldberg: This sociologist's view is that the differences between males and females are not due to environment but to inborn differences that direct the emotions and behaviours of the two genders.

Marvin Harris: This anthropologist suggested that male dominance grew out of the greater strength that men had which made them better suited for the hand-to-hand combat of tribal societies; women became the reward to entice men into battle.

Gerda Lerner: Lerner concluded that in all societies women—as a group—have never had decision-making power over men.

Catharine McKinnon: McKinnon is an activist lawyer who published a book identifying sexual harassment as a structural problem in workplaces.

George Murdock: This anthropologist surveyed 324 premodern societies around the world and found that in all of them activities were sex-typed.

Alice Rossi: This feminist sociologist has suggested that women are better prepared biologically for "mothering" than are men.

Felice Schwartz: Schwartz is associated with the notion of dual career tracks—one for women who want to combine work and motherhood (the mommy track) and the other for women who want to devote their time and energies to a career (the fast track).

Jean Stockard and Miriam Johnson: These sociologists observed boys playing basketball and heard them exchange insults that reflect a disrespect and devaluation of women.

Samuel Stouffer: In his classic study of combat soldiers during World War II, Stouffer noted the general devaluation of things associated with women.

Christine Williams: Williams found that men in non-traditional careers and occupations often experience a glass escalator—moving more quickly than women into desirable work assignments, higher-level positions, and larger salaries.

K SELF-TEST

After completing this self-test, check your answers against the Answer Key at the back of this Study Guide and against the text on page(s) indicated in parentheses.

MULTIPLE CHOICE QUESTIONS

1. Which of the following statements about gender stratification is *incorrect*? (146)
    a. it cuts across all aspects of social life
    b. it cuts across all social classes
    c. it refers to the unequal access to power, prestige, and property on the basis of sex
    d. unlike class stratification, it is not a structured feature of society

2. To what does the term "sex" refer? (146)
    a. the social characteristics that a society considers proper for its males and females
    b. the biological characteristics that distinguish females and males
    c. masculinity and femininity
    d. all of the above

3. If biology is the principal factor in human behaviour, around the world what would we find? (148)
    a. things to be just like they are
    b. men and women to be much more like each other than they currently are
    c. women to be one sort of person and men another
    d. none of the above

4. Patriarchy: (147)
    a. is a society in which men dominate women
    b. has existed throughout history
    c. is universal
    d. All of the above

5. What is the association of behaviours with one sex or the other called? (149)

a. sex-typing
b. sex-association
c. sex-discrimination
d. sex-orientation

6. When anthropologist George Murdock surveyed 324 premodern societies, which of the following was *not* one of his findings? (149)
   a. Activities were sex-typed in all of them.
   b. Every society associates activities with one sex or the other.
   c. Biological requirements were the basis for men and women being assigned different tasks.
   d. Activities considered "female" in one society may be considered "male" activities in another.

7. In regard to the prestige of work: (149)
   a. greater prestige is given to activities which are considered to be of great importance to a society, regardless of whether they are performed by females or males.
   b. greater prestige goes to female activities that males can't do, like pregnancy and lactation.
   c. greater prestige is given to male activities—regardless of what those activities are.
   d. none of the above

8. Which statement concerning global discrimination is *incorrect*? (150)
   a. Of about 1 billion adults around the world who can't read, two-thirds are women.
   b. Canada leads the world in the number of women who hold public office.
   c. Around the globe, women average less pay than men.
   d. A global human rights issue has become violence against women.

9. Worldwide ____ percent of men, compared with ____ percent women are literate. (149)
   a. 100, 50
   b. 85, 76
   c. 20, 70
   d. 50, 50

10. In 2004 worldwide, women held only ___percent of seats in parliaments or congresses. (149)
    a. 16
    b. 20
    c. 25
    d. 35

11. Historically in Canada, women: (152)
    a. did not have the right to vote until the 1950s.
    b. were allowed to make legal contracts but had to be represented by an attorney because it was assumed that they were like children.
    c. could not serve on juries or hold property in their own name.
    d. could spend their own wages but had to tell their fathers how the money was spent.

12. A "second wave" of protest and struggle against gender inequalities: (153)
    a. occurred when women began to compare their working conditions with those of men.
    b. began in the 1960s.
    c. had as its goals everything from changing work roles to changing policies on violence against women.
    d. all of the above

13. Gender inequality in education: (154)
    a. has virtually disappeared today.
    b. is allowed by law.
    c. is perpetuated by the use of sex to sort students into different academic disciplines.
    d. disappears by the time men and women enter graduate school.

14. Researchers who have studied conversation patterns between men and women conclude that: (155)
    a. women talk more and interrupt men more frequently than the other way around.
    b. men and women are social equals when it comes to everyday conversation.
    c. even in everyday conversation, the talk between a man and a woman reflects social inequality.
    d. men interrupt more in conversations, but women control the topics that are discussed.

15. The pay gap between men and women: (156)
    a. is found primarily among those with less than a high school education.
    b. is found primary among those with college and graduate education.
    c. is found at all educational levels.
    d. largely has disappeared.

16. The glass ceiling: (157)
    a. keeps both men and women out of non-traditional occupations.
    b. has largely been shattered by today's generation of business women.
    c. refers to the invisible barrier that keeps women from reaching the executive suite.
    d. all of the above

17. Another form of violence against women is "honour killings," found in such societies as (150)
    a. Pakistan.
    b. Jordan.
    c. India.
    d. all of the above

18. Felice Schwartz suggested that corporations create two parallel career paths. These are: (158)

   a. the college-bound and the vocational-technical.
   b. the "partner-material" path and the "non-partner-material" path.
   c. the "mommy track" and the "daddy track."
   d. the "mommy track" and the "fast track."

19. What is true of sexual harassment? (160)
   a. It is still exclusively a female problem.
   b. Targets of sexual harassment are usually men.
   c. Male victims are less likely than female victims to receive a sympathetic ear.
   d. Male victims of sexual harassment receive more sympathy than female victims.

20. The pattern of date rape shows: (162)
   a. that it is not an isolated event.
   b. that it is more likely to happen with couples who have dated for a period of time.
   c. that it is difficult to prosecute.
   d. all of the above

21. Which of the following is *not* among feminist explanations for gender violence? (163)
   a. higher testosterone levels in males
   b. males reassert their declining power and status
   c. the association of strength and virility with violence
   d. cultural traditions that are patriarchal

22. Women continue to be underrepresented in politics because: (164)
   a. they are not really interested in pursuing political careers.
   b. they are not viewed as serious candidates by the voters.
   c. their roles as mothers and wives are incompatible with political roles.
   d. they lack the proper educational backgrounds.

23. In many parts of Canada today, the primary concern of voters is: (164)
   a. the gender of the candidate.
   b. whether the candidate can win.
   c. whether the candidate is the primary caregiver of young children.
   d. how much money the candidate spends.

24. What is most likely to break the stereotypes locking us into traditional gender activities?
   (166)
   a. stricter laws
   b. equal pay
   c. increased female participation in the decision-making processes of social institutions
   d. increased male participation in nurturing activities

25. What is it that keeps most males and females locked into fairly rigid gender roles? (166)
    a. social structural obstacles
    b. socialization
    c. stereotypes
    d. all of the above

TRUE-FALSE QUESTIONS

T F 1. The terms sex and gender basically mean the same thing to sociologists. (146)

T F 2. The study of the medical accident that led to the sex change operation conclusively supports the view that biology is destiny. (148)

T F 3. Universally, there is great variability in terms of the amount of prestige accorded to male and female activities. (149)

T F 4. Female circumcision was never practiced. (150)

T F 5. As China has begun the cautious transition to capitalism, the situation of women within that country has improved. (151)

T F 6. Men, who are reluctant to abandon their privileged positions, use various cultural devices to keep women subservient. (152)

T F 7. In Canada, the reason for under representation of women in politics is that they are still under represented in law and business, the careers from which most politicians come. (164)

T F 8. A gender gap in earnings shows up at all levels of education. (156)

T F 9. Super Jockey, a popular nationally-run comedy show in Japan involves a degree of violence against women as a source of entertainment. (162)

T F 10. Because gender socialization gives men and women different orientations to life, they enter higher education with gender-linked aspirations. (154)

T F 11. Throughout Canada, women are less likely to be full professors, the highest, most prestigious rank. (154)

T F 12. In a study of World War II combat soldiers, Samuel Stouffer reported that officers used feminine terms as insults to motivate soldiers. (155)

T F 13. Women are more likely to interrupt a conversation and to control changes in topics. (155)

T F 14. Research by Fuller and Schoenberger found that women college graduates were able to close the income gap within five years of graduating. (156)

T F 15. The "glass ceiling" and "mommy track" both have a more negative impact on women than on men in corporations and the professions. (156)

T F 16. The "glass escalator" refers to the opportunities that women have to advance quickly in traditional male occupations. (157)

T F 17. Until the 1970s the term of sexual harassment was unknown. (160)

T F 18. Male victims of sexual harassment are less likely than female victims to receive a sympathetic ear. (160)

T F 19. Women in Canada are greatly outnumbered by men in political office. (164)

T F 20. The only reason there are not more women in public office is because men keep them out. (164)

FILL-IN QUESTIONS

1. Males' and females' unequal access to power, prestige, and property on the basis of sex reflects _____. (146)
2. _____ refers to biological characteristics that distinguish females and males, consisting of primary and secondary sex characteristics. (146)
3. The social characteristics that a society considers proper for its males and females make up an individual's _____. (146)
4. You inherit your _____, but you learn your _____ as you are socialized into specific behaviours and attitudes. (146)
5. A society in which women dominate men is called a _____. (147)
6. When activities become associated with one sex or the other they are said to be _____. (149)
7. Violence against women has taken many forms, such as_____ in China (150)
8. _____ is a particular form of violence directed exclusively against women. (150)
9. A _____ is a group that is discriminated against on the basis of its members' physical characteristics. (150)
10. _____ is the philosophy that men and women should be politically, economically, and socially equal. (152-153)
11. The _____ prevents women from advancing to top executive positions. (157)
12. Men who move into traditionally female occupations are likely to climb onto a _____, moving very quickly into more desirable work assignments, higher level positions, and larger salaries. (157)
13. The proposed _____ would address the stresses that many working women experience when they attempt to combine careers and families. (157-158)
14. The abuse of one's position of authority to force unwanted sexual demands on someone is referred to as _____. (160)
15. _____ most commonly occurs between couples who have known each other about a year. (162)
16. The number of women in _____and high-tech occupations doubled between 1991 and 2001. (157)
17. On the eve of International Women's Day in 2002, the Norwegian Government announced a plan whereby it would force companies to guarantee that at least_____ board room seats are held by women. This proposal also called for at least _____male board members.

MATCH THESE SOCIAL SCIENTISTS WITH THEIR CONTRIBUTIONS

__1.	Janet Chafetz	a.	*surveyed 324 societies and found evidence of sex-typed activities*
__2.	Alice Rossi	b.	*men in non-traditional occupations often experience a glass escalator*
__3.	Felice Schwartz	c.	*male dominance grew out of the greater strength men had*
__4.	Christine Williams	d.	*study supports the view that things feminine are generally devalued*
__5.	Gerda Lerner	e.	*associated with the notion mommy tack and fast track*

__6.	Catharine McKinnon	f.	*differences between males and females are due to inborn differences*
__7.	George Murdock	g.	*women are better prepared biologically for "mothering" than are men*
__8.	Samuel Stouffer	h.	*identified sexual harassment as a structural problem in work places*
__9.	Marvin Harris	i.	*patriarchy may have had different origins around the globe*
__10.	Steven Goldberg	j.	*male dominance developed with the origin of private property*
__11.	Friedrich Engels	k.	*noted the devaluation of things associated with women among soldiers*
__12.	Douglas Foley	l.	*studied the second wave of feminism in the 1960s*

ESSAY QUESTION

1. Before examining inequalities of gender, consider why men and women act differently—is it due to biology or culture? What is the dominant sociological position?
2. Compare and contrast the two waves of the feminist movement in Canada by identifying the forces that contributed to both waves.
3. Evaluate the pros and cons of the two parallel career paths available to women; the "fast track" and the "mommy track."
4. Why was rape renamed "sexual assault" under the reformed criminal code?

"DOWN-TO-EARTH SOCIOLOGY"

1. Read "Thinking Critically About Social Controversy" on page 147. Select one view or the other to adopt (at least temporarily) as your own and prepare a statement in which you justify your position. If you have taken the side of nurture, consider all of the forces that shape our behaviour and attitudes as men or women. On the other hand, if you take the side of nature, consider whether or not this means that male dominance and discrimination against women is inevitable. After you have considered one side, try doing the same thing with the opposing side. Then come up with an argument that combines elements of both.
2. After reading about the experiences of women in China (151), what do you see as some of the factors that make it difficult for women there to improve their status today? Which do you think is a more powerful force in shaping women's position in society—economics or politics?
3. Did you realize before reading "Making the Invisible Visible" on page 153 that physicians often do not take women's medical complaints as seriously as those of men? How can this type of problem be a matter of life or death? Do you think gender bias ever affects your own perceptions and behaviour?
4. One of the central issues raised by contemporary Canadian feminists is that women should be granted reproductive rights—that their bodies are their own and they alone

should have the right to decide what happens to them. Yet after reading about reproductive technologies on page 160, you can see that there are still areas in which women do not have this right. How do you feel—should women have exclusive control, or do men and the state have certain rights?

5. What is your view on the recent incidents involving sexual harassment in the military in the United States (161)? After reading this chapter, do you think that the problem is between individuals—young men with overactive sex drives—or social structural—related to society and the inequalities based on gender?

CHAPTER 8
INEQUALITIES OF RACE AND ETHNICITY

CHAPTER SUMMARY

- In a sense race is in the eye of the beholder. Humans show such a mixture of characteristics that there is no inevitable, much less universal way to classify our many biological differences. Therefore, race is a complex and often misunderstood concept. Sociologists, however, stress that what we call races are social classifications, not biological categories. Modern geneticists conclude that there is only ONE racial (genotype) category of humans: homo sapiens. The idea that there are superior or "pure" races is a myth. Nevertheless, the idea of race is powerful, shaping basic relationships between people.

- Ethnic and ethnicity refer to a group of people who identify with one another on the basis of common ancestry and cultural heritage. A minority group is defined as one, singled out for unequal treatment by members of the dominant group, and that regards itself as the object of collective discrimination. Both race and ethnicity can be a basis for unequal treatment.

- Prejudice refers to an attitude and discrimination to unfair treatment. Individual discrimination is the negative treatment of one person by another, while institutional discrimination is discrimination built into society's social institutions.

- Psychological theories explain the origin of prejudice in terms of stress frustration that gets directed towards scapegoats and in terms of the development of authoritarian personalities. Sociologists emphasize how different social environments affect levels of prejudice. They look at the benefits and costs of discrimination, the exploitation of racial-ethnic divisions by those in power, and the self-fulfilling prophecies that are the outcome of labelling.

- Dominant groups typically practice one of six policies toward minority groups: genocide, population transfer, internal colonialism, segregation, assimilation, multiculturalism, or pluralism.

- The major classifications in Canada are: the Native peoples, including status Indians, Métis, and Inuit; the two "Charter Groups," the French and English white settlers; and immigrant groups from other regions of the world.

- Canadian society has been described as a "vertical mosaic"—a pyramid in which the apex is composed of one dominant group, the English.

- The primary issues in Canada today around questions of race and ethnicity are demands for greater political autonomy from Quebec and new challenges of racial and ethnic diversity due to the immigration of people from the less developed nations of the world.

LEARNING OBJECTIVES

As you read Chapter 8, use these learning objectives to organize your notes. After completing your reading, briefly state an answer to each of the objectives, and review the text pages in parentheses.

1. Explain how race can be both a reality and a myth and distinguish between the concepts of race and ethnicity. (169-170)
2. Define the term "minority group," explain the process by which a group becomes a minority, and identify five characteristics shared by minority groups worldwide. (170-171)
3. Differentiate between prejudice and discrimination. (171)

4. Provide examples of prejudice and discrimination among racial and ethnic groups and relate these examples to the concept of racism. (171)
5. Compare and contrast individual and institutional discrimination and give examples of each type of discrimination. (171)
6. Discuss the different psychological perspectives on prejudice. (171-172)
7. Outline the functionalist, conflict, and symbolic interactionist perspectives on prejudice. (172-173)
8. Postmodernist position on understanding racism and discrimination maintains that it is only through the "voices" of the disaffected minorities who have directly experienced racism and discrimination that we can come to understand what it means. (173)
9. Postcolonial theory seeks to understand the ways in which the colonial legacy of racism persists on the so-called post colonial societies and interacts with the refusal of the members of such societies to accept white European notions of race, ethnicity, and cultural identity. (173-174)
10. Critical race theory accepts that racism is an "endemic" facet of life in our society and that neutrality, objectivity, colourblindness, and meritocracy are all questionable constructs. (174)
11. List and describe the six patterns of intergroup relations. (174-176)
12. Describe the multiracial feminist point of view. (173)
13. Discuss Canadian government policy with respect to Native peoples. (176-177)
14. Identify the two Charter Groups and explain why John Porter termed Canada a "vertical mosaic." (177-180)
15. Compare and contrast the experiences of immigrants from Europe, Africa, Latin and Central America, and Asia. (180-181)
16. Identify the key issues facing Canadians that are tied to race and ethnicity. (180-181)

CHAPTER OUTLINE

I. **Laying the Sociological Foundation**
    A. Race, a group with inherited physical characteristics that distinguish it from another group, is both a myth and a reality.
        1. It is a reality in the sense that humans come in different colours and shapes.
        2. It is a myth because there are no pure races; what we call "races" are social classifications, not biological categories. In addition, it is a myth that any one race is superior to another.
        3. The myth makes a difference for social life because people believe these ideas are real and they act on their beliefs.
    B. Race and ethnicity are often confused due to the cultural differences people see and the way they define race. Ethnicity and ethnic refers to cultural characteristics that distinguish a people. Physical or cultural differences can lead to unfair treatment.
    C. Minority groups are people singled out for unequal treatment and who regard themselves as objects of collective discrimination.
        1. They are not necessarily in the numerical minority. Sociologists refer to those who do the discriminating as the dominant group—they have greater power, more privileges, and higher social status. The dominant group attributes its privileged position to its superiority, not to discrimination.

    2. A group becomes a minority through expansion of political boundaries by another group. Another way for a group to become a minority is by migration into a territory, either voluntarily or involuntarily.

    3. Shared characteristics of minorities worldwide: (1) membership is ascribed involuntarily through birth; (2) the physical or cultural traits that distinguish them are held in low esteem by the dominant group; (3) they are unequally treated by the dominant group; (4) they tend to marry within their own group; and (5) they tend to feel strong group solidarity.

D. Prejudice and discrimination exist throughout the world, in, for example, Canada, Israel, and Japan.

    1. Discrimination is unfair treatment directed toward someone. When based on race, it is known as racism. It also can be based on features such as age, sex, sexual preference, religion, or politics.

    2. Prejudice is prejudging of some sort, usually in a negative way.

    3. Ethnocentrism is so common that each racial/ethnic group views other groups as inferior in at least some way. Studies confirm that there is less prejudice among the more educated and among younger people.

E. Sociologists distinguish between individual discrimination (negative treatment of one person by another) and institutional discrimination (negative treatment of a minority group that is built into a society's institutions).

II. Theories of Prejudice

A. Psychological Perspectives

    1. According to John Dollard, prejudice results from frustration: people unable to strike out at the real source of their frustration find scapegoats to unfairly blame.

    2. According to Theodor Adorno, highly prejudiced people are insecure, intolerant people who long for the firm boundaries established by strong authority; he called this complex of personality traits the authoritarian personality.

    3. Subsequent studies have generally concluded that people, who are older, less educated, less intelligent and from a lower social class are more likely to be authoritarian.

B. Sociological Perspectives

    1. To functionalists, the social environment can be deliberately arranged to generate either positive or negative feelings about people. Prejudice is functional in that it creates in-group solidarity and out-group antagonism. Functionalists do not justify what they discover but simply identify functions and dysfunctions of human action.

    2. To conflict theorists, the ruling class systematically pits group against group; by splitting workers along racial ethnic lines the ruling class benefits, because solidarity among the workers is weakened. The higher unemployment rate of minorities creates a reserve labour force from which owners can draw when they need to expand production temporarily. The existence of the reserve labour force is a constant threat to white workers, who modify their demands rather than lose their jobs to unemployment.

3. To symbolic interactionists, the labels people learn colour their perception, leading people to see certain things and be blind to others. Racial and ethnic labels are powerful because they are shorthand for emotionally laden stereotypes. Symbolic interactionists stress that people learn prejudices in interactions with others.

4. The stereotypes that we learn not only justify prejudice and discrimination, but they also lead to a self-fulfilling prophecy—stereotypical behaviour in those who are stereotyped.

5. Multiracial feminists point out that the analysis of inequality must include the experiences of women and men of different racial and ethnic groups and their class differences.

III. Global Patterns of Intergroup Relations

A. Genocide is the actual or attempted systematic annihilation of a race or ethnic group that is labelled as less than fully human. The Holocaust is an example.

B. Population transfer is involuntary movement of a minority group. Indirect transfer involves making life so unbearable that members of a minority then leave; direct transfer involves forced expulsion.

C. Internal colonialism is a society's policy of exploiting a minority, by using social institutions to deny it access to full benefits. Slavery is an extreme example.

D. Segregation is the formal separation of groups. It accompanies internal colonialism.

E. Assimilation is the process by which a minority is absorbed into the mainstream. Forced assimilation occurs when the dominant group prohibits the minority from using its own religion, language, and customs. Permissive assimilation is when the minority adopts the dominant group's patterns in its own way and/or at its own speed.

F. Multiculturalism, also called pluralism, permits or encourages ethnic variation.

IV. The Major Classifications in Canada

A. Canadians can be classified into three categories: Native peoples; the two "Charter Groups" (French and English); and all the other ethnic groups that have settled in Canada through immigration over the past century.

B. Native peoples in Canada comprise a rich diversity of customs, languages, and cultural differences that stretch back to pre-European contact.

1. Native peoples constitute approximately 3.7 percent of Canada's population.

2. These include status Indians, non-status Indians, Métis, and Inuit.

3. The federal government has made efforts to gain Native Canadians' support for the Charter of Rights and Freedoms by making provision for their self-government. However, it takes the consent of seven provincial governments to agree to any amendments, and this has yet to be achieved.

C. The two "Charter Groups" refer to the linguistic and culturally distinct white "settler" groups, the French and British.

1. The early history of French-English relations was characterized by struggles over the colonization of North America.

2. The century leading up to Confederation witnessed the growth of the two Charter Groups. Each controlled its own institutional elite: the British

controlled commerce, while the French Catholics held onto the professions (lawyers, doctors, clergy) and farming.
    3. As Canada developed politically and economically, it developed into a "vertical mosaic": a pyramid in which the apex was composed of one dominant Charter Group, the English.
  D. Canada also includes a rich diversity of immigrants and refugees from different parts of the world. Today, the majority of Canadians have neither British nor French ancestry.
    1. New immigrants create more jobs than they fill, rather than taking employment away from other Canadians.
    2. Faced with unemployment and discrimination, however, up to 20 percent of some immigrant groups have returned to their native countries.

V.   Looking Toward the Future
  A. There will be two major issues facing Canadians in relation to questions of race and ethnicity. First, the continued demands for political autonomy from within Quebec. Second, new challenges of racial and ethnic diversity due to immigration, and arrivals of refugees, from less developed nations of the world.

KEY TERMS

After studying the chapter, review the definition for each of the following terms.

assimilation: the process of being absorbed into the mainstream culture

authoritarian personality: Theodor Adorno's term for people who are prejudiced and rank high on scales of conformity, intolerance, insecurity, respect for authority, and submissiveness to superiors

compartmentalize: to separate acts from feelings or attitudes

discrimination: an act of unfair treatment directed against an individual or a group

dominant group: the group with the most power, greatest privileges, and highest social status

dual labour market: also called **split labour market**, work is divided along racial, ethnic, and gender lines.

ethnic (and ethnicity): having distinctive cultural characteristics

genocide: the systematic annihilation or attempted annihilation of people based on their presumed race or ethnicity

individual discrimination: the negative treatment of one person by another on the basis of that person's perceived characteristics

institutional discrimination: negative treatment of a minority group that is built into a society's institutions; also called systemic discrimination

internal colonialism: the policy of economically exploiting a minority group

minority group: people who are singled out for unequal treatment, and who regard themselves as objects of collective discrimination

multiculturalism (also called pluralism): a philosophy or political policy that permits or encourages ethnic variation

population transfer: involuntary movement of a minority group

postcolonialism: the theory concerned with how to understand the cultural products (print and visual media, literature, the arts, and, of course, language) coming from societies that were once colonies of Europe

prejudice: an attitude or prejudging, usually in a negative way

race: inherited physical characteristics that distinguish one group from another

racism: prejudice and discrimination on the basis of race

reserve labour force: the unemployed; unemployed workers are thought of as being "in reserve"—capitalists take them "out of reserve" (put them back to work) during times of high production and lay them off (put them back in reserve) when they are no longer needed

scapegoat: an individual or group unfairly blamed for someone else's troubles

segregation: the policy of keeping racial or ethnic groups apart

selective perception: seeing certain features of an object or situation but remaining blind to others

KEY PEOPLE

Review the major theoretical contributions or findings of these people.

Theodor Adorno: Adorno identified the authoritarian personality type.

Emery Cowen, Judah Landes and Donald Schaet: In an experiment these psychologists found that students directed frustrations onto people who had nothing to do with their problem.

John Dollard: This psychologist first suggested that prejudice is the result of frustration and scapegoats become the targets for frustration.

Raphael Ezekiel: This sociologist did participant observation of neo-Nazis and the Ku Klux Klan in order to examine racism from inside racist organizations.

John Porter: Porter studied patterns of economic inequality in Canadian society and noted the dominant position of the English Charter Group

Muzafer and Carolyn Sherif: The Sherifs researched the functions of prejudice and found that it builds in-group solidarity.

W.I. Thomas: Thomas observed that once people define a situation as real, it is real in its consequences.

Charles Wagley and Marvin Harris: These anthropologists identified the characteristics of minorities worldwide.

Louis Wirth: Wirth offered a sociological definition of minority group.

Eugene Hartly: He discovered that people can be prejudiced against people they have never met, and even against groups that do not exist.

Mette Spencer: Her research has thrown light on the economic experience of moving to and living in Canada.

SELF-TEST

After completing this self-test, check your answers against the Answer Key at the back of this Study Guide and against the text on page(s) indicated in parentheses.

MULTIPLE CHOICE QUESTIONS

1. Race: (169)
   a. means having distinctive cultural characteristics.
   b. means having inherited physical characteristics that distinguish one group from another.
   c. means people who are singled out for unequal treatment.
   d. is relatively easy to determine.

2. People often confuse race and ethnicity because: (170)
   a. they dislike people who are different from them.
   b. of the cultural differences people see and the way they define race.
   c. they are unaware of the fact that race is cultural and ethnicity is biological.
   d. all of the above

3. Which are the characteristics shared by minorities worldwide?: (171)
   a. Membership in a minority group is an ascribed status.
   b. Physical or cultural traits that distinguish the group are held in low esteem.
   c. They are unequally treated by the dominant group.
   d. all of the above

4. What is true of relations with "minority groups"? (170)
   a. Minority groups are people singled out for unequal treatment.
   b. Minority groups regard themselves as objects of collective discrimination.
   c. Minority groups do not necessarily refer to a numerical minority.
   d. all of the above

5. Prejudice and discrimination: (171)
   a. are less prevalent in Canada than in other societies.
   b. are more prevalent in Canada than in other societies.
   c. appear to characterize every society, regardless of size.
   d. appear to characterize only large societies.

6. Prejudice: (171)
   a. is an attitude.
   b. may be positive or negative.
   c. often is the basis of discrimination.
   d. all of the above

7. Racism is: (171)
   a. unique to the United States.
   b. an example of individual discrimination.
   c. present only in people with authoritarian personalities.

    d. discrimination based on race.

8. The negative treatment of one person by another on the basis of personal characteristics is: (171)
    a. individual discrimination.
    b. individual prejudice.
    c. institutional discrimination.
    d. institutional prejudice

9. What did Eugene Hartley's study show about prejudice? (171)
    a. Prejudice does not necessarily depend on negative.
    b. People can be prejudiced against people they have never met.
    c. People can be prejudiced against groups that do not exist.
    d. all of the above

10. At times discrimination is woven into the fabric of society to such an extent that: (171)
    a. it becomes routine.
    b. it becomes social policy.
    c. a and b
    d. none of the above

11. The Muzafer and Carolyn Sherif (1953) study shows that: (172)
    a. the social environment can be deliberately arranged to generate either positive or negative feelings about people.
    b. prejudice is never functional to a group.
    c. prejudice never creates in-group solidarity.
    d. lifelong friends remain loyal friends despite being put in a competing group.

12. According to conflict theorists, prejudice: (172)
    a. benefits capitalists by splitting workers along racial or ethnic lines.
    b. contributes to the exploitation of workers, thus producing a split-labour market.
    c. keeps workers from demanding higher wages and better working conditions.
    d. all of the above

13. Symbolic interactionists stress that prejudiced people: (173)
    a. are born that way.
    b. have certain types of personalities.
    c. learn their prejudices in interaction with others.
    d. none of the above

14. The_____ provide an outstanding example of multiculturalism, made up of four separate groups—French, Italian, German, and Romansh—living in harmony. (176)
    a. French
    b. Swiss
    c. Germans
    d. Austrians

15. Genocide: (169-174)
    a. occurred when Hitler attempted to destroy all Jews.
    b. is the systematic annihilation of a race or ethnic group.
    c. often requires the cooperation of ordinary citizens.
    d. all of the above

16. When a minority is expelled from a country or from a particular area of a country, the process is called: (174)
    a. population redistribution.
    b. direct population transfer.
    c. indirect population transfer.
    d. expelled population transfer.

17. A society's policy of exploiting a minority group, using social institutions to deny the minority access to the society's full benefits, is referred to as: (174-175)
    a. segregation.
    b. pluralism.
    c. internal colonialism.
    d. genocide.

18. The process of being absorbed into the mainstream culture is: (175)
    e. pluralism.
    f. assimilation.
    g. cultural submersion.
    h. internal colonialism.

19. Another term for pluralism is: (176)
    a. assimilation.
    b. melting pot.
    c. ethnic unity.
    d. multiculturalism.

20. The term "Charter Groups" refers to: (177)
    a. status and non-status Indians.
    b. French and English white settlers.
    c. Métis and Inuit.
    d. all of the above

21. Which of the following is true of the federal governments relations with Native Canadians? (176)
    a. It has made efforts to gain Native Canadians support for the Charter of Rights and Freedoms.
    b. On April 1, 1999, the territory of Nunavut was created.
    c. Nunavut territory is nearly one fifth the size of Canada.
    d. all of the above

22. Despite the much publicized conflict with Natives, (177)
    a. Quebec has better record than rest of Canada with dealing with Native peoples.
    b. there is evidence of a favourable rate of Native language retention.
    c. there is lower rate of imprisonment of Natives compared with non-Natives.
    d. all of the above

23. According to John Porter, Canadian society is a "vertical mosaic" because: (177-180)
    a. it is structured like a pyramid, with the English at the top.
    b. it is a diverse society, representative of the interests of many ethnic groups.
    c. each of the major ethnic groups in Canada has representatives in the political elite.
    d. all of the above

24. Which of the following statements about the English charter group in Canada is *incorrect*? (179)
    a. It could be found in the country's political elites.
    b. It could be found in the country's media elites.
    c. It was not part of the trade union elites.
    d. It was even in the upper echelons of the Protestant clergy.

25. According to Metta Spencer, what factor(s) contribute to some immigrants deciding to return to their native countries? (180)
    a. policies of assimilation
    b. differences in educational requirements for some professions
    c. lack of formal protection under the Charter of Rights and Freedoms
    d. unemployment and discrimination

TRUE-FALSE QUESTIONS

T F   1.   Modern genetics conclude that there is only ONE racial (genotype) category of humans: homo sapiens. (169)
T F   2.   Jews are more properly considered an ethnic group than a race. (170)
T F   3.   The system known as apartheid in South Africa is an example of institutional discrimination. (171)
T F   4.   In Israel, Ashkenazie Jews discriminates against Sephardie Jews. (171)
T F   5.   Minorities tend to marry within their own group. (171)
T F   6.   Minorities often have a shared sense of identity and of common destiny. (171)
T F   7.   Discrimination is unfair treatment based solely on racial characteristics. (171)
T F   8.   Discrimination is often the result of an attitude called prejudice—a prejudice of some sort, usually in a negative (171)
T F   9.   Psychologist John Dollard suggested that prejudice is the result of frustration (171)
T F   10.   Sociologists believe that individual discrimination is an adequate explanation for discrimination. (171)
T F   11.   Hartley found that people who are prejudiced against one racial or ethnic group tend to be prejudiced against other groups. (171)
T F   12.   Persons with an authoritarian personality are characterized by prejudice and high rankings on scales of conformity, intolerance, insecurity, and excessive respect for authority. (172)

T F 13. The Sherif study demonstrates that the social environment can be deliberately arranged to generate either positive or negative feelings about people. (172)

T F 14. Functionalists focus on the role of the capitalist class in exploiting racism and ethnic inequalities. (172)

T F 15. Unemployment is a useful weapon to help maintain a split labour market. (172)

T F 16. Genocide is facilitated by labelling the rejected group as less than fully human. (174)

T F 17. Segregation allows the dominant group to exploit the labour of the minority while maintaining social distance. (175)

T F 18. The Constitution Act of 1982 recognizes Native Indians, Inuit, and Metis. (176)

T F 19. Porter found that members of the English Charter Group dominate Canada's political and media elites. (179)

T F 20. Based on the 2001 Canadian census, except for Canada's native peoples, and Jamaicans, all groups reported higher levels of university qualifications than the national average. (180)

FILL-IN QUESTIONS

1. _____ is inherited physical characteristics that distinguish one group from another. (169)

2. Membership in a minority group is a(n) _____ status; that is, it is not voluntary, but comes through birth. (171)

3. _____ is discrimination on the basis of race. (171)

4. _____ discrimination is the negative treatment of a minority group that is built into a society's institutions. (171)

5. Theodor Adorno's term for people who are prejudiced and rank high on scales of conformity, intolerance, insecurity, respect for authority, and submissiveness to superiors is _____. (172)

6. _____ theorists believe that prejudice can be both functional and dysfunctional. (172)

7. The dual labour market is used by _____ theorists to explain how racial and ethnic strife can be used to pit workers against one another. (172)

8. The term used to describe the unemployed who can be put to work during times of high production and then discarded when no longer needed is _____. (172)

9. _____ is the ability to see certain points but remain blind to others. (173)

10. The systematic annihilation or attempted annihilation of a race or ethnic group is _____. (174)

11. The types of population transfer are: (1) _____ and (2) _____. (174)

12. _____ is facilitated by labelling the targeted group as less than fully human. (174)

13. _____ is the process of being absorbed into the mainstream culture. (175)

14. _____ is a philosophy or political policy that permits or even encourages ethnic variation. (176)

15. _____ is Porter's term to describe the economic and political dominance of Canada by the English Charter Group. (177)

16. The system of reserves for Canada's Native peoples is an example of _____.(175)

17. Derived from the Greek language, _____ and _____ are terms that refer to people who identify with one another on the basis of common ancestry and cultural heritage. (170)

MATCH THESE SOCIAL SCIENTISTS WITH THEIR CONTRIBUTIONS

___ 1. Theodor Adorno
___ 2. W.I. Thomas
___ 3. John Dollard

___ 4. John Porter
___ 5. Louis Wirth
___ 6. Eugene Hartley
      experience
___ 7. Munzafer and
      Carolyn Sherif

a. *suggested that prejudice is the result of frustration*
b. *offered a sociological definition of minority group*
c. *observed that defining a situation as real makes it real in its consequences*
d. *identified the authoritarian personality type*
e. *in The Vertical Mosaic he used the term Charter Groups*
f. *suggested that prejudice does not depend on negative*

g. *suggested that prejudice is a function and shaped by the social environment*

ESSAY QUESTIONS

1. Explain what the authors mean when they say that race is both a myth and a reality.
2. Which of the six patterns of inter group relations in Figure 8.1 have been or are part of the Canadian experience?
3. Explore how both psychological and sociological theories can be used together to gain a deeper understanding of prejudice and discrimination.

"DOWN-TO-EARTH SOCIOLOGY"

1. What are the new challenges posed by Multiracial feminism? (173)
2. What were the rationales given by the Canadian federal government to support the relocation of Inuit peoples (177)? What were the impacts of these relocations? Is some form of restitution in order? What would be an appropriate form of compensation?
3. What does the history of Louis Riel (178) tell us about French-English relations? About relations with Native peoples? To what extent is Riel's legacy still felt today?

CHAPTER 9
INEQUALITIES OF AGE

CHAPTER SUMMARY

- The authors of the chapter clearly feel that "examining the ways in which we, as a society, are socially constructing aging is important" for our own future life course, as well as for understanding social inequalities in Canada. Aging is as much a socially constructed process as a biological process.
- With industrialization, urbanization, and modernization came a dramatic increase in people's lifespan. Today a Canadian woman can expect to live to age 82 and a man to 77.
- In Canada, the rising proportion of older people in the population is referred to as the "greying of Canada."
- Seniors organize: as seniors have become an ever more prominent demographic and economic element in Canadian society, they have established their own support groups and organizations.
- Aging differs by gender, social class, and ethnicity. There are no universal attitudes, beliefs or policies regarding the aged.
- The symbolic interaction perspective identifies four factors that influence when people label themselves as "old": biological changes, biographical events, gender roles, and cultural timetables. Ageism is based on stereotypes that are influenced by the mass media.
- Conflict theorists study the potential for conflict created by issues related to aging (e.g., struggles by seniors to protect pension programs).
- Problems of dependency for the elderly include inadequate nursing homes, elder abuse, and poverty. About one-third of elderly men and one-half of women will spend at least some time in nursing homes.

LEARNING OBJECTIVES

As you read Chapter 9, use these learning objectives to organize your notes. After completing your reading, briefly state an answer to each of the objectives, and review the text pages in parentheses.

1. Appreciate that aging is as much a socially constructed process as a biological process. Explain the importance of the "social construction of aging." (185)
2. Recognize the demographic effects of industrialization, urbanization, and modernization, and describe the effect of the "baby boom." (185-186)
3. Examine what the term "graying of Canada" means and discuss differences in aging based on gender and ethnicity. (188)
4. Understand some of the societal implications of the dramatic increase in the proportion of seniors in the population in Canada and around the globe. (188)
5. Describe how seniors have become an ever more prominent demographic and economic element in Canadian society. (189)
6. Describe differences in aging by gender, social class, and ethnicity. (190)
7. Look at aging from a variety of useful perspectives: symbolic interactionist, feminist, and conflict theories. (191-199)

8. Review how the meaning of old age has changed over time in Canada and consider some of the factors that contributed to this change. Discuss also the ways in which media influence and perpetuate these ideas. (193-195)
9. Discuss the pros and cons of mandatory retirement. (197-199)
10. Explain why critical social gerontologists have a valid concern, when they point out the necessity to take seriously the plight of mentally and physically disabled, regardless of age or cause. (202)
11. Discuss the problems that often emerge in finding resources to provide adequate care as seniors become dependent on social and family resources. How such problems are intensified by poverty and debilitating illnesses. (200-202)
12. Why is elderly abuse increasingly becoming a current issue? (202)

CHAPTER OUTLINE

I.   **The "Age-Quake"**
  A. With industrialization, urbanization, and modernization came a dramatic increase in men and women's lifespan and a remarkable increase in the numbers of seniors in the population.
    1. The demographic effects of industrialization were further magnified by World War II.
    2. The net result was the "baby boom"—a dramatic increase in the population generated between 1946 and 1965.
    3. In the period following 1965, there has been a decline in the numbers of children born into a typical family.
    4. The net result is that the age pyramid that characterizes most traditional societies—many children, fewer adults, and very few elders—has been increasingly turned on its head, and older Canadians increasingly predominate in the population.
    5. Median age (the point at which exactly one-half of the population is older and the other half is younger) of Canadians was 22.7 in 1901, 37.6 in 2001, and is expected to go up to 41.0 by 2011.
  B. This shift in Canada toward an older society poses significant issues.
    1. Will older citizens who continue to occupy positions in the labour force block the entry and advancement of younger Canadians?
    2. Or will older workers be increasingly the victims of ageist discrimination in the workplace?
    3. Will seniors who are disabled or ill become an overwhelming burden for young citizens who are directly or indirectly (through taxation) involved in the provision of care for the elderly?
    4. As the seniors' population continues to grow, particularly the population of aged seniors (80 years of age and over), it is likely that debates over not only social security taxes but also other public expenditures, such as health care, will greatly intensify.
    5. This raises the question of how scarce resources will be allocated when the interests of seniors conflict with those of the young. For example, should limited research funding be directed toward the diseases of the elderly—e.g.

arthritis, heart disease—or the health concerns of the young—e.g. reproductive technologies?

C. In Canada, the "greying of Canada" refers to the proportion of older persons in Canada's population.

    1. According to the 2001 census, there are 3.9 million Canadian seniors, comprising 13 percent of the population.

    2. In large measure, this is the result of marked improvements in Canadian life expectancy. It is startling to realize that 100 years ago the clear majority of Canadians would not live to see age 65.

    3. Today, a Canadian woman can expect to live to age 82 and a man to 77.

    4. What is not clear and has momentous implications is whether the growing senior population will be able to participate as productive members of society or whether many—in particular aged seniors—will continue to experience high rates of disability, frailty, and dependency.

    5. The impact of this aging population has not been felt uniformly across the country. There are regional differences, the Atlantic Provinces and Quebec having older populations than the Canadian average.

D. Seniors organize: as seniors have become an ever more prominent demographic and economic element in Canadian society, they have predictably established their own support groups and organizations.

    1. Some of these efforts have been intended to provide assistance and support to seniors in terms of specific issues and concerns, while others are intended more generally to provide a sense of community and solidarity as well as to advance the interests and perspectives of seniors.

    2. The first significant step in this direction was taken in the 1960s when Margaret Kuhn helped to establish the Gray Panthers in the United States.

    3. Since then a growing number of organizations have flourished in both Canada and the United States, such as Fédération de l'Age d'Or du Québec that lobbies Quebec government on seniors' issues, Alberta Council of Aging, Grandparents Raising Grandchildren, and Ontario Network for the Prevention of Elder Abuse.

    4. A dramatic example of the ability of Canadian seniors to mobilize effectively and quickly around a social issue was the seniors' immediate and overwhelming response to the 1985 government efforts to de-index government pensions. Finance Minister Michael Wilson proposed that the Old Age Security (OAS) and Guaranteed Income Supplement (GIS) pensions no longer be automatically increased in response to increases in the cost of living (the Consumer Price Index). Seniors and their supporters made it a front-page issue; their nationwide efforts were capped in the summer of 1985 with a massive protest on Parliament Hill.

    5. Anti-poverty advocates pointed out that the proposed changes would consign hundreds of thousands of low-income seniors to poverty. In the face of five weeks of these protests, the federal government backed down and abandoned the legislation.

    6. Since that time, seniors have become not only more numerous but better organized. The Canadian Association of Retired Persons (CARP, now known as Canada's Association for the Fifty-Plus) with local chapters across Canada has launched a vigorous Canada-wide campaign against age discrimination. In

Ontario, working with the Ontario Human Rights Commission, the group has helped to create a province-wide campaign to increase public awareness of ageism and its impact.

    7. Not all organizations by seniors are so formal or mainstream; there is for example, The Raging Grannies.

E. Aging differs by gender, social class, and ethnicity.

    1. Currently, women make up 57 percent of Canadians 65 years of age and older and more than 65 percent of those 80 years of age or older.

    2. In old age, as in other stages in the life course, having enough money improves your prospects for health and longevity.

    3. Clearly, social class—in complex association with gender—colours the aging experience.

    4. Twenty-five years ago the sheer numbers of poor Canadian seniors was a social embarrassment. Although the situation has much improved, thanks in large measure to improved government income support through OAS, GIS, and Canada/Quebec Pension Plans, many seniors still do live in poverty and near the poverty line.

    5. Senior women who are divorced or separated figure among the poorest of the poor.

    6. Finally, there is a variety of research suggesting that ethnic and cultural differences intersect with social class and gender to affect the structure and experience of aging. People living in remote and northern areas of Canada, the majority of whom are Aboriginal, have markedly lower life expectancies than the average Canadian. People living in Region de Nunavik in Quebec have the lowest life expectancy in Canada, at 66.7 years for both males and females, more in line with individuals living in Dominican Republic than urban Canada.

    7. Not only how many years you will spend as a senior, but the quality of that life appear to be affected by ethnicity.

II. **Theoretical Perspectives on Aging: Symbolic Interactionism**

A. Symbolic Interactionist Perspectives on aging: to study how aging is socially constructed, symbolic interactionists examine how the symbols associated with age affect our perceptions.

    1. There are several factors that push people to apply the label "old."

    2. Biology changes how a person looks and feels; the person adopts the role of "old" (acts the way old people are thought to act) upon experiencing these changes.

    3. Personal history (an injury that limits mobility) or biography (becoming a grandmother at an early age) may affect self-concept regarding age.

    4. Gender age also plays a part. The relative values that culture places on men's ages is less than that of women's ages.

    5. When a particular society defines a person as "old," the person is likely to feel "old." These timetables are not fixed; groups sometimes adjust expectations about the onset of old age.

B. Aging is relative; when it begins and what it means varies from culture to culture.

1. One cultural group may choose a particular birthday, such as the sixtieth or sixty-fifth, or a particular physical event, such as menopause, to signal the onset of old age.

2. To grow old in traditional Inuit society meant voluntary death. Inuit society was so precarious that a person no longer able to pull his or her own weight was expected to simply go off and die.

C. Robert Butler coined the term ageism to refer to prejudice, discrimination, and hostility directed at people because of their age.

   1. Having acknowledged that the history of aging is complex and contradictory, it can, however, be argued that the Industrial Revolution corresponded not only with an increase in the numbers of seniors but also with a significant downturn in the social position of the great majority of seniors—those who were working class, female, immigrants, and/or disabled.

   2. Modern Canadian society has inherited long-held contradictory perspectives on aging and the elderly, along with the economic marginalization of many seniors. Certainly, being old is not seen as necessarily synonymous with being disabled, frail, incompetent, or dependent—and positive notions of older citizens do appear. However, research suggests that since seniors tend to have been denied important productive social roles, they do tend to be stereotyped in often negative terms.

D. The popular media tend to reflect an ambivalent perception of older Canadians; positive representations exist alongside persistent negative stereotypes.

   1. The consumer market economy—which relies on the creation of personal dissatisfaction and needs—has tapped into our societal and personal discomfort with aging. The net result has been a billion-dollar market in goods and services designed to delay, counteract, or camouflage aging.

   2. An enormous amount of economic activity is directed towards the message that age is a personal problem and a stigma that must be constantly battled if self-worth is to be maintained.
   Canadian researchers Julie Ann McMullin and John Cairney (2004) explored the relationship between self-esteem, age, class, and gender. Their results lend credence to the view that aging is socially constructed as a negative experience in contemporary Canada.

E. Today, ageism is an increasingly central feminist concern and, at the same time, feminists have played a key role in challenging mainstream gerontology, and articulating a critical approach to the study of aging. Aging exacerbates the problem of power and inequality for women.

   1. While aging is seen as empowering for many men, it is not so for women. On men, greying hair and wrinkles may be seen as signs of "maturing," while on women those same features are likely to be interpreted as signs of being "old."

   2. As Abu-Laban and McDaniel (2005) comment, "The prospects for women of colour, Aboriginal women, women with disabilities, or lesbian women are even worse."

F. Much contemporary postmodern feminism has been exploring the ways in which gender and age are reproduced in the discourses embedded in cultural representations such as art, literature, and the mass media. The U.S. feminist Betty Friedan examined mass media images of older women. The implicit message was that most seniors, except the rich, famous, and powerful, do not count and that this is especially true of senior women.

III. **Theories of Aging: the Conflict Perspective**
   A. Conflict theorists examine social life as a struggle between groups for scarce resources. Pension legislation is an example of that struggle.
      1. Until recently, almost all Canadians were required by law to retire at age 65. This tradition reflects a standard established in 1889 by Count Otto von Bismarck, Germany's first chancellor.
      2. At this point in history, most citizens in industrialized economies were in physical decline by age 65 and were increasingly unable to work; few would survive many years past retirement.
      3. Conflict theorists state that pension legislation was not a result of generosity, but rather of competition among interest groups.
   B. Since equilibrium is only a temporary balancing of social forces, some form of continuing conflict between the younger and the older appears inevitable.
      1. The huge costs of government pension funds have become a national concern. The dependency ratio (number of workers compared with number of recipients) is currently four working-age Canadians paying to support each person over 65, but is expected to drop to a ratio of 2-to-1 by 2030.
      2. The federal and provincial governments have increasingly introduced policies to provide some measure of economic security for seniors. Currently Canadian seniors are supported by a three-level retirement system which includes the Old Age Security System, the Canada and Quebec Pension Plan, and Registered Retirement Savings Plans.
      3. A movement has emerged, powered in part by seniors' groups, professional organizations, and employers, intent on ending the policy of mandatory retirement at age 65.
      4. Currently, only Manitoba bans mandatory retirement through its human rights legislation.
      5. Older women workers may be particularly affected by mandatory retirement provisions since typically they have been able to spend less time in the paid labour force and, as a result, have built up fewer retirement resources.
      6. For some youth there is a popular belief that the good jobs and the prospects for a prosperous life are being obstructed by a "boomer bottleneck" in which older Canadians continue to hang on to opportunities for privilege, power, and wealth.
      7. Employers do not tend to assume one clear position on the issue of retirement.
      8. Segments of the labour movement are vigorously opposed to efforts to do away with retirement legislation. The right to retire and draw upon pension funds was a hard-won victory for workers who, during the early industrial period, were simply expected to work until they died.
   C. Critical social gerontology challenges the traditional approaches to the study of seniors. In particular, the tendency to approach age in bio-medical terms, almost as an ailment which can be "cured" by medical intervention, has been extensively

criticized as has the tendency to homogenize seniors rather than acknowledging the important differences amongst them.

1. Canadian sociologist Susan McDaniel has made a particularly important contribution with her concept of intergenerational inter-linkages (IGILs). Each generation is both receiving and giving, and transfers between generations are monetary, public, and global. In short, McDaniel is challenging our assumptions about seniors and family life and opening up a wide array of research doors, in particular to "whether or how generation works with or against other dimensions of societal cleavage such as class, gender, ethnicity, and/or immigrant recency."

2. A useful example of this new approach to aging issues is its perspective on the popular notion of the "sandwich generation." According to the 2002 General Social Survey, 30 percent of Canadians aged 45 to 64 with unmarried children under age 25 living at home were also caring for a senior.

3. Drawing on McDaniel's concept of inter-linkages, Joseph Tindale et al. (2002) suggest that we need an approach that is not premised on generational conflict between seniors and their caregivers and that recognizes the possibility of intergenerational support between parents in their 70s and their children in their 40s and 50s.

4. Critical social gerontologists press for the necessity of locating older people as participants in these new global realities, which are more fluid, mobile, and uncertain than prior social arrangements.

IV. The Dependency Crisis

A. With increasing age, there is no question that most seniors will become increasingly vulnerable to physical and mental disability. Most Canadian seniors (81 percent) living at home have at least one chronic health problem—heart disease, diabetes, rheumatism, or arthritis—and that one in four are living with chronic pain.

1. The eldercare scene in Canada is currently characterized by an uneven mix of home care, hospital care, and institutional care. About 5 percent of seniors over age 65 and 18 percent of those 80 and over are cared for in an institution.

2. Women are expected to provide family care and service—to the likely detriment of their careers and economic well-being—only to end up living by themselves in old age. However, paid community providers and institutional caregivers are not necessarily the solution. Recent media coverage of the abuse and neglect.

3. Neglect of seniors in seniors' residences underscores these concerns.

4. The composite of isolation, disability, illness, and dependency accounts for many of the social problems with which aged seniors are identified, and are seen as root cause of increased suicides. Of course, for some aged seniors, suicide may be a valued escape from chronic suffering and disease.

5. Currently, only the Netherlands and the state of Oregon in the U.S. allow assisted suicide.

6. Polls indicate that three-quarters of Canadians support doctor-assisted suicide for the terminally ill; this speaks strongly to the fact that death and dying, like aging, are as much socially constructed as biological events.

7. Seriously addressing the plight of the mentally and physically disabled, regardless of age or cause and that of their caregivers necessarily raises fundamental questions about the social value placed online, the meaning of "quality of life," and the responsibility of the state and community in maintaining minimal standards of life.

KEY TERMS

After studying the chapter, review the definition for each of the following terms.

ageism: prejudice, discrimination, and hostility directed against people because of their age; can be directed against any age group, including youth

dependency ratio: the number of workers required to support dependent persons—those 64 and older and those 15 and younger

greying of Canada: a term that refers to the rising proportion of older persons as a percentage of the Canadian population

life expectancy: the number of years that an average newborn can expect to live

timetables: the signals societies use to inform their members they are old.

KEY PEOPLE

Review the major theoretical contributions or findings of these people.

Robert Butler: Butler coined the term "ageism" to refer to prejudice, discrimination and hostility directed against people because of their age.

Marcel Danesi: He argues that contemporary Western culture has embraced the view that age is bad and youth is good.

Susan McDaniel: A Canadian sociologist who developed the concept of intergenerational interlinkages (IGILs). She suggests that intergenerational linkages should be explored in a variety of directions, contexts, and forms in a three generational typology—parents, children, and grandchildren—each generation both receiving and giving.

Ann McMullin and John Cairney: explored the relationship between self-esteem, age, class, and gender.

Joseph Tindale et. al: proposed that "lasagna" is a better metaphor than "sandwich generation" to recognize the more nuanced perspective of intergenerational support between parents and children.

SELF-TEST

After completing this self-test, check your answers against the Answer Key at the back of this Study Guide and against the text on page(s) indicated in parentheses.

MULTIPLE CHOICE QUESTIONS

1. By 1999, the International Year of Older Persons, (185)
   a. the federal government had established the national Advisory Council on Aging.
   b. scholars had established the Canadian Association of Gerontology.
   c. almost very university in Canada had created a gerontology or aging studies program.
   d. all of the above

2. Which of the following contributes to an increase in the number of people who reach older ages? (185)
   a. changing social attitudes about aging
   b. reduction in warfare
   c. later retirement
   d. industrialization

3. The process by which older persons make up an increasing proportion of Canada's population is referred to as: (188)
   a. the aging process.
   b. the greying of Canada.
   c. the gentrification process.
   d. none of the above

4. What explains the fact that Native Canadians have lower life expectancy? (191-192)
   a. different cultural attitudes about aging
   b. biological differences and susceptibility to disease
   c. some groups are inherently less healthy
   d. higher rates of improvement and social marginalization

5. There are important regional differences in the greying of Canada: (188-189)
   a. Atlantic provinces and Quebec have older populations than the Canadian average.
   b. As a result of low fertility and outmigration, Atlantic Canada is expected to continue to age more rapidly than the rest of Canada.
   c. The increased pressure on the health care system is expected to be felt disproportionately across Canada.
   d. all of the above

6. Factors that may push people to apply the label of old to themselves include: (192)
   a. personal history or biography.
   b. cultural signals about when a person is old.
   c. biological factors.
   d. all of the above

7. Feminist analysts point out that the aging process for women (196)
   a. exacerbates the problem of power and inequality.
   b. complicates economic well-being when divorced.
   c. subjects them to cultural standards of femininity.
   d. all of the above

8. Which of the following factors spur people to apply the label "old" to themselves? (192)
   a. biological changes
   b. personal history
   c. society's timetables
   d. all of the above

9. Modern Canadian society has inherited long-held contradictory perspectives on aging and the elderly, which is reflected in: (194)
   a. the popular acceptance of a variety of stereotypes about the elderly.
   b. being old is not seen as necessarily synonymous with being disabled, frail, or dependent.
   c. positive notions of older citizens do appear.
   d. all of the above

10. What is true of older women's economic situation? (196)
    a. It is related to women's traditional role in the economy.
    b. They have devoted their lives to home and family.
    c. They often interrupt their careers or work part-time.
    d. all of the above

11. Which of the following characteristics of older women cause them extra hardships? (196-197)
    a. being aboriginal or a woman of colour
    b. having disabilities
    c. being lesbian
    d. all of the above

12. Conflict theorists believe that some of the following factors could possibly rupture our retirement and health care system in the next 30 years. (197-198)
    a. retirement of the Boomer Generation
    b. rising life expectancies
    c. falling birth rates
    d. all of the above

13. Currently, only _____ bans mandatory retirement:(198)
    a. Manitoba
    b. British Columbia
    c. Ontario
    d. Alberta

14. In recent years analysts have increasingly challenged traditional gerontological approaches by pointing to: (199)
    a. the tendency to approach age in biological terms as an "ailment" to be cured.
    b. the tendency to homogenize seniors rather than acknowledging their important differences.
    c. the need for an improved awareness of the diversity that characterizes the aging population.
    d. all of the above

15. Research with family caregivers suggests the following problem(s): (200)
    a. difficulty in balancing work and family
    b. lack of free time
    c. responsibility for an ailing senior may be exhausting so the care-giver wishes someone else would take over
    d. all of the above

16. Researchers have found that elder abuse: (200)
    a. occurs less frequently than one might think, given the level of abuse shown in the media.
    b. is fairly extensive.
    c. is most often caused by workers in nursing homes.
    d. is easy to study because the victims are so visible.

17. Canadian seniors (65 and older) are now deriving between _____ and _____ percent of their total incomes from government transfer payments: (198)
    a. 91 and 95
    b. 81 and 85
    c. 71 and 75
    d. 61 and 65

18. According to feminists, _____ is an important ingredient in becoming a victim as a senior. (202)
    a. being a woman
    b. being a man
    c. being a recent immigrant
    d. a. and c.

19. In trying to explain suicide rates of senior men over 75, sociologists see as root causes: (201)
   a. isolation.
   b. disability and illness.
   c. dependency.
   d. all of the above

TRUE-FALSE QUESTIONS

T F 1. To study how aging is socially constructed, symbolic interactionists examine how the symbols associated with age affect our perceptions. (191)

T F 2. The demographic effects of industrialization were further magnified by World War II. (185)

T F 3. Today a Canadian woman can expect to live to age 82 and a man to 77. (188)

T F 4. According to the symbolic interactionists, a person's perception of "old" and what it means to be old is influenced by the signals societies use to inform their members they are old. (192)

T F 5. The difference in the social evaluation of "old women" and "mature men" is revealed when older male news anchors are likely to be retained, while female anchors that turn the same age are more likely to be transferred to less visible positions. (196)

T F 6. There was once a "golden era" in human history when a society's elderly were uniformly respected and valued. (193)

T F 7. In movies, older men are much more likely than older women to play leads. (196)

T F 8. Death and dying, like aging, are as much socially constructed as biological events. (202)

T F 9. In Canada the first national survey of elder abuse was undertaken in 1992. (202)

T F 10. According to conflict theorists, the ongoing dispute over mandatory retirement provides a revealing example of the complexities and contradictions in age-based struggles. (197)

T F 11. The dependency ratio is the number of workers compared to the number of QPP/CPP recipients. (197-198)

T F 12. Currently only the Netherlands and the State of Oregon in the U.S. allow assisted suicide. (201)

T F 13. Elder abuse includes abuse from both professional caregivers and family members. (202)

T F 14. The income level of Canada's seniors has declined since 1980. (190)

T F 15. For some aged seniors, suicide may be a valued escape from chronic suffering and disease. (201)

FILL-IN QUESTIONS

1. The process by which older persons make up an increasing proportion of Canada's population is called _____. (188)

2. The _____ of an average newborn is the number of years he or she can expect to live. (188)

3. The impact of this aging population has not been felt _____ Canada. (188)

4. While aging is seen as _____ for many men, it is not seen to be so for women. (196)
5. Women's lack of _____ is related to women's traditional role in the economy. (196)
6. _____ is the discrimination against the elderly because of their age. (193)
7. The _____ send the implicit message that most seniors, except the rich, famous, and powerful, do not count. (197)
8. Hundreds of years ago the _____ of Canadians would not live to see age 65. (188)
9. Having enough money improves your prospects for _____ and _____. (190)
10. Not only how many years you will spend as a senior, but the _____ of that life appear to be affected by_____. (191)
11. The number of workers required to support the portion of the population aged 64 and older is the _____. (197)
12. Founded in the 1960s by Margaret Kuhn, the _____ encourages people of all ages to work for the welfare of both the old and the young. (189)
13. Resistance to government efforts to _____ provides a telling example of the ability of seniors to mobilize effectively. (189)
14. The _____ (CARP) with local chapters across Canada has launched a vigorous Canada-wide campaign against _____. (189-190)
15. _____are the signals societies use to inform their members they are old. (192)

MATCH THESE SOCIAL SCIENTISTS WITH THEIR CONTRIBUTIONS

___1. Robert Butler   a. *Explored the relationship between self-esteem, age, class, and gender*

___2. Susan McDaniel   b. *Suggested the use of " lasagna" rather than " sandwich generation for intergenerational support structure*

___3. Marcel Danesi   c. *coined "ageism" to refer to prejudice or discrimination based on age*

___4. Ann McMullin and   d. *Developed the concept intergenerational interlinkages*
       John Cairnes

___5. Joseph Tindale et.al.   e. *Argues that contemporary Western culture has embraced the view that age is bad and youth is good*

ESSAY QUESTIONS

1. Choose one of the theoretical perspectives on aging and discuss how that perspective approaches the subject of aging. Consider both the strengths as well as the weaknesses of the perspective you chose.
2. Explain why aging is as much a socially constructed process as a biological process.

"DOWN-TO-EARTH SOCIOLOGY"

1. The Feminist Perspective" on pages 196-197 discusses the gendered character of aging. What specific issues face women as they age? In what ways does feminist analysis construct aging as a positive experience? What types of social change are needed to ensure that aging does not result in marginalization?

2. Do you think the QPP/CPP system will still be there when you retire? How might we change the current system so that it not only provides for today's retired workers but will also provide for future retirees? (197-199)

3. What kind of life do you hope to have when you reach your senior years? Given the current conditions, do you think your view will remain accurate?

CHAPTER 10
BUREAUCRACY AND FORMAL ORGANIZATIONS

CHAPTER SUMMARY

- The rationalization of society refers to a major transformation in the way people think—from a desire to protect time-honoured ways to a concern with efficiency and practical results. Max Weber traced the rationalization of society to Protestantism, while Marx attributed it to capitalism.

- As a result of the emphasis on rationality, formal organizations—secondary groups designed to achieve explicit objectives—have become a central feature of contemporary society. Their most common form is a bureaucracy, which Weber characterized as having a hierarchy of authority, a division of labour, written rules, written communications, and impersonality. Weber's characteristics of bureaucracy are an "ideal type" which typify the organization.

- The dysfunctions of bureaucracies include alienation, red tape, lack of communication between units, goal displacement, and incompetence. In Weber's view, the impersonality of bureaucracies tends to produce alienation among workers. In Marx's view, workers experience alienation when they lose control of the work process and are cut off from the finished product of their labour.

- In Canada voluntary associations—groups made up of volunteers who organize on the basis of some mutual interest—have also proliferated.

- The iron law of oligarchy is the tendency of formal organizations to be dominated by a small, self-perpetuating elite. What many find depressing about the iron law of oligarchy is that it applies even to organizations strongly committed to democratic principles.

- The concept of corporate culture refers to the organization's traditions, values, and norms. Much of this culture is invisible. It can affect its members, either negatively or positively, depending upon the members' opportunity structure.

- Humanizing work settings involves strategies to develop human potential. More humane bureaucracies expand opportunities on the basis of ability and contributions rather than personal characteristics, provided a more even distribution of power, less rigid rules, and more open decision-making. Conflict theorists claim that these efforts merely conceal the fundamental goal of employers to exploit workers.

- Co-operatives as an alternative form of organization are owned by members who collectively make decisions, determine goals, evaluate resources, set salaries, and assign work tasks.

- The Japanese corporate model provides a contrast to the North American corporate model. Virtual organizations are companies " without walls," often transcending time, space, and culture. Revolution in microtechnology has transformed work and affected skills and the division of labour.

LEARNING OBJECTIVES

As you read Chapter 10, use these learning objectives to organize your notes. After completing your reading, briefly state an answer to each of the objectives, and review the text pages in parentheses.

1. Explain what is meant by the "rationalization of society," and differentiate between the views of Max Weber and Karl Marx on this process. (206-207)
2. State the definition of formal organizations and list the characteristics of bureaucracies. (207-209)
3. Describe the difference in "ideal" versus "real" bureaucracy. (210)
4. Discuss the dysfunctions of bureaucracies, and give examples of each type of problem. (210-211)
5. Explain the sociological significance of bureaucracies. (213)
6. Indicate the roles of voluntary associations, the different motivations for joining, and explain how the problem of oligarchy occurs in such organizations. (213-216)
7. Identify the consequences of hidden values in the corporate culture, especially noting their impact on women and minority participants. (217)
8. Discuss the characteristics of management strategies, focusing on scientific management, humanizing work, quality circles, employee stock ownership, small work groups, and workplace day care. (218-221)
9. Discuss an alternative to corporate capitalism. (221)
10. Explain the criticisms made by conflict theorists of the move to humanize the workplace. (221)
11. Describe how computer technology can be used to control workers. (222)
12. Describe the contribution of virtual organizations to contemporary society.
13. Compare and contrast the Japanese and North American corporate organizational models. (223-224)

CHAPTER OUTLINE

I. **The Rationalization of Society**
   A. Rationality—the acceptance of rules, efficiency, and practical results as the right way to approach human affairs—is a characteristic of industrial societies.
   B. The contribution of Max Weber
      1. Historically, the traditional orientation to life had been based on the idea that the past is the best guide for the present; however, this orientation stood in the way of industrialization.
      2. In *The Protestant Ethic and the Spirit of Capitalism* Weber proposed that a set of behaviours rooted in Protestantism led to the development of capitalist activity and the rationalization of society.
      3. Weber argued that because of the Calvinistic belief in predestination, people wanted to show they were among the chosen of God. Financial success in life became a sign of God's approval; however, money was not to be spent on oneself. Rather, the investment of profits became an outlet for people's excess money, while the success of those investments became a further sign of God's approval.

4. Because capitalism demanded rationalization (the careful calculation of practical results), traditional ways of doing things, if not efficient, had to be replaced, for what counted were the results.

C. Marx on rationalization

   1. Unlike Weber, Karl Marx attributed the growth of rationality to capitalism instead of religion.

   2. Marx said that the change to capitalism changed the way people thought about life, not the other way around. Marx criticized capitalism's rationality and emphasis on efficiency. He argued that the values and practices of capitalism contributed to feelings of alienation.

II.   **Formal Organizations and Bureaucracy**

A. Formal organizations—secondary groups designed to achieve explicit objectives—have become a central feature of contemporary life.

B. The essential characteristics of bureaucracies are:

   1. a hierarchy where assignments flow downward and accountability flows upward;

   2. a division of labour;

   3. written rules;

   4. written communications and records; and

   5. impersonality.

C. Weber's characteristics of bureaucracy describe an ideal type—a composite of characteristics based on many specific examples. The real nature of bureaucracy often differs from its ideal image.

D. Weber's model only accounts for part of the characteristics of bureaucracies. Dysfunctions can also be identified.

   1. Red tape, or the strict adherence to rules, often results in nothing getting accomplished.

   2. A lack of communication between units means that they are sometimes working at cross purposes; sometimes one unit "undoes" what another unit has accomplished because the two fail to inform one another of what each is doing.

   3. Bureaucratic alienation, a feeling of powerlessness and normlessness, occurs when workers are assigned to repetitive tasks in order for the corporation to achieve efficient production, thereby cutting workers off from the product of their labour.

   4. To resist alienation, workers form primary groups within the larger secondary organization, relating to one another not just as workers, but as people who value one another.

   5. The alienated bureaucrat is one who feels trapped in the job, does not take initiative, will not do anything beyond what she or he is absolutely required to do, and uses rules to justify doing as little as possible.

   6. Goal displacement occurs when an organization adopts new goals after the original goals have been achieved and there is no longer any reason for it to continue.

7. Bureaucratic incompetence is reflected in the Peter principle—members of an organization are promoted for good work until they reach their level of incompetence. In reality, bureaucracies are remarkably successful.

E. To the sociologist, bureaucracies are significant because they represent a fundamental change in how people relate to one another. Prior to this rationalization, work focused on human needs—for instance, making sure that everyone had an opportunity to earn a living; with rationalization, the focus shifts to efficiency in performing tasks and improving the bottom line.

III. Voluntary Associations

A. Voluntary associations are groups made up of volunteers who have organized on the basis of some mutual interest.

B. Voluntary associations represent no single interest or purpose. The idea of mutual interest is characteristic of all voluntary associations; a shared interest in some view or activity is the tie that binds members together.
1. The motivation for joining a group differs widely among its members, from the expression of strong convictions to the cultivation of personal contacts.
2. Because of this, membership turnover tends to be high.

C. Within voluntary associations is an inner core of individuals who stand firmly behind the group's goals and are firmly committed to maintaining the organization. If this inner core loses commitment, the group is likely to fold.

D. Some volunteer work such as the requirement in Ontario that high school students complete a minimum of forty hours of volunteer work before graduation, raises the question, "who benefits from this program?" Is voluntarism confused with coercion, is discussed by Norene Pupo in Thinking Critically About Social Controversy.

E. Building on the term oligarchy, a system in which many are ruled by a few, sociologist Robert Michels coined the term iron law of oligarchy to refer to how formal organizations come to be dominated by a small, self perpetuating elite.

IV. Careers in Bureaucracies

A. As sociologist Rosabeth Moss Kanter stresses, the corporate culture is crucial in determining people's corporate fate. She explains how a corporation's "hidden values"—those not officially part of the organization—operate as self-fulfilling stereotypes. These function to keep the elite in power and also provide better access to information, networking, and "fast tracks" for workers like themselves, usually white and male.
1. Workers who fit in are given opportunities to advance; they outperform others and are more committed.
2. Those who are judged outsiders and experience few opportunities think poorly of themselves, are less committed, and work below their potential.
3. These hidden values create this self-fulfilling prophecy and contribute to the iron law of oligarchy.

B. When women and minorities do not match the hidden values of the corporate culture they may be treated differently. They may experience "showcasing"—being put in highly visible positions with little power so that the company is in compliance with affirmative action—and "slow-track" positions—jobs where promotions are slow because accomplishments in these areas seldom come to the attention of top management.

C. Morale is influenced by the level one achieves in an organization; the higher people go, the higher their morale.

V. Management Strategies and the Corporate Culture

A. Corporations have developed many strategies to manage work forces, harness people's energies to specific goals, and monitor progress to those goals.

B. Management strategies include:

1. Scientific Management. This is a strategy used to establish management control over the pace of work, the level of production, and all decisions pertaining to the labour process. Scientific management involves dividing complex work tasks into simple sub-tasks and separating conceptual work from the execution of work tasks.

2. Humanizing Work. This refers to efforts to organize the workplace in such a way that it develops rather than impedes human potential. Characteristics of more humane work are: the availability of opportunities on the basis of ability and contributions rather than personal characteristics; the more equal distribution of power; and less rigid rules and more open decision-making. However, the pursuit of efficiency and profit relegates social relationships and people's needs or interests to the "back court." The sweat shops of the garment industry are a good example of this and are found around the world.

3. Quality Circles. These are small groups of workers and a manager or two who meet regularly to try to improve the quality of the work setting and the product.

4. Employee Stock Ownership. On average, companies with at least ten percent of a stock owned by employees are more profitable than other firms, probably because the workers are more committed and managers take a longer-term view. Employee ownership of a company's stock does not eliminate problems between workers and management; profitability, not ownership appears to be the key to reducing these problems.

5. Work Teams. Within these groups workers are able to establish primary relationships with other workers so that their identities are tied up with their group; the group's success becomes the individual's success.

6. Workplace Day Cares. These ease the strain on parents, leading to reduced turnover, less absenteeism, and shorter maternity leaves.

C. The cooperative represents an alternative to bureaucracy. These are collectives owned by members who collectively make decisions, determine goals, evaluate resources, set salaries, and assign work tasks. The economic results of cooperatives have been mixed—some are more profitable than private organizations, some are less.

D. Conflict theorists point out that the basic relationship between workers and owners is confrontational regardless of how the work organization is structured.

E. While the computer has the capacity to improve the quality of people's lives, it also holds the potential of severe abuse.

1. Computers allow managers to increase surveillance without face-to-face supervision.

2. Computers can create the "maximum-security workplace," potentially keeping track of every movement a worker makes while on the job. Some worry that it is only a short step from this type of workplace to the "maximum-security society."

F. Virtual organizations are companies "without walls," often transcending time, space, and culture. Professor Ursula Huws notes that information technology has affected skills, the division of labour and sometimes removed work from the centre to distant locations.

VI. The Japanese Corporate Model

A. The Japanese production technique is often referred to as *lean production*. Lean production uses a just-in-time (JIT) strategy to reduce the need for large warehouses and work stations. Lean production relies on flexible work assignments and a strategy of continuous improvement, which may result in job elimination and work intensification. William Ouchi lists five ways in which this model differs from the North American system:

1. Hiring and promotion: The Japanese model features a team approach; a starting cohort of workers gets the same salary, is rotated through the organization, and develops intense loyalty to one another and to the organization. In the North American model, employees are hired on the basis of what the individual can contribute; the emphasis is on competition; and individual loyalty is to the individual himself or herself, not to the company.

2. Lifetime security: The Japanese model takes lifetime security for granted; the company is loyal to the employee, and expects the employee to be loyal to the company. In the North American model, lifetime security is unusual; continued employment is based on good and/or bad economic conditions; and workers are expected to look out for themselves.

3. Almost total involvement: Work is like a marriage in Japan in that the company and the employee are committed to each other. In North America, the work relationship is highly specific; fulfill your job obligations and the rest of your time is your private life, separated from the firm.

4. Broad training: In Japan, workers move from one job to another within the corporation. In North America, employees are expected to perform one job well and then be promoted to a job with more responsibility.

5. Decision-making by consensus: In Japan, decision-making occurs after lengthy deliberations in which each person to be affected by a decision is included in the process. In North America, the individual responsible for the unit does as much consulting as she or he thinks necessary and then makes the decision.

B. Research on Japanese corporations suggests that the Japanese corporate model fails to adequately reflect the reality of Japanese corporate life.

KEY TERMS

After studying the chapter, review the definition for each of the following terms.

alienation: Marx's term for the experience of being cut off from the product of one's labour, which results in a sense of powerlessness and normlessness

assimilation: the process by which the dominant group absorbs a minority group

bureaucracy: a formal organization with a hierarchy of authority; a clear division of labour; emphasis on written rules, communications, and records; and impersonality of positions

capitalism: the investment of capital with the goal of producing profits

corporate culture: the orientations that characterize corporate work settings

formal organization: a secondary group designed to achieve explicit objectives

goal displacement: a goal displaced by another, in this context, the adoption of new goals by an organization; also known as *goal replacement*

humanizing a work setting: organizing a workplace in such a way that it develops rather than impedes human potential

iron law of oligarchy: Robert Michels's phrase for the tendency of formal organizations to be dominated by a small, self-perpetuating elite

just-in-time (JIT): a strategy to reduce parts inventories to the amount needed at the time, thereby reducing the demand for huge parts warehouses and large work stations

kaizen: means continuous improvement; a system where production techniques are constantly evaluated in search of more efficient and improved methods

McDonaldization: increasing rationalization of the routine tasks of everyday life

Peter Principle: a bureaucratic "law," according to which the members of an organization are promoted for good work until they reach their level of incompetence, the level at which they can no longer do good work

Principles of Scientific Management: (often referred to as Taylorism) refers to the reduction of waste inefficiency in production

quality circles: perhaps a dozen workers and a manager or two who meet regularly to try to improve quality of work setting and company's products

rationality: the acceptance of rules, efficiency, and practical results as the right way to approach human affairs

rationalization of society: a widespread acceptance of rationality and a social organization built around this idea

sweating: working conditions in the garment industry

traditional orientation: the idea, characteristic of tribal, peasant, and feudal societies, that the past is the best guide for the present

virtual organization: companies "without walls," often transcending time, space, and culture

voluntary association: a group made up of volunteers who have organized on the basis of some mutual interest

walmartization: profound transformations in regional and global economies through the sheer size, influence, and power of big-box department store Walmart

KEY PEOPLE

Review the major theoretical contributions or findings of these people.

Rosabeth Moss Kanter: Kanter studied the "invisible" corporate culture, which for the most part continually reproduces itself by promoting those workers who fit the elite's stereotypical views.

Gary Marx: Marx has written about the "maximum security" workplace, given the increased use of computers to control workers.

Karl Marx: Marx believed that the emergence of rationality was due to capitalism. Capitalism changed the way people thought about life, rather than people's orientation to life producing capitalism.

Robert Michels: Michels first used the term "the iron law of oligarchy" to describe the tendency for the leaders of an organization to become entrenched.

William Ouchi: Ouchi studied the Japanese corporation and identified defining qualities of this corporate model.

George Ritzer: Ritzer coined the term the "McDonaldization of society" to describe the increasing rationalization of modern social life.

Joyce Rothchild and Allen Whitt: These sociologists researched the history of cooperatives.

Max Weber: Weber studied the rationalization of society by investigating the link between Protestantism and capitalism and identifying the characteristics of bureaucracy.

Shoshana Zuboff: Zuboff has researched the degree to which computer technology increases managers' ability to carry out surveillance on workers without face-to-face interaction.

SELF-TEST

After completing this self-test, check your answers against the Answer Key at the back of this Study Guide and against the text on page(s) indicated in parentheses.

MULTIPLE CHOICE QUESTIONS

1. What is rationality? (206)
   a. the idea that the past is the best guide for the present
   b. making excuses for bureaucratic incompetence
   c. the acceptance of rules, efficiency, and practical results as the right way to approach human affairs
   d. None of the above

2. The idea that the past is the best guide for the present is referred to as: (206)
   a. traditional orientation.
   b. modern orientation.
   c. status quo.
   d. rationalization.

3. What was one of the major obstacles to industrialization? (206)
   a. the medieval church
   b. a traditional orientation
   c. money lenders
   d. the traditional family

4. According to Max Weber, capitalism: (206)
    a. is the investment of capital in the hopes of producing profits.
    b. became an outlet for the excess money of Calvinists.
    c. produced success for many that became a sign of God's approval.
    d. All of the above

5. In reconciling Weber's and Marx's views on rationality, sociologists feel that: (207)
    a. Weber was most correct.
    b. Marx was most correct.
    c. Weber and Marx were both incorrect.
    d. no analyst has yet reconciled the opposing views satisfactorily.

6. Prior to industrialization, only a few formal organizations existed, but today is different: (208)
    a. Secondary groups have become common.
    b. We take the existence of secondary groups for granted.
    c. All of us spend a good deal of time in secondary groups.
    d. all of the above

7. All of the following are characteristics of bureaucracy, *except*: (208-209)
    a. a division of labour.
    b. a hierarchy with assignments flowing upward and accountability flowing downward.
    c. written rules, communications, and records.
    d. impersonality.

8. Ideal types: (210)
    a. are composites of characteristics based on many specific examples.
    b. are the model or perfect way to do something.
    c. largely are not used in sociology because they are unrealistic.
    d. none of the above

9. George Ritzer used the term "the McDonaldization of society" to refer to: (209)
    a. the preference for McDonald's over Burger King.
    b. the spread of McDonald's world-wide.
    c. the increasing rationalization of daily living.
    d. none of the above

10. Ritzer extends his concept of "the McDonaldization of society" to apply to which of the following? (209)
    a. shopping malls as controlled environments
    b. travel agents with prepackaged tours of 10 European capitals in 14 days
    c. television production of the same type of bland instant news each day
    d. all of the above

11. Dysfunctions of bureaucracies include: (210-213)
    a. alienation.
    b. goal displacement.
    c. red tape.
    d. all of the above

12. 12. As a worker in a large corporation, Linda is often unhappy. At work she often feels that no one appreciates her and that the work she does is boring and repetitive. Which of the following best describes Linda's situation? (212)
    a. bureaucratic incompetence
    b. alienation
    c. goal displacement
    d. goal frustration

13. How do workers resist alienation? (212)
    a. by forming primary groups
    b. by praising each other and expressing sympathy when something goes wrong
    c. by putting pictures and personal items in their work areas
    d. all of the above

14. According to your text, what is the alienated bureaucrat likely to do? (212)
    a. quit his or her job once unhappiness and dissatisfaction sets in
    b. seek counselling to overcome the problem
    c. not do anything for the organization beyond what he or she is required to do
    d. return to school for further training in order to move up in the organization

15. The reason why the War Amps is a good example of good displacement is (213)
    a. that the organization never achieved its stated goals.
    b. that the population of war amputees declined and amputees drew on other existing sources and programs in their communities.
    c. that War Amps turned its attention to child amputees and started the Child Amputee Program.
    d. b and c above

16. The Peter Principle: (213)
    a. states that each employee of a bureaucracy is promoted to his or her level of competence.
    b. states that each employee of a bureaucracy is promoted to his or her level of incompetence.
    c. is generally true and explains why so many bureaucracies fail.
    d. was first stated by Max Weber.

17. What is true of voluntary associations in North America? (213)
    a. Already in the 1830's there was evidence of voluntary associations in the United States.
    b. Alexis de Tocqueville (1835), as an outsider, observed that Americans joined a lot of voluntary associations.
    c. Like their American neighbours, Canadians are very proud of their commitment to voluntary organizations.
    d. all of the above

18. What is true of people involved in voluntary associations in Canada? (213-214)
    a. People aged 35 to 44 have the highest rate of volunteerism.
    b. Seniors (people aged 55 and over) who volunteer their time spend more hours per week than others.
    c. Major organizations, such as hospitals, sometimes hire full time volunteer coordinators to provide training and support to volunteers.
    d. all of the above

19. What is the term that describes the tendency for organizations to be dominated by a small, self-perpetuating elite? (216)
    a. the Peter Principle
    b. bureaucratic engorgement
    c. the iron law of oligarchy
    d. the corporate power struggle

20. According to Rosabeth Moss Kanter, what is the nature of the corporate culture? (217)
    a. The corporate culture determines an individual's corporate fate.
    b. The people with the best qualifications typically will rise to the top of an organization.
    c. The employees who work the hardest and are the most cooperative have the greatest likelihood of being promoted.
    d. none of the above

21. What does it mean to humanize a work setting? (219)
    a. organizing work in such a way that it develops rather than impedes human potential
    b. offering access to opportunities on the basis of ability and contribution rather than personal characteristics
    c. distributing power and decision making more equally
    d. all of the above

22. Research on the costs and benefits of employer-financed day care (at Union Bank, Monteray, California) demonstrated that: (220-221)
    a. such a benefit is costly to the employer because of strict government regulations that must be met.
    b. such a benefit cuts into stockholders' dividends by eating up profits.
    c. few employees took advantage of the benefit.
    d. such a benefit can save the employer money by reducing turnover and absenteeism.

23. Which type of organization attempts to allow members to work towards their own goals? (221)
   a. corporations
   b. cooperatives
   c. collectives
   d. small businesses

24. Which of the following reflects the views of conflict theorists? (221)
   a. Quality circles, employee stock ownership, and small work groups are excellent ways to solve the problems encountered in bureaucracies.
   b. The interests of workers and owners both may be met by humanizing the work setting.
   c. The interests of workers and owners are fundamentally opposed and, in the final analysis, workers are always exploited.
   d. There is less conflict in the Japanese corporate model than in the North American model.

25. Computers in the workplace: (222)
   a. have the potential of improving the quality of work life.
   b. could lead to more surveillance of workers by managers.
   c. may be the first step towards a society in which every move a citizen makes is recorded.
   d. all of the above

TRUE-FALSE QUESTIONS

T F   1.   Capitalism demands rationalization, the careful calculation of practical results. (206)
T F   2.   A central orientation of a traditional society is to protect the status quo. (206)
T F   3.   Max Weber believed that the growth of capitalism contributed to the rise of the Protestant ethic. (206)
T F   4.   Calvinists believed that thrift was a virtue and that money should not be spent on the luxuries of life. (206)
T F   5.   Marx argued that the switch to rationality was due to capitalism itself. (207)
T F   6.   Either primary or secondary groups can be formal organizations. (207)
T F   7.   Weber identified five essential characteristics of bureaucracy. (208-209)
T F   8.   Most colleges and universities do not have written systems of accountability for faculty members. (208-209)
T F   9.   In bureaucracy, it is the office that is important, not the individual who holds the office. (209)
T F   10.   The characteristics of bureaucracy identified by Max Weber are ideal types. (210)
T F   11.   Marx argued that the values and practices of capitalism contributed to feelings of alienation. (210)
T F   12.   All workers can successfully resist becoming alienated if they work at it. (212)
T F   13.   The Peter Principle has been proven to be mostly true. (213)
T F   14.   Voluntary associations are made up of volunteers who have organized on the basis of some mutual interest. (213-215)
T F   15.   Voluntary associations can be reactionary or can demand social change. (215)
T F   16.   The iron law of oligarchy was defined by Robert Michels. (216)
T F   17.   Bureaucracies are likely to disappear as our dominant form of social organization in the near future. (224)

T F   18.   Scientific management, quality circles, employee stock ownership, and small work groups are four examples of management strategies. (218-220)

T F   19.   Another way to humanize the work setting is to set up day care facilities at workplaces. (220)

T F   20.   The Japanese corporate model incorporates the practice of kaizen, which means continuous improvement. (223)

FILL-IN QUESTIONS

1.   In a_____ assignments flow downward and accountability flows upward. (208)

2.   The idea that the past is the best guide for the present is known as _____. (206)

3.   _____ was written by Max Weber and emphasizes that religion holds the key to understanding the development of certain types of economic systems. (206)

4.   The investment of capital in the hope of producing profits is called _____. (206)

5.   _____ are organizations owned by members who collectively make decisions, determine goals, evaluate resources, set salaries, and assign work tasks. (221)

6.   George Ritzer has coined the term _____ to refer to the increasing rationalization of life's routine tasks. (209)

7.   _____ is a feeling of powerlessness and normlessness; the experience of being cut off from the product of one's labour. (207)

8.   _____ occurs when new goals are adopted by an organization to replace previous goals which may have been fulfilled. (213)

9.   A group made up of volunteers who have organized on the basis of some mutual interest is called a(n) _____. (213)

10. _____ refers to the tendency of formal organizations to be dominated by a small, self-perpetuating elite. (216)

11. The orientation that characterizes corporate work settings is referred to as _____. (216-217)

12. Women and minorities are often _____, which means that they are placed in highly visible positions with little power in order to demonstrate to the public and affirmative action officials how progressive the company is. (217)

13. _____ consist of perhaps a dozen workers and a manager or two who meet regularly to try to improve the quality of the work setting and of the company's products. (220)

14. Professor Ursula Huws has studied the revolution in _____ and the ways in which it has transformed _____ (222)

15. Lean production, almost total involvement, broad training, and collective decision making are characteristics of the _____ model. (223-224)

MATCH THESE SOCIAL SCIENTISTS WITH THEIR CONTRIBUTIONS

___1.   Max Weber   a.   *the iron law of oligarchy*

___2.   Robert Michels   b.   *the McDonaldization of society*

___3. William Ouchi   c. *hidden values in the corporate culture*
___4. Karl Marx   d. *exploitation of workers by capitalists*
___5. Rosabeth Moss Kanter   e. *rationalization of society*
___6. George Ritzer   f. *Japanese corporate model*

ESSAY QUESTIONS

1. Explain what an ideal type is and why such constructs are useful.
2. Discuss the differences between the Japanese and North American corporations.
3. Discuss the impact of McDonaldization as a process occurring throughout the society.

"DOWN-TO-EARTH SOCIOLOGY"

1. Acquire a copy of the organizational chart for your own college or university. Compare it with Figure 10.1 (208) to determine ways in which the charts are similar and ways in which they differ. What are some of your own experiences with bureaucratic dysfunctions?
2. What was your reaction to the "Down-to-Earth Sociology" box on page 209? Can you see evidence of McDonaldization in your own life? What do you see as the advantages of this trend? What do you see as the disadvantages? Do you agree with the author when he says that "to resist [this trend] will be futile"?
3. Why did the female insurance executive say that women in her work organization have no other choice than to play corporate games in order to achieve their objectives (217)? Do you agree or disagree? What has been your own experience with the hidden culture in offices in which you have worked?
4. After reading about diversity training on page 218, what would you say are the advantages of these types of programs? What are the drawbacks?
5. After reading "Cracks in the Corporate Facade" (224), how has your thinking about the Japanese corporate model changed? What are the forces behind the changes in corporate Japan? How does this compare with the situation in North America?

CHAPTER 11
THE ECONOMY: MONEY AND WORK

CHAPTER SUMMARY

- The earliest hunting and gathering societies were characterized by subsistence economies; economic systems became more complex as people discovered first how to domesticate and cultivate (horticultural and pastoral societies), then to farm (agricultural societies) and finally to manufacture (industrial societies).

- In the least complex societies, people exchanged goods and services through barter. As societies and economies evolved, certain items were assigned uniform value and became the mediums of exchange. Today we rely increasingly on electronic transfer of funds with credit and debit cards.

- The two major economic systems are capitalism, in which the means of production are privately owned, and socialism, in which the means of production are state owned. There are different forms of both capitalism (laissez-faire capitalism and welfare capitalism) and socialism (democratic socialism). In recent years each system has adopted features of the other.

- Two new ideologies are emerging, neoliberalism and social conservatism.

- Corporations dominate modern capitalism; an inner circle—a group of leaders from the major corporations—are mutually interested in making certain that corporate capitalism is protected. The sociological significance of global capitalism is that the interests of the inner circle extend beyond national boundaries.

- Symbolic interactionists analyze such things as factors that distinguish professions from jobs and the aspects that lead to work satisfaction. Functionalists state that work is a fundamental source of social solidarity; preindustrial societies foster mechanical solidarity while industrial societies, with their more complex division of labour, are characterized by organic solidarity. Conflict theorists focus on power, noting how the new technologies and global capitalism affect workers and owners; workers lose jobs while the inner circle maintains it power and profits.

- Most Canadian workers today are employed in the tertiary sector, as opposed to either the primary or secondary sectors. A quiet revolution has occurred due to the dramatic increase in the number of married women who work for pay. The underground economy, economic activity that is not reported to the government, runs perhaps 15 to 20 percent of the regular economy. While Canada's banks and other corporations report record profits, household income has declined dramatically in the past two decades.

- Patterns of leisure change with the life course and amount of time spent at work.

- Work will continue to be restructured as a result of downsizing, new technologies, and the expansion of global capitalism.

LEARNING OBJECTIVES

As you read Chapter 11, use these learning objectives to organize your notes. After completing your reading, briefly state an answer to each of the objectives, and review the text pages in parentheses.

1. Trace the transformation of the economic systems through each of the historical stages and state the degree to which social inequality existed in each of the economies. (228-229)
2. Explain what the "medium of exchange" means and how it is vital to society. (230)
3. State the essential features of capitalism and socialism. (231-232)
4. Identify variations on models of "pure" capitalism and socialism and explain why these exist. (234-235)
5. State criticisms of capitalism and socialism. (233)
6. Describe the recent changes in both capitalist and socialist economies, and explain why some theorists believe the two systems are converging. (234-235)
7. Explain the significance of the following terms: the corporation, oligopolies, and corporate capitalism. (235)
8. Discuss how the wealthy use interlocking directorates to maintain power. (235)
9. Define the concepts "multinational corporations" and explain why the emergence of global capitalism has sociological significance. (236-238)
10. Explain the difference between a profession and a job, using the symbolic interactionist perspective. (238)
11. Contrast mechanical and organic solidarity as Durkheim originally envisioned them, discuss changes in the global economy that have contributed to a new meaning of organic solidarity, and explain the consequences of this new form of interdependency. (239)
12. Outline the conflict perspective on economic life and explain the role of the inner circle. (239)
13. Review recent changes in the Canadian economy, including the shift in employment among the three economic sectors, the employment of women outside the home, the growth of the underground economy, the decline in real wages, and patterns of work and leisure. (240-244)
14. Consider what impact expanding global trade, new technologies, and downsizing will have on the Canadian economy and society in the years to come. (245-246)

CHAPTER OUTLINE

I. **The Transformation of Economic Systems**
    A. Market, or economy, is the mechanism by which values are established in order to exchange goods and services.
        1. The economy, which may be one of our most important social institutions, is the system of distribution of goods and services.
        2. The economy today is radically different from that of the past; it is impersonal and global in nature.
    B. As societies developed, a surplus emerged which fostered social inequality.
        1. Earliest hunting and gathering societies had subsistence economies, characterized by little trade with other groups, and a high degree of social equality.

2. In pastoral and horticultural economies, people created more dependable food supplies. The creation of a surplus allowed groups to grow in size, to settle in a single place, to develop a specialized division of labour, and to trade with other groups, all of which fostered social inequality.

3. Agricultural economies brought even greater surpluses, magnifying prior trends in social, political and economic inequality. More people were freed from food production, a more specialized division of labour developed, and trade expanded.

C. The surplus (and greater inequality) grew in industrial societies. As the surplus increased emphasis changed from production of goods to consumption (Thorstein Veblen coined the term conspicuous consumption).

D. The "information explosion" and the global village are key elements of postindustrial society.

1. According to Daniel Bell, postindustrial economies have six traits: (1) extensive trade among nations; (2) a large surplus of goods; (3) a service sector employing the majority of workers; (4) a wide variety and amount of goods available to the average person; (5) an information explosion; and (6) a global village with instantaneous, worldwide communications.

2. Consequences of the information explosion are uneven. Due to political and economic arrangements, some will prosper while others suffer.

3. Overall, the postindustrial economy has brought a greater availability of goods, but it has not resulted in income equality either in the United States or Canada.

4. We may be on the verge of yet another new type of society that is being ushered in by advances in biology and the "marriage" of biology and economics.

II. **The Transformation of the Medium of Exchange**

A. A medium of exchange is the means by which people value and exchange goods and services.

B. One of the earliest mediums of exchange was barter, the direct exchange of one item for another.

C. In agricultural economies, people came to use gold and silver coins. Deposit receipts which transferred ownership of a specified amount of gold or bushels of wheat, etc., on deposit somewhere were used. Toward the end of this period, the receipts were formalized into currency (paper money). Currency represented stored value; no more could be issued than the amount of gold or silver the currency represented.

D. In industrial economies, bartering largely disappeared and gold was replaced by paper currency. The gold standard (a dollar represents a specified amount of gold) kept the number of dollars that could be issued to a specific limit. When "fiat money" came into existence, the currency no longer could be exchanged for gold or silver.

1. Even without a gold standard, the amount of paper money that can be issued is limited: prices increase if a government issues currency at a rate higher than the growth of its gross national product. Issuing more produces inflation: each unit of currency will purchase fewer goods and services.

2. Checking accounts and credit cards have become common in industrial economies, largely replacing currency.

E. In postindustrial economies paper money is being replaced by checks, credit cards, and debit cards. Spending eventually becomes an electronic transfer of numbers residing in computer memory banks.

III. World Economic Systems

A. Capitalism has three essential features: (1) the private ownership of the means of production; (2) the pursuit of profit; and (3) market competition.

1. Pure (laissez-faire) capitalism exists only when market forces are able to operate without interference from the government.

2. Canada today has welfare (or state) capitalism. Private citizens own the means of production and pursue profits, but do so within a vast system of laws designed to protect the public welfare.

3. Under welfare capitalism the government supports competition but establishes its own monopoly over "common good" items, e.g., those presumed essential for the common good of the citizens.

B. Socialism also has three essential features: (1) the public ownership of the means of production; (2) central planning; and (3) the distribution of goods without a profit motive.

1. Under socialism, the government owns the means of production, and a central committee determines what the country needs instead of allowing market forces (supply and demand) to control production and prices. Socialism is designed to eliminate competition, to produce goods for the general welfare, and to distribute them according to people's needs, not their ability to pay.

2. Socialism does not exist in pure form. Although the ideology of socialism calls for resources to be distributed according to need rather than position socialist nations found it necessary to offer higher salaries for some jobs in order to entice people to take greater responsibilities.

3. Some nations (e.g., Sweden and Denmark) have adopted democratic or welfare socialism: both the state and individuals engage in production and distribution, although the state owns certain industries (steel, mining, forestry, telephones, television stations, and airlines) while retail stores, farms, and most service industries remain in private hands.

C. The primary criticism of capitalism is that it leads to social inequality (a top layer of wealthy, powerful people, and a bottom layer of people who are unemployed or underemployed). Socialism has been criticized for not respecting individual rights, and for not being capable of producing much wealth (thus the greater equality of socialism actually amounts to almost everyone having an equal chance of being poor).

D. In recent years, fundamental changes have taken place in these two economic systems.

1. Over the years Canada has adopted many public welfare policies—universal health care, accessible and free public education, employment insurance, the Canada Pension Plan, and Old Age Security.

2. In 1989, the former Soviet Union concluded that its system of central planning had failed. It began to reinstate market forces.

3. Despite the firm stand that Chinese leaders took in regard to Tiananmen Square, they too began to endorse capitalism, soliciting western investment, allowing the use of credit cards, and approving a stock market. While still proclaiming Marxist-Leninist-Maoist principles, the Communist Party, under the slogan "One China, two systems," is trying to make Shanghai the financial centre of East Asia.

4. As the two systems continue to adopt features of each other, convergence theory predicts that they will eventually converge, creating a hybrid economic system. The reality is that the two remain far from "converged" and the struggles between them continue, although they are more muted than in the past. With the pullback of socialism around the world, capitalism—in its many varieties—has a strong lead.

E. Two new ideologies are emerging, neoliberalism and social conservatism.

1. As a capitalist business and political ideology, neoliberalism is not the same as the classical market liberalism even though they share a belief in the centrality of private property, its inheritance, and the pursuit of profit. Neoliberalism refers to a new expansion in time and space of the free market; nothing less than a 24-hour global economy will satisfy neoliberals.

2 Social conservatism, a set of beliefs often linked to the economic changes, associated with neoliberalism, is on the rise. It is a value system characterized by a belief in conventional morality and social mores and a desire to preserve them.

IV. Capitalism in a Global Economy

A. The corporation (joint ownership of a business enterprise, whose liabilities are separate from those of its owners) has changed the face of capitalism.

1. One of the most significant aspects of large corporations is the separation of ownership and management. Unlike most businesses, it is not the owners who run the day-to-day affairs of the company but managers who are to treat it as though it were their own.

2. Oligopolies, several large companies that dominate a single industry, dictate pricing, set the quality of their products, and protect the market. Often they use their wealth and connections for political purposes (e.g., favourable legislation giving them special tax breaks or protecting their industry from imports).

3. Corporate capitalism refers to economic domination by giant corporations.

B. Interlocking directorates occur when individuals serve as directors of several companies, concentrating power and minimizing competition.

C. Out growing national boundaries, the larger corporations move investments and production from one part of the world to another.

D. The sociological significance of global capitalism is that the multinational corporations owe allegiance only to profit and market share, not to any nation, nor even to any particular culture.

E. On the positive side, these corporations' global interconnections have increased the standard of living for many in the developed and the newly emerging industrial nations.

V. **Applying Sociological Theories**
  A. The symbolic interactionist perspective is useful in understanding the distinctions between a job and a profession.
     1. The characteristics that make work a profession include: (1) rigorous education including graduate school and an admission examination; (2) the education is theoretical, not practical or "how to do it"; (3) self-regulation by the profession; (4) authority over clients based on specialized education and theoretical understanding; and (5) service to society.
  B. The functionalist perspective states that work is functional for society because important tasks are accomplished.
     1. It binds people together according to Durkheim's principles of mechanical solidarity (unity from being involved in similar occupations or activities) and organic solidarity (interdependence resulting from mutual need as each individual fulfills his or her job).
     2. Today organic solidarity has expanded far beyond anything Durkheim envisioned, creating interdependencies that span the globe. These global interdependencies suggest the need for a new term—perhaps "superorganic solidarity."
     3. The world's nations are dividing into three primary trading blocs: North and South America dominated by the U.S., Europe dominated by Germany, and Asia dominated by Japan.
     4. The multinational corporate giants, benefiting from this new world structure, are promoting free trade. If free trade is put into practice world wide, its functions will include greater competition over scarce resources on a global scale and vast loss of production jobs in most industrialized nations.
  C. Conflict theorists are concerned that the wealthy will benefit from changing technology at the expense of workers and that an inner circle of corporate and government leaders will wield too much economic and political power.
     1. With the introduction of new technologies, low-level workers, living from paycheck to paycheck, are most directly affected by the uncertainty, the loss of jobs and the lower wages. The result is that profits increase by lowering production costs.
     2. The multinationals are headed by an inner circle. This group, while in competition with one another, is united by a mutual interest in preserving capitalism. Sometimes this leads to a misuse of their enormous power, as was the case when ITT plotted with the CIA to unseat Chile's elected government. When this failed they succeeded in the assassination of the Chilean president, Salvador Allende.
  D. The "first wave" feminists were primarily concerned with the political right of voting and were known as "suffragists." The "second wave" struggled in the work place. The "third wave" offers very little to our understanding of inequality in the work place.

VI.   Work in Canadian Society

   A. Sociologists divide economic life into primary (extracting natural resources), secondary (turning raw materials into goods), and tertiary (service-oriented) sectors. In postindustrial societies, most of the labour force works in the tertiary sector.

   B. A sharp increase in the number of women working outside the home has occurred in Canada.

   1. How likely a woman is to work depends on several factors, such as her education, marital status, and the age of her children; race and ethnicity have little influence.

   2. Men and women have different work experiences and different models for success.

   3. The quiet revolution refers to the continually increasing proportions of women in the labour force. This transformation affects consumer patterns, relations at work, self-concepts, and familial relationships.

   C. The underground (informal) economy is exchange of goods and services not reported to the government, including income from work done "on the side" and from illegal activities (e.g., drug dealing). Estimates place the underground economy at 15 to 20 percent of the regular economy, which means it may run close to $140 billion. As a result, Revenue Canada loses millions of dollars in taxes a year.

   D. In Canada, household income growth declined during the past two decades. For some, trying to stay even has meant having to work more hours or more jobs.

   E. Leisure is time not taken up by work or required activities such as eating/sleeping. Patterns of leisure change with the life-course as seen in Figure 11.5. Patterns of work and leisure are changing in the post-industrial society.

VII.   The Future: Facing the Consequences of Global Capitalism

   A. Predictions for a shorter work week and more meaningful jobs have not yet materialized.

   1. Jobs are being transformed and new jobs created, particularly in the knowledge/ information services sector. However, this change has also meant thousands of lost jobs.

   B. There is a great deal of uncertainty with respect to the future of work for Canadians. Consider some of the issues in "New Technology and Restructuring of Work."

KEY TERMS

After studying the chapter, review the definition for each of the following terms.

barter: the direct exchange of one item for another

capitalism: an economic system characterized by the private ownership of the means of production, the pursuit of profit, and market competition

conspicuous consumption: Thorstein Veblen's term for a change from the Protestant ethic to an eagerness to show off wealth by the elaborate consumption of goods

convergence theory: the view that as capitalist and socialist economic systems each adopt features of the other, a hybrid (or mixed) economic system may emerge

corporate capitalism: the domination of the economic system by giant corporations

corporation: the joint ownership of a business enterprise, whose liabilities and obligations are separate from those of the owners

credit card: a device that allows its owner to purchase goods but be billed later

currency: paper money

debit card: a device that allows its owner to charge purchases against his or her bank account

democratic socialism: a hybrid economic system in which capitalism is mixed with state ownership

deposit receipts: a receipt stating that a certain amount of goods is on deposit in a warehouse or bank; the receipt is used as a form of money

economy: a system of distribution of goods and services

fiat money: currency issued by a government that is not backed by stored value

glass ceiling: refers to the barriers to social advancement that many women face in some organizations.

gold standard: paper money backed by gold

gross national product (GNP): the amount of goods and services produced by a nation

inflation: an increase in prices

interlocking directorates: the same people serving on the board of directors of several companies

job ghettoes: (also called **pink ghettoes**) are those employment areas where women dominate

laissez-faire capitalism: unrestrained manufacture and trade (literally, "hands off" capitalism)

leisure: time not taken up by work or required activities such as eating, sleeping, commuting, childcare, and housework

market: any process of buying and selling; on a more formal level, the mechanism that establishes values for the exchange of goods and services

market competition: the exchange of items between willing buyers and sellers

market forces: the law of supply and demand

market restraints: laws and regulations that limit the capacity to manufacture and sell products

mechanical solidarity: Durkheim's term for the unity that comes from being involved in similar occupations or activities

medium of exchange: the means by which people value goods and services in order to make an exchange, for example, currency, gold, and silver

money: any item (from sea shells to gold) that is used as a medium of exchange; today, currency is the most common form

neoliberalism: it refers to a new expansion in time and space of the free market. Nothing less than 24-hour global economy will satisfy neoliberals

oligopoly: the control of an entire industry by several large companies

organic solidarity: Durkheim's term for the interdependence that results from people's needing others to fulfill their job

primary sector: that part of the economy that extracts raw materials from the environment

private ownership of the means of production: the ownership of machines and factories by individuals, who decide what shall be produced

profession: an occupation characterized by rigorous education, a theoretical perspective, self-regulation, authority over clients, and service to society (as opposed to a job)

quiet revolution (the): the fundamental changes in society that occurred as a result of vast numbers of women entering the work force

secondary sector: that part of the economy in which raw materials are turned into manufactured goods

social conservatism: a value system characterized by a belief in conventional morality and social mores and desire to preserve them

socialism: an economic system characterized by the public ownership of the means of production, central planning, and the distribution of goods without a profit motive

stored value: the backing of a currency by goods that are stored and held in reserve

subsistence economy: the type of economy in which human groups live off the land with little or no surplus

tertiary sector: that part of the economy that consists of service-oriented occupations

underemployment: the condition of having to work at a job beneath one's level of training and abilities, or of being able to find only part-time work

underground economy: exchanges of goods and services that are not reported to the government and thereby escape taxation

welfare (state) capitalism: an economic system in which individuals own the means of production but the state regulates many economic activities for the welfare of the population

KEY PEOPLE

Review the major theoretical contributions or findings of these people.

Daniel Bell: Bell identified six characteristics of the postindustrial society.

Wallace Clement: Followed in John Porter's footsteps and showed the increasing concentration of corporate power in Canada.

Emile Durkheim: Durkheim contributed the concepts of mechanical and organic solidarity to our understanding of social cohesion.

John Porter: The first Canadian sociologist to identify the highly concentrated character of Canada's corporate elite.

R. Jack Richardson: Compared corporate concentration in several developed economies.

Michael Useem: Using a conflict perspective, Useem studied the activities of the "inner circle" of corporate executives.

Thorstein Veblen: Veblen created the term "conspicuous consumption" to refer to the eagerness to show off one's wealth through the elaborate consumption of material goods.

SELF-TEST

After completing this self-test, check your answers against the Answer Key at the back of this Study Guide and against the text on page(s) indicated in parentheses.

MULTIPLE CHOICE QUESTIONS

1. What is a market? (228)
   a. It is any process of buying and selling.
   b. It is the mechanism that establishes values for the exchange of goods and services.
   c. It means the movement of vast amounts of goods across international borders.
   d. all of the above

2. Which of the following characterize hunting and gathering societies? (228)
   a. market economy
   b. surplus economy
   c. subsistence economy
   d. maintenance economy

3. The primary sociological significance of surplus and trade was: (228)
   a. the development of hunting.
   b. the expansion of gathering societies.
   c. fostering of social inequality.
   d. none of the above

4. Which of the following is *not* a feature of industrial economies? (228)
   a. Machines are powered by fuels.
   b. a creation of larger surpluses than ever before
   c. The steam engine was invented and became the basis for the economy.
   d. A service sector developed and employed the majority of workers.

5. What did Veblen label the lavishly wasteful spending of goods designed to enhance social prestige? (228)
   a. prestigious consumption
   b. wasteful consumption
   c. conspicuous prestige
   d. conspicuous consumption

6. Which of the following is *not* a defining characteristics of postindustrial economies? (229)
   a. a marked shortage of goods
   b. extensive trade among nations
   c. information explosion
   d. a "global village"

7. In which type of society was money first used extensively? (230)
   a. agricultural
   b. industrial
   c. postindustrial
   d. pastoral and horticultural

8. What term is used to describe the total goods and services that a nation produces? (230)
   a. the gross national product
   b. the net national product
   c. the national debt
   d. the medium of exchange

9. The debit card came into existence in the: (230)
    a. agricultural economy.
    b. industrial economy.
    c. postindustrial economy.
    d. none of the above.

10. Which of the following are features of capitalism? (231)
    a. private ownership of the means of production
    b. pursuit of profit
    c. market competition
    d. all of the above

11. "Pure" capitalism is: (231)
    a. the type of capitalism dominant in Canada.
    b. an ideal type used to develop models of capitalism in Western Europe.
    c. a system where market forces operate without interference from government.
    d. a system where market forces are moderated by some government interference.

12. In the few Socialist/Communist economies that remain in the world (China, North Korea, and Cuba), which means of production does the government own? (232)
    a. the factories
    b. the land and railroads
    c. the oil wells and gold mines
    d. all of the above

13. Dissatisfied with the greed of capitalism and the lack of individual freedom of socialism, some Western nations (Sweden, Denmark) developed: (232)
    a. welfare capitalism.
    b. democratic socialism.
    c. post industrialism.
    d. laissez-faire capitalism.

14. Which of the following are criticisms levelled at capitalism? (233)
    a. Capitalism produces a tiny top layer of wealthy and powerful people.
    b. The tiny top layer exploits a vast bottom layer of poorly paid workers.
    c. The tiny top layer wields vast political power.
    d. all of the above

15. The primary criticism levelled against socialism is that (233)
    a. it does not respect individual right.
    b. central planning is grossly inefficient.
    c. it is not capable of producing sufficient quantities of consumer goods.
    d. all of the above

16. What is oligopoly? (235)
    a. the control of an entire industry by several large companies
    b. the control of an entire industry by a single company
    c. illegal in Canada
    d. none of the above

17. .Neoliberalism is not the same as classical market liberalism. Neoliberalism _____
    . (234)
    a. refers to a new expansion in time and space of the free market
    b. has its origins in the Enlightenment ideas of human rights to life, liberty, and the pursuit
       of property
    c. believes in conventional morality and desires to preserve them
    d. none of the above

18. The elites who sit on the boards of directors of multiple companies are referred to as: (235)
    a. vertical integrators.
    b. interlocking trustees.
    c. interlocking directorates.
    d. oligopolies.

19. Which of the following characteristics describes a profession? (238)
    a. rigorous educational training
    b. authority over clients based on the specialized training
    c. professional culture geared at service to society
    d. All of the above are among the characteristics of a profession.

20. Which perspective views work as the tie which binds us together? (239)
    a. functionalist
    b. conflict
    c. symbolic interactionist
    d. ethnomethodological

21. As societies industrialize, they become based on: (239)
    a. mechanical solidarity.
    b. organic solidarity.
    c. social solidarity.
    d. none of the above

22. According to conflict theory, which group bears the brunt of technological change? (239)
    a. middle management
    b. top-level executives
    c. low-level workers
    d. labourers in the least industrialized nations

23. Workers who package fish, process copper into electrical wire, and turn trees into lumber and paper are in the: (240)
    a. primary sector.
    b. secondary sector.
    c. tertiary sector.
    d. none of the above

24. What term is used to describe the fundamental changes in society that follow the movement of vast numbers of women from the home to the work force? (275)
    a. the feminization of work
    b. the "mommy movement"
    c. the quiet revolution
    d. the backlash

25. What is the underground, also known as the informal economy? (242)
    a. It is an exchange of goods and services that is not reported to the government.
    b. It helps many Canadians avoid what they consider exorbitant taxes.
    c. It includes illegal activities such as drug dealing .
    d. all of the above

TRUE-FALSE QUESTIONS

T F   1.   Hunting and gathering societies were the first economies to have a surplus. (228)

T F   2.   As agricultural societies developed, trade expanded and gave rise to trading centres, which blossomed into cities. The result was greater social, political, and economic equality. (228)

T F   3.   The characteristics of postindustrial economies were identified by Daniel Bell. (229)

T F   4.   By the late 1960's, U.S. paper money was still exchangeable for gold or silver. (230)

T F   5.   The richest fifth of Canadians earn about 47 percent of all the income in Canada. (230)

T F   6.   Even without the gold standard governments have a practical limit on the amount of paper money they can issue. (230)

T F   7.   Credit cards and debit cards are the same thing. (230)

T F   8.   In welfare capitalism, private citizens own the means of production and pursue profits, but do so within a vast system of laws. (231)

T F   9.   The Canadian capitalism is welfare or state capitalism. (231)

T F 10.   Socialism involves the distribution of goods without a profit motive. (232)

T F 11.   While still proclaiming Marxist-Leninist-Maoist principles, the Communist Party, under the slogan "One China, two systems," is trying to make Shanghai the financial centre of East Asia. (234)

T F 12.   Corporations have so changed capitalism that the term corporate capitalism is used to indicate that giant corporations dominate the economic system. (235)

T F 13.   The sociological significance of multinational corporations is that they owe allegiance only to profits and market share, not to any nation, not even any particular culture. (236)

T F 14.   Members of a profession claim that only they possess sufficient knowledge to determine the profession's standards and to certify those qualified to be admitted. (238)

T F   15.   Durkheim's concept of organic solidarity is an adequate concept for understanding the interdependency that exists among various occupational sectors. (239)

T F   16.   The inner circle is made up of the heads of the largest multinational corporations. (239)

T F   17.   Researchers have found that both men and women workers are equally concerned with maintaining a balance between their work and family lives. (242)

T F   18.   The "quiet revolution" refers to the continually increasing proportions of women who have joined the ranks of paid labour. (242)

T F   19.   While Canada's banks and corporations report record profits, household income growth has declined dramatically over the past twenty years. (242)

T F   20.   In recent decades, Canada has followed the lead of the western nations in terms of a gradually shrinking work week and an increase in leisure. (244)

FILL-IN QUESTIONS

1.   _____ is the term for a system of distribution of goods and services. (228)

2.   Toward the end of the agricultural period_____ or paper money came into use. (230)

3.   A _____ allows its owners to purchase goods but to be billed later. A _____ allows its owners to charge purchases against his or her bank account. (230)

4.   The economic system where market forces operate without interference from government is called _____. (231)

5.   _____ is the condition of having to work at a job beneath one's level of training and abilities, or of being able to find only part-time work. (233)

6.   A _____ is a business that is treated in law as a person. (235)

7.   One way in which the wealthy use corporations to wield power is by means of _____, or serving as directors of several companies simultaneously. (235)

8.   Durkheim's term for the unity that comes from being involved in similar occupations or activities is _____. (239)

9.   Members of the _____ may compete with one another, but they are united by a mutual interest in preserving capitalism. (239)

10.   That part of the economy in which raw materials are turned into manufactured goods is the _____. (240)

11.   In the _____ sector, workers are primarily involved in providing services. (240)

12.   The _____ has contributed to a transformation of consumer patterns, relations at work, self-concepts, and relationships with family and friends. (242)

13.   The _____ consists of economic activities, whether legal or illegal, that people don't report to the government. (242)

14.   _____ is time not taken up by work or required activities such as eating and sleeping. (243)

MATCH THESE SOCIAL SCIENTISTS WITH THEIR CONTRIBUTIONS

___1. Daniel Bell   a.   *studied the activities of the "inner circle"*
___2. Emile Durkheim   b.   *studied the concentration of corporate power in Canada*
___3. Michael Useem   c.   *identified six characteristics of postindustrial society*
___4. Wallace Clement   d.   *created the term "conspicuous consumption"*
___5. Thorstein Veblen   e.   *contributed the concepts of mechanical and organic solidarity*

ESSAY QUESTIONS

1. Discuss the advantages and disadvantages of both capitalism and socialism as ideologies and as economic systems.
2. Identify the defining characteristics of professions and discuss the usefulness of this framework for understanding work.
3. Discuss the sociological significance of global capitalization, the underground economy, and shrinking pay checks of Canadian households.
4. In what way is neoliberalism different from classical market liberalism?

"DOWN-TO-EARTH SOCIOLOGY"

1. After reading "Selling the North American Dream" (233), can you think of ways in which advertising is able to increase your desire to consume products, even when you previously felt no need for them? How does advertising affect what you wear? What you eat? What you do for recreation? How does advertising affect the way you feel about yourself?
2. What impact does Globalization of Capitalism have on Canada? (236-237)
3. When you read "Finding Work" (243), were you surprised to learn that trends of job security are different now than they were 40 years ago? What are the social implications of this change?
4. Do your concerns about technology and work mirror those voiced in "New Technology and the Restructuring of Work"? (245-246)? What kinds of social, political, and economic conditions would have to be present for either of the future alternatives to come true?

CHAPTER 12
POLITICS: POWER AND AUTHORITY

CHAPTER SUMMARY

- The essential nature of politics is power, the ability to carry out one's will despite resistance; every group is political. Micropolitics refers to the exercise of power in everyday life while macropolitics refers to large-scale power, such as governing a nation.
- Authority refers to the legitimate use of power, while coercion is its illegitimate use. The state is a political entity that claims a monopoly on violence over a particular territory. Three types of authority, traditional, rational-legal, and charismatic, were identified by Max Weber as ideal type constructs. The orderly transfer of authority at the death, resignation, or incapacitation of a leader is critical for social stability.
- Three forms of government are monarchies (power is based on hereditary rule), democracies (power is given by the citizens), and dictatorships and oligarchies (power is seized by an individual or a small group).
- Canada has a federal system of government. This means that some areas of legal jurisdiction or real powers of enforcement are reserved for the federal parliament and other, residual powers are distributed among the provincial and municipal governments. Many democracies in Europe have a system of proportional representation which encourages the formation of coalition governments. The Canadian system has evolved from two-party to multi-party system.
- Functionalists and conflict theorists have very different views on who rules Canada. According to the functionalists, no one group holds power; the outcome is that the competing interest groups balance one another (pluralism). According to conflict theorists, Canada is governed by a ruling class made up of members drawn from the elite (power elite).
- War is a common means to implement political objectives; however, dehumanization of the enemy is a particularly high cost of war. The seeds of future wars and terrorism are sown by selling advanced war technology to the least industrialized nations and by nuclear proliferation.
- The global expansion of communication, transportation, and trade, the widespread adoption of capitalism and the retreat of socialism, as well as the trend toward larger political unions suggest that a new international world order may be in the process of emerging. The oppositional trend is for fierce nationalism to emerge.

LEARNING OBJECTIVES

As you read Chapter 12, use these learning objectives to organize your notes. After completing your reading, briefly state an answer to each of the objectives, and review the text pages in parentheses.

1. Define the term power and distinguish between micropolitics and macropolitics. (250)
2. Explain the difference between authority and coercion and why the state claims a monopoly on legitimate violence. (250)

3. Describe the sources of authority identified by Weber, indicate why these are "ideal types," and explain how the orderly transfer of authority is achieved under each type of authority. (250-252)
4. Differentiate between monarchies, democracies, and dictatorships and oligarchies. (253-255)
5. Explain how the political system is structured in Canada. (255-256)
6. Describe the Parliamentary system in Canada. (256)
7. Discuss the evolution of Canada's political party system. (256-258)
8. Analyze the impact of the Quiet Revolution and the Quebec sovereignty movement on Canadian politics. (258-260)
9. Compare Canadian democracy with democratic systems found in Europe. (260)
10. Distinguish between the functionalist and conflict perspectives on how the Canadian political process operates, and discuss the power elite perspectives of C. Wright Mills and John Porter. (260-261)
11. Discuss the conditions that lead to war and analyze the dehumanizing aspects of war. (262-263)
12. Evaluate the possibility for global political and economic unity in the future and what impact the resurgence of nationalism could have on this new world order. (264)

CHAPTER OUTLINE

I. **Micropolitics and Macropolitics**
   A. Power is the ability to carry out one's will despite resistance.
   B. Symbolic interactionists use micropolitics to refer to exercise of power in everyday life. Macropolitics is the exercise of large-scale power over a broad group.

II. **Power, Authority, and Violence**
   A. Authority is legitimate power that people accept as right, while coercion is power that people do not accept as just.
   B. The state is the source of legitimate force or violence in society; violence is the ultimate foundation of political order. A government that is viewed as legitimate is more stable than one that is not; revolution (armed resistance to overthrow a government) is a rejection by the people of a government's claim to rule and of its monopoly on violence.
   C. Three sources of authority were identified by Max Weber.
      1. Traditional authority (based on custom) is prevalent in preliterate groups, where custom sets relationships. When society changes, traditional authority is undermined, but does not die, even in postindustrial societies. For example, parental authority is a traditional authority.
      2. Rational-legal authority (based on written rules, also called bureaucratic authority) derives from the position an individual holds, not from the person. Everyone (no matter how high the office) is subject to the rules.
      3. Charismatic authority (based on an individual's personal following) may pose a threat. Because this type of leader works outside the established political system and may threaten the established order, the authorities are often quick to oppose this type of leader.

D. Weber's three types of authority are ideal types representing composite characteristics found in real life examples. In rare instances, traditional and rational-legal leaders possess charismatic traits, but most authority is one type or another. A Canadian example of a leader who combined a rational-legal and charismatic authority was Pierre Elliot Trudeau.

E. Orderly transfer of authority upon death, resignation, or incapacity of a leader is critical for stability. Succession is more of a problem with charismatic authority than with traditional or rational-legal authority. Routinization of charisma refers to the transfer of authority from a charismatic leader to either traditional or rational-legal authority.

III.   Types of Government

A. A monarchy is a government headed by a king or queen.
1. As cities developed, each city-state (an independent city whose power radiated outward, bringing adjacent areas under its rule) had its own monarchy.
2. As city-states warred with one another, the victors would extend their rule, eventually over an entire region. As the size of these regions grew, people developed an identification with the region; over time this gave rise to the state.

B. A democracy is a government whose authority derives from the people.
1. Direct democracy (eligible voters meet to discuss issues and make decisions) emerged about 2,000 years ago in Athens.
2. Representative democracy (voters elect representatives to govern and make decisions on their behalf) emerged as Canada became more populous, making direct democracy impossible.
3. Today, citizenship (people have basic rights by virtue of birth or residence) is taken for granted in Canada; this idea is quite new to the human scene. Universal citizenship (everyone having the same basic rights) came into practice very slowly and only through struggle.

C. Dictatorship is government where power is seized and held by an individual; oligarchy results when a small group of individuals seizes power. Dictators and oligarchies can be totalitarian; this is when the government exercises almost total control of a people.

IV.   The Canadian Political System

A. Canada is a parliamentary democracy.
1. Parliament is the highest political authority in the country.
2. Provincial governments have a number of separate and significant powers of their own.
3. Canada's system of government lays in-between the models of a unitary state (where all power resides with the central government) and a confederal union (where provinces have most power).

B. The Parliamentary system in Canada is made up of three levels of national government: the Queen, the Senate, and Parliament.
1. The Queen has no powers to make laws in Canada, and the Senate is a minor player in the lawmaking process.

2. While Parliament is the highest lawmaking authority, there are limits to its powers; it cannot make laws in areas of provincial jurisdiction and, since 1982, parliaments formal powers have been limited by the Charter of Rights and Freedoms.

3. Opposition parties play an adversarial role, debating the government's policies.

4. The federal bureaucracy includes employees in the armed forces, the RCMP, various government agencies, and the public service.

5. The Canadian government has enacted policies of employment equity to provide more opportunities for women, aboriginal peoples, visible minorities, and peoples with disabilities in the federal public service.

6. Politics in Quebec are tied to the struggles over French language and French-Canadian culture.

C. Not all democracies around the world are Parliamentary systems like ours.

1. Most European countries use proportional representation (legislative seats divided according to the proportion of votes each political party received).

2. The European system encourages minority parties. Non-centrist parties (representing marginal ideas) develop in European systems with proportional representation.

3. Three main results follow from proportional representation: (1) minority parties can gain access to the media, which keeps their issues alive; (2) because many parties compete in the elections, no single party is likely to gain a majority of the seats in the national legislature but must form a coalition; (3) because coalitions break down, governments tend to be less stable.

V. Who Rules Canada?

A. The functionalists say that pluralism, the diffusion of power among many interest groups, prevents any one from gaining control of the government and using it to oppress the people.

1. From the functionalist perspective the Canadian government functions like a healthy human body; special-interest groups negotiate with one another, reach compromises and conflict is minimized.

B. According to the conflict perspective, the power elite make the decisions that direct the country and shape the world.

1. C. Wright Mills took the position that those decisions that have the greatest impact on the lives, not only of Americans but people across the globe, are made by a coalition of individuals whose interests coincide and who have access to the centre of political power. Mills called them power elite.

2. John Porter identified several elites in Canadian society, not just the industrial-military complex identified by Mills for the United States.

3. The Canadian economic elite attend the same schools and social clubs, and recruit one another to serve on various boards of directors.

VI. War: A Means to Implement Political Objectives

A. The state uses violence to protect citizens from individuals and groups, turning violence against other nations. War (armed conflict between nations or politically distinct groups) often is part of national policy.

B. War is simply one option that groups may choose for dealing with disagreements; but not all societies choose this option.

C. Nicholas Timasheff identified three essential conditions of war.
1. There is a cultural tradition of war; because they have fought wars in the past, leaders see war as an option.
2. An antagonistic situation exists, with two or more states confronting incompatible objectives.
3. A "fuel" heats the antagonistic situation to the boiling point, so that people move from thinking about war to actually engaging in it; Timasheff identified six fuels.

D. Despite the fact war is costly to society, it continues to be a common technique for pursuing political objectives.

E. The Most Industrialized Nations relentlessly pursue profits by selling powerful weapons to the Least Industrialized Nations—Russia and the United States are the chief merchants of death to the Least Industrialized Nations.

F. Today terrorism directed against civilian populations is a danger.
1. Suicide terrorism is one of the few options available to a weaker group that wants to retaliate against a powerful country.
2. The real danger is from nuclear, chemical, and biological weapons.

G. War has an effect on morality.
1. Exposure to brutality and killing often causes dehumanization (reducing people to objects that do not deserve to be treated as humans).
2. Characteristics of dehumanization include: (1) increased emotional distance from others; (2) an emphasis on following procedures; (3) inability to resist pressures; and (4) a diminished sense of personal responsibility.
3. Dehumanization does not always insulate the self from guilt; after the war ends, returning soldiers often find themselves disturbed by what they did during the war. Although most eventually adjust, some live with the guilt forever.

VII. **A New World Order?**
A. The globalization of capitalism, accompanied by the world wide flow of information, capital, and goods is little affected by national boundaries. There are many examples of nations working together to solve mutual problems—the North American Free Trade Agreement (NAFTA), the European Union (EU), and the United Nations (UN).
B. Similarly, the United Nations, transcending national borders and moderating disputes between countries, can authorize the use of international force against individual nations. The rising tension between nations and states is explored in the "Cultural Diversity around the World of Nationalism" perspective box.

KEY TERMS

After studying the chapter, review the definition for each of the following terms.

authority: power that people accept as rightly exercised over them; also called *legitimate power*

charismatic authority: authority based on an individual's outstanding traits, which attract followers

citizenship: the concept that birth (and residence) in a country impart basic rights

city-state: an independent city whose power radiates outward, bringing the adjacent areas under its rule

coalition government: a government in which a country's largest party aligns itself with one or more smaller parties

coercion: power that people do not accept as rightly exercised over them; also called *illegitimate power*

confederal union: a form of government where power resides in provinces, rather than a central government

dehumanization: the act or process of reducing people to objects that do not deserve the treatment accorded humans

democracy: a system of government in which authority derives from the people, derived from two Greek words that translate literally as "power to the people"

dictatorship: a form of government in which power is seized by an individual

direct democracy: a form of democracy in which the eligible voters meet together to discuss issues and make their decisions

macropolitics: the exercise of large-scale power, the government being the most common example

micropolitics: the exercise of politics in everyday life, such as deciding who is going to do the housework

monarchy: a form of government headed by a king or queen

nationalism: a strong identity with a nation, accompanied by the desire for the nation to be dominant

non-centrist party: a political party that represents marginal ideas

oligarchy: a form of government in which power is held by a small group of individuals; the rule of the many by the few

pluralism: the diffusion of power among many interest groups, preventing any single group from gaining control of the government

power: the ability to carry out one's will, even over the resistance of others

power elite: C. Wright Mills's term for those who rule Canada; the top people in the leading corporations, the most powerful generals and admirals of the armed forces, and certain elite politicians

proportional representation: an electoral system in which seats in a legislature are divided according to the proportion of votes each political party receives

rational-legal authority: authority based on law or written rules and regulations; also called *bureaucratic authority*

representative democracy: a form of democracy in which voters elect representatives to govern and make decisions on their behalf

revolution: armed resistance designed to overthrow a government

routinization of charisma: the transfer of authority from a charismatic figure to either a traditional or a rational-legal form of authority

state: a political entity that claims a monopoly on the use of violence in some particular territory; commonly known as a country

totalitarianism: a form of government that exerts almost total control over the people

traditional authority: authority based on custom

unitary state: a state in which all power resides with the central government

universal citizenship: the idea that everyone has the same basic rights by virtue of being born in a country (or by immigrating and becoming a naturalized citizen)

war: armed conflict between nations or politically distinct groups

KEY PEOPLE

Review the major theoretical contributions or findings of these people.

Peter Berger: Berger argued that violence is the ultimate foundation of any political order.

Wallace Clement: Clement classified three components of Canada's corporate elite: a Canadian component, a foreign (mostly U.S.) component, and a "comprador" elite.

Everett Hughes: Hughes studied the industrialization of rural Quebec and the division of labour between English-speaking Protestants and French-speaking Catholics.

C. Wright Mills: Mills suggested that power resides in the hands of an elite made up of the top leaders of the largest corporations, the most powerful generals of the armed forces, and certain elite politicians.

John Porter: Porter identified an economic elite, as well as elites in the media, religion, organized labour, and the political sector of Canadian society.

Nicholas S. Timasheff: Timasheff identified three essential conditions of war—a cultural tradition of war, an antagonistic situation in which two or more countries have incompatible objectives, and a fuel which moves the antagonisms into conflict situations.

Max Weber: Weber identified three different types of authority: traditional, rational-legal, and charismatic.

SELF-TEST

After completing this self-test, check your answers against the Answer Key at the back of this Study Guide and against the text on page(s) indicated in parentheses.

MULTIPLE CHOICE QUESTIONS

1. Which of the following relates to power? (250)
   a. Max Weber used the term authority to refer to legitimate power.
   b. It is the ability to carry out one's will in spite of resistance from others.
   c. We perceive power as either legitimate or illegitimate .
   d. all of the above

2. Governments, whether dictatorships or the elected forms, are examples of: (250)
   a. coercion.
   b. macropolitics.
   c. micropolitics.
   d. none of the above

3. The state (government) claims the exclusive right to use _____ and the right to punish everyone else who does: (250)
   a. laws
   b. elections
   c. violence
   d. leaders

4. Which of the following are examples of traditional authority: (250-251)
   a. someone becomes king or queen because of birth into a social location
   b. custom of widows to wear black
   c. parental authority
   d. all of the above.

5. Pierre Elliott Trudeau: (252)
   a. combined rational-legal and charismatic authority.
   b. was a purely charismatic leader.
   c. is an example of a traditional leader.
   d. none of the above

6. The example of the Ayatollah Khomeini of Iran shows that: (252-253)
   a. charismatic and traditional authority can also overlap.
   b. he was a charismatic leader .
   c. he was holder of the traditional position of ayatollah.
   d. all of the above

7. A government run by a single person who has seized power is a: (255)
   a. democracy
   b. dictatorship
   c. oligarchy
   d. monarchy

8. Which form of government exerts almost total control over the people? (255)
   a. monarchy
   b. dictatorship
   c. totalitarian regime
   d. oligarchy

9. Canada's political system is: (255)
   a. a parliamentary democracy.
   b. a unitary state.
   c. a confederal state.
   d. none of the above

10. What does the history of the political party system in Canada demonstrate? (256-257)
    a. Third parties have generally promoted left-wing policies.
    b. The party system evolved into a multi-party system during the twentieth century.
    c. The Liberals and Conservatives are the only important political parties.
    d. all of the above

11. What event(s) in Quebec have transformed Canadian politics? (258-259)
    a. the Quiet Revolution
    b. the rise of the sovereignty movement
    c. (a) and (b)
    d. the Meech Lake Accord

12. Most European countries base their elections on a system of: (260)
    a. parliamentary democracy.
    b. multi-party competition.
    c. pluralism.
    d. proportional representation.

13. Functionalists see that _____ prevent(s) any one group from having total government control. (260)
    a. the existence of a powerful elite
    b. pluralism
    c. coalition governments
    d. all of the above

14. Which perspective suggests that conflict is minimized as special-interest groups negotiate with one another and reach compromises? (260)
    a. functionalists
    b. conflict theorists
    c. symbolic interactionists
    d. political sociologists

15. Members of Canada's corporate elite are drawn from: (261)
    a. banking.
    b. insurance.
    c. the industrial-military complex only.
    d. a. and b.

16. According to conflict theorists, the ruling class is: (261)
    a. made up of a group of dissimilar people.
    b. a group that came from the ranks of the working class.
    c. made up of people whose backgrounds and orientations to life are so similar that they automatically share the same goals.
    d. involved in a grand conspiracy.

17. War: (262)
    a. is armed conflict between nations or politically distinct groups.
    b. is universal.
    c. is chosen for dealing with disagreements by all societies at one time or another.
    d. all of the above

18. Which of the following is *not* one of the essential conditions of war identified by Nicholas Timasheff? (262)
    a. the existence of a strong, well-armed military force
    b. a cultural tradition of war
    c. an antagonistic situation in which two or more states confront incompatible objectives
    d. the presence of a "fuel" that heats the antagonistic situation to boiling point

19. Timasheff found that war is likely if a country's leaders see the antagonistic situation as an opportunity to: (262)
    a. exact revenge or settle "old scores."
    b. dictate their will to a weaker nation.
    c. save the nation's "honour."
    d. all of the above

20. The world has about 5000 nations. Which of the following makes each a nation? (264)
    a. Its people share a language and culture.
    b. Its people share a political organization.
    c. Its people share a territory.
    d. all of the above

TRUE-FALSE QUESTIONS

T F 1. In every group, large or small, some individuals have power over others. (250)

T F 2. Coercion refers to legitimate power. (250)

T F 3. The state claims a monopoly on violence within some designated territory. (250)

T F 4. Even in port-industrial societies, parental authority provides an excellent example of traditional authority. (251)

T F 5. Rational-legal authority derives from the position that an individual holds, not from the person who holds the position. (251)

T F 6. Because the authority of charismatic leaders is based on their personal ability to attract followers, they pose no threat to the established political system. (252)

T F 7.   Weber's classification of authority into traditional, rational-legal, and charismatic represents ideal types of authority. Any given leader may show a combination of these characteristics. (252)

T F 8.   Weber used the term routinization of charisma to refer to the transition of authority from a charismatic leader to rational-legal authority. (253)

T F 9.   The orderly transfer of authority from one leader to another is critical for social stability. (253)

T F 10. Direct democracy is not possible with the larger populations of Canada and the United States. (253)

T F 11. There is nothing "natural" (inevitable) about citizenship—it is simply one way in which people choose to define themselves. (253)

T F 12. The idea of universal citizenship caught on quickly in Canada. (254)

T F 13. The Conservative Party of Canada is the latest addition to the federal political landscape. (258)

T F 14. Taken together all categories of public sector employees at all levels of government make up over 40 percent of the total labour force. (258)

T F 15. The European system of democracy is not that different from our own. (260)

T F 16. Functionalists believe that pluralism prevents any one group from gaining control of the government and using it to oppress the people. (260)

T F 17. Conflict theorists think that the behaviour of the ruling class stems from some grand conspiracy to control the country. (261)

T F 18. Some groups do not even have a word for war in their language. (262)

T F 19. Sociologists attribute the causes of war to human factors such as aggressive impulses. (262)

T F 20. "Suicide terrorism" is one of the few options open to a weaker political group looking for ways to retaliate against a powerful enemy country. (263)

FILL-IN QUESTIONS

1. The exercise of power in everyday life, such as deciding who is going to do the housework is referred to as _____. (250)

2. _____ is synonymous with government; the source of legitimate violence in society. (250)

3. A _____ is armed resistance designed to overthrow a government. (250)

4. _____ is authority based on custom. (250)

5. Bureaucratic authority is also called _____. (251)

6. _____ may have had mass appeal in English Canada, but he was far from a hero in his home province of _____. (252)

7. _____ is a form of democracy in which the eligible voters meet together to discuss issues and make their decisions. (253)

8. The concept that birth and residence in a country impart basic rights is known as _____. (254)

9. A form of government that exerts almost total control over the people is _____. (255)
10. An electoral system in which seats in a legislature are divided according to the proportion of votes each political party receives is called _____. (260)
11. A _____ is a government where the party with the most seats aligns itself with one or more of the smaller parties to maintain power. (260)
12. _____ were the first type of government. (253)
13. Canada has a _____ system of government, but the _____ have evolved a number of separate and significant powers of their own. (255)
14. The act or process of reducing people to objects that do not deserve the treatment accorded humans is _____. (263)
15. Today _____, a strong identity with a nation, accompanied by the desire for that nation to be dominant, challenges efforts to forge a new world order. (264)

MATCH THESE SOCIAL SCIENTISTS WITH THEIR CONTRIBUTIONS

___ 1. Peter Berger   a. *power elite*
___ 2. John Porter   b. *violence is the foundation of the political order*
___ 3. C. Wright Mills   c. *three types of authority*
___ 4. Max Weber   d. *identified Canadian elite*
___ 5. Nicholas Timasheff   e. *Classified three components of Canada's corporate elite*
___ 6. Wallace Clement   f. *essential conditions of war*

ESSAY QUESTIONS

1. Distinguish between macropolitics and micropolitics, explaining what each is and which perspectives are associated with each, and provide your own examples to illustrate each.
2. Compare and contrast the systems of democracy found in Canada and Europe.
3. Discuss the impact of voter turnout at federal elections in Canada. How different would the distribution of seats in the parliament be, if voter turnout would be 90 percent? What is the sociological impact of the non-voters on Canadian politics.

"DOWN-TO-EARTH SOCIOLOGY"

1. What are your views of political parties, political leadership and the electoral process? Which perspective (functionalist, conflict, or feminist) best reflects your own views? Do you vote? If not, why not? (260-262)
2. Based on "The Rise of Nationalism Versus the Globalization of Capitalism: Implications for a New World Order," (264), do you agree that the next twenty years may be bloody if the world cannot find a better way to answer the demands of newly emboldened nations? Why or why not? How can the needs of these new nations for national identities be balanced against the demands of an increasingly global economy?

CHAPTER 13
THE FAMILY: INITIATION INTO SOCIETY

CHAPTER SUMMARY

- Because there are so many cultural variations, family structure is hard to define. Nevertheless, family is defined broadly as two or more people who consider themselves related by blood, marriage or adoption. Marriage and family patterns vary remarkably across cultures, but four universal themes in marriage are mate selection, descent, inheritance, and authority.
- There is no one clear standard for the family. In some cultures, men are expected to have more than one wife and in others women have more than one husband.
- According to the functionalist perspective, the family is universal because it serves six essential functions: economic production, socialization of children, care of the sick and aged, recreation, sexual control, and reproduction. Conversely, conflict theorists focus on how changing economic conditions affect families, especially gender relations. Symbolic interactionists focus on the contrasting experiences and perspectives of men and women that are played out in marriage.
- The family life cycle is analyzed in terms of love and courtship, marriage, childbirth, child rearing, and the family in later life. Within Canada, marriage, childbirth, and child rearing all vary by social class.
- Family diversity in Canadian society is based on racial and ethnic differences, as well as social class. As well, one-parent families, childless families, blended families, same-sex, and intentional families represent some of the different types of families today.
- Trends in Canadian families include postponement of marriage and parenting, common-law marriage, and the emergence of the "sandwich generation" who are caught between caring for their own children and caring for their elderly parents.
- Various studies have focused on problems of divorce, children of divorce, ex-spouses, and remarriage. Research suggests that children can suffer long-term negative effects from divorce. However, researchers have noted that the impacts of divorce are complex, not uniform.
- Violence and abuse—including child abuse, battering, spousal violence , and incest —are the "dark side" of family life. Researchers have identified variables that help marriages last and be happy such as being wealthy, religious, college-educated, not living common-law before marriage, and postponing marriage to at least twenty. Further, those who devote energy to maintaining their marriage will reap benefits in terms of the marital bond.
- The trends for the future include a continued increased in cohabitation, mother headed families, and blended families. The continuing growth in the numbers of working wives will impact on marital balance of power.

LEARNING OBJECTIVES

As you read Chapter 13, use these learning objectives to organize your notes. After completing your reading, briefly state an answer to each of the objectives, and review the text pages in parentheses.

1. Explain why it is difficult to define the term "family," including the different ways in which family systems can be classified. (268)
2. Identify the common cultural themes that run through marriage and the family. (269)
3. Explain why is it important to avoid a "monolithic bias" when defining the family. (270)
4. Contrast the functionalist, conflict, and symbolic interaction perspectives regarding marriage and family. (271-276)
5. Outline the major developments in each stage of the family life cycle and discuss the social factors that produce variations within each of these stages. (276-279)
6. State examples of the impact of racial and ethnic diversity on Canadian family life. (279-280)
7. Identify the major concerns of one-parent families, families without children, blended families, gay families, and intentional families. (280-283)
8. Describe the current trends affecting marriage and family life in Canada. (283-285)
9. Outline the legislative changes in Canadian society that facilitated increased divorce rates. (285-287)
10. Note some of the adjustment problems of children of divorce. (287-288)
11. Explain the statement that "family life can be rewarding or brutal" and give examples of abuse within the family setting. (288-290)
12. List some of the characteristics which tend to be present in marriages that work. Explain why happy and unhappy couples approach problems differently. (280-290)
13. Summarize conclusions regarding the future of marriage and family in Canada. (290-291)

CHAPTER OUTLINE

I.   **Marriage and Family in Global Perspective**
   A. Defining Family
      1. The term "family" is difficult to define because there are many types.
      2. In some societies men have more than one wife (polygyny) or women have more than one husband (polyandry).
   B. Common Cultural Themes
      1. Each group establishes norms to govern whom you can and cannot marry. Endogamy is the practice of marrying within one's own group, while exogamy is the practice of marrying outside of one's own group. Some norms of mate selection are written into law, others are informal.
      2. Three major patterns of descent (tracing kinship over generations) are: (a) bilateral (descent traced on both the mother's and the father's side); (b) patrilineal (descent traced only on the father's side); and (c) matrilineal (descent traced only on the mother's side).
      3. Mate selection and descent are regulated in all societies in order to provide an orderly way of passing property, etc., to the next generation. In a bilateral system, property passes to males and females; in a patrilineal system, property passes only to males; in a matrilineal system, property passes only to females.
      4. Patriarchy is a social system in which men dominate women, and runs through all societies. No historical records exist of a true matriarchy. In an egalitarian social system authority is more or less equally divided between men and women. Today, in Canada, Europe and elsewhere many, especially young women are embracing more egalitarian attitudes.

C. The Problem of Monolithic Bias
   1. A broad definition of family is two or more people who consider themselves
       related by blood, marriage, or adoption, and live together (or have lived
       together).
   2. A household, in contrast to a family, is all the people occupying the same
       housing unit.
   3. The family of orientation is the family in which a person grows up, while the
       family of procreation is the family formed when a couple's first child is born.
   4. Marriage is a group's approved mating arrangements, usually marked by a
       ritual.
   5. Canadian sociologists have rejected a "monolithic" approach to studying
       families, and argue that the vision of the nuclear family supports a very limited
       view of family life.
   6. They note that a monolithic bias can also contribute to a conservative bias, or
       a "normalizing" of the heterosexual, nuclear family.

II. **Marriage and Family in Theoretical Perspective**
   A. The functionalist perspective stresses how the family is related to other parts of
       society and how it contributes to the well-being of society.
      1. The family is universal because it serves functions essential to the well-being
          of society: economic production, socialization of children, care of the sick and
          aged, recreation, sexual control, and reproduction.
      2. The incest taboo (rules specifying which people are too closely related to have
          sex or marry) helps the family avoid role confusion and forces people to look
          outside the family for marriage partners, creating a network of support.
      3. Industrialization has made the family more fragile by weakening its functions
          and removing reasons for a family to struggle together against hardship,
          leading to higher rates of divorce.
      4. The nuclear family has few people it can depend on for material and emotional
          support; thus, the members of a nuclear family are vulnerable to "emotional
          overload." The relative isolation of the nuclear family makes it easier for the
          "dark side" of families (incest and other types of abuse) to emerge.
   B. Central to the conflict perspective is the struggle over scarce resources; in the
       family this struggle centres around housework.
      1. Research of Meg Luxton and others found that women did the lion's share of
          housework in Canada.
      2. Arlie Hochschild found that after an eight-hour day at work, women typically
          work a "second shift" at home; this means that wives work an extra month of
          24-hour days each year. There seems to be continued male resistance to
          household equality. The result is that working wives feel deep discontent.
   C. Using the symbolic interactionist perspective, we can explore the different meaning
       that housework has for men and women and how each sex experiences marriage
       differently.
      1. When men's and women's earnings are about the same, men are more likely to
          share in the housework; when women earn more than their husbands, the men
          are least likely to do housework. A wife's higher earnings tend to threaten a
          man's gender identity; doing "woman's work" is a further threat.

2. Men and women perceive their marriages differently. A gulf exists because each holds down different corners of the marriage. Jessie Bernard argued that every marriage actually contains two separate marriages—his and hers.
3. Men and women seem to have different perceptions of housework and even love making. Marriage remains a central social value.

III. The Family Life Cycle

A. Romantic love provides the ideological context in which Canadians seek mates and form families. Romantic love has two components: (1) emotional, a feeling of sexual attraction; and (2) cognitive, the feeling we describe as being "in love."
B. The social channels of love and marriage in Canada include age, education, social class, race, and religion.
   1. Homogamy is the tendency of people with similar characteristics to marry one another usually resulting from propinquity (spatial nearness).
C. Facts contradict the popular image that having a baby makes a couple deliriously happy.
   1. Marital satisfaction usually decreases with the birth of a child. Having a child usually means less time, less sleep, and heavier expenses.
D. As more mothers today are employed outside the home, child care has become an issue. While the majority of Canadians (90 percent) think that it is preferable for one parent to stay at home with children, two thirds of Canadian wives with young children are working for pay.
   1. As a result, in 2001, 53 percent of Canadian children aged six months to five years were in some form of child care. Research suggests that the children of employed parents do feel loved and valued, provided they know they are their parents' priority.
   2. Marital dissolution appears to have a particularly negative impact on the role of the father in child rearing.
E. Later stages of family life bring both pleasures and problems.
   1. The empty nest is a married couple's domestic situation after the last child has left home. The empty nest is thought to signal a difficult adjustment for women; however Lillian Rubin argues that this syndrome is largely a myth because women's satisfaction generally increases when the last child leaves home. Many couples report a renewed sense of companionship at this time.
   2. With prolonged education and a growing cost of establishing households, Canadian children are leaving home much later, or are returning after having left (boomerang kids).
   3. Women are more likely than men to face the problem of adjusting to widowhood, for not only does the average woman live longer than a man but she has also married a man older than herself.

IV. Diversity in Canadian Families

A. Cultural diversity influences the structures and practices of Canadian families. More than 14 percent of Canadians are visible minorities.
   1. Some differences, as national costume, or dates of religious events, may seem trivial, but many such differences as mother tongue or cultural beliefs and values, may have profound effect on family life.

B. The lives of Canadian families are also profoundly influenced by patterns of discrimination and economic inequality.
   1. The family life of First Nations peoples is conditioned by long-standing patterns of economic and social marginalization.
   2. Aboriginal analysts are pointing to the importance of families—extended family networks in rural communities and reserves; nuclear families and two generation families in urban and rural communities, and "unintentional families" of the heart—in supporting efforts to create a vibrant, new Aboriginal presence in Canada.
   3. Historically, immigration policies have intentionally blocked family formation among working-class Chinese, South Asian, and Japanese men and women, and more recently black Caribbean women. Government policies have ensured that these visible immigrants remained "single," provided temporary labour, and then returned to their country of origin.
C. There has been an increase in one-parent families.
   1. In 2001, one in four Canadian families with children was headed by a single parent, 81 percent headed by a woman.
   2. To understand many one-parent families, we need to view them through the lens of poverty, for that is often the primary source of strain.
   3. Children from poor families are penalized in terms of physical, mental, and social health.
D. Overall, about 41 percent of Canadian families never have children.
   1. According to Kathleen Gerson, there are a number of reasons why couples choose to be childfree—unstable marriages, lost career opportunities, and the expenses involved are among the reasons.
   2. For many families, choice is not the reason they have no children; they are infertile. Some adopt, while a few turn to new reproductive technologies.
E. A blended family is one whose members were once part of other families (two divorced persons marry, bringing children into a new family unit). Blended families are increasing in number. One in five Canadian children are not born into the "traditional" family of mother, father and joint children.
F. In 1989, Denmark was the first country to legalize marriage between people of the same sex. Since then, Netherlands, Norway, and Sweden have followed and done the same. In 1998, British Columbia became the first jurisdiction in North America to give same-sex couples the same privileges and obligations as opposite-sex couples (including custody, access, and child support). On July 12, 2002, the Ontario Superior Court ruled that the current legal definition of marriage is discriminatory and ordered it changed to include recognition of same sex marriages and in June 2005 the Canadian Federal Government fully recognized and legalized same sex unions. These changes reflect great social acceptance of the 34,200 same sex couples enumerated in the 2001 Census. Recent survey reports that almost half of Canadians approve of same sex marriages.
G. To overcome the loneliness and isolation that often accompanies the segmented relationships of contemporary society, many people form intentional families.

V.   **Trends in Canadian Families**

A. The average age of Canadian brides is older than at any time in the twentieth century.

B. Despite increases in the number of Canadians, the number of marriages declined to an all time low in 2000. There is also a marked reduction in fertility. Since the 1981 census—the first time the number of common-law families was counted—the numbers have increased by 200 percent.

C. The "sandwich generation" refers to people who find themselves sandwiched between two generations, responsible for the care of their children and for their own aging parents. The result can be considerable stress, but many are also satisfied and have a strengthened relationship with their elderly family members.

D. Divorce and Remarriage

1. Although many marriages end in divorce, most divorces end in remarriages, except in Quebec.

2. From Confederation until 1968, adultery was the only grounds for divorce.

3. After rising for a century, the Canadian divorce rate levelled off and has even declined; the rate today is lower than it was in 1980.

4. Men are more likely to remarry and remarry more quickly than women.

5. Women who possess very high levels of education and income are less likely to remarry than their less-educated, less well-to-do counterparts.

E. The number of children affected by divorce increased by 300 percent from the 1970s to the 1990s. Divorce profoundly affects a child's world.

1. The more frequently children experience disruptions (divorce, death) in the parental structure of the family, the less likely they are as adults to report that they had a very happy childhood.

2. The overwhelming majority of adult children of divorce (80 percent) indicate that their childhood experiences "strengthened their resolve to have lasting relationships" as adults.

3. After the reform of divorce laws in 1968, divorce rates kept going up until they peaked in 1987 and levelled off by 1997.

4. Today, about 38 percent of Canadians will divorce, but the rate varies across the country. Only 17 percent of Newfoundlanders, but 50 percent of Quebecers divorce.

VI.   **Two Sides of Family Life**

A. Child Abuse, battering, marital rape, and incest represent the dark side of family life.

1. Currently, we do not have statistics that capture the extent of child abuse across Canada. However, police statistics indicate that 61 percent of the sexual assaults reported to police were against children and 43 percent were perpetrated by a family member.

2. Thanks in large measure to Canada's landmark 1993 *Canadian Violence against Women* Survey, and now yearly family violence statistical profiles, we have good statistics on wife battering. In the survey, almost one in three women, who had ever married or lived in common-law relationships, revealed at least one episode of violence by husband or partner.

3. Incest is sexual relations between relatives, such as brothers and sisters or parents and children. It is most likely to occur in families that are socially isolated, and is more common than it previously was thought to be.
4. Also, sibling violence is very common.
5. Increased attention is paid to violence against men in intimate relationships.

B. There are a number of factors that help predict "lasting" marriages: being wealthy, religious, college-educated, and not living common-law before marriage. Further, research suggests that those who devote energy to maintaining their marriages will reap benefits in terms of the marital bond.

VII.   The Future of Marriage and Family

A. It is likely that cohabitation will increase, as will the age at first marriage, and the number of women joining the work force, with a resulting shift in marital power. Finally, more families will struggle with the twin demands of raising children and caring for aging parents.

KEY TERMS

After studying the chapter, review the definition for each of the following terms.

bilateral (system of descent): a system of reckoning descent that counts both the mother's and the father's side

blended family: a family whose members were once part of other families

conservative bias: see monolithic bias

egalitarian: authority more or less equally divided between people or groups, in this instance between husband and wife

endogamy: the practice of marrying within one's own group

exogamy: the practice of marrying outside one's group

extended family: a nuclear family plus other relatives, such as grandparents, uncles and aunts, who live together

family: two or more people who consider themselves related by blood, marriage, or adoption

family of orientation: the family in which a person grows up

family of procreation: the family formed when a couple's first child is born

homogamy: the tendency of people with similar characteristics to marry one another

household: all persons who occupy the same housing unit

incest: sexual relations between specified relatives, such as brothers and sisters or parents and children

intentional family: people who declare themselves a family and treat one another as members of the same family; originated in the late twentieth century in response to the need for intimacy not met due to distance, divorce, and death

marriage: a group's approved mating arrangements, usually marked by a ritual of some sort

matriarchy: authority vested in females; female control of a society or group

matrilineal (system of descent): a system of reckoning descent that counts only the mother's side

monolithic bias: this implies that the "normal" and "natural" family is composed of two heterosexual adults with their children.

monolithic structure: perception that there is only one type of family

nuclear family: a family consisting of a husband, wife, and child(ren)

patriarchy: authority vested in males; male control of a society or group

patrilineal (system of descent): a system of reckoning descent that counts only the father's side

polyandry: a marriage in which a woman has more than one husband

polygyny: a marriage in which a man has more than one wife

romantic love: feelings of erotic attraction accompanied by an idealization of the other

system of descent: how kinship is traced over the generations

KEY PEOPLE

Review the major theoretical contributions or findings of these people.

Jessie Bernard: Bernard studied marriages and concluded that husbands and wives have different conceptions of marriage, resulting in two marriages within every union.

Margrit Eichler: Eichler suggested that the sociological definition of the nuclear family supports a very limited view of family life.

Kathleen Gerson: Gerson found that there are different reasons why some couples choose not to have children—weak marriages, expenses associated with raising children, diminished career opportunities.

Arlie Hochschild: Hochschild conducted research on families in which both parents are employed full-time in order to find out how household tasks are divided up. She found that women did more of the housework than their husbands, resulting in women putting in a *second shift* at home after their workday has ended.

William Jankowiak and Edward Fischer: These anthropologists surveyed data on 166 societies and found that the majority of them contained the ideal of romantic love.

Jeanette and Robert Lauer: These sociologists interviewed 351 couples who had been married fifteen years or longer in order to find out what makes a marriage successful.

Meg Luxton: studied the movement of women into the paid labour force in Canada and the effects on the division of labour within the household

Janice Ristock: reports that lesbians, like straight women, may be subject to severe physical, verbal, and sexual abuse.

Lillian Rubin: Rubin also interviewed both career women and homemakers found that the notion of the "empty nest" as being a difficult time for women is largely a myth and that most women's satisfaction increased when the last child left home.

Diana Russell: Russell found that incest victims who experience the most difficulty are those who have been victimized the most often, over longer periods of time, and whose incest was "more intrusive."

SELF-TEST

After completing this self-test, check your answers against the Answer Key at the back of this Study Guide and against the text on page(s) indicated in parentheses.

MULTIPLE CHOICE QUESTIONS

1. Polyandry is: (268)
   a. a marriage in which a woman has more than one husband.
   b. a marriage in which a man has more than one wife.
   c. male control of a society or group.
   d. female control of a society or group.

2. Endogamy: (270)
   a. is the practice or marrying outside one's group.
   b. is the practice of marrying within one's own group.
   c. is the practice of marrying someone within one's own family.
   d. none of the above

3. In a matrilineal system: (270)
   a. descent is figured only on the mother's side.
   b. children are not considered related to their mother's relatives.
   c. descent is traced on both the mother's and the father's side.
   d. descent is figured only on the father's side.

4. The family of orientation: (270)
   a. is the family formed when a couple's first child is born.
   b. is the same thing as an extended family.
   c. is the same as the family of procreation.
   d. none of the above

5. According to functionalists, the family is universal because it: (271)
   a. serves no essential functions for modern society.
   b. serves certain essential functions in all societies.
   c. has very few functions left.
   d. is no longer universal.

6. The incest taboo: (271)
   a. is rules specifying the degrees of kinship that prohibit sex or marriage.
   b. helps families avoid role confusion.
   c. facilitates the socialization of children.
   d. all of the above

7. According to research findings, which of the following feels most threatened by doing housework, and consequently does the least? (274)
   a. Men who earn significantly more money than their wives.
   b. Men who earn about the same amount of money as their wives.
   c. Men who earn less money than their wives.
   d. Men who are employed in occupations that are highly sex-typed as masculine.

8. Meg Luxton and June Corman wrote an award-winning book: (275)

    a. Getting by in Hard Times
    b. Hired Hand
    c. The Working Man
    d. Getting Away from It All

9. Why do husbands and wives disagree on an answer to such a basic question as how frequently they have sex? (276)
    a. Men are embarrassed to say the real answer for fear of being viewed as inadequate.
    b. Husbands and wives have different perspectives on the motivation for love-making.
    c. Women don't want to say how much sex they have because they think it is socially inappropriate.
    d. Husbands and wives won't tell the truth because they don't trust the interviewer and don't know what the purpose of the research really is.

10. The tendency of people with similar characteristics to marry one another is: (277)
    a. propinquity.
    b. erotic selection.
    c. homogamy.
    d. heterogamy.

11. According to Lillian Rubin, when does a woman's marital satisfaction increase? (278)
    a. during the initial stages of child rearing
    b. when the last child leaves home
    c. prior to childbirth
    d. when the first child leaves home

12. In 2001, _____ percent of Canadian children aged six months to five years were in some form of child care. (278)
    a. 53
    b. 83
    c. 43
    d. 23

13. The increasing number of young adults who return home and who are continuing to live with their parents are called: (278)
    a. Bommerang kids.
    b. Hip Hop generation.
    c. walking disasters.
    d. none of the above

14. According to your text, which of the following contributes to family diversity in Canada: (279)
    a. language
    b. cultural beliefs
    c. cultural values
    d. all of the above

15. While individual lives vary, simply by reason of being a Native Canadian you are more likely to be: (280)
    a. in a low income category.
    b. more likely to commit suicide.
    c. less likely to have a high level of formal education.
    d. all of the above

16. Children from poor families are penalized in terms of: (280)
    a. physical health.
    b. mental health.
    c. social health.
    d. all of the above

17. According to 2001 census data, _____ percent of families made up of married couples having no children living at home. (281)
    a. 41
    b. 21
    c. 11
    d. 51

18. Sociologist Kathleen Gerson found that there were different reasons why couples choose not to have children. Which of the following is *not* one of the reasons identified by Gerson? (281)
    a. having children would limit their options in life
    b. diminishing career opportunities
    c. selfish and immature attitudes
    d. too expensive

19. A family whose members were once part of other families, sociologist call a: (281)
    a. reconstituted family.
    b. mixed family.
    c. blended family.
    d. multiple nuclei family.

20. With few exceptions, when picking a marriage partner the trend is to choose a person with: (277)
    a. similar education.
    b. similar ethnicity.
    c. similar age .
    d. all of the above

21. The "sandwich generation" refers to: (285)
    a. stay-at-home moms who spend their days making sandwiches for their preschoolers.
    b. people who are sandwiched between two sets of family relations because of the increase in divorce today.
    c. young children who consume a lot of sandwiches and whose needs are often overlooked by parents whose time is stretched by work and household responsibilities.
    d. people who find themselves caught between two generations, simultaneously responsible for the care of their children and their aging parents.

22. Only 31 percent of divorces involve custody orders, with _____ percent of primary custody arrangements being awarded mothers, _____ percent to fathers, and 42 percent joint custody: (286)
    a. 48, 10
    b. 10, 48
    c. 50, 50
    d. 25, 75

23. Research indicates that children growing up in lone-parent families: (287)
    a. have poorer scores in terms of academic achievement.
    b. have worse health.
    c. have poorer relationships.
    d. all of the above

24. According to research who are victims of incest who suffer most? (290)
    a. those victimized the longest.
    b. those victimized most often.
    c. whose incest was "more intrusive."
    d. all of the above

25. According to the author, what trend(s) are likely to continue into the next century? (290)
    a. increase in cohabitation
    b. increase in mother headed families
    c. increase in blended families
    d. all of the above

TRUE-FALSE QUESTIONS

T F 1. Polygyny is a marriage in which a man has more than one wife. (268)

T F 2. Most people in North America marry within their own "racial" group. (270)

T F 3. Families are people who live together in the same housing unit. (270)

T F 4. The popular vision of the nuclear family supports a very limited view of family life. (270)

T F 5. Functionalists believe that the incest taboo helps the family to avoid role confusion. (271)

T F 6. The closer the amounts of a husband's and wife's earnings, the more likely they are to share housework. (274)

T F 7. Bibby report shows that two thirds of Canadian wives with young children (under three years) are working for pay. (277)

T F 8. According to Arlie Hochschild men willingly take on household duties. (273)

T F 9. Symbolic interactionists have found that husbands and wives generally share the same meanings about their marriages. (276)

T F 10. Love and marriage channels include age, education, social class, race, and religion. (277)

T F 11. Most husbands who get laid off reduce their housework. (274)

T F 12. The burden of the second shift creates deep discontent in wives. (274)

T F   13.   Researchers have found that most husbands and wives experience the empty nest when their last child leaves home. (278)

T F   14.   Women are about as likely as men to face the problem of adjusting to widowhood. (278)

T F   15.   According to recent research, the majority of newlyweds now indicate intentions to remain childless. (281)

T F   16.   Two divorced people who marry and each bring their children into a new family unit become a blended family. (281)

T F   17.   Marriage between same-sex couples is legal in most countries, including Sweden. (282)

T F   18.   97 percent of Canadians in a recent survey indicated that they would agree or strongly agree that their marriages were happy or pretty happy. (290)

T F   19.   The "sandwich generation" are people who must care for both their parents and their children. (285)

T F   20.   At present we do not have statistics that capture the full extent of child abuse across Canada. (288)

FILL-IN QUESTIONS

1. A marriage in which a man has more than one wife is _____. (268)
2. _____ is the practice of marrying outside one's group. (270)
3. Female control of a society or group is a(n) _____. (270)
4. _____ is a group who consider themselves related by blood, marriage, or adoption. (270)
5. A(n) _____ is a family consisting of a husband, wife, and child(ren). (271)
6. Rules specifying the degrees of kinship that prohibit sex or marriage are _____. (289-290)
7. _____ is the tendency of people with similar characteristics to get married. (277)
8. A married couple's domestic situation after the last child has left home is sometimes referred to as the _____. (278)
9. A _____ may or may not be also a family. (270)
10. Historically _____ have intentionally blocked family formation among working-class Chinese, South Asian, and Japanese men and women, and more recently black Caribbean women. (280)
11. In 1998, British Columbia became the first jurisdiction in North America to grant custody, access and child support rights to _____. (282)
12. To overcome such problems as loneliness, some have started _____ families. (283)
13. The term _____ refers to people who find themselves caught between two generations and responsible for the care of both. (285)
14. From the time of Confederation until 1968, _____ was the only grounds for divorce in most of Canada. (286)
15. Sexual relations between specified relatives, such as brothers and sisters, or parents and children, is _____. (289)

MATCH THESE SOCIAL SCIENTISTS WITH THEIR CONTRIBUTIONS

__1.	Jessie Bernard	a.	*noted the existence of two marriages within one union*
__2.	Meg Luxton	b.	*found that women's satisfaction increased after last child moved out*
__3.	Kathleen Gerson	c.	*studied incest victims*
__4.	Margrit Eichler	d.	*identified reasons why couples choose to be child-free*
__5.	Lillian Rubin	e.	*suggested that the definition of the nuclear family supports a very limited view of family life*
__6.	Diana Russell	f.	*studied the gendered division of household labour*

ESSAY QUESTIONS

1. Consider the impact on families of the Reform of divorce laws in Canada in 1968 and later in 1985.
2. Explain the social forces that have contributed to the emergence of intentional families.
3. Discuss the impact that divorce has on family members—men, women, and children.

"DOWN-TO-EARTH SOCIOLOGY"

1. Consider what would be the pros and cons of polygyny and polyandry. (268)
2. Do you think that male resistance to household labour (274) is a temporary problem or a long-range problem in many families? How will you resolve problems such as this in your family?
3. After reading about high-tech reproductive technologies on page 281, what are your own views on the subject? Consider both the pluses (infertile couples are able to become parents) and the minuses (the ethical considerations, the costs of the procedures) and then develop a convincing argument in favour or opposition.

CHAPTER 14
EDUCATION AND RELIGION

CHAPTER SUMMARY

- Industrialized societies have become credential societies; employers use diplomas and degrees to determine who is eligible for jobs, even when these qualifications may be irrelevant to the particular work. Educational certification provides evidence of a person's ability.

- In earlier societies, education consisted of informal learning and was synonymous with acculturation. Today, education is no longer the same as informal acculturation, for the term now refers to a group's formal system of teaching knowledge, values, and skills.

- Functionalists emphasize the functions of education, including teaching knowledge and skills, transmitting cultural values, social integration, gatekeeping, and promoting personal and social change.

- Conflict theorists view education as a mechanism for maintaining social inequality and keeping people in line. Accordingly, they stress such matters as the way in which education reflects the social structure of society (the correspondence principle), unequal funding of schools, culturally biased IQ tests, tracking, and the hidden curriculum.

- Symbolic interactionists examine classroom interaction. They study how teacher expectations cause a self-fulfilling prophecy, producing the very behaviour the teacher is expecting. Labels are powerful. They can set people on courses of action that affect the rest of their lives.

- Problems facing the current Canadian educational system include cheating, illegal essay-writing services, grade inflation, social promotion, functional illiteracy, teen pregnancy, and violence in schools. Suggestions to improve Canadian education include implementing and maintaining a secure and safe learning environment, and reforms directed at the structure of the educational system. There are also questions regarding the intersection of race and education: many teachers and students have preconceived ideas about racial minorities.

- The sociological study of religion involves the analysis of the relationship between society and religion to gain insight into the role of religion in people's lives. For Durkheim, the key elements of religion are: beliefs separating the profane from the sacred, rituals, and a moral community.

- According to functionalists, religion meets basic human needs such as answering questions about ultimate meaning, providing emotional comfort, social solidarity, guidelines for everyday life, social control, adaptation, support for the government, and social change. Functionalists also believe religion has two main dysfunctions: war and religious persecution.

- Symbolic interactionists focus on how religious symbols communicate meaning and how ritual and beliefs unite people into a community.

- Conflict theorists see religion as a conservative force that serves the needs of the ruling class by reflecting and reinforcing social inequality.

- Unlike Marx, who asserted that religion impedes social change by encouraging people to focus on the afterlife, Weber saw religion as a powerful force for social change. He analyzed how Protestantism gave rise to an ethic that stimulated "the spirit of capitalism." The result was capitalism, which transformed society.

- The world's major religions include Judaism, Christianity, Islam, Hinduism, Buddhism, and Confucianism. Just as different religions have distinct teachings and practices, so within a religion different groups contrast sharply with one another.

- Sociologists have identified cults, sects, denominations, churches, and ecclesia as distinct types of religious organizations. Both cults and sects represent belief systems that are at odds with the prevailing beliefs and values of the broader society. If a sect grows, and its members make peace with the rest of society, it changes into a church. Ecclesiae, or state religions, are rare.

- Religion in Canada is characterized by diversity and a degree of continuity with the past. As well, Canadians differ dramatically from Americans in terms of those expressing no religious affiliation.

- Feminist spirituality in both Judaism and Christianity questions the male dominance of these religious traditions.

- There is little doubt that religion could last as long as humanity lasts, or until humans develop adequate functional alternatives.

LEARNING OBJECTIVES

As you read Chapter 14, use these learning objectives to organize your notes. After completing your reading, briefly state an answer to each of the objectives, and review the text pages in parentheses.

1. Explain why Canada has become a credential society. (294)
2. Describe the development of modern education. (294-295)
3. Discuss the beginning of universal education in Canada. (295-296)
4. List and briefly explain the manifest and latent functions of education. (296)
5. Explain how education maintains social inequality using the conflict perspective. (301)
6. Summarize symbolic interaction research regarding teacher expectations and the self-fulfilling prophecy. (305)
7. Identify the major problems that exist within Canadian education today and discuss solutions. (305-308)
8. Define religion and Durkheim's concepts of sacred and profane elements of religion. (309)
9. Discuss the functionalist view of religion, and list the functions and dysfunctions of religion as a social institution. (310)
10. Discuss the importance of rituals, symbols, and beliefs for the creation of a community. (311-312)
11. Describe the conflict perspective on religion. (312-313)
12. Describe the relationship Weber proposed between religion and capitalism. (314)
13. Describe the history and characteristics of the world's major religions. (314-316)
14. Describe the differences among types of religious groups (cult, sect, denomination, church, and ecclesia) and their relationships to the dominant culture. (316-318)
15. Describe the main characteristics of religion in Canada today. (318-319)
16. Discuss feminist themes in the sociological study of religion. (313)
17. On the basis of sociological knowledge, speculate on the future of religion in human societies. (319-320)

CHAPTER OUTLINE

I.   **Today's Credential Society**

A.   A credential society is one in which employers use diplomas and degrees to determine job eligibility. The sheer size, urbanization and consequent anonymity of Canadian society is a major reason why credentials are required. Diplomas/degrees often serve as sorting devices for employers; because they don't know the individual personally, they depend on schools to weed out the capable from the incapable.

B.   Without the right credentials, a person will not get hired despite the person's ability to do the job better than someone else.

II. **The Development of Modern Education**

A.   In earlier societies, education was synonymous with acculturation (transmission of culture from one generation to the next), not with a separate institution.

1.   In societies where a sufficient surplus developed, a separate institution arose. Some individuals devoted themselves to teaching, while those who had leisure became their students. Education gradually came to refer to a group's formal system of teaching knowledge, values, and skills.

2.   During the Dark Ages, only the monks and a handful of the wealthy nobility could read and write.

3.   Industrialization created a need for the average citizen to be able to read, write, and work with figures because of the new machinery and new types of jobs.

B.   The development of universal education in Canada was linked to the development of the industrial economy.

1.   Before Confederation (1867) it was religious groups that were the most involved in providing education. They used education to attempt to assimilate Native Canadians. Church influence over education ensured that guidance in Christian morality and obedience were taught.

2.   The development of universities was also connected to religious bodies, such as the Church of England.

3.   The beginnings of a system of universal education were entrenched by the time of Confederation. Education became a matter of political socialization.

4.   By 1920 most provinces had compulsory education laws that required children to attend school until they had either completed eighth grade or turned 16.

5.   As industrialization developed, graduating with a postsecondary certificate or degree has become more common.

6.   Those who do not complete high school experience higher rates of unemployment, lower earnings, and are less likely to hold secure jobs.

III. **The Functionalist Perspective: Providing Social Benefits**

A.   Manifest and latent functions of education include: (1) teaching knowledge and skills; (2) cultural transmission of values (individualism, competition, and patriotism); (3) individualism; (4) competition; (5) patriotism; (6) social integration; (7) gatekeeping; (8) mainstreaming (incorporating people with disabilities into regular social activities); and (9) assuming many functions previously fulfilled by the family (e.g., child care and sex education).

IV. **The Conflict Perspective: Reproducing the Social Class Structure**
  A. Conflict theorists see that the educational system is a tool used by those in the controlling sector of society to maintain their dominance.
  B. The hidden curriculum is unwritten rules of behaviour and attitude (e.g., obedience to authority, conformity to cultural norms) taught in school in addition to the formal curriculum. Education tends to reproduce the class structures.
  C. Conflict theorists criticize IQ (intelligence quotient) testing because it not only measures intelligence but also culturally acquired knowledge.
      1. The tests focus only on certain components of intelligence—mathematical, spatial, symbolic, and linguistic abilities—while ignoring others.
      2. Questions regarding who composes the test questions and how they are geared toward should be raised.
      3. Standardized testing neglects learning disabilities.
  D. Because public schools are largely financed by local property taxes, there are rich and poor school districts. Unequal funding stacks the deck against minorities and the poor.
  E. The correspondence principle is how schools correspond to (or reflect) the social structure of society. The educational system reinforces the status quo, because what is taught in a nation's schools corresponds to the characteristics of that society. Thus education perpetuates society's prevailing inequalities.
  F. Schools reproduce social class inequalities, as children of the wealthy are more likely to attend university than poorer students. The education system helps pass privilege (or lack thereof) across generations.

V. **The Symbolic Interaction Perspective: Teacher Expectations and the Self-Fulfilling Prophecy**
  A. Symbolic interactionists study face-to-face interaction inside the classroom. They have found that expectations of teachers are especially significant in determining what students learn.
  B. The Rist research (participant observation in an African-American grade school with an African-American faculty) found tracking begins with teachers' perceptions.
      1. After eight days, with social class as the underlying basis, teachers divided the class into fast, average, and slow learners; and seated them accordingly.
      2. Students from whom more was expected did the best; students in the slow group were ridiculed and they disengaged themselves from classroom activities.
      3. The labels applied in kindergarten tended to follow the child through school. What occurred was a self-fulfilling prophecy (Robert Merton's term for an originally false assertion that becomes true simply because it was predicted).
  C. The significance of Rist's research is that labels are powerful and can affect the rest of people's lives. Teachers shaped the experiences the students had within the classroom.
      1. Teachers' own middle-class background and racial attitudes influence their interactions with students.

VI.   Rethinking Schools: Problems and Solutions

    A.   A variety of factors have been identified as the major problems facing the Canadian educational system today. These problems include: cheating and illegal essay-writing services; grade inflation, and how it relates to social promotion and functional illiteracy; and violence in schools.

       A number of solutions have been offered to address these problems, including implementing and maintaining a secure and safe learning environment and programs to prevent students from committing the "offensive" behaviour in the first place.

VII.   What Is Religion?

    A.   According to Durkheim, religion is the beliefs/practices separating the profane from the sacred, uniting the adherents into a moral community. Sacred refers to aspects of life having to do with the supernatural that inspire awe, reverence, deep respect, or deep fear. Profane refers to the ordinary aspects of everyday life. Durkheim defined religion by three elements: (1) beliefs that some things are sacred (forbidden, set off from the profane); (2) practices (rituals) concerning things considered sacred; (3) a moral community (a church) resulting from a group's beliefs and practices.

VIII.   The Functionalist Perspective

    A.   Religion performs certain functions: (1) answering questions about ultimate meaning (the purpose of life, why people suffer); and existence of after life; (2) providing emotional comfort; (3) uniting believers into a community that shares values and perspectives; (4) providing guidelines for life; (5) controlling behaviour; (6) helping people adapt to new environments; (7) providing support for the government; and (8) spearheading social change on occasion (as the formation of the Cooperative Commonwealth Federation that led the New Democratic Party.

    B.   War and religious persecution are dysfunctions of religion.

IX.   The Symbolic Interactionist Perspective

    A.   Religions use symbols to provide identity and social solidarity for members. For members, these are not ordinary symbols, but sacred symbols evoking awe and reverence, which become a condensed way of communicating with others.

    B.   Rituals are ceremonies or repetitive practices helping unite people into a moral community by creating a feeling of closeness with God and unity with one another.

    C.   Symbols, including rituals, develop from beliefs. A belief may be vague ("God is") or specific ("God wants us to prostrate ourselves and face Mecca five times each day."). Religious beliefs not only include values (what is considered good and desirable) but also a cosmology (unified picture of the world).

    D.   Shared meanings that come through symbols, rituals, and beliefs unite people into a moral community, which is powerful. It provides the basis for mutual identity and establishes norms that govern the behaviour of members. Not only are members bound together by shared beliefs and rituals, but they are also separated from those who do not share their symbolic world.

X.   The Conflict Perspective
   A. Conflict theorists are highly critical of religion. Karl Marx called religion the "opium of the people" because he believed that the workers escape into religion. He argued that religion diverts the energies of the oppressed from changing their circumstances because believers focus on the happiness they will have in the coming world rather than on their suffering in this world.
   B. Religious teachings and practices reflect a society's inequalities. Gender inequalities are an example: when males completely dominated Canadian society, women's roles in churches and synagogues were limited to "feminine" activities, a condition which is beginning to change.
   C. Religion legitimates social inequality; it reflects the interests of those in power by teaching that the existing social arrangements of a society represent what God desires.

XI.   The Feminist Perspective
   There are four main categories of feminists:
   A. Revisionists who believe that the basic message of the major religions is liberating.
   B. Reformists who advocate revealing the "liberating core" of religious teachings with female imagery.
   C. Revolutionaries who seek to change the established orthodoxy by importing language, images, and rituals from other traditions.
   D. Rejectionists who judge the traditional teachings to be hopelessly sexist and have abandoned them in order to establish a new spiritual tradition.
   E. Postmodernism extols the intrinsic worth of socially contextualized individual experience, spirituality, and cultural diversity.

XII.   Religion and the Spirit of Capitalism
   A. Weber saw religion as a force for social change, observing that European countries industrialized under capitalism. Thus, religion held the key to modernization (transformation of traditional societies into industrial societies).
   B. Weber concluded that:
      1. The spirit of capitalism (desire to accumulate capital as a duty, as an end in itself) was a radical departure from the past.
      2. Religion (including a Calvinistic belief in predestination and the need for reassurance as to one's fate) is the key to why the spirit of capitalism developed in Europe.
      3. A change in religion (from Catholicism to Protestantism) led to a change in thought and behaviour (the Protestant ethic), which resulted in the "spirit of capitalism."
   C. Today the spirit of capitalism and the Protestant ethic are by no means limited to Protestants; they have become cultural traits that have spread throughout the world.

XIII.   The World's Major Religions
   A. The founding of Judaism marked a fundamental change in religion, in that it was the first religion based on monotheism, the belief in only one God.

1. Contemporary Judaism has three main branches: Orthodox (adheres to the laws espoused by Moses), Reform (more liberal, uses the vernacular in religious ceremonies, and has reduced much of the ritual); and Conservative (falling somewhere between).
2. The history of Judaism is marked by conflict and persecution (anti-Semitism).

B. Christianity developed out of Judaism and is based on the belief that Christ is the Messiah God promised the Jews.
   1. During the first 1,000 years of Christianity, there was only one church organization, directed from Rome; during the eleventh century, Greek Orthodoxy was established.
   2. Although Martin Luther's original goal was to reform the Roman Catholic church, the Protestant Reformation of the sixteenth century began the splintering of Christianity, today divided into hundreds of groups.

C. Islam (whose followers are known as Muslims) began in the same part of the world as Judaism and Christianity; Islam is the world's third monotheistic religion.
   1. The founder, Muhammad, established a theocracy, a government based on God being the ruler, his laws the statutes of the land, and priests his earthly administrators, and founded the Muslim empire. His teachings were written in the Koran.
   2. After Muhammad's death, a struggle for control over the empire split Islam into two branches that remain today: the Shi'ite which is more conservative and inclined to fundamentalism (the belief that true religion is threatened by modernism and that faith as it was originally practiced should be restored), and the Sunni which is generally more liberal.

D. Hinduism, the chief religion of India, goes back about 4,000 years, but has no specific founder or canonical scripture (texts thought to be inspired by God). Instead several books expound on the moral qualities people should strive to attain.
   1. Hindus are polytheists (believe there are many gods) and believe in reincarnation, a cycle of life, death, and rebirth.

E. About 600 B.C., Siddhartha Gautama founded Buddhism, which emphasizes self-denial and compassion.
   1. Buddhism spread rapidly into many parts of Asia. Today it flourishes in Sri Lanka, Myanmar, Tibet, Laos, Cambodia, Thailand, China, Korea, and Japan.

F. Confucius (China 551-479 B.C.) urged social reform and developed a system of morality based on peace, justice, and universal order. His teachings were incorporated into writings called the Analects.
   1. The basic moral principle of Confucianism is to maintain *jen* (sympathy or concern for other humans). The basic principle is to treat those who are subordinate to you as you would like to be treated by those superior to you.
   2. He taught that right relationships within the family (loyalty, respect) should be the model for society.

XIV. Types of Religious Groups
A. A cult is a new religion with few followers, whose teachings and practices put it at odds with the dominant culture and religion.

      1. All religions began as cults. Cults often begin with the appearance of a charismatic leader (exerting extraordinary appeal to a group of followers).
      2. Each cult meets with rejection from society.
      3. The cult demands intense commitment, and its followers confront a hostile world.
      4. Although most cults ultimately fail because they are unable to attract a large enough following, some succeed and make history.

B. A sect is larger than a cult. Its members still feel a fair amount of tension with the prevailing beliefs and values of the broader society.
      1. Like cults, sects also stress evangelism, the active recruitment of new members.
      2. If a sect grows, its members tend to become respectable in the eyes of society, and the sect changes into institutionalized religion.

C. Institiutional religion, a highly organized religious group with formal, sedate services and less emphasis on personal conversion. The religious group is highly bureaucratized (including national and international offices that give directions to local congregations). Most new members come from within the church, from children born to existing members, rather than from outside recruitment.

D. An ecclesia is a religious group so integrated into the dominant culture that it is difficult to tell where one begins and the other leaves off.
      1. Ecclesiae are also called state religions. The government and religion work together to try to shape the society.

E. Not all religions go through all stages, although all religions began as cults, not all varieties of a religion have done so.
      1. Some die out because they fail to attract members; some remain sects. Few become ecclesia.
      2. A denomination is a "brand name" within a major religion (e. g., Methodist).

F. Three major patterns of adaptation occur when religion and the culture in which it is embedded find themselves in conflict.
      1. Members of a religion may reject the dominant culture and withdraw from it socially, although they continue to live in the same geographic area.
      2. A cult or sect rejects only specific elements of the prevailing culture.
      3. The society rejects the religious group entirely, and may even try to destroy it.

XV. Characteristics of Religion in Canada

A. Religion in Canada is very diverse and changing, but reflects a degree of continuity with the past.
      1. Canada has been, historically, predominantly Christian. The population has been divided between Protestants, living outside Quebec, and Roman Catholics, living within Quebec.
      2. The only religious groups that have grown significantly in recent years are the eastern non-Christian religions of Islam, Hinduism, and Buddhism.
      3. Since the 1961 census, the number of Canadians reporting "no religion" has increased dramatically. Since the post-World War II period, attendance at religious services has dropped. Nonetheless, a vast majority still indicate a belief in God.

XVI.   The Future of Religion
   A.   Marx was convinced religion would crumble when the workers threw off the chains of oppression; however, after communist countries were established (and despite persecution) people continued to be religious.
   B.   Neither science nor political systems can replace religion, and religion will last as long as humanity lasts.

KEY TERMS

After studying the chapter, review the definition for each of the following terms.

acculturation: the transmission of culture from one generation to the next

anti-Semitism: prejudice, discrimination, and persecution directed against Jews

charismatic leader: literally, someone to whom God has given a gift; more commonly, someone who exerts extraordinary appeal to a group of followers

correspondence principle: the sociological principle that schools correspond to (or reflect) the social structure of society

cosmology: teachings or ideas that provide a unified picture of the world

credential society: the use of diplomas and degrees to determine who is eligible for jobs, even though the diploma or degree may be irrelevant to the actual work

cult: a new religion with few followers, whose teachings and practices put it at odds with the dominant culture and religion

cultural transmission: in reference to education, the ways in which schools transmit a society's culture especially its core values

denomination: a "brand name" within a major religion, for example, Methodist or Baptist

ecclesia: a religious group so integrated into the dominant culture that it is difficult to tell where the one begins and the other leaves off; also called a *state religion*

education: a formal system of teaching knowledge, values, and skills

evangelism: an attempt to win converts

fundamentalism: the belief that true religion is threatened by modernism and that the faith as it was originally practiced should be restored

gatekeeping: the process by which education opens and closes doors of opportunity; another term for the social placement function of education

hidden curriculum: the unwritten goals of schools, such as obedience to authority and conformity to cultural norms

institutionalized religion: highly bureaucratized sect with rules, controlled finances and more

latent functions: unintended consequences of people's actions

mainstreaming: helping people to become part of the mainstream of society

manifest functions: intended consequences of people's actions

modernization: the transformation of traditional societies into industrial societies

monotheism: the belief that there is only one God

moral community: simply a group of people united by their religious practices

political socialization: the way young people are inculcated with beliefs, ideas, and values to ensure they embrace the civil order

profane: Durkheim's term for common elements of everyday life

Protestant ethic: Weber's term to describe the ideal of a self-denying, highly moral life, accompanied by hard work and frugality

reformists: liberating religious teachings with female imagery and sex-neutral language

reincarnation: in Hinduism and Buddhism, the return of the soul after death in a different form

rejectionists: are feminists who judge the traditional teachings to be hopelessly sexist.

religion: is defined by beliefs, practices, and a moral community; according to Durkheim beliefs and practices that separate the profane from the sacred and unite adherents into a moral community

revisionists: believe that the basic message of the major religions is liberating.

revolutionaries: seek to change the established orthodoxy (language, images, rituals)

rituals: ceremonies or repetitive practices; in this context, religious observances or rites often intended to evoke a sense of awe of the sacred

sacred: Durkheim's term for things set apart or forbidden, that inspire fear, awe, reverence, or deep respect

sect: a group larger than a cult that still feels substantial hostility from and toward society

self-fulfilling prophecy: Robert Merton's term for an originally false assertion that becomes true simply because it was predicted

social placement: a function of education that funnels people into a society's various positions

spirit of capitalism: Weber's term for the desire to accumulate capital as a duty—not to spend it, but as an end in itself—and to constantly reinvest it

tracking: the sorting of students into different educational programs on the basis of real or perceived abilities

values: what is considered good and desirable—how we ought to live

KEY PEOPLE

Review the major theoretical contributions or findings of these people.

Samuel Bowles and Herbert Gintis: Bowles and Gintis used the term correspondence principle to refer to the ways in which schools reflect the social structure of society.

Randall Collins: Collins studied the credential society.

Kingsley Davis and Wilbert Moore: Davis and Moore argue that a major task of society is to fill social positions with capable people and that one of the functions of schools is gatekeeping — the funnelling of people into these positions based on merit.

Emile Durkheim: Durkheim investigated world religions and identified elements that are common to all religions—separation of sacred from profane, beliefs about what is sacred, practices surrounding the sacred, and a moral community.

Harry Gracey: Gracey conducted a participant observation study of kindergarten and concluded that the purpose of kindergarten is to socialize students into the student role. He referred to kindergarten as a boot camp.

Donald Hayes and Loreen Woller: state that "dumbed down" textbooks and less reading by students cause smaller vocabulary and less rigour in thought and verbal expression.

John Hostetler: Hostetler is known for his research and writings on the Amish.

Benton Johnson: Johnson analyzed types of religious groups—cults, sects, churches, and ecclesiae.

William Kephart and William Zellner: These sociologists also investigated the Amish religion and way of life.

Karl Marx: Marx was critical of religion, calling it the opium of the masses.

Robert Merton: Merton coined the expression "self-fulfilling prophecy" to refer to an originally false assumption of what is going to happen that comes true simply because it is predicted.

Randle Nelsen: argues today's education in schools is infused with popular culture and is "edu-tainment."

Talcott Parsons: Another functionalist who suggested that a function of schools is to funnel people into social positions.

Liston Pope: Another sociologist who studied types of religious groups.

Ray Rist: This sociologist's classic study of an African-American grade school uncovered some of the dynamics of educational tracking.

Johanna Stuckey: Stuckey outlined four main categories of the feminist study of spirituality: revisionists, reformists, revolutionaries, and rejectionists.

Ernst Troeltsch: Yet another sociologist who is associated with types of religious groups from cults to eccelsiae.

Max Weber: Weber studied the link between Protestantism and the rise of capitalism, and found that the ethic associated with Protestant denominations was compatible with the early needs of capitalism.

SELF-TEST

After completing this self-test, check your answers against the Answer Key at the back of this Study Guide and against the text on page(s) indicated in parentheses.

MULTIPLE CHOICE QUESTIONS

1. Using diplomas to hire employees, even when diplomas are irrelevant to the work, is: (294)
   a. a credential society.
   b. a certification mill.
   c. employer discretion in hiring.
   d. none of the above

2. In earlier societies: (294)
   a. there was no separate social institution called education.
   b. education was synonymous with acculturation.
   c. persons who already possessed certain skills taught them to others.
   d. all of the above

3. Education: (294-296)
   a. is a formal system of teaching knowledge, values, and skills.
   b. is the same as informal acculturation.
   c. is very similar in countries throughout the world.
   d. all of the above

4. According to functionalists, all of the following are functions of education, *except*: (296-298)
   a. maintaining social inequality.
   b. transmitting cultural values.
   c. helping to mould students into a more or less cohesive unit.
   d. teaching patriotism.

5. The function of education that sorts people into various positions on the basis of merit is: (300)
   a. functional placement.
   b. social placement.
   c. railroading .
   d. social promotion.

6. The hidden curriculum refers to: (301)
   a. the extra curriculum costs that are buried in school budgets.
   b. the lessons that teachers hide from the eyes of prying school boards.
   c. the unwritten rules of behaviour and attitudes that are taught in school.
   d. all of the above

7. Public schools are largely supported by: (303)
   a. provincial funding.
   b. federal funding.
   c. local property taxes.
   d. none of the above

8. The ways in which schools correspond to, or reflect, the social structure of society is: (304)
   a. the reproduction of social class.
   b. the correspondence principle.
   c. the status quo quotient.
   d. the status maintenance process.

9. From a conflict perspective, the real purpose of education is to: (304)
   a. reproduce existing social inequalities.
   b. provide educational opportunities for students from all types of backgrounds.
   c. teach patriotism, teamwork, and cooperation.
   d. replace family functions which most families no longer fulfill.

10. Teacher expectations and the self-fulfilling prophecy are of interest to _____ theorists. (304-305)
    a. functionalist
    b. conflict
    c. symbolic interaction
    d. educational

11. Ray Rist found that _____ was the underlying basis for assigning children to different tables in a kindergarten classroom. (305)

    a. ability
    b. maturity level
    c. social class
    d. gender

12. A self-fulfilling prophecy: (305)
    a. is an originally false assertion that becomes true simply because it was predicted.
    b. is an originally true assertion that becomes false because a person decides to prove that the label is incorrect.
    c. is a term coined by Ray Rist.
    d. all of the above

13. When compared to grades of forty years ago, today's grades: (306)
    a. are lower.
    b. are higher.
    c. have remained about the same.
    d. none of the above

14. High school graduates who have difficulty with basic reading and writing are known as: (307)
    a. "boneheads."
    b. functional literates.
    c. functional illiterates.
    d. underachievers.

15. What was Durkheim's purpose in writing *The Elementary Forms of the Religious Life*? (309)
    a. He wanted to explain the development of Protestantism.
    b. He set out to chart the history of world religions.
    c. He wanted to study the development of religion from sect to church.
    d. He wanted to identify elements common to all religions.

16. According to Durkheim, a moral community: (310)
    a. is a large, highly organized religious group.
    b. has little emphasis on personal conversion.
    c. is a group of people united by their religious practices.
    d. all of the above

17. All of the following are functions of religion, *except*: (310)
    a. encouraging wars for holy causes
    b. support for the government
    c. social change
    d. social control

18. War and religious persecution are: (310)
    a. manifest functions of religion.
    b. latent functions of religion.
    c. dysfunctions of religion.
    d. functional equivalents of religion.

19. Religion is the opium of the people according to some: (312)
    a. conservatives.
    b. functionalists.
    c. conflict theorists.
    d. all of the above

20. Weber believed that religion held the key to: (314)
    a. modernization.
    b. bureaucratization.
    c. institutionalization.
    d. socialization.

21. The spirit of capitalism is: (314)
    a. the desire to accumulate capital so one can spend it to show how one "has it made."
    b. Marx's term for the driving force in the exploitation of workers.
    c. to accumulate money (capital) as an end in itself and to consider it a duty to invest money in order to make a profit..
    d. none of the above

22. Polytheism is the belief: (315)
    a. that God is a woman.
    b. that there is only one God.
    c. that there are many gods.
    d. that God does not exist.

23. What is the essence of feminist/female religiosity? (313)
    a. commitment to diversity
    b. recognition that the spiritual is deeply personal
    c. Women have been neglected in religious studies.
    d. all of the above

24. The religion with no specific founder is: (315)
    a. Islam.
    b. Hinduism.
    c. Buddhism.
    d. Confucianism.

25. Islam, whose followers are known as _____ , began in the same part of the world as Judaism and Christianity: (315)
    a. Hindus.
    b. Muslims.
    c. Confucians.
    d. none of the above

26. A cult: (317)
    a. is a new religion with few followers.
    b. has teachings and practices which put it at odds with the dominant culture.
    c. often is at odds with other religions.
    d. all of the above

27. Although larger than a cult, a _____ still feels substantial hostility from society. (317)
    a. commune
    b. ecclesia
    c. sect
    d. church

28. In Canada, the only religious group that grew in any significant degree between 1986 and 1996 was: (319)
    a. Eastern non-Christian religions.
    b. Christians.
    c. Atheists.
    d. those who believe in God but don't attend church.

TRUE-FALSE QUESTIONS

T F   1.   Canada is a credential society. (294)
T F   2.   In earlier societies there was a separate social institution called education. (294)
T F   3.   By 1920, most Canadian provinces had compulsory education laws. (295)
T F   4.   The rates of high school graduation are approximately equal across the provinces. (296)
T F   5.   Education's most obvious manifest function is to teach knowledge and skills. (296)
T F   6.   Canadian schools discourage individualism and encourage teamwork. (297)
T F   7.   Students everywhere are taught that their country is the best country in the world. (297)
T F   8.   Parental influence is strong enough to challenge the influence of peer culture when it comes to moulding students' appearance, ideas, speech patterns, and interactions with the opposite sex. (299)
T F   9.   Functional theorists believe that social placement is harmful to society. (300)
T F   10. Bullying is considered a serious problem. (299)
T F   11. Greater percentage of the population age over 35 in the relatively richer provinces have university degrees. (303)

T F 12. According to conflict theorists, unequal funding for education automatically stacks the deck against children from lower income families. (303)

T F 13. The correspondence principle states that schools correspond to the social structure of society. (304)

T F 14. Research by Ray Rist concluded that the child's journey through school was preordained by the end of the first year of kindergarten. (305)

T F 15. Teacher expectations of student ability are not related to the class background of teachers or students. (305)

T F 16. The goal of the sociological study of religion is to determine which religions are most effective in people's lives. (309)

T F 17. According to Durkheim, all religions separate the sacred from the profane. (309)

T F 18. Functionalists believe that religion is universal because it meets basic human needs. (310)

T F 19. The Crusades are an example of the dysfunctions of religion. (310)

T F 20. Karl Marx believed that religion is the opium of the people. (312)

T F 21. Conflict theorists believe that religion reduces social inequalities and social conflict. (312)

T F 22. Emile Durkheim wrote The Protestant Ethic and the Spirit of Capitalism. (314)

T F 23. Contemporary Judaism comprises two main branches. (314)

T F 24. Fundamentalism is the belief that modernism threatens religion and that the faith as it was originally practiced should be restored. (315)

T F 25. The Northwest Territories do not have a university. (303)

T F 26. Feminist spirituality is a recent development within second-wave feminism. (313)

T F 27. Unlike cults, sects do not stress evangelism. (317)

T F 28. Islam in Iran and Iraq is an example of ecclesia. (318)

T F 29. In Canada, the incidence of those reporting "no religion" has not changed over the past four decades. (319)

T F 30. Feminist approaches to spirituality advocate for a maintenance of women's traditional roles within religious traditions. (313)

FILL-IN QUESTIONS

1. Using diplomas and degrees to determine eligibility for jobs occurs in a _____. (294)

2. _____ is the transmission of culture from one generation to the next. (294)

3. A formal system of teaching knowledge, values, and skills is the definition for _____. (294-295)

4. Tracking and social placement both contribute to the _____ function of education. (300)

5. A new function of education today is _____, incorporating people with disabilities into regular social activities. (300)

6. The unwritten rules of behaviour and attitude, such as obedience to authority and conformity to cultural norms, are referred to as the _____. (301)

7. _____ theorists believe that culturally biased IQ tests favour the middle classes and discriminate against minorities and students from lower-class backgrounds. (302)

8. The idea that schools reflect the social structure of society is the _____. (304)
9. _____ theorists found that the expectations of teachers are especially significant for determining what students learn. (305)
10. _____ refers to the trend of giving higher grades for the same work, so that there is a general rise in student grades despite the fact that learning may be declining. (306-307)
11. It is not uncommon today for schools to practise _____, which involves passing students to the next grade even though they have not mastered basic material. (306)
12. Someone who has graduated from high school but still has difficulties with reading and writing is considered _____. (307)
13. Durkheim's term for common elements of everyday life was _____. (309)
14. Answering questions about ultimate meaning, providing emotional comfort, and uniting believers into a community are _____ of religion. (310)
15. Ceremonies or repetitive practices that help unite people into a moral community are_____ (311-312)
16. _____ is teachings or ideas that provide a unified picture of the world. (312)
17. According to conflict theorists, religion is the _____. (312)
18. _____ is Weber's term to describe the ideal of a highly moral life, hard work, industriousness, and frugality. (314)
19. The belief that there is only one God is _____. (314)
20. Hindus are _____, believing there are many gods. (315)
21. _____ is the belief that true religion is threatened by modernism and that the faith as it originally was practised should be restored. (315)
22. A(n) _____ is someone who exerts extraordinary appeal to a group of followers. (316)
23. A group larger than a cult that still feels substantial hostility from and toward society is a(n) _____. (317)
24. A(n) _____ is a religious group so integrated into the dominant culture that it is difficult to tell where the one begins and the other leaves off. (318)
25. Within the categories of feminist spirituality, _____ seek to change the established orthodoxy by importing language, images, and rituals from other traditions. (313)

MATCH THESE SOCIAL SCIENTISTS WITH THEIR CONTRIBUTIONS

___1.	Randall Collins	a.	*gatekeeping sorts people on the basis of merit*
___2.	Bowles and Gintis	b.	*credential society*
___3.	Ray Rist	c.	*correspondence principle*
___4.	Karl Marx	d.	*tracking and expectations of kindergarten teachers*
___5.	Harry Gracey	e.	*kindergarten as boot camp*
___6.	Davis and Moore	f.	*cult-sect-church-ecclesia typology*
___7.	George Farkas	g.	*students are rewarded for signals they send teachers*
___8.	Emile Durkheim	h.	*The Protestant Ethic and the Spirit of Capitalism*
___9.	Johanna Stuckey	i.	*"religion is the opium of the people"*
___10.	Max Weber	j.	*The Elementary Forms of Religious Life*
___11	John Hostetler	k.	*outlined four categories of feminist spirituality*
___12.	Ernst Troeltsch	l.	*studied "shunning"*

ESSAY QUESTIONS

1. Explain the link between democracy, industrialization and universal education.
2. Select one of the three perspectives and design a research project to test the claims of that perspective about the nature of education.
3. Assume that you have been asked to make a presentation about religion to a group of people who have absolutely no idea what religion is. Prepare a speech in which you define religion and explain why it exists.
4. Which element defines religion?

"DOWN-TO-EARTH SOCIOLOGY"

1. After reading "Kindergarten as Boot Camp" (302), do you agree with Harry Gracey's ideas? Did you attend kindergarten? If so, which experiences do you remember the most vividly? Do you think it would be accurate to refer to college as a "boot camp"?
2. Have you ever been involved in a distance learning course like the ones described on page 306? If you have, what aspects of the course did you like? What aspects did you dislike? What changes would have improved the course? In what ways might distance learning change the way in which education is organized and instruction is delivered? Thinking about the different sociological perspectives on education, analyze how each might "see" this new development in terms of addressing problems as well as creating new problems.
3. After reading this chapter, and particularly the box on Heaven's Gate (317), do you understand why some people are attracted to cults and willing to give their lives for them? Why do you think cults rise up at certain points in history—like the 1970s and the 1990s? What is going on in society that would make them especially attractive?
4. What explanations are provided by the functionalist, symbolic interactionist, conflict, and feminist perspectives for the existence of religion in society?

CHAPTER 15
MEDICINE: HEALTH AND ILLNESS IN CANADA

CHAPTER SUMMARY

- Sociologists study medicine as a profession, a bureaucracy, and publicly funded social institution. In the midst of our publicly funded, universally accessible medicare system in Canada stands the Health-Industrial Complex, comprised of pharmaceutical industries, the private health insurance companies, the privately operated home care and many non-profit industries that extend over the health and medicine sector of our economy. Sociologists study how this important sector of our society is influenced by our ideas of self-regulation, bureaucratic structure and public policy. Sociologists also study the social construction of illness and health.

- Symbolic interactionists view health and illness as intimately related to cultural beliefs and practices; definitions of illness vary from one group to the next. Functionalists study the sick role and the ways in which the rules governing this role excuse people from normal responsibilities but obligate them to get well in order to resume those responsibilities. The conflict perspective stresses that health care is one of the scarce resources over which groups compete.

- The primary focus of feminist theorists is how sexism pervades our social institutions and social life. Here is how sexism works in medicine and health: bias against women's reproductive organs; male dominance in medicine; gender differences in the experience.

- Historical patterns of health and illness and patterns of mental health are profiled.

- In Canada, universal government-funded medical, hospital and health insurance has been available since 1971. The purpose of the national health system is to eliminate financial barriers to health care. The Canada Health Act was enacted in 1984, setting out provisions for national standards. The Act outlines five basic criteria: comprehensive scope, universal coverage, public administration, portability, and accessibility.

- Current issues in medical and health care include depersonalization, sexism, gendered differences in experiences of health and illness, the medicalization of society, and questions related to medically assisted suicide.

- Major threats to health today include AIDS, the globalization of disease, smoking, alcohol abuse, and disabling environments.

- Alternatives to the current health-care system include individuals taking more responsibility for their health and a fundamental shift in the medical establishment toward "wellness" and preventive medicine.

LEARNING OBJECTIVES

As you read Chapter 15, use these learning objectives to organize your notes. After completing your reading, briefly state an answer to each of the objectives, and review the text pages in parentheses.

1. Define the sociological perspective in studying medicine. (325)
2. Discuss the symbolic interactionist perspective on the role of culture in defining health and illness. (325)
3. Explain the components of health. (325)

4. Identify the functionalist perspective on the purpose of the sick role and explain why everyone is not given the same right to claim this role. (325-326)
5. Consider the conflict perspective on consequences of global stratification in terms of health, illness, and access to medical treatment. (326)
6. Consider the feminist perspective on health; how does sexism pervade health care and medicine (327)
7. Answer the question, "Were Canadians healthier in the past?" (329-331, 334)
8. Outline and briefly explain the major issues in Canadian health and health care. (329-334)
9. Discuss these threats to health: AIDS, drugs, and disabling environments. (334)
10. Analyze the prospects for change in medicine which might be possible through preventive medicine. (337)

CHAPTER OUTLINE

I. **Sociology and the Study of Medicine**
   A. Medicine is a society's standard way of dealing with illness and injury. In Canada, medicine is a profession, a bureaucracy, and a publicly funded institution.
   B. Sociologists study how medicine is influenced by ideals of professional self-regulation, the bureaucratic structure, and the profit motive; they also are interested in how illness and health are related to cultural beliefs, lifestyle, and social class.

II. **The Symbolic Interactionist Perspective**
   A. Health is affected by cultural beliefs. In Western culture a person who hears voices and sees visions might be locked up; in a tribal society, such an individual might be a shaman, the healing specialist who attempts to control the spirits thought to cause a disease or injury.
   B. Health is a human condition measured by three components: physical, mental, and social. The consideration of feminist and postmodernist views a fourth, "spiritual" component is added. What makes someone healthy varies from culture to culture. Sociologists analyze the effects that people's ideas of health and illness have on their lives and even how people determine that they are sick.

III. **The Functionalist Perspective**
   A. Functionalists point out that societies must set up ways to control sickness. They develop a system of medical care as well as make rules to keep too many people from "being sick."
   B. The sick role is a social role that you are forced to play when you are not well.
      1. It has four elements—you are not held responsible for being sick, you are exempt from normal responsibilities, you don't like the role, and you will get help so you can return to your usual routines. People who don't seek competent help are considered responsible for being sick and can not claim sympathy from others.
      2. Often there is ambiguity between the well role and the sick role; a decision to claim the sick role typically is more of a social than a physical matter.
      3. Parents and physicians are the primary gatekeepers to the sick role. They mediate between our feelings of our illness and our claim to being sick.

IV.   The Conflict Perspective

    A. The primary focus of conflict theorists is the struggle over scarce resources, including medical treatment.

    B. One consequence of global domination by the Developed Industrialized Nations is the international stratification of medical care.

        1. The Least Industrialized Nations cannot afford the same life-saving technology available in highly industrialized nations. Differences in life expectancy and infant mortality rates illustrate the consequences of global stratification.

        2. Global stratification even changes the face of diseases. People living in the Least Industrialized Nations located in the tropics face illness and death from four major sources: malaria, internal parasites, diarrhea, and malnutrition.

V.   The Feminist Perspective

    A. The primary focus of feminist theorists is how sexism pervades our social institutions and social life; this includes how sexism works in medicine and health.

VI.   Historical Patterns of Health

    A. Epidemiology is the study of the distribution of medical disorders throughout a population; it provides answers about patterns of health and illness over time.

    B. Were Canadians healthier in the past? If being healthier is measured by life span, then Canadians are healthier than their ancestors.

    C. When it comes to mental health, no rational basis for comparisons exists, since we do not even know how extensive mental illness is today.

VII.   Issues in Health Care

    A. The provision of health care in Canada is a provincial responsibility; however, the federal government has played a major role in providing funding.

        1. Universal government-funded health care has been available since 1971. The purpose of universal health care is to eliminate financial barriers to health care.

        2. Physicians are reimbursed on a fee-for-service basis; but these fees are determined by province-wide, negotiated uniform fee schedules.

        3. Private insurance companies offer coverage only for additional services not covered by federal funding.

        4. The Canada Health Act was introduced in 1984 to ensure that health services would be available to all Canadians. The Act sets out national standards for health care based on five basic criteria: comprehensive scope, universal coverage, public administration, portability, and accessibility.

    B. The sociology of health in Canada has passed through at least two major stages, the first focusing on issues related to the complexity of the health care system, and the second on issues such as the impact of population aging on the provision of health care.

        1. Research in the field of health care has used large surveys to determine the health status of Canadians.

    2. The ongoing longitudinal National Population Health Survey has examined the causal links between social status and heath status, with a specific focus on factors such as socioeconomic status, gender, age, and ethnicity.

C. Depersonalization is the practice of dealing with people as though they were cases and diseases, not individuals.

    1. Many patients get the impression that they are being treated by a physician who while talking to them is impatiently counting the minutes.

    2. Although students begin medical school wanting to "treat the whole person," as they progress through school, their feelings for patients are overpowered by the need to be efficient.

D. Medicine is not immune to sexism; there is evidence that women and men are treated differently by the medical establishment.

    1. Physicians don't take women's health complaints as seriously as they do men's.

    2. Women may receive unnecessary surgery, such as total hysterectomy, as some male doctors work hard to "sell" the operation in order to make money.

    3. Male dominance of medicine in Canada underlies this sexism (less than 30 percent of Canadian physicians are women). The situation is improving, however, as today women earn 40.5 percent of all medical degrees in Canada.

E. There are gendered differences in men's and women's experiences of health and illness. Sociologists have advanced five different theories to account for these gendered differences. These theories focus on (1) role accumulation; (2) role overload and role conflict; (3) gendered patterns of socialization; (4) caregiver responsibilities of women; (5) gendered differences in engagement in risky behaviour.

F. Sociologists use the term medicalization to refer to the process of turning something that was not previously considered medical into a medical matter. Examples include balding, weight, wrinkles, acne, anxiety and depression—yet there is nothing inherently medical in such conditions.

G. With modern technology, machines can perform most bodily functions even when the person's mind no longer works; this has created the question "Who has the right to pull the plug?"

    1. A living will (that people in good health sign to make clear what they wish medical personnel to do should they become dependent on artificial life-support systems) is an attempt to deal with this issue.

VIII.   Threats to Health

A. AIDS (Acquired Immune Deficiency Syndrome) is probably the most pressing health issue in Canada and globally.

    1. Its exact origin is unknown.

    2. AIDS is transmitted through the passing of bodily fluids such as blood and semen, and in rare cases by mother's milk to newborns. AIDS cannot be transmitted by casual contact.

    3. One of the most significant sociological aspects of AIDS is the stigma, which contributes to its spreading because people are afraid to be tested and stigmatized.

4. The stigma is so great in Africa and in some Asian countries that government official refuse to acknowledge how widespread AIDS is
5. Drugs have been found to slow the progress of AIDS, but there is no cure. If this disease is to be brought under control, its stigma must be overcome.

B. AIDS is an example of a disease that has globalized; an outbreak of Ebola in Zaire threatened to spread to other parts of the globe. Modern travel has wiped out the frontiers that used to contain disease. Older diseases have mutated and produced "super bugs" that are immune to antibiotics. Antibiotics are also ineffective against many of the new diseases.

C. Alcohol and nicotine are the most frequently used drugs in Canada.
1. Alcohol is the standard recreational drug in Canada. While limited amounts of alcohol reduce the risk of heart attacks and blood vessel diseases, alcohol consumption has been linked to increased risks of cancer and stroke.
2. It has been estimated that smoking kills three times more Canadians prematurely than car accidents, suicides, drug abuse, murder, and AIDS combined.

D. A disabling environment is one that is harmful to health.
1. Some occupations have high health risks which are evident (e.g., mining, construction, etc.). In others, the risk becomes evident only years after people have worked at what they thought was a safe occupation (e.g., labourers who worked with asbestos).
2. Industrialization not only increased the world's standard of living, but it also threatens to disable the basic environment of the human race, posing what may be the greatest health hazard of all time, the greenhouse effect produced by burning vast amounts of carbon fuels and warming the earth that may change the globe's climate, melt its polar icecaps, and flood the earth's coastal shores. Use of fluorocarbon gases threatens the ozone shield. In humans, this high-intensity ultraviolet radiation causes skin cancer.

IX.   **The Search for Alternatives:** What alternatives are there to the way medicine is usually practised. It is suggested that we shift the emphasis from treatment of disease to the prevention of it.
A. Values and lifestyles have a major impact on health.
1. Many of the threats to health are preventable. Individuals can exercise regularly, eat nutritious food, having protected sex , and avoid smoking and alcohol abuse in order to prevent disease.
2. Instead of treatment, the Canadian medical establishment have "wellness" as its goal. To implement a national policy of "prevention not intervention" would require a program of education in the schools and the media, showing how some practices of nutrition, exercise, sex and judicious prescription drug use pay off with healthier lives.
3. On a broader scale, there needs to be a systematic attempt to eliminate disabling environments and the use of harmful drugs.

KEY TERMS

After studying the chapter, review the definition for each of the following terms.

depersonalization: dealing with people as though they were objects; in the case of medical care, as though patients were merely cases and diseases, not persons

disabling environment: an environment that is harmful to health

epidemiology: the study of disease and disability patterns in a population

euthanasia: mercy killing

health: a human condition measured by four components: physical, mental, social, and spiritual

living will: a statement people in good health sign that clearly expresses their feelings about being kept alive on artificial life support systems

medicalization: the transformation of something into a matter to be treated by physicians

medicine: one of the major social institutions that sociologists study; a society's organized ways of dealing with sickness and injury

shaman: the healing specialist of a preliterate tribe who attempts to control the spirits thought to cause a disease or injury; commonly called a witch doctor

sick role: a social role that excuses people from normal obligations because they are sick or injured, while at the same time expecting them to seek competent help and cooperate in getting well

KEY PEOPLE

Review the major theoretical contributions or findings of these people.

Sue Fisher: Fisher did participant observation in a hospital where she discovered doctors recommending total hysterectomies even when no cancer was present, because the reproductive organs were "potentially disease-producing" organs that were no longer needed once a woman had passed her child-bearing years.

Erich Goode: This sociologist compared the health of smokers and nonsmokers and found that smokers are three times as likely to die before reaching age 65.

Jack Haas and William Shaffir: These sociologists did a participant observation of medical students and discovered that, over the course of medical school, students' attitudes change from wanting to "treat the whole person" to needing to be efficient in treating the specific ailment.

Talcott Parsons: Parsons was the first sociologist to analyze the sick role, pointing out that it has four elements—not being responsible for your sickness, being exempt from normal responsibilities, not liking the role, and seeking competent help in order to return to daily routines.

Diana Scully: Scully interviewed residents about their attitudes towards surgical procedures involving women's reproductive organs and found that doctors try to "sell" women on the procedure, not because women need it, but because the doctor wants to make money.

Leonard Stein: This physician analyzed doctor-nurse interactions in terms of a game in which the nurse (lower-status role) disguises her recommendations about patient care to the doctor (higher-status role).

SELF-TEST

After completing this self-test, check your answers against the Answer Key at the back of this Study Guide and against the text on page(s) indicated in parentheses.

MULTIPLE CHOICE QUESTIONS

1. Sociologists focus on medicine as: (325)
   a. a profession.
   b. a bureaucracy.
   c. a business.
   d. all of the above

2. A _____ is the healing specialist of a preliterate tribe who tries to control the spirits thought to cause a disease or injury. (325)
   a. soothsayer.
   b. high priest.
   c. shaman.
   d. medicine man.

3. Which of the following is an example of gatekeeping of the sick role? (326)
   a. Parents call the school to excuse a sick child's absence.
   b. Parents decide if child is faking illness.
   c. "doctor's excuse" to a person's employer
   d. all of the above

4. How would a sick or injured person who can't fulfill normal role obligations be described? (325-326)
   a. a hypochondriac
   b. in the sick role
   c. deviant
   d. all of the above

5. Which of the following is an element of the "sick role," identified by the functionalist Talcott Parsons? (326)
   a. You are not responsible for being sick.
   b. You are exempt from normal responsibilities.
   c. You do not like the role and generally try to get help.
   d. all of the above

6. Life expectancy in the Least Developed Nations is lower than in the Developed Industrial Nations in part because of: (326)
   a. lack of access to affordable medical technology.
   b. malnutrition.
   c. higher risk of catching life-threatening disease.
   d. all of the above

7. The field of epidemiology is the study of : (329)
    a. the development of medical knowledge.
    b. the professionalization of medicine.
    c. how medical disorders are distributed throughout a population.
    d. patterns of social stratification of medical care.

8. According to recent data the top causes of death for Canadians are: (369)
    a. cancer, heart diseases, cerebrovascular diseases.
    b. related to cigarette and alcohol addictions.
    c. not related to physical health, but are due to mental disorders.
    d. a result of violent crimes.

9. The criteria of the Canada Health Act are: (330)
    a. comprehensive scope
    b. universal coverage and public administration
    c. portability and accessibility
    d. all of the above—see fig.15.2

10. The most significant findings of the National Population Health Survey point to the fact that: (331-332)
    a. the organization of work and family are not important predictors of health status of Canadians.
    b. most of Canadian health care is privately administered.
    c. social factors such as class, gender, age, and ethnicity influence health.
    d. the federal government's share of health care funding has been dramatically increased.

11. Which of the following statements about depersonalization is *incorrect*? (332)
    a. It is less common today because of the development of the Canada Health Act.
    b. It is the practice of dealing with people as though they were objects.
    c. It means treating patients as though they were merely cases and diseases.
    d. It occurs when an individual is treated as if he or she was not a person.

12. Doctor recommendations for total hysterectomies even when there is no cancer is present is an example of: (327)
    a. sexism in medicine.
    b. medicalization of society.
    c. monopolization of medicine.
    d. holistic medicine.

13. Which is a reason given for gender differences in the experience of health and illness? (328)
    a. different life expectations between men and women
    b. demands on health created by role accumulation
    c. the demands of the "double day" duty of women
    d. b. and c.

14. The term medicalization refers to: (332)
    a. the increasing availability of public, accessible medical care.
    b. the growing awareness of new medical problems.
    c. the process of turning something that was not previously medical into a medical matter.
    d. the use of medical procedures to treat criminal behaviour.

15. AIDS is known to be transmitted by: (334)
    a. casual contact between a carrier and a non-carrier in which bodily fluids are exchanged.
    b. exchange of blood and/or semen.
    c. airborne passage of the virus from carrier to non-carrier through coughing or sneezing.
    d. none of the above

16. A cure for AIDS: (334-335)
    a. has been found with drugs.
    b. can be found as soon as the one virus which causes AIDS is identified.
    c. has not been found.
    d. will never be found because pharmaceutical companies won't pool their research.

17. Which factors contribute to new health threats? (335)
    a. Older diseases have mutated and produced "super bugs" immune to antibiotics.
    b. Antibiotics are ineffective against the 28 new diseases that have recently appeared.
    c. Modern travel has wiped out the frontiers that used to contain disease.
    d. all of the above

18. Which of the following statements is not correct about smoking? (336)
    a. Of all drugs, nicotine is the least harmful to health.
    b. Smoking doubles the risk of blindness in old age
    c. Quebec remains a holdout where smokers can light up in most bars and restaurants.
    d. Smokers in their thirties are six times as likely to have heart attacks as non-smokers of the same age.

19. An environment that is harmful to health is referred to as a(n): (375)
    a. disabling environment.
    b. health hazard.
    c. harmful setting.
    d. crippling environment.

20. Prevention implies both an individual and a group responsibility. What do the textbook authors suggest should be done if prevention is the goal? (337-338)
    a. on individual level, doing exercise regularly, eating nutritious food, avoiding smoking and alcohol
    b. on broader level, eliminating disabling environments and use of harmful drugs
    c. on the group level, practising preventive medicine
    d. all of the above

TRUE-FALSE QUESTIONS

T F   1.   Health is a relative matter. (325)

T F   2.   People who don't seek competent help when they are sick are just behaving as expected, according to the social definition of the sick role. (326)

T F   3.   In traditional tribal societies shaman's role is to diagnose and treat medical problems. (325)

T F   4.   Born in the Least Industrialized Nations you would be likely to face illness and death from four major sources: malaria, internal parasites, diarrhea, and malnutrition. (326)

T F   5.   Epidemiology is the study of mental illness within a population. (329)

T F   6.   Women engage in more risky behaviours, detrimental to health, such as smoking and alcohol than do men. (329)

T F   7.   Because many people today live longer than their ancestors, it is possible to conclude that contemporary Canadians are healthier. (329)

T F   8.   Since we do not even know how extensive mental illness is today, we certainly can not judge how much there was in the past. (329)

T F   9.   In Canada, universal government-funded medical, hospital, and related health insurance has been available since the early years of the post-World War II period. (330)

T F   10.   Canadian physicians are reimbursed on a fee-for-service basis, as are physicians in the United States. (330)

T F   11.   The Canada Heath Act sets out guidelines for health care that vary across the provinces. (330)

T F   12.   Studies on the health of Canadians have confirmed that the organization of work is an important predictor of health status. (332)

T F   13.   Medicine in Canada is male dominated. (327)

T F   14.   Male dominance of medicine is not a worldwide phenomenon. (327)

T F   15.   There is a lack of consensus about the practice of euthanasia. (333)

T F   16.   The U.S Census Bureau projects that by 2010, as a result of AIDS deaths and the loss of future population from the deaths of women of child-bearing age, sub-Saharan Africa will have 71 million fewer people than it would otherwise have. (335)

T F   17.   In Canada, the number of deaths due to AIDS has been increasing since the mid-1990s. (335)

T F   18.   Alcohol consumption reduces the risk of heart attacks and blood vessel diseases and does not increase the risk for other diseases. (336)

T F   19.   In general, people are very aware when they are working in a disabling environment, one that is harmful to their health. (336)

T F   20.   Strategies for preventative medicine require both individual and group responsibility. (337)

FILL-IN QUESTIONS

1. The healing specialist of a preliterate tribe who attempts to control the spirits thought to cause a disease or injury is a _____. (325)

2. _____ is a human condition measured by four components: physical, mental, social, and spiritual. (325)

3. The _____ is a social role that excuses people from normal obligations because they are sick or injured. (325-326)
4. Parents and physicians are the primary _____ to the sick role. (326)
5. One consequence of the inequitable distribution of economic and military power between nations is the _____ of medical care. (326)
6. The study of disease and disability patterns in a population is _____. (329)
7. In 1984, the _____ was enacted to ensure that health services would be available to all Canadians. (330)
8. The practice of dealing with people as though they are cases, not individuals, is termed _____. (332)
9. The percentage of Canadian medical degrees earned by women has risen from only _____ percent in 1975 to _____ percent today. (327)
10. The theory of _____ suggests that due to socialization, women are more likely to accept help in dealing with their health problems than are men. (328)
11. The term _____ refers to the process of turning something that was not previously considered medical into a medical matter. (332)
12. A(n) _____ is a statement people in good health sign, that clearly expresses their feelings about being kept alive on artificial life-support systems. (333)
13. One of the most significant sociological aspects of AIDS is its _____. (334)
14. The origin of _____ is _____. (334)
15. Lumberjacking, mining, and the construction industry are all examples of _____. (336)

MATCH THESE SOCIAL SCIENTISTS WITH THEIR CONTRIBUTIONS

___1.   Talcott Parsons   a.   *compared health of smokers and nonsmokers*
___2.   Erich Goode   b.   *sick role*
___3.   Haas/Shaffir   c.   *transformation of medical students*
___4.   Leonard Stein   d.   *interaction games played by doctors and nurses*

ESSAY QUESTIONS

1. Describe the elements of the sick role and identify variations in the pattern of claiming this role.
2. Explain the pattern of the worldwide AIDS epidemic and suggest reasons why this threat to the health of the world's population has not been addressed more aggressively.
3. Discuss the obstacles to developing preventive medicine and suggest ways in which these obstacles can be overcome.
4. Describe the development of universal health care in Canada.

"DOWN-TO-EARTH SOCIOLOGY"

1. Do you think "The Doctor-Nurse Game" on page 328 is an accurate description of the relationship between most doctors and nurses today? If nurses spend more time with patients, why are they not in charge of determining what care the patients should receive? What function does this "game" that goes on between doctors and nurses serve?
2. After reading "Euthanasia in the Netherlands" on page 333, what do you think about this subject? Why do you think leading Dutch physicians who practise euthanasia oppose its legalization in the United States? Do you agree?
3. Consider the description of the events to the SARS outbreak in 2003 see fig.15.4 (332) What can we learn from this event?

CHAPTER 16
CRIME AND SOCIAL DEVIANCE

CHAPTER SUMMARY

- Norms make social life possible by making behaviour predictable.
- Deviance, which refers to violations of social norms, is relative; what people consider deviant varies from one culture to another and from group to group within a society. It is not the act itself, but the reaction to the act, that makes something deviant. To explain deviance, biologists and psychologists look for reasons within people, such as genetic predispositions or personality disorders, while sociologists look for explanations in social relationships.
- Symbolic interactionists use differential association theory, control theory, and labelling theory to analyze how group membership influences people's behaviours and views of the world.
- Many people succeed in neutralizing the norms of society and are able to commit deviant acts while thinking of themselves as conformists. Primary, secondary, and tertiary deviance refer to stages in people's reactions to their own socially unacceptable behaviours. Although most people resist being labelled deviant, there are those who embrace deviance.
- According to Emile Durkheim, social deviance, including crime is functional to society. Functionalists stress how the many groups in a pluralistic society coexist. If some group threatens to upset the equilibrium, efforts are made to restore balance. This view may be called the Canadian Mosaic or the pluralistic theory of social control.
- Functionalists argue that crime is a natural part of society. Sociologist Robert Merton developed a typology of deviance (Table 16.1), using what is known as strain theory to explain the means by which people try to reach societal goals. The most common path is the use of institutionalized means to reach cultural goals. The socioeconomically disadvantaged people tend to have a difficult time identifying with these norms, resorting to innovation, ritualism, retreatism and rebellion.
- The social class position is an important predictor of economic success in our society. The school system, which constitutes the common route to success, fails the poor. A different door, called illegitimate opportunity structure is into the texture of life in poor urban neighbourhoods. For some people deviance becomes functional.
- The more privileged are not crime free but while white-collar crime tends to be less severely punished than street crime.
- Conflict theorists argue that the group in power imposes its definitions on other groups— the ruling class directs the criminal justice system, the police, courts, and prisons.
- The conclusions of both symbolic interactionists and conflict theorists cast doubts on the accuracy of official crime statistics. Feminist theories of social deviance connect patterns of male violence against women to systems of patriarchy, which are rooted in ideologies of male superiority.
- Postmodernist theories of deviance emphasize the need to "deconstruct" the meaning of such concepts as "law and order" and the "criminal justice system." They also argue that we live in a media created "risk society."
- All these theories have merit.

- Reactions to deviance include negative sanctions, degradation ceremonies, and imprisonment.
- Society may deal with deviance by medicalizing it and calling it mental illness. Thomas Szasz disagrees, claiming that deviance involves just problem behaviours, not mental illness.
- With deviance inevitable, the larger issues are how to protect people from deviant behaviours that are harmful to their welfare, to tolerate those that are not, and to develop systems of fairer treatment for deviants.

LEARNING OBJECTIVES

As you read Chapter 16, use these learning objectives to organize your notes. After completing your reading, briefly state an answer to each of the objectives, and review the text pages in parentheses.

1. Explain what sociologists mean when they say that deviance is relative. (342)
2. Compare and contrast the functionalist and the conflict views on social control. (346-351)
3. Explain the importance of norms and their relation to a system of social order. (341-342)
4. Compare biological, psychological, and sociological explanations of deviance. (341-342)
5. State the key components of the symbolic interaction perspective on deviance, and briefly explain differential association theory, and labelling theory. (343-346)
6. Distinguish between primary, secondary, and tertiary deviance. Give examples of each. (345)
7. Summarize these reactions by deviants to their own behaviour: neutralizing deviance and embracing deviance. (344-346)
8. Discuss the major reasons why functionalists view deviance as functional for society. (346-347)
9. Describe Merton's strain theory, and list and briefly explain the four types of responses to anomie. (347-348)
10. Identify the relationship between social class and crime by using the illegitimate opportunity theory and perspectives on white-collar crime. (349-350)
11. Explain the conflict view of the relationship between class, crime, and the criminal justice system. (350)
12. State why official statistics may not accurately reflect the nature and extent of crime. (351)
13. Discuss feminist theories of social deviance, focusing on issues of male violence against women and Canadian public policy. (351-352)
14. Describe the "postmodern" approach to "law and order" and the " criminal justice system," and what they mean by media-created "risk society." (352-353)
15. State why there is a need to use more than one theory of deviance in trying to explain this behaviour and discuss how the different theories can be combined. (353)
16. Describe the reactions to deviance by explaining sanctions, degradation ceremonies, and imprisonment. (355-356)
17. Explain what is meant by the medicalization of deviance and discuss how social conditions like homelessness can contribute to mental illness, just as mental illness is seen as contributing to these same conditions. (357-358)

CHAPTER OUTLINE

I. **Gaining a Sociological Perspective of Deviance**
   A. Sociologists use the term deviance to refer to a violation of norms.
      1. According to sociologist Howard S. Becker, it is not the act itself that makes an action deviant, but rather how society reacts to it.
      2. Because different groups have different norms, what is deviant to some is not deviant to others.
      3. Deviants are people who violate rules, whether the infraction is minor (jaywalking) or serious (murder). To sociologists, all people are deviants because everyone violates rules from time to time.
      4. Erving Goffman used "stigma" to refer to attributes that discredit one's claim to a "normal" identity. These attributes include norms of ability (e.g. handicaps) and appearance (e.g. obesity) as well as involuntary membership in stigmatized groups (AIDS victims). The stigma becomes a person's master status, superceding all other statuses the person occupies.
   B. Norms make social life possible by making behaviour predictable. Without norms, social chaos would exist. The reason deviance is seen as threatening is because it undermines predictability. Thus, social control (the formal and informal means of enforcing norms) is necessary for social life.
   C. Comparing Biological, Psychological, and Sociological Explanations
      1. Psychologists and sociobiologists explain deviance by looking within individuals; some psychologists focus on abnormalities within the individual, on what are called personality disorders.
      2. Biological explanations of deviance focus on genetic predispositions—factors such as intelligence, "XYY" theory, or body type.
      3. In contrast to the biological and psychological perspectives, sociologists search for the explanatory factors outside the individual. Sociological explanations search outside the individual: crime is a violation of norms written into law, and each society has its own laws against certain types of behaviour, but social influences—such as socialization, subcultural group memberships, or social class (people's relative standing in terms of education, occupation, income and wealth)—may "recruit" some people to break norms.
   D. In trying to answer the question of where definitions of deviance come from, sociologists use symbolic interactionist, functionalist, conflict, feminist, and postmodernist perspectives.
      1. In tribal societies, agreement on how life should be lived is relatively simple, because these societies are small with strong social bonds. In industrial societies, because there are many competing groups, techniques of social control are set up to enforce different groups' version of what is good.
      2. To functionalists, social control emerges as individuals and groups attempt to achieve a balance between competing interest groups. According to the pluralistic theory of social control, in societies like Canada, the central government often plays a mediating role between groups.
      3. To conflict theorists, the purpose of social control is to maintain power for an elite group, primarily consisting of wealthy, white males who work behind

the scenes to control government. Official deviance (the statistics on victims, lawbreakers, and the outcome of criminal investigations and sentencing) reflects the elite's concern with protecting its interests.

II.   The Symbolic Interactionist Perspective
    A. Differential association is Edwin Sutherland's term to indicate that those who associate with groups oriented toward deviant activities learn an "excess of definitions" of deviance and, thus, are more likely to engage in deviant activities.
        1. The key to differential association is the learning of ideas and attitudes favourable to following the law or favourable to breaking it. Some groups teach members to violate norms (e.g., families involved in crime may set their children on a lawbreaking path; some friends and neighbourhoods tend to encourage deviant behaviour; even subcultures contain particular attitudes about deviance and conformity that are learned by their members).
        2. Symbolic interactionists stress that people are not mere pawns, because individuals help produce their own orientation to life and their choice of association helps to shape the self.
    B. Control Theory—Canadian Mosaic or the pluralistic theory of social control.
        1. Functionalists stress how many groups in a pluralistic society coexist.
        2. If some group threatens to upset equilibrium, efforts are made to restore balance.
        3. This view of mediation and balance among competing groups is broadly representative of what may be called the Canadian Mosaic or the pluralistic theory of social control.
    C. Labelling theory is the view that the labels people are given affect their own and others' perceptions of them, thus channelling their behaviour either into deviance or into conformity.
        1. Gresham Sykes and David Matza use the term "techniques of neutralization" to describe the strategies deviants employ to resist society's label. These are (1) denial of responsibility ("I didn't do it"); (2) denial of injury ("Who really got hurt?"); (3) denial of a victim ("She deserved it"); (4) condemnation of the condemners ("Who are you to talk?"); and (5) appeal to higher loyalty ("I had to help my friends").
        2. Sometimes an individual's deviant acts begin casually, and he or she gradually slides into more serious deviance.
        3. Edwin Lemert identified primary deviance as fleeting acts that are not absorbed into an individual's self-concept and secondary deviance as deviant acts that are absorbed into one's self-concept. As a consequence, the deviant individual often redefines deviant behaviour as non deviant; this is referred to as tertiary deviance.
        4. Most people resist being labelled deviant, but some revel in a deviant identity (e.g., motorcycle gangs may pride themselves on getting into trouble, laughing at death, etc.).
        5. William J. Chambliss's study of the Saints (boys from respectable middle class families) and the Roughnecks (boys from working class families who hang out on the streets) provides an excellent illustration of labelling theory—labels given to people affect how others perceive them and how they

perceive themselves, thus channelling their behaviour into deviance or conformity. The study showed how labels open and close doors of opportunity for the individuals involved.

III.   The Functionalist Perspective

A. Emile Durkheim stated that deviance, including crime, is functional, for it contributes to social order.

  1. Deviance clarifies moral boundaries (a group's ideas about how people should act and think) and affirms norms.

  2. Deviance promotes social unity (by reacting to deviants, group members develop a "we" feeling and collectively affirm the rightness of their own ways).

  3. Deviance promotes social change (if boundary violations gain enough support, they become new, acceptable behaviours).

B. Robert Merton developed strain theory to analyze what happens when people are socialized to desire cultural goals but denied the institutionalized means to reach them.

  1. Merton used "anomie" (Durkheim's term) to refer to the strain people experience when they are blocked in their attempts to achieve those goals.

  2. The most common reaction to cultural goals and institutionalized means is conformity (using lawful means to seek goals society sets); most people in industrialized societies follow this socially acceptable road.

  3. Merton identified four types of deviant responses to anomie table 16.1: innovation (using illegitimate means to achieve societal goals); ritualism (giving up on achieving cultural goals but clinging to conventional rules of conduct); retreatism (rejecting cultural goals, dropping out); and rebellion (seeking to replace society's goals).

  4. According to strain theory, deviants are not pathogenic individuals but the products of society.

C. Illegitimate Opportunity Theory

  1. Social classes have distinct styles of crime due to differential access to legitimate institutionalized means to cultural goals.

  2. Illegitimate opportunity structures are opportunities for remunerative crime woven into the texture of life, according to sociologists Richard Cloward and Lloyd Ohlin. For some then, such illegal income producing activities are functional.

  3. Edwin Sutherland used the term white-collar crime to refer to crimes that people of respectable and high social status commit in the course of their occupations. Such crimes exist in greater numbers than commonly perceived, and can be very costly. They can involve physical harm and sometimes death; for instance, unsafe working conditions due to executive decisions to put profits ahead of workers' safety killed workers in 2002 worldwide, according to the International Labour Organization (ILO).

IV.   The Conflict Perspective
   A. The state's machinery of social control represents the interests of the wealthy and powerful; this group determines the laws whose enforcement is essential for maintaining its power.
   B. The law is an instrument of oppression, a tool designed to maintain the powerful in privileged positions and keep the powerless from rebelling and overthrowing the social order. When members of the working class get out of line, they are arrested, tried, and imprisoned in the criminal justice system.
   C. Caution is needed in interpreting official statistics because the reactions of authorities are influenced by social class of the offender.
   D. The criminal justice system directs its energies against violations by the working class; while it tends to overlook the harm done by the owners of corporations. Flagrant violations by members of the capitalist class are occasionally prosecuted to preserve visible evidence of the fairness of the criminal justice system.

V.   Feminist Theories and Male Violence Against Women
   A. When it comes to feminist theories of social deviance —more specifically, male violence against women—a number of common principles are shared by all feminist theories, of which the most important is patriarchy. First and foremost, patriarchy is characterized as a "sexual system of power in which the male possesses superior power and economic priviledge" (Eisenstein, 1980, p.16). Michael Smith (1990) has identified two related forms of patriarchy, the "social" and the "familial."
   B. Public policy strategies to address the problem of male violence against women include policing initiatives, job creation, social services, and anti-sexist male collectives.

VI.   The Need for Multiple Theories
   A. All of the different theories have merit in helping to explain deviance.
   B. The postmodern approach emphasizes the need to "deconstruct" or decode the meaning of concepts such as "law and order" and the "criminal justice system." Postmodern theorists also argue that we live in a media-created "risk society."
   C. Besides a need for multiple theories, there is also a need for better understanding of The Canadian Criminal Justice System which comprises three principal components: the police, the courts, and the corrections. Each division is made up of its own subsystems that include both public and private sectors. Some provinces, such as Ontario and Quebec, have their own provincial police forces.
   The court system in Canada is composed of four basic levels. Whereas in the United States, states' rights prevail in criminal matters, in Canada the federal government has exclusive authority over the procedures in the criminal court. The highest level of court of appeal is the Supreme Court, which has nine judges, three of whom must be from Quebec.

VII.   Reactions to Deviance
   A. Sanctions are either negative sanctions (punishments ranging from frowns and gossip to imprisonment, exile, and capital punishment) or positive sanctions (rewards for desired behaviour, ranging from smiles to awards).

1. Most negative sanctions are informal.
2. Reacting to deviance is vital to the welfare of groups; by reacting, the boundaries that establish the unique identity of the group are maintained.

B. Degradation ceremonies are rituals designed to mark an individual with the status of an outsider. Typically, an individual is called before a group and denounced; when the individual is pronounced guilty, steps are taken to strip the individual of his/her identity as a group member. Such proceedings signal that the individual is no longer a group member.

C. Imprisonment—follows a degradation ceremony involving a public trial/pronouncement that the person is unfit to live among law-abiding people for a specified period of time.

D. Medicalization of deviance is the view of deviance as a symptom of some underlying illness that needs to be treated by physicians.

1. Thomas Szasz argues that mental illness is simply problem behaviours: some forms of "mental" illnesses have organic causes (e.g., depression caused by a chemical imbalance in the brain); while others are responses to troubles with various coping devices.
2. Some sociologists find Szasz's analysis refreshing because it indicates that social experiences, and not some illness of the mind, underlie bizarre behaviours.
3. Being mentally ill can sometimes lead to other problems like homelessness; but being homeless can lead to unusual and unacceptable ways of thinking that are defined by the wider society as mental illness.

VIII. The Need for a More Humane Approach

A. With deviance inevitable, one measure of a society is how it treats its deviants.

B. The larger issues are how to protect people from deviant behaviours that are harmful to their welfare, to tolerate those that are not, and to develop systems of fairer treatment for deviants.

KEY TERMS

After studying the chapter, review the definition for each of the following terms.

crime: the violation of norms that are written into law

criminal justice system: the system of police, courts, and prisons set up to deal with people who are accused of having committed a crime

cultural goals: the legitimate objectives held out to the members of a society

degradation ceremonies: rituals designed to strip an individual of his or her identity as a group member; for example, a court martial or the defrocking of a priest

differential association: Edwin Sutherland's term to indicate that associating with some groups results in learning an "excess of definitions" of deviance, and, by extension, in a greater likelihood that one will become deviant

genetic predispositions: inborn tendencies, in this context, to commit deviant acts

illegitimate opportunity structures: opportunities for crimes woven into the texture of life

institutionalized means: approved ways of reaching cultural goals

labelling theory: the view, developed by symbolic interactionists, that the labels people are given affect their own and others' perceptions of them, thus channelling their behaviour either into deviance or into conformity

medicalization of social deviance: to make deviance a medical matter, a symptom of some underlying illness that needs to be treated by physicians

negative sanction: a punishment or negative reaction for disapproved behaviour, for deviance

official social deviance: a society's statistics on lawbreaking; its measures of crime, victims, lawbreakers, and the outcomes of criminal investigations and sentencing

patriarchy: is characterized as a "sexual system of power in which the male possesses superior power and economic privilege"

personality disorders: the view that a personality disturbance of some sort causes an individual to violate social norms

pluralistic theory of social control: the view that society is made up of many competing groups, whose interests manage to become balanced

positive sanction: reward or positive reaction for approved behaviour, for conformity

primary social deviance: Edwin Lemert's term for acts of deviance that have little effect on the self-concept

risk society: postmodern theorists argue that we live in a "risk society" created by the media

secondary social deviance: Edwin Lemert's term for acts of deviance incorporated into the self-concept, around which an individual orients his or her behaviour

social control: a group's formal and informal means of enforcing norms

social deviance: any violation of social norms

social order: a group's usual and customary social arrangements, on which its members depend and on which they base their lives

stigma: "blemishes" that discredit a person's claim to a "normal" identity

strain theory: Robert Merton's term for the strain engendered when a society socializes large numbers of people to desire a cultural goal (such as success) but withholds from many the approved means to reach that goal; one adaptation to the strain is crime, the choice of an innovative means (one outside the approved system) to attain the cultural goal

street crime: crimes such as mugging, rape, and burglary

techniques of neutralization: ways of thinking or rationalizing that help people deflect society's norms

tertiary social deviance: "normalizing" behaviour considered deviant by mainstream society; relabelling behaviour as nondeviant

white-collar crime: Edwin Sutherland's term for crimes committed by people of respectable and high social status in the course of their occupations; for example, bribery of public officials, securities violations, embezzlement, false advertising, and price fixing

KEY PEOPLE

Review the major theoretical contributions or findings of these people.

Howard Becker: Becker observed that an act is not deviant in and of itself, but only when there is a reaction to it.

William Chambliss: Chambliss demonstrated the power of the label in his study of two youth gangs—the Saints and the Roughnecks.

Richard Cloward and Lloyd Ohlin: These sociologists identified the illegitimate opportunity structures that are woven into the texture of life in urban slums and provide an alternative set of opportunities for slum residents when legitimate ones are blocked.

Nanette Davis: Davis studied young girls in order to find out what led them to become prostitutes. She found that they had experienced a gradual slide from promiscuity to prostitution.

Emile Durkheim: Durkheim noted the functions that deviance has for social life.

Robert Edgerton: This anthropologist's studies document how different human groups react to similar behaviours, demonstrating that what is deviant in one context is not in another.

Harold Garfinkel: Garfinkel used the term degradation ceremonies to describe formal attempts to mark an individual with the status of an outsider.

Erving Goffman: Goffman wrote about the role of stigma in the definition of who and what is deviant.

Travis Hirschi: Hirschi studied the strength of the bonds an individual has to society in order to understand the effectiveness of inner controls.

Ruth Horowitz: studied subcultures and their redefinitions of what is a crime.

Edwin Lemert: Lemert distinguished between different types of deviance—primary, secondary, and tertiary deviance—in terms of the degree to which the deviant label has been incorporated into the individual's identity.

Robert Merton: Merton developed strain theory to explain patterns of deviance within a society.

Walter Reckless: Reckless developed control theory, suggesting that our behaviour is controlled by two different systems, one external (outer controls like the police, family and friends) and the other internal (inner controls like our conscience, religious principles, and ideas of right and wrong).

Edwin Sutherland: Sutherland not only developed differential association theory, but was the first to study and give a name to crimes that occur among the middle class in the course of their work—white collar crime.

Gresham Sykes and David Matza: These sociologists studied the different strategies delinquent boys use to deflect society's norms—techniques of neutralization.

Thomas Szasz: Szasz argued that mental illness represents the medicalization of deviance.

Mark Watson: Watson studied motorcycle gangs and found that these people actively embraced the deviant label.

SELF-TEST

After completing this self-test, check your answers against the Answer Key at the back of this Study Guide and against the text on page(s) indicated in parentheses.

MULTIPLE CHOICE QUESTIONS

1. In sociology, to what does the term deviance refer? (342)
    a. behaviour that sociologists believe is bad enough to warrant being punished by society
    b. all violations of social rules
    c. the violation of serious rules only
    d. crime only

2. Erving Goffman used the term stigma to refer: (343)
    a. to attributes that discredit people
    b. to violation of norms of ability
    c. to certain norms of appearance
    d. all of the above

3. Which of the following is NOT a pluralistic theory of social control explanation? (347)
    a. If some group threatens to upset the equilibrium between groups, efforts are made to restore balance.
    b. In Canada federal and provincial governments mediate demands of the various groups.
    c. The Supreme Court of Canada mediates the demands of various groups.
    d. Law is an instrument of oppression.

4. According to conflict theorists, social control: (350)
    a. is based on balancing tensions between competing groups in society.
    b. represents the interests of the wealthy and powerful.
    c. represents the interests of the general public.
    d. is important for mediation in a pluralistic society.

5. Differential association theory is based on the: (343)
    a. functionalist perspective.
    b. conflict perspective.
    c. symbolic interactionist perspective.
    d. psychological perspective.

6. Which socially deviant paths are included in Merton's typology? (348)
    a. innovators
    b. ritualists
    c. retreatists
    d. all of the above

7. Which of the following are techniques of neutralizing deviance? (344-345)
    a. denial of injury and of victim
    b. denial of responsibility
    c. condemnation of the condemners
    d. all of the above

8. What is the term for acts of deviance that have little effect on the self-concept? (345)
    a. primary deviance
    b. secondary deviance
    c. tertiary deviance
    d. none of the above

9. At the tertiary social deviance stage, most people: (345)
    a. accept that what they do is terribly wrong.
    b. are first labelled deviant.
    c. simply reject the judgment that the behaviour is wrong.
    d. are fully accepted into mainstream society.

10. What does William Chambliss's study of the Saints and the Roughnecks suggest? (346)
    a. Labels are easy to cast off once a person gets away from the group doing the labelling.
    b. People often live up to the labels that a community gives them.
    c. People often rebel against the labels given them and lead a completely different life.
    d. Sociological research on labelling has produced few conclusions.

11. Mark Watson's study revealed that: (346)
    a. "Saints" and "Roughnecks" both were involved in deviant activities.
    b. teachers and authorities saw "Roughnecks" as headed for trouble.
    c. teachers and authorities expected good, law-abiding, behaviour from the "Saints."
    d. all of the above

12. Durkheim argued that according to functionalism: (346-347)
    a. crime and social deviance clarify moral boundaries.
    b. crime and social deviance promote social unity.
    c. crime and social deviance promote social change.
    d. all of the above

13. All of the following are responses to anomie as identified by Robert Merton, except: (348)
    a. ritualism.
    b. rebellion.
    c. retreatism.
    d. recidivism.

14. Who are the most committed type of rebels, according to Merton's strain theory? (348)
    a. conformists
    b. revolutionaries
    c. neurotics
    d. ritualists

15. Which of the following are part of the illegitimate opportunity structure: (349)
    a. gambling
    b. hustling
    c. glamorous "easy money"
    d. all of the above

16. What are crimes committed by high status people in the course of their occupations called? (349)
    a. upper-class crime
    b. crimes of respectability
    c. white-collar crime
    d. tuxedo crime

17. Why do conflict theorists see the law as an instrument of oppression? (350)
    a. It penalizes corporate executives.
    b. It is used by the powerful to maintain their privileged position.
    c. It facilitates male violence against women.
    d. all of the above

18. Symbolic interactionists as they enforce the law point out that police use: (351)
    a. a symbolic system.
    b. the idea of "typical criminals."
    c. the idea of "typical good citizens."
    d. all of the above

19. Feminist theorists relate male violence against women to: (351)
    a. biological tendencies towards violent behaviour within men.
    b. systemic inequality rooted in capitalist exploitation.
    c. patriarchal ideologies, which promote male superiority.
    d. lack of proper socialization.

20. Public policy strategies to address male violence include: (352)
    a. job creation programs.
    b. expanded social services.
    c. anti-sexist self-help groups for violent men.
    d. all of the above

21. Of what are frowns, gossip, and crossing people off guest lists all examples? (355)
    a. retribution
    b. degradation ceremonies
    c. negative sanctions
    d. institutionalized means to achieve goals

22. A court martial where the guilty officer is publicly stripped of his rank is an example of: (355-356)
    a. degradation ceremonies.
    b. humiliation ceremonies.
    c. stigmatization.
    d. deinstitutionalization.

23. What experience follows a public pronouncement that a person is "unfit to live among decent, law-abiding people"? (356)
   a.   retribution
   b.   imprisonment
   c.   rehabilitation
   d.   deterrence

24. The medicalization of deviance refers to: (357)
   a.   the castration of sex offenders.
   b.   use of lethal injections for the death penalty.
   c.   viewing deviance as a medical matter.
   d.   all of the above

25. A more humane approach to dealing with social deviance is needed because: (358)
   a.   social deviance is inevitable.
   b.   deviance is often the result of systems of inequality.
   c.   a measure of a society is how it treats deviant behaviour.
   d.   all of the above

TRUE-FALSE QUESTIONS

T F   1.   The nature of, and the reaction to, violence in sports depends on a society's culture. (341)

T F   2.   Sociologists use the term social deviance only for crime. (342)

T F   3.   Social control includes both formal and informal means of enforcing norms. (341)

T F   4.   Functionalists agree with the pluralistic theory of social control. (347)

T F   5.   Conflict theorists maintain that an elite group of wealthy, white males maintains power by controlling the government. (350)

T F   6.   According to the biological explanation of crime, genetic predispositions are seen as explanations of crime. (341)

T F   7.   According to differential association theory, the source of deviant behaviour may be found in a person's socialization, or social learning. (343)

T F   8.   Primary social deviance refers to fleeting acts that deviate from societal norms and do not become part of self-concept. (345)

T F   9.   No one embraces deviance or wants to be labelled with a deviant identity. (346)

T F   10.   Social deviance can be viewed as a social continuum with minor rule or norm breaking at one end and serious criminal violations on the other. (343)

T F   11.   In the study by Chambliss, the Saints and the Roughnecks both turned out largely as their labels would have predicted. (346)

T F   12.   Functionalists agree that crime is a natural part of society. (346-347)

T F   13.   According to strain theory, everyone has a chance to get ahead in society, but some people prefer to use illegal means to achieve their goals. (347-348)

T F   14.   According to strain theory, some people experience greater pressures to deviate from society's norms because of their social location. (348-349)

T F   15.   Illegitimate opportunity structures are readily available in poor urban neighbourhoods. (349)

T F   16.   White-collar crime is not as costly as street crime. (349)
T F   17.   Both functionalists and conflict theorists agree that the criminal justice system functions for the well-being of all citizens. (351)
T F   18.   Official statistics are accurate counts of the crimes committed in our society. (351)
T F   19.   Feminist theories connect male violence against women to patriarchal ideologies of male violence. (351)
T F   20.   The purpose of positive sanctions is to express disapproval of deviance from social norms. (355)

FILL-IN QUESTIONS

1. _____ is the violation of rules or norms. (342)
2. Erving Goffman used the term _____ to refer to attributes that discredit people. (343)
3. Formal and informal means of enforcing norms constitute a system of _____. (341)
4. According to the _____ perspective, society is made up of competing groups, and the group that holds power uses social control to maintain its position of privilege. (350)
5. _____ make social life possible by making behaviour predictable. (341)
6. _____ is a group's usual and customary social arrangements, on which its members depend and on which they base their lives. (341)
7. Labelling theory is used to show what strategies people use to neutralize _____ (344)
8. _____ social deviance refers to fleeting acts that do not become part of the self-concept. (345)
9. Strain theory is based on the idea that large numbers of people are socialized into desiring _____ (the legitimate objects held out to everyone) but many do not have access to _____ in order to achieve those goals. (347)
10. _____ are the ones in Merton's typology of deviance who accept both cultural goals and the institutionalized means to reach those goals. (348)
11. Edwin Sutherland used the term _____ to refer to crimes that people of respectable and high social status commit in the course of their occupations. (349)
12. In combination the policy, courts, and prisons that deal with people who are accused of having committed crimes make up the _____ . (350)
13. Steps to strip an individual of his or her identity as a group member occur during _____ . (355-356)
14. The view that deviance, including crime, is the product of mental illness is referred to as _____ . (357)

MATCH THESE SOCIAL SCIENTISTS WITH THEIR CONTRIBUTIONS

__1. Edwin Sutherland

__2. Robert Merton

__3. Erving Goffman

__4. Thomas Szasz

__5. Emile Durkheim

__6. William Chambliss

__7. Gresham Sykes and David Matza

__8. Harold Garfinkel

a. *strain theory*

b. *myth of mental illness*

c. *degradation ceremonies*

d. *white-collar crime*

e. *functions of deviance*

f. *effects of labelling*

g. *importance of stigma*

h. *techniques of neutralization*

ESSAY QUESTIONS

1. Discuss how the different sociological perspectives could be combined in order to provide a more complete picture of deviance.
2. Explain how forms of deviance such as street gangs can be both functional and dysfunctional at the same time.
3. Compare the societal harm caused by white-collar and street crime.

"DOWN-TO-EARTH SOCIOLOGY"

1. What can we learn about deviance from a subcultural perspective (p.344)? Can you think of some examples of subcultural differences in definition of what is considered a "crime"?
2. What did you think of the description of hockey and sports violence? Should sports be allowed to police themselves? (p.340-341)
3. Describe how youth unemployment affects different young people differently. (See "Mean Streets and Hard Times"). (p.348)

CHAPTER 17
POPULATION, URBANIZATION, AND THE ENVIRONMENT

CHAPTER SUMMARY

- Demography is the study of the size, composition, growth, and distribution of human populations. Over 200 years ago Thomas Malthus observed that populations grow geometrically while food supplies increase arithmetically; this meant, he argued, that if births go unchecked the population of the world would eventually outstrip its food supply.

- The New Malthusians point out that the world's population is following an exponential growth curve. In just the time it takes to read this chapter, another 15.000 to 20.000 babies will be born!

- From Figure 17.3 we can conclude that some countries produce more food than their people are able to consume, others less than they need for survival. In short, the cause of starvation is an imbalance between supply and demand.

- People in the Least Industrialized Nations have large families because motherhood and fatherhood are socially valued; children are viewed as gifts from God, and they represent parents source of security.

- To project population trends, demographers use what they call the basic demographic equation: Growth Rate = Births – Deaths + Net Migration. But social factors—economic booms and busts, wars, plagues, and famines—push rates up or down

- Cities can only develop if there is an agricultural surplus; the primary impetus to the development of cities was the invention of the plow about five or six thousand years ago. A city, in fact, can be defined as a place in which a large number of people are permanently based and do not produce their own food. Although cities are not new to the world scene urbanization is. Urbanization refers to masses of people moving to cities, giving cities a growing influence on society. Urbanization is worldwide. The year 2007 is expected to mark the historic moment when more than half of humanity will live in cities. Urbanization is so extensive today that some cities have become metropolises; in some cases metropolises have merged to form a megalopolis. Three major models have been proposed to explain how cities expand: the concentric-zone, sector, and multiple-nuclei models. These models fail to account for medieval cities, as well as many European cities and those in the Least Industrialized Nations.

- Some people find a sense of community in cities; others find alienation. To develop community in the city, people personalize their shopping, identify with sports teams, and even become sentimental about objects in the city. An essential element in determining whether someone finds community or alienation in the city is that person's social networks.

- Forces such as suburbanization, deindustrialization, and globalization have transformed Canadian cities.

- Contrary to common assumptions, environmental problems are not new on the human scene. Several civilizations destroyed themselves by destroying the environment on which their very existence depended. Although environment degradation is not new, the frontal assault on the natural environment did not begin in earnest until nations industrialized.

- Today we face such environmental problems as acid rain, global warming, and the greenhouse effect. Environmental problems are worldwide, brought about by industrial production and urbanization, the pressures of population growth, and inadequate environmental regulation; the world today is facing a basic conflict between the lust for profits through the exploitation of the world's resources and the need to produce a sustainable environment. In response, a worldwide environmental movement has emerged, which seeks solutions in education, legislation, and political activism. If we are to survive, we must seek harmony between technology and the environment.

LEARNING OBJECTIVES

As you read Chapter 17, use these learning objectives to organize your notes. After completing your reading, briefly state an answer to each of the objectives, and review the text pages in parentheses.

1. Discuss the Malthus theorem and identify key issues in the debate between New Malthusians and Anti-Malthusians regarding the specter of overpopulation. (362-363)
2. Outline the feminist perspective on the population debates. (364)
3. Explain why there is starvation. (364-365)
4. Explain why people in the Least Industrialized Nations have so many children and note the implications of different rates of population growth. (366)
5. State the three demographic variables used in estimating population growth and explain why it is difficult to forecast population growth. (367-368)
6. Describe urbanization and outline the history of how cities came into existence. (370)
7. Identify the trends contributing to the emergence of metropolises and megalopolises. (370)
8. Discuss urban patterns in Canada. (370-371)
9. Review the three models of urban growth and critique each of them. (371-372)
10. Explain why many people feel a sense of alienation by living in large urban areas. (372-373)
11. Define the urban village and briefly describe the different types of people who live in the city as identified by sociologist Herbert Gans. (374)
12. Describe ways in which city people create a sense of intimacy for themselves in large urban areas (373-374)
13. Outline the major changes facing Canadian cities regarding suburbanization, deindustrialization, and globalization. (374-375)
14. Describe the environmental problems in past civilizations. (375)
15. State ways in which nations at different stages of industrialization may have contributed to global environmental problems. (375)
16. Discuss the goals and activities of the environmental movement. (376-377)
17. List the assumptions of environmental sociology. (377-378)
18. Describe some of the actions which would be necessary to reach the goal of harmony between technology and the environment. (379)

CHAPTER OUTLINE

I. **A Planet with No Space to Enjoy Life?**

   A. Demography is the study of size, composition, growth, distribution of populations.

   B. Thomas Malthus wrote *An Essay on the Principle of Population* (1798) stating the Malthus theorem—population grows geometrically while food supply increases arithmetically; thus, if births go unchecked, population will outstrip food supplies.

   C. New Malthusians believe Malthus was correct. The world population is following an exponential growth curve (where numbers increase in extraordinary proportions): 1800, one billion; 1930, two billion; 1960, three billion; 1975, four billion. Right now, the world population has reached six billion.

   D. Anti-Malthusians believe that people do not blindly reproduce until there is no room left.

      1. They cite three stages of the demographic transition in Europe as an example. Stage 1, a fairly stable population (high birth rates offset by high death rates); Stage 2, "population explosion" (high birth rates and low death rates); and Stage 3, population stability (low birth rates and low death rates).

      2. They assert this transition will happen in the Least Industrialized Nations, which currently are in the second stage.

      3. Population shrinkage (a country's population is smaller because birth rate and immigration cannot replace those who die and emigrate) has occurred in Europe.

      4. Today, Canada's birth rate continues to drop. Statistics Canada's latest report states that Canada's birth rate for 2002 was the lowest since vital statistics were first taken, in 1921.

   E. Who is correct? Only the future will prove the accuracy of either the projections of the New Malthusians or the Anti-Malthusians.

      1. The New Malthusians interpret population growth negatively, while the Anti-Malthusians view the figures positively.

   F. Feminists reject the population control strategies advanced by the New Malthusians, such as forced sterilization of women in the industrializing and least industrialized countries. They claim that these policies deprive women of freedom to make decisions about their own bodies.

      1. Feminists argue that women's rights, particularly the right to decide one's reproductive future, must be recognized as human rights.

      2. Feminist strategies to achieve population control include providing economic opportunities, education about birth control, and improving women's rights.

   G. Why are people starving?

      1. Anti-Malthusians note that the amount of food produced for each person in the world has increased: famines are not the result of too little food production, but result from maldistribution of existing food.

      2. Recently, famines have been concentrated in Africa. However, these famines are not due to too many people living on too little land. Rather, these famines are due to outmoded farming techniques and ongoing political instability that disrupt harvests and food distribution.

II.   **Population Growth**

A. In short, stress the Anti-Malthusians, the world's problem will not be a population explosion, but population shrinkage—too few children in the world, not too many.

B. Three reasons poor nations have so many children are: (1) the status that parenthood provides; (2) the community supports this view; and (3) children are considered to be economic assets (the parents rely on the children to take care of them in their old age). People in the Most Industrialized Nations see children as economic liabilities.

    1. The symbolic interactionist perspective stresses that we need to understand these patterns within the framework of the culture and society in which the behaviour occurs.

    2. Feminists stress that in the Least Industrialized Nations, men dominate women in all spheres of life, including that of reproduction. There is an emphasis on male virility and dominance, including the fathering of many children, as a means of achieving status in the community.

C. Estimated population growth is based on three demographic variables:

    1. Fertility, measured by the fertility rate (number of children an average woman bears), is sometimes confused with fecundity (number of children a woman theoretically can bear). To compute a country's fertility rate, demographers use crude birth rate (annual number of births per 1,000 people).

    2. Mortality is measured by the crude death rate (number of deaths per 1,000 people).

    3. Migration is measured by the net migration rate (difference between the number of immigrants moving in and emigrants moving out per 1,000 population); it may be voluntary or forced. Push factors make people want to leave where they are living (e.g., persecution, lack of economic opportunity); pull factors attract people (e.g., opportunities in the new locale).

D. The growth rate equals births less deaths, plus net migration.

    1. Economic changes, government policies, and behavioural changes make it difficult to forecast population growth. The primary unknown factor that influences a country's growth rate is its rate of industrialization—in every country that industrializes, the growth rate declines.

    2. Because of the difficulties in forecasting population growth, demographers formulate several predictions simultaneously, each depending on different assumptions.

III.   **The Challenge of the Twenty-First Century**

A. Today modern technology could be used to solve problems such as malnutrition. starvation, resource depletion, unrest, enforced migration, and armed conflict.

B. Technological advances are occurring in the Most Industrialized Nations, where there is slow population growth. The areas of the world where populations are rapidly expanding, and where there are many problems produced by this rapid expansion, do not have access to the technology to solve the problems.

C. The challenge is how to make technology available to the Least Industrialized Nations.

IV. **Urbanization**

   A. A city is a place in which a large number of people are permanently based and do not produce their own food. Small cities with massive defensive walls existed as far back as 10,000 years ago.

   B. The Industrial Revolution drew people to cities to work. Today urbanization not only means that more people live in cities, but also that today's cities are larger; about 300 of the world's cities contain one million people or more.

   C. Urbanization is the process by which an increasing proportion of a population lives in cities. It is expected that by the year 2007 more than half of all humanity will live in cities. There are specific characteristics of cities, such as size and anonymity, that give them their unique urban flavour.

      1. Metropolis refers to cities that grow so large that they exert influence over a region; the central city and surrounding smaller cities and suburbs are connected economically, politically, and socially.

      2. Megalopolis refers to an overlapping area consisting of at least two metropolises and their suburbs, connected economically, socially, and sometimes politically.

   D. In 1871, only about 18 percent of Canadians lived in small cities; by 1921, almost 50 percent of the Canadian population lived in urban areas; today, over four-fifths of Canadians live in cities.

      1. There is a hierarchy of cities in Canada, as not all Canadian cities are the same size, nor do they carry the same commercial or financial weight.

      2. Between 1996 and 2001 six of the ten fastest-growing metropolitan areas were in Ontario: Oshawa, Toronto, Kitchener, Windsor, Ottawa-Hull, and Hamilton.

      3. For 2001, the CMAs with the largest population were Toronto, Montreal, Vancouver, Ottawa-Hull, and Calgary.

V. **Models of Urban Growth**

   A. To explain how cities expand, sociologists created models of urban growth.

   B. Ernest W. Burgess proposed the concentric-zone model.

      1. The city consists of a series of zones emanating from its centre, with each characterized by a different group of people and activity: Zone 1—central business district; Zone 2—in transition with deteriorating housing and rooming houses; Zone 3—an area to which thrifty workers have moved to escape the zone in transition while maintaining access to work; Zone 4—more expensive apartments, single-family dwellings, and exclusive areas where the wealthy live; and Zone 5—commuter zone consisting of suburban areas or satellite cities that have developed around rapid transit routes.

      2. Burgess intended this model to represent the tendency for towns and cities to expand outward from the central business district; however, no city fits perfectly this ideal scheme.

   C. The sector model sees urban zones as wedge-shaped sectors radiating out from the centre.

      1. A zone might contain a sector of working-class housing, another sector of expensive housing, a third of businesses, and so on, all competing with one another for the same land.

2. In an invasion-succession cycle poor immigrants move into a city, settling in the lowest-rent area available; as their numbers grow, they begin to encroach on adjacent areas. As the poor move closer to the middle class, the middle class leave, expanding the sector of lower-cost housing.

3. Gentrification is the movement of middle-class people into rundown areas of a city. As a consequence of gentrification, the poor are often displaced from their neighbourhoods.

D. The multiple-nuclei model views the city as comprised of multiple centres or nuclei, each of which focuses on a specialized activity (e.g., retail districts, automobile dealers, etc.).

E. These models tell only a partial story of how cities develop. These models are time-bound, also geography-bound and do not account for urban planning policies, such as "green-belts" in the United Kingdom.

VI.   City Life

A. Cities provide opportunities but also create problems. Humans have a need for community, which some people have a hard time finding in cities.

B. Louis Wirth argued that the city undermines kinship and neighbourhood, which are the traditional bases of social control and social solidarity.

1. Urban dwellers live in anonymity, their lives marked by segmented and superficial encounters which make them grow aloof from one another and indifferent to other people's problems.

2. This is similar to the idea that *Gemeinschaft* (a sense of community that comes from everyone knowing everyone else) is ripped apart as a country industrializes, and *Gesellschaft* (a society characterized by secondary, impersonal relationships which result in alienation) replaces it.

C. The city is made up of a series of smaller worlds, within which people find a sense of community, or belonging.

D. Herbert Gans identified types of people who live in the city.

1. Cosmopolites—intellectuals and professionals, students, writers, and artists who live in the inner city to be near its conveniences and cultural benefits.

2. Singles—young, unmarried people who come seeking jobs and entertainment.

3. Ethnic villagers—live in tightly knit neighbourhoods that resemble villages and small towns, united by race and social class.

4. The trapped—who consist of four subtypes: those who could not afford to move when their neighbourhood was invaded by another ethnic group; downwardly mobile persons who have fallen from a higher social class; elderly people who have drifted into the slums because they are not wanted elsewhere and are powerless to prevent their downward slide; and alcoholics and drug addicts.

E. The city is divided into worlds that people come to know down to the smallest detail.

1. City people create a sense of intimacy for themselves by personalizing their shopping (by frequenting the same stores and restaurants, people become recognized as "regulars").

2. Spectator sports also engender community identification.

3. City dwellers develop strong feelings for particular objects and locations in the city such as trees, buildings, rivers, lakes, parks, and even street corners.

F. An essential element in determining whether someone finds community or alienation in a city is that person's social networks; community is found in relationships, not in buildings and space.

G. Suburbanization is the movement from the city to the suburbs. For the past 100 years, people have moved to towns next to the cities in which they worked.

H. The development of a global market has led to deindustrialization. Manufacturing firms have relocated from the inner city to areas where production costs are lower.

    1. Hundreds of thousands of manufacturing jobs were eliminated.

    2. The inner-city economies have not been able to provide alternative employment for poor residents, thereby locking them out of the economy. As a result, many are left in despair.

VII. The Natural Environment

A. Environmental problems are not new to the human scene. Several civilizations were destroyed because the environment on which their existence depended was destroyed.

B. Industrialization led to a major assault on the environment. While it has been viewed as good for the nation's welfare, it has also contributed to today's environmental problems.

    1. Many of our problems today—depletion of the ozone layer, acid rain, the greenhouse effect, and global warming—are associated with our dependence on fossil fuels.

    2. There is an abundant source of natural energy that would provide low-cost power and therefore help to raise the living standards of human across the globe. More technology is needed to harness this energy supply. From a conflict perspective, such abundant sources of energy present a threat to the multinationals' energy monopoly. We cannot expect the practical development and widespread use of alternative sources of power until the multinationals have cornered the market on the technology that will harness them.

C. Environmental degradation is also a problem in the industrializing nations, as these countries rushed into global industrial competition without the funds to purchase expensive pollution controls.

    1. Pollution was treated as a state secret in the former Soviet Union. With protest stifled, no environmental protection laws to inhibit pollution, and production quotas to be met, environmental pollution was rampant.

    2. Almost one-half of Russia's arable land is unsuitable for farming, air pollution in cities is ten times higher than that which is permitted in the U.S., and half the tap water is unfit to drink.

    3. The consequence of these conditions is that Russian life expectancy has dropped.

D. The combined pressures of population growth and almost nonexistent environmental regulations destine least industrialized nations to become the earth's major source of pollution. Some companies in industrialized nations use the least industrialized nations as a garbage dump for hazardous wastes and for producing chemicals no longer tolerated in their own countries.

    1. As tropical rain forests are cleared for lumber, farms and pastures, the consequence may be the extinction of numerous plant and animal species.

    2. As the rain forests disappear at a rate of nearly 2500 acres every hour, it is estimated that 10,000 species are made extinct each year.

E. The globalization of capitalism underlies today's environmental decay.

    1. The highly industrialized nations continue to push for economic growth, the industrializing nations strive to achieve faster economic growth, and the least industrialized nations, anxious to enter the race, push for even faster growth.

    2. If our goal is a sustainable environment, we must stop turning the earth's natural resources into trash.

    3. The Kyoto Protocol is an agreement, entered into by a number of countries, intended to reduce greenhouse gases (global warming) and thereby contribute to global sustainable development. One hundred and forty-one countries ratified Kyoto, the most glaring exception being the largest single polluter in the world, the United States. Ironically, two of the worst—and steadily worsening—polluters, India and China, have not, and are not required to sign on to Kyoto because they are industrializing nations.

F. Concern about the world's severe environmental problems has produced a worldwide social movement. In some countries, the environment has become a major issue in local and national elections. This movement seeks solutions in education, legislation, and political activism. In Europe, especially Germany, green parties campaign in local and national elections.

G. Environmental sociology examines the relationship between human societies and the environment. Its basic assumptions include: (1) the physical environment is a significant variable in sociological investigation; (2) humans are but one species among many that are dependent on the environment; (3) because of intricate feedbacks to nature, human actions have many unintended consequences; (4) the world is finite, so there are potential physical limits to economic growth; (5) economic expansion requires increased extraction of resources from the environment; (6) increased extraction of resources leads to ecological problems; (7) these ecological problems place restrictions on economic expansion; and (8) the state creates environmental problems by trying to create conditions for the profitable accumulation of capital.

H. If we are to have a world that is worth passing on to the coming generations, we must seek harmony between technology and the natural environment.

I. Ecofeminism and the environment—Ecofeminists believe human beings are connected to one another and to the non-human world whether it is animal, vegetable, or mineral.

KEY TERMS

After studying the chapter, review the definition for each of the following terms.

acid rain: rain containing sulfuric and nitric acid (produced by the reaction of sulfur dioxide and nitrogen oxide with moisture when released into the air with the burning of fossil fuels)

basic demographic equation: growth rate = births – deaths + net migration

city: a place in which a large number of people are permanently based and do not produce their own food

community: a place people identify with, where they sense that they belong and that others care what happens to them

crude birth rate: the annual number of births per 1,000 population

crude death rate: the annual number of deaths per 1,000 population

demographic transition: a three-stage historical process of population growth; first, high birth rates and high death rates; second, high birth rates and low death rates; and third, low birth rates and low death rates

demographic variables: the three factors that influence population growth: fertility, mortality, and net migration

demography: the study of the size, composition, growth, and distribution of human populations

environmental sociology: a subdiscipline of sociology that examines how human activities affect the physical environment and how the physical environment affects human activities

exponential growth curve: a pattern of growth in which numbers double during approximately equal intervals, thus accelerating in the latter stages

fecundity: the number of children that women are theoretically capable of bearing

fertility rate: the number of children that the average woman bears

gentrification: the displacement of the poor by the relatively affluent, who renovate the former's homes

global warming: an increase in the earth's temperature due to the greenhouse effect

greenhouse effect: the buildup of carbon dioxide in the earth's atmosphere that allows light to enter but inhibits the release of heat; believed to cause global warming

growth rate: the net change in a population after adding births, subtracting deaths, and either adding or subtracting net migration

invasion-succession cycle: the process of one group of people displacing a group whose racial-ethnic or social class characteristics differ from their own

Malthus theorem: an observation by Thomas Malthus that although the food supply increases only arithmetically (from 1 to 2 to 3 to 4 and so on), population grows geometrically (from 2 to 4 to 8 to 16 and so forth)

megalopolis: an urban area consisting of at least two metropolises and their many suburbs

metropolis: a central city surrounded by smaller cities and their suburbs

net migration rate: the difference between the number of immigrants and emigrants per 1,000 population

population shrinkage: the process by which a country's population becomes smaller because its birth rate and immigration are too low to replace those who die and emigrate

suburb: the communities adjacent to the political boundaries of a city

suburbanization: the movement from the city to the suburbs

sustainable environment: a world system that takes into account the limits of the environment, produces enough material goods for everyone's needs, and leaves a heritage of a sound environment for the next generation

urbanization: the process by which an increasing proportion of a population live in cities

zero population growth: a demographic condition in which women bear only enough children to reproduce the population

KEY PEOPLE

Review the major theoretical contributions or findings of these people.

Ernest Burgess: Burgess developed the concentric zone model of urban development.

William Faunce: Writing about the far-reaching implications of exponential growth, this sociologist's views are consistent with those of the New Malthusians.

Herbert Gans: Gans studied urban neighbourhoods, with the result that he documented the existence of community within cities and identified the several different types of urban dwellers that live there.

Chauncey Harris and Edward Ullman: These two geographers developed the multiple-nuclei model of urban growth.

Homer Hoyt: Hoyt modified Burgess's model of urban growth with the development of the sector model.

David Karp and William Yoels: These sociologists note that identification with a city's sports teams can be so intense that even after an individual moves away from the city, he or she continues to root for the team.

Thomas Malthus: Malthus was an economist who made dire predictions about the future of population growth.

Steven Mosher: This anthropologist, an anti-Malthusian, predicts that the world's population will decline sharply after peaking at about 7 billion in the year 2030.

Robert Park: Park coined the term "human ecology" to describe how people adapt to their environment.

Kathleen Riel: Riel is a Canadian sociologist who studies matters affecting the environment.

Victor Rodriguez: This sociologist points out that many U.S. industries have abandoned local communities and moved their factories to places where labour costs are lower because of competitive pressures of a global market.

Julian Simon: Simon is an anti-Malthusian who believes people do not just reproduce blindly but act intelligently and plan rationally. Simon has also argued that immigrants are a net contributor on the U.S. economy.

Gregory Stone: Stone observed how city people create a sense of intimacy for themselves by personalizing their shopping.

Louis Wirth: Wirth wrote a classic essay, "Urbanism as a Way of Life," in which he argued that city life undermines kinship and neighbourhood.

Richard Wohl and Anseim Strauss: These sociologists have pointed out that city dwellers even develop strong feelings for particular objects and locations in the city.

SELF-TEST

After completing this self-test, check your answers against the Answer Key at the back of this Study Guide and against the text on page(s) indicated in parentheses.

MULTIPLE CHOICE QUESTIONS

1. Who studies the size, composition, growth, and distribution of human population? (362)
   a. population experts
   b. growth specialists
   c. demographers
   d. social development professionals

2. The proposition that the population grows geometrically while food supply increases arithmetically is known as the: (362)
   a. food surplus equation.
   b. Malthus theorem.
   c. exponential growth curve.
   d. demographic transition.

3. Which of the following statements is consistent with beliefs of the Anti-Malthusians? (363)
   a. People will blindly reproduce until there is no room left on earth.
   b. It is possible to project the world's current population growth into the indefinite future.
   c. Most people do not use intelligence and rational planning when it comes to having children.
   d. The demographic transition provides an accurate picture of what the future looks like.

4. The three-stage historical process of population growth is known as the: (363)
   a. demographic equation.
   b. demographic transition.
   c. exponential growth curve.
   d. implosion growth curve.

5. The process by which a country's population becomes smaller because its birth rate and immigration are too low to replace those who die and emigrate is: (364)
   a. population transfer.
   b. population annihilation.
   c. population shrinkage.
   d. population depletion.

6. What is true of the Supply and demand for food? (364-366)
   a. A cause of starvation is an imbalance between supply and demand.
   b. When famine ravished West Africa, Canadian farmers had trouble selling their grain.
   c. Africa has 22 percent of the earth's land surface and contains some of the world's untapped land suitable for agriculture.
   d. all of the above

7. Why do people in the Least Industrialized Nations have so many children? (366)
   a. Parenthood provides status.
   b. Children are considered to be an economic asset.
   c. The community encourages people to have children.
   d. all of the above

8. What are the factors that influence population growth called? (367)
   a. demographic variables
   b. demographic transitions
   c. demographic equations
   d. demographic constants

9. Which of the following will have an impact on the country's population growth rate? (367)
   a. economic booms and busts
   b. wars
   c. plagues and famines
   d. all the above

10. The annual number of deaths per 1,000 population is the: (367)
    a. crude death rate.
    b. crude mortality rate.
    c. crude life expectancy rate.
    d. net death rate.

11. What factors might push someone to migrate? (367)
    a. poverty
    b. lack of religious and political freedom
    c. political persecution
    d. all of the above

12. Which of the following is not a demographic variable used to project population trends? (367)
    a. poverty
    b. fertility
    c. mortality
    d. net migration

13. The process by which an increasing proportion of a population lives in cities is: (370)
    a. suburbanization.
    b. gentrification.
    c. megalopolitanism.
    d. urbanization.

14. What is not true of the process of urbanization? (370)
    a. In 1800 only 3 percent of world's population lived in cities.
    b. In 2007 it is expected that 27 percent of all humanity will live in cities.
    c. Today 75 percent of those who live in the least industrialized nations live in cities.
    d. Today over 70 percent of Canadians live in cities.

15. Who first proposed the concentric-zone model? (371)
    a. Herbert Gans
    b. Ernest Burgess
    c. Robert Park
    d. Homer Hoyt

16. When a new group of immigrants enter a city, they tend to settle in low-rent areas. As their numbers increase, those already living in the area begin to move out; their departure creates more low-cost housing for the immigrants. How do sociologists refer to this process? (371)
    a. progressive population replacement
    b. reverse gentrification
    c. cycle of assimilation
    d. invasion-succession cycle

17. The model which suggests that land use in cities is based on several centres, such as a clustering of restaurants or automobile dealerships, is the: (371)
    a. sector model.
    b. concentric-zone model.
    c. multiple-nuclei model.
    d. commerce model.

18. How do urban dwellers counteract alienation? (374)
    a. by personalizing their shopping
    b. by frequenting taverns, restaurants, and Laundromats
    c. by attending spectator sports events
    d. all of the above

19. According to Gans's typology, the trapped include: (374)
    a. downwardly mobile persons.
    b. elderly persons.
    c. alcoholics and drug addicts.
    d. all of the above

20. What is suburbanization? (374)
    a. movement from the suburbs to edge cities
    b. movement from the city to the suburbs
    c. movement from rural areas to suburbs
    d. displacement of the poor by the relatively affluent, who renovate the former's homes

21. According to Gans's typology, cosmopolitans include: (374)
    a. city's students.
    b. city's intellectuals and professionals.
    c. city's musicians, artists, and entertainers.
    d. all of the above

22. How do conflict theorists explain the energy shortage? (376)
    a. They note that the earth has a limited supply of energy, and that multinational corporations are rapidly depleting it.
    b. There is no reliable alternative to the internal combustion engine.
    c. They argue that multinational corporations are unwilling to develop alternative energy sources, because it would threaten their monopoly over existing fossil fuels and cut into their profits.
    d. As a result of the past exploitation of natural resources by profit-hungry multinational corporations, there are no longer alternative energy resources that are reliable.

23. Which of the following presents the greatest threat to the survival of numerous plant and animal species? (376)
    a. the continued burning of fossil fuels
    b. the dumping of toxic waste in the least industrialized nations
    c. the disappearance of the world's rain forests
    d. the greenhouse effect

24. Environmental sociology examines: (377-378)
    a. how the physical environment affects human activities.
    b. how human activities affect the physical environment.
    c. the unintended consequences of human actions.
    d. all of the above

25. What is the goal of environmental sociologists? (378)
    a. to stop pollution
    b. to do research on the mutual impact that individuals and environments have on one another
    c. to empower those who are disadvantaged by environmental threats so that the quality of their lives will be improved
    d. to lobby for alternatives to fossil fuels

TRUE-FALSE QUESTIONS

T F 1.   Thomas Malthus was a sociologist at the University of Chicago in the 1920s. (362)
T F 2.   Anti-Malthusians, such as economist Julian Simon and anthropologist Steven Mosher, argue that people simply do not blindly reproduce until there is no room left. (363)
T F 3.   Anti-Malthusians say that the world's problem will not be a population explosion, but a population shrinkage . (364)
T F 4.   The Anti-Malthusians believe that Europe's demographic transition provides a more accurate population prediction than Malthus. (363)

T F 5. The amount of food produced for each person in the world is now less than it was in 1950. (364)

T F 6. The major reason why people in the Least Industrialized Nations have so many children is because they do not know how to prevent conception. (366)

T F 7. Demographers study fertility, mortality, and migration to project population trends. (367)

T F 8. The imbalance of supply and demand of food is the cause of starvation. (364)

T F 9. Migration rates do not affect the global population. (367)

T F 10. It is difficult for demographers to forecast population growth. (368)

T F 11. The rate and extent of urbanization in recent years is new to the world scene. (370)

T F 12. The concentric-zone model is based on the idea that cities expand radially from their central business district. (371)

T F 13. The multiple-nuclei model is the most accurate model of urban growth. (371)

T F 14. The Urban Villagers was written by Herbert Gans. (374)

T F 15. Sports teams often engender community identification in urban areas. (374)

T F 16. Environmental problems have only recently emerged on the human scene. (375)

T F 17. Rain containing sulfuric and nitric acid, released into the air with the burning of fossil fuels, is a cause of the greenhouse effect. (375)

T F 18. Scientists are in agreement that the problems of acid rain and the greenhouse effect must be solved quickly. (375)

T F 19. Environmental sociology that examines the relationship between human societies and the environment, emerged in 1970 as a sub discipline of sociology. (377)

T F 20. The goal of environmental sociology is to reduce pollution levels on a global scale. (378)

FILL-IN QUESTIONS

1. From demographers' point of view, we will be at _____population growth with every 1000 women giving birth to _____ children. (368)

2. A pattern of growth in which numbers double during approximately equal intervals, thus accelerating in the latter stages is the _____. (362)

3. The Anti-Malthusians believe that Europe's _____, a three-stage historical process of population growth, provides an accurate picture of the future. (363)

4. When the people in a society do not produce enough children to replace the people who die, there is concern about _____. (364)

5. The _____ refers to the number of children that the average woman bears. (367)

6. The basic demographic equation is *growth* = _____ − _____ + _____. (367)

7. When women bear only enough children to replace the population, _____has been achieved. (368)

8. _____ is a place in which a large number of people are permanently based and do not produce their own food. (370)

9. _____ is the process by which an increasing number of people live in cities. (370)

10. A central city, surrounded by smaller cities and their suburbs, forming an interconnected urban area, is a _____. (370)

11. The _____, for example, produces more energy than humanity could ever use. (375)
12. The displacement of the poor by the relatively affluent, who renovate the former's homes, is _____. (371)
13. _____ exists when people identify with an area and with one another. (372)
14. The greenhouse effect is believed to produce _____. (375)
15. Two of the worst polluters, _____ and _____ have not, and are not required to sign on to Kyoto because they are industrializing nations. (376)

MATCH THESE SOCIAL SCIENTISTS WITH THEIR CONTRIBUTIONS

___ 1.   Thomas Malthus   a.   *theorem on population growth*
___ 2.   Ernest Burgess   b.   *human ecology*
___ 3.   Herbert Gans   c.   *concentric-zone model*
___ 4.   Homer Hoyt   d.   *urban villagers*
___ 5.   Robert Park   e.   *sector model*

ESSAY QUESTIONS

1. State the positions of the New Malthusians and the Anti-Malthusians and discuss which view you think is more accurate, based on the information provided about each position.
2. Identify the problems that are associated with forecasting population growth.
3. Describe the dilemma of China's and India's unwanted baby girls and what happens to them—see Perspectives Box. (369)
4. Will cities of the least industrialized nations satisfy the people's longing for a better life? See Perspectives Box. (372)

"DOWN-TO-EARTH SOCIOLOGY"

1. What was your reaction after reading "Killing Little Girls" on page 369? Why is this practice common in certain cultures and not others? What social, economic or political changes would contribute to the elimination of this practice?
2. As we look to the 21st century, we need to find ways to use technology to improve the quality of life around the globe (369). This might involve reproductive technologies or those that boost food production and create employment. If you lived in a least industrialized nation how would you view these things? Would you see them as enhancing your life, or threatening it?
3. How does the picture of urban living painted on page 372 match your own "picture" of what life is like in the Least Industrialized Nations? Do the lives of people in these nations have any bearing on your life? Why or why not?
4. Do you think "Ecosabotage," (377), is ever justified? Do you think radical acts can do more harm than good? Do they alienate or unite supporters of the movement?

CHAPTER 18
SOCIAL MOVEMENTS AND SOCIAL CHANGE

CHAPTER SUMMARY

- Early theorists argued that individuals are transformed by crowds, losing all capacity for rationality. Terms such as "herd mentality," "collective mind," and "circular reaction" were developed to explain why people behaved as they did when in the midst of a crowd. According to Herbert Blumer, crowds go through five stages before they become an acting crowd: social unrest, an exciting event, milling, a common object of attention, and common impulses.

- Contemporary explanations emphasize the rationality of the crowd, the emergence of norms to govern behaviour; collective behaviour is seen as directed toward a goal, even if it is cruel and destructive behaviour.

- Some of the major forms of collective behaviour are riots, panics, moral panics, rumours, fads, fashions, and urban legends. Conditions of discontent and uncertainty provide fertile ground for collective behaviour.

- Social movements usually involve more people, are more prolonged, are more organized, and focus on social change. At the heart of social movements lie grievances and dis-satisfactions. For some people, a current condition of society is intolerable, and their goal is to promote social change. Theirs is called a proactive social movement. In contrast, others feel threatened because some condition of society is changing, and they organize to resist that change. Theirs is a reactive social movement. Depending on whether their target is individuals or society and the amount of change desired is partial or complete, social movements can be classified as alternative, redemptive, reformative, or transformative.

- Tactics are chosen on the basis of a group's levels of membership, its publics, and its relationship to authority. Because the mass media are the gatekeepers, their favourable or unfavourable coverage greatly affects a social movement and tactics are chosen with the media in mind.

- Mass society theory, relative deprivation theory and ideological commitment theory all attempt to explain why people join social movements.

- Social movements go through distinct stages: initial unrest and agitation; resource mobilization; organization; institutionalization; organizational decline and possible resurgence. Resource mobilization is the crucial factor that enables social movements to make it past the first stage.

- Social change, the alteration of culture and society over time, is a vital part of social life.

- William Ogburn identified three processes of social change. Technology can lead to social change through innovation, discovery, and diffusion. Cultural lag refers to the changes in the symbolic culture in response to changes in technology.

- Technology is a driving force in social change, and it can shape an entire society by changing existing technology, social organization, ideology, values, and social relationships, as is evident when analyzing the impact that both the automobile and the computer have had on Canadian society.

- Other theories of social change include: evolutionary theories (both unilinear and multilinear), Marxist conflict theories, cyclical theories, feminist theories, and postmodern theories.

- Social movements rarely solve all of society's social problems. However, many have become powerful forces for social change.

LEARNING OBJECTIVES

As you read Chapter 18, use these learning objectives to organize your notes. After completing your reading, briefly state an answer to each of the objectives, and review the text pages in parentheses.

1. Discuss early explanations of collective behaviour and note how these explanations focused on the transformation of the individual. (383)
2. Compare and contrast the minimax strategy and the emergent norm theory. (384)
3. Describe the forms of collective behaviour, including riots and demonstrations, panic, moral panic, rumours, fads and fashions, and urban legends. (385-388)
4. Compare and contrast proactive and reactive social movements. (388)
5. List the different types of social movements, classifying them according to their target and the amount of change they seek, alterative, redemptive, reformative, and transformative social movements. (389-390)
6. Describe the role that each of the following plays in influencing leadership choice of tactics: membership levels, publics, and relationships to authorities. (390-391)
7. Define propaganda and discuss the role of the mass media in social movements. (391-392)
8. Compare the different explanations of why people join social movements. (392-393)
9. Discuss the role of the agent provocateur in social movements. (393)
10. Identify the five stages that social movements go through as they grow and mature. (394)
11. Identify the double meaning of technology and discuss the role of technology in postmodern societies. (394-395)
12. Identify and define Ogburn's three processes of social change, explain what is meant by "cultural lag," and evaluate the utility of Ogburn's theory. (395-396)
13. Using automobiles or computers, explain how technology transforms society. (397-398)
14. State the impact that computers will have on social inequality in the twenty-first century. (399)
15. Outline the alternative theories of social change, including evolutionary, Marxist, cyclical, feminist, and postmodern theories. (400)
16. Study the benefits and drawbacks of increased surveillance in the work place facilitated by computers. (399)

CHAPTER OUTLINE

I.   **Early Explanations of Collective Behaviour: The Transformation of the Individual**
     A. Collective behaviour is characterized by a group of people becoming emotionally aroused and engaging in extraordinary behaviour, in which the usual norms do not apply.
     B. In 1852, Charles Mackay concluded that when people were in crowds, they sometimes went "mad" and did "disgraceful and violent things;" just as a herd of cows will stampede, so people can come under the control of a "herd mentality."
     C. Based on Mackay's idea, Gustave LeBon stressed that the individual is transformed by the crowd.

      1. In a crowd, people feel anonymous, not accountable for what they do; they develop feelings of invincibility, believing that together they can accomplish anything. A collective mind develops.

      2. They become highly suggestible; this paves the way for contagion, a kind of collective hypnosis, which releases the destructive instincts that society has so carefully repressed.

D. Herbert Blumer synthesized LeBon's ideas withy another sociologist Robert Park.

E. Using symbolic interaction theory and synthesizing both LeBon's and Park's ideas, Herbert Blumer identified five stages of collective behaviour.

      1. A background condition of social unrest exists—when people's routine activities are thwarted or when they develop new needs that go unsatisfied.

      2. An exciting event occurs—one so startling that people are preoccupied with it.

      3. People engage in milling—the act of standing or walking around as they talk about the exciting event and circular reaction sets in.

      4. A common object of attention emerges—people's attention becomes riveted on some aspect of the event.

      5. Stimulation of the common impulses occurs—people collectively agree about what they should do. Social contagion, described as a collective excitement passed from one person to another, becomes the mechanism that stimulates these common impulses. The end result is an acting crowd—an excited group that collectively moves toward a goal, which may be constructive or destructive.

II.   The Contemporary View: The Rationality of the Crowd

A. Richard Berk pointed out that people use a minimax strategy (trying to minimize their costs and maximize their rewards) whether in small groups or in crowds; the fewer the costs and the greater the rewards that people anticipate, the more likely they are to carry out a particular act.

B. Ralph Turner and Lewis Killian noted that human behaviour is regulated by the normative order—socially approved ways of doing things that make up our everyday life —but when an extraordinary event occurs and existing norms do not cover the new situation, people develop new norms to deal with the problem (emergent norms).

      1. There are five kinds of crowd participants: (1) the ego-involved, who feel a high personal stake in the event; (2) the concerned, who have a personal interest in the event, but less than the ego-involved; (3) the insecure, who have little concern about the issue but have sought out the crowd because it gives them a sense of power and security; (4) the curious spectators, who are inquisitive and may cheer the crowd on even though they do not care about the issue; and (5) the exploiters, who do not care about the issue but use it for their own purposes (e.g., hawking food or T-shirts).

      2. The concept of emergent norms is important because it points to a rational process as the essential component of collective behaviour.

III.   Forms of Collective Behaviour

A. Riots, such as the one that erupted in Los Angeles after the verdict in the Rodney King trial, are usually caused by frustration and anger at deprivation.

   1. Frustration develops from a perception of being kept out of the mainstream society—limited to a meager education, denied jobs and justice, and kept out of good neighbourhoods—and builds to such a boiling point that it takes only a precipitating event to erupt in collective behaviour.

   2. It is not only the deprived who participate in riots or demonstrations; others, who are not deprived, but who still feel frustration at the underlying social conditions that place them at a disadvantage, also get involved.

   3. The event that precipitates a riot is much less important than the riot's general context.

B. Panic, like the one which occurred following the broadcast of H. G. Wells's "War of the Worlds," is behaviour that results when people become so fearful that they cannot function normally.

   1. One explanation as to why people panic is because they are anxious about some social condition.

   2. This is why it is against the law to shout "Fire!" in a public building when no such danger exists—if people fear immediate death, they will lunge toward the nearest exit in a frantic effort to escape.

   3. Sociologists have found that not everyone panics in these situations, and some employees, such as some of those at the supper club, engage in role extension—the incorporation of additional activities into a role—to try to help people to safety.

C. Moral panics occur when large numbers of people become intensely concerned, even fearful, about some behaviour that is perceived as a threat to morality—the threat is seen as enormous and hostility builds toward those thought responsible.

   1. Like other panics, moral panics centre around a sense of danger. But, because they involve larger numbers of people and are fostered by the mass media, moral panics, as opposed to other forms of panic, do not arise as quickly.

   2. Moral panics are often fed by rumour, information for which there is no discernible source and which is usually unfounded.

   3. Moral panics also thrive on uncertainty and anxiety.

D. Rumours thrive in conditions of ambiguity, functioning to fill in missing information.

   1. Most rumours are short-lived and arise in a situation of ambiguity, only to dissipate when they are replaced either by another rumour or by factual information. A few rumours have a long life because they hit a responsive cord (e.g., rumours of mass poisoning of soft drink products that spread to many countries).

   2. Three main factors in why people believe rumours are that they: (1) deal with a subject that is important to an individual; (2) replace ambiguity with some form of certainty; and (3) are attributed to a creditable source.

E. A fad is a temporary pattern of behaviour that catches people's attention, while fashion is a more enduring version of the same.

   1. John Loftand identified four types of fads: (1) object fads, such as the hula hoop or pet rocks; (2) activity fads, such as eating goldfish or playing Trivial Pursuit: (3) idea fads, such as astrology; and (4) personality fads, such as Elvis Presley, Vanna White, and Michael Jordan.

2. Fashion is a behaviour pattern that catches people's attention, lasting longer than a fad. Most often thought of in terms of clothing fashions, it can also refer to hairstyles, home decorating, design and colours of buildings, and language.

F. Urban legends are stories with an ironic twist that sound realistic but are false. Jan Brunvand, who studied the transmission of urban legends, concluded that urban legends are passed on by people who think that the event really happened to someone, such as a "friend of a friend"; the stories have strong appeal and gain credibility from naming specific people or local places; and they are "modern morality stories," with each teaching a moral lesson about life.

IV. **Social Movements**
   A. Social movements consist of large numbers of people, who, through deliberate and sustained efforts, organize to promote or resist social change. At the heart of social movements lie grievances and dissatisfactions.
   B. Proactive social movements promote social change because a current condition of society is intolerable. In contrast, reactive social movements resist changing conditions in society that they perceive as threatening. To further their goals, people develop social movement organizations.
   C. The National Action Committee on the Status of Women, The Council of Canadians, and the National Indian Brotherhood are all examples of social movement organizations in Canada whose goal is to promote social change.

V. **Types and Tactics of Social Movements**
   A. David Aberle classified social movements into four broad categories according to the type and amount of social change they seek.
      1. Two types seek to change people but differ in terms of the amount of change desired: alternative social movements seek to alter only particular aspects of people (e.g., Mothers Against Drunk Driving); while redemptive social movements seek to change people totally (e.g., a religious social movement such as fundamental Christianity that stresses conversion).
      2. Two types seek to change society but also differ in terms of the amount of change desired: reformative social movements seek to reform only one part of society (e.g., the environment); transformative social movements seek to change the social order itself and to replace it with their own version of the ideal society (e.g., revolutions in the American colonies, France, Russia, and Cuba).
      3. Today some social movements, called new social movements, have a global orientation, committed to changing a specific condition throughout the world. The women's, environmental, and animal rights movements are examples.
   B. Tactics of social movements are best understood by examining levels of membership, publics they address, and their relationship to authorities.
      1. Three levels of membership are the inner core (the leadership that sets goals, timetables, etc.); people committed to the goals of the movement, but not to the same degree as members of the inner core; and people who are neither as committed nor as dependable.

2. Publics can be described as just outside the third circle of members, and blending into it, is the sympathetic public. Sympathy with the movement's goals makes this public fertile ground for recruiting new members. The second public is hostile; it is keenly aware of the group's goals and dislikes them. The public wants to stop social movement, for the movement's values go against its own. The third public consists of disinterested people. They are either unaware of the social movement, or if aware, indifferent to it.

3. The movement's relationship to the authorities is important in determining tactics: if authorities are hostile to a social movement, aggressive or even violent tactics are likely; if authorities are sympathetic, violence is not likely. If a social movement is institutionalized, accepted by the authorities and given access to resources they control, the likelihood of violence is very low.

4. Other factors that can influence the choice of tactics include the nature of friendships, race, and even the size of towns.

C. In selecting tactics, leaders of social movements are aware of their effects on the mass media. Their goal is to influence public opinion about some issue.

1. Propaganda is a key to understanding social movements. Propaganda simply means the presentation of information in an attempt to influence people.

2. The mass media play a critical role in social movements. They can in effect, become the gatekeepers to social movements. If those who control and work in the mass media are sympathetic to a "cause," it will receive sympathetic treatment. If the social movement goes against their own biases, it will either be ignored or receive unfavourable treatment.

3. A case in point is the widely televised "LIVE 8—The Long Walk to Justice" concerts in 2005, staged in the major cities of the G8 countries and Johannesburg, South Africa, on the eve of the G8 summit in Gleneagles, (near Edinburgh), Scotland. Three billion people world wide watched these concerts. The aim was to pressure the leaders of the G8 nations to do three things—to eliminate poverty in Africa: cancel the debt owed by African nations to rich countries, and to make trade fairer.

VI. **Why People Join Social Movements**

A. In the mass society theory, William Kornhauser proposed that social movements offer a sense of belonging to people who have weak social ties.

1. Mass society, characterized as an industrialized, highly bureaucratized, impersonal society, makes many people feel isolated and, as a result, they are attracted to social movements because they offer a sense of belonging.

2. However Doug McAdam (who studied those involved in civil rights movements) found that many who participate in social movements have strong family and community ties, and joined such movements to right wrongs and overcome injustice, not because of isolation. The most isolated (the homeless) generally do not join anything except food lines.

B. According to deprivation theory people who are deprived of things deemed valuable in society—whether money, justice, status, or privilege—join social movements with the hope of redressing their grievances.

1. Absolute deprivation is people's actual negative condition; relative deprivation is what people think they should have relative to what others have, or even compared with their own past or perceived future.
2. While the notion of absolute deprivation provides a beginning point for looking at why people join social movements, it is even more important to look at relative deprivation in trying to understand why people join social movements.
3. Improved conditions fuel human desires for even better conditions, and thus can spark revolutions.

C. James Jasper and Dorothy Nelkin note that people join a particular social movement because of moral issues and an ideological commitment to the movement. It is the moral component, they argue, that is a primary reason for some people's involvement in social movements.

D. An agent provocateur is a special type of social movement participant.
1. An agent of the government or of a social movement, the agent provocateur's job is to spy on the leadership and sabotage their activities. Some are recruited from the membership itself, while others go underground and join the movement.
2. On occasion a police agent is converted to the social movement on which he or she is spying. Sociologist Gary Marx noted that this occurs because the agent, to be credible, must share at least some of the class, age, ethnic, racial, religious, or sexual characteristics of the group. This makes the agent more likely to sympathize with the movement's goals and to become disenchanted with the means being used to destroy the group.
3. Sometimes the agent provocateur will go to great lengths, even breaking the law, to push the social movement into illegal activities.

VII.   On the Success and Failure of Social Movements

A. Social movements have a life course; that is, they go through five stages as they grow and mature.
1. Initial unrest and agitation because people are upset about some social condition; at this stage leaders emerge who verbalize people's feelings.
2. Mobilization of resources such as time, money, people's skills, technologies, attention by the mass media, and legitimacy among the public and authorities.
3. An organization emerges with a division of labour, with leadership that makes policy decisions and a rank and file that actively supports the movement.
4. Institutionalization occurs as the movement becomes bureaucratized and leadership passes to career officials who may care more about their position in the organization than about the movement itself.
5. The organization declines, but there may be a possibility of resurgence. Some movements cease to exist; others become reinvigorated.

VIII.   An Overview of Social Change

A. Social change is a shift in the characteristics of culture and societies over time. Before being able to interpret these changes, we need to consider the importance of technology.

IX.   How Technology Changes Society

A. Technology refers to both the tools used to accomplish tasks and to the skills or procedures to make and use those tools.

1. Technology is an artificial means of extending human abilities.

2. Although all human groups use technology, it is the chief characteristic of postindustrial societies because it greatly extends our abilities to analyze information, to communicate, and to travel.

3. The way technology alters people's way of life is of great significance. These new technologies allow us to do what had never been done in history: probe space and other planets and communicate instantaneously anywhere on the globe.

B. Modernization (the change from traditional to modern societies) produces sweeping changes in societies, but they should be interpreted as "more or less" not either or.

C. William Ogburn identified three processes of social change.

1. *Inventions* can be either material (computers) or social (capitalism); *discovery* is a new way of seeing things; and *diffusion* is the spread of an invention, discovery, or idea, from one area to another.

2. Ogburn coined the term cultural lag to describe the situation in which some elements of a culture adapt to an invention or discovery more rapidly than others. We are constantly trying to catch up with technology by adapting our customs and ways of life to meet its needs.

D. Ogburn has been criticized because of his view that technology controls almost all social change. Some find Ogburns analysis too one-directional.

1. People also take control over technology, developing the technology they need and selectively using existing technology. Both can happen—technology leads to social change, and social change leads to technology.

E. New technologies can reshape an entire society. Five ways in which technology can shape an entire society are (1) Transformation of existing technologies; (2) Changes in social organization; (3) Changes in ideology; (4) Transformation of values; and (5) Transformation of social relationships.

F. The automobile is an example of technological change. The automobile has pushed aside old technology; it has changed the shape of cities; it has changed architecture; it has changed courtship practices and sexual norms; and it has had a major effect on the lives of women.

G. The computer is another example, changing medicine, education, and the workplace. On the negative side are increased surveillance of workers and depersonalization.

H. With the information superhighway, homes and businesses are connected by a rapid flow of information. The implications of this superhighway for national and global stratification are severe.

1. On a national level, we may end up with information have-nots, thus perpetuating existing inequalities.

2. On a global level, the highly industrialized nations will control the information superhighway, thereby destining the least industrialized nations to a perpetual pauper status.

X. **Contemporary Theories of Social Change**
   A. Alternative theories of social change include: Evolutionary theories (unilinear or multilinear); Marxist conflict theories; Cyclical theories; Feminist theories; and Postmodern theories.

XI. **The Difficult Road to Success**
   A. Social movements rarely solve all of society's social problems, as movements must appeal to a broad constituency in order to effectively mobilize resources. However, many have become powerful forces for social change, as they highlight problems and provide direction towards a resolution. Others become powerful forces in resisting undesirable social change. Quebec sovereignty movement and trade unions in Canada come to mind.

KEY TERMS

After studying the chapter, review the definition for each of the following terms.

acting crowd: Herbert Blumer's term for an excited group that collectively moves toward a goal

agent provocateur: someone who joins a group in order to spy on it and to sabotage it by provoking its members to commit illegal acts

alienation: Marx's term for workers' lack of connection to the product of their labour, caused by their being assigned repetitive tasks on a small part of a product

alterative social movement: a social movement that seeks to alter only particular aspects of people

collective behaviour: extraordinary activities carried out by groups of people; includes lynchings, rumours, panics, urban legends, and fads and fashions

collective mind: Gustave LeBon's term for the tendency of people in a crowd to feel, think, and act in extraordinary ways

cultural lag: Ogburn's term for human behaviour lagging behind technological innovation.

demonstrations: participation in collective action such as riots

diffusion: the spread of invention or discovery from one area to another; identified by William Ogburn as the final of three processes of social change

discovery: a new way of seeing reality; identified by William Ogburn as the second of three processes of social change

emergent norms: Ralph Turner and Lewis Killian's term for the development of new norms to cope with a new situation, especially among crowds

fad: a temporary pattern of behaviour that catches people's attention

fashion: a pattern of behaviour that catches people's attention, which lasts longer than a fad

invention: the combination of existing elements and materials to form new ones; identified by William Ogburn as the first of three processes of social change

mass society: industrialized, highly bureaucratized, impersonal society

mass society theory: an explanation for participation in social movements based on the assumption that such movements offer a sense of belonging to people who have weak social ties

milling: a crowd standing or walking around as they talk excitedly about some event

minimax strategy: Richard Berk's term for the effort people make to minimize their costs and maximize their rewards

modernization: the process by which a traditional society is transformed into a modern society

moral panic: a fear that grips large numbers of people that some evil group or behaviour threatens the well-being of society, followed by intense hostility, sometimes violence, toward those thought responsible

new social movement: social movement with a new emphasis on the world, instead of on a condition in a specific country

panic: the condition of being so fearful that one cannot function normally, and may even flee

postmodern society: another term for postindustrial society; its chief characteristic is the use of tools that extend the human abilities to gather and analyze information, to communicate, and to travel

proactive social movement: a social movement that promotes social change

propaganda: in its broad sense, the presentation of information in the attempt to influence people; in its narrow sense, one-sided information used to try to influence people

public: a dispersed group of people who usually have an interest in the issue on which a social movement focuses; the sympathetic and hostile publics have such an interest, but a third public is either unaware of the issue or indifferent to it

public opinion: how people think about some issue

reactive social movement: a social movement that resists social change

redemptive social movement: a social movement that seeks to change people totally

reformative social movement: a social movement that seeks to change only particular aspects of society

relative deprivation theory: the belief that people join social movements based on their evaluations of what they think they should have compared with what others have

resource mobilization: a theory that social movements succeed or fail based on their ability to mobilize resources such as time, money, and people's skills

riot: violent crowd behaviour aimed against people and property

role extension: the incorporation of additional activities into a role

rumour: unfounded information spread among people

social change: the alteration of culture and societies over time

social movement: a large group of people who are organized to promote or resist social change

social movement organization: an organization developed to further the goals of a social movement

technology: often defined as the applications of science, but can be conceptualized as tools, items used to accomplish tasks, along with the skills or procedures necessary to make and use those tools

transformative social movement: a social movement that seeks to change society totally

urban legend: a story with an ironic twist that sounds realistic but is false

KEY PEOPLE

Review the major theoretical contributions or findings of these people.

David Aberle: Aberle classified social movements into four types: alternative, redemptive, reformative, and transformative based on the amount of intended change and the target of the change.

William Bainbridge: examined several modern instances of whether panics occurred.

Richard Berk: Berk developed the minimax strategy to explain collective behaviour; this is that people are more likely to act when costs are low and anticipated rewards high.

Herbert Blumer: Blumer identified five stages that precede the emergence of an active crowd (an excited group that moves towards a goal. These are tension or unrest; an exciting event; milling; a common object of attraction; and common impulses.

Jan Brunvand: This folklorist studied urban legends and suggests that they are modern morality stories.

Hadley Cantril: This psychologist suggests that people panicked after hearing the famous *War of the Worlds* because of widespread anxiety about world conditions.

James Flink: Flink examined the numerous ways in which the automobile has transformed U.S. society and culture, from architecture to women's roles.

James Jasper and Dorothy Nelkin: These sociologists argue that many become involved in social movements because of moral issues and an ideological commitment.

William Kornhauser: Kornhauser proposed mass society theory to explain why people are attracted to social movements. He suggested that these movements fill a void in some people's lives by offering them a sense of belonging.

Gustave LeBon: LeBon argued that a collective mind develops within a crowd and people are swept away by any suggestion that is made.

Alfred and Elizabeth Lee: These sociologists found that propaganda relies on seven basic techniques, which they labelled "tricks of the trade."

John Loftand: Lofiand identified four different types of fads: object fads, activity fads, idea fads, and personality fads.

Charles Mackay: Mackay was the first to study collective behaviour; he suggested that a "herd mentality" takes over and explains the disgraceful things people do when in crowds.

Gary Marx: This sociologist investigated the agent provocateur and found that some are converted to the movement because they share the some of the same social characteristics as the movement's members.

Karl Marx: Marx analyzed the emergence of capitalism and saw changes in the factory system as a source of alienation.

Doug McAdam: McAdam challenged the mass society theory on the basis of research findings related to people's decision to become involved in the civil rights struggle. He found they were well integrated into society, rather than isolated from it as mass society theory suggests.

William Ogburn: Ogburn identified three processes of social change: invention, discovery, and diffusion. He also coined the term "cultural lag" to describe a situation in which some elements of culture adapt to an invention or discovery more rapidly than others.

Robert Park: Park suggested that social unrest is the result of the circular reaction of people in crowds.

Victor Rodriguez: This sociologist suggests that minorities in the middle class might participate in riots when they feel frustrated with being treated as second-class citizens even when they are employed and living stable lives.

Ellen Scott: Scott studied the movement to stop rape and found that close friendships, race, and even size of town are important in determining tactics.

Ralph Turner and Lewis Killian: These sociologists use the term "emergent norm" to explain the rules that emerge in collective behaviour.

SELF-TEST

After completing this self-test, check your answers against the Answer Key at the back of this Study Guide and against the text on page(s) indicated in parentheses.

MULTIPLE CHOICE QUESTIONS

1. Which of the following statements about Charles Mackay is *incorrect*? (383)
   a. He noticed that ordinary people did disgraceful things when in a crowd.
   b. He suggested that people have a "herd mentality" when in a crowd.
   c. He proposed that a collective mind develops once a group of people congregate.
   d. His work marked the beginnings of the field of collective behaviour.

2. Gustave LeBon's term for the tendency of people in a crowd to feel, think, and act in extraordinary ways is: (383)
   a. social unrest.
   b. the "herd mentality."
   c. collective behaviour.
   d. collective mind.

3. Which of the following is not one of Blumer's stages that precede what is called the "acting crowd"? (383)
   a. social calm
   b. exciting event
   c. milling behaviour
   d. common object and common impulse

4. Acting crowd: (383)
   a. is a term coined by Herbert Blumer.
   b. is an excited group that collectively moves toward a goal.
   c. is the end result of the five stages of collective behaviour.
   d. all of the above

5. Richard Berk used the term "minimax strategy" to describe the tendency for: (384)
   a. crowds to operate with a minimum of strategy.
   b. humans to minimize costs and maximize rewards.
   c. those in authority to maximize the costs of an action in order to minimize rewards.
   d. society to respond to even the most minimum of social movements.

6. According to Turner and Killian, when new norms emerge, not everyone in the crowd has the same point of view. Which kinds of participants did they NOT include in these? (385)
   a. ego involved
   b. the concerned
   c. the agitators
   d. the exploiters

7. Urban riots are usually caused by which of the following factors? (385-386)
   a. People tended to be frustrated for being kept out of mainstream society.
   b. People had limited education and were kept out of good jobs and neighbourhoods.
   c. People's frustration had built up to such a level that it took only a precipitating event to erupt in collective violence.
   d. all of the above

8. Failure to function normally, and even fleeing, is the result of _____ .(386)
   a. disturbance
   b. panic
   c. fad
   d. riot

9. Sociologists have found that not everyone panics when disaster strikes; they use the term _____ to describe these actions of those who do not panic. (387)
   a. role extension
   b. role reverse
   c. role strain
   d. role replacement

10. Which statement about moral panics is *incorrect*? (387)
    a. Moral panics occur when people are concerned about something viewed as immoral.
    b. Moral panics are generally based on an event that has been verified as true.
    c. Moral panics thrive on uncertainty and anxiety.
    d. Moral panics are fueled by the mass media.

11. Sociologists refer to unfounded information spread among people as: (387)
    a. hearsay.
    b. scuttlebutt.
    c. rumour.
    d. gossip.

12. A temporary pattern of behaviour that catches people's attention is a: (388)
    a. panic.
    b. trend.
    c. fashion.
    d. fad.

13. Eating goldfish and bungee jumping are both examples of: (388)
    a.   object fads.
    b.   urban legends.
    c.   activity fads.
    d.   rumours.

14. Social movements that seek to change people totally are: (389)
    a.   alternative social movements.
    b.   redemptive social movements.
    c.   reformative social movements.
    d.   transformative social movements.

15. A social movement that seeks to change society totally is a(n): (390)
    a.   alternative social movement.
    b.   redemptive social movement.
    c.   reformative social movement.
    d.   transformative social movement.

16. Levels of membership in social movements include: (390)
    a.   the inner core.
    b.   the committed.
    c.   a wider circle of members.
    d.   all of the above

17. The public that social movements face can really be divided into: (391)
    a.   supporters and opponents.
    b.   informed supportive public, informed oppositional public, and uninformed mass.
    c.   receptive audience, hostile audience, and disinterested mass.
    d.   sympathetic public, hostile public, and disinterested people.

18. How people think about some issue is: (391)
    a.   irrelevant to most social scientists.
    b.   public opinion.
    c.   propaganda.
    d.   mass-society theory.

19. Which statement about propaganda is *incorrect?* (391)
    a.   Propaganda plays a key role in social movements.
    b.   Propaganda generally involves negative images.
    c.   Propaganda has become a regular and routine part of modern life.
    d.   Propaganda is the presentation of information in an attempt to influence people.

20. Advertising is: (391)
    a.   a type of propaganda.
    b.   an organized attempt to manipulate public opinion.
    c.   a one-sided presentation of information that distorts reality.
    d.   all of the above

21. The mass media: (391-392)
    a. are the gatekeepers to social movements.
    b. engage in biased reporting, controlled by people who have an agenda to get across.
    c. are sympathetic to some social movements, while ignoring others; it all depends on their individual biases.
    d. all of the above

22. According to mass society theory, social movements offer people: (392)
    a. a set of rules or guidelines to govern their behaviour.
    b. an outlet for leisure activities.
    c. a sense of belonging.
    d. answers to basic questions concerning morality.

23. In order to turn a group of people who are upset about a social condition into a social movement, there must be: (394)
    a. agitation
    b. resource mobilization.
    c. organization.
    d. institutionalization.

24. The alteration of culture and society over time is: (394)
    a. social transformation.
    b. social metamorphose.
    c. social alternation.
    d. social change.

25. Technology refers to: (394)
    a. items that people use to accomplish a wide range of tasks.
    b. skills and procedures that are employed in the development and utilization of tools.
    c. tools ranging from combs or hairbrushes to computers and the Internet.
    d. all of the above

26. Ogburn called the process of change that involves new ways of seeing reality: (395-396)
    a. invention.
    b. discovery.
    c. diffusion.
    d. exploration.

27. The situation in which some elements of a culture adapt to an invention or discovery more rapidly than others is: (396)
    a. cultural downtime.
    b. cultural lag.
    c. cultural delay.
    d. cultural drag.

28. According to Karl Marx, the change-over to the factory system produced: (397)
    a. rationality.
    b. alienation.
    c. efficiency.
    d. worker satisfaction.

29. The automobile: (397-398)
    a. has changed the shape of cities.
    b. has stimulated mass suburbanization.
    c. has altered dating and courting rituals.
    d. all of the above

30. A new development that allows doctors in one state or country to check the heart condition of a patient in an entirely different location is: (399)
    a. electronic imaging technology.
    b. remote heart monitoring.
    c. telemedicine.
    d. cardiac computerization.

31. One concern about the expansion of the information superhighway is that: (399)
    a. interest in accessing it will outstrip capacity to carry so many users.
    b. social inequalities will become greater, both on a national and global basis.
    c. people will tie up the services with non-essential activities.
    d. people will become even more alienated as they relate more and more through their computers and less and less face to face.

32. The least industrialized nations become dependent on countries that have already industrialized and they are unable to develop their own resources according to: (400)
    a. dependency theory.
    b. capitalist exploitation theory.
    c. evolutionary theory.
    d. multilinear evolution theory.

33. _____ theories assume that all societies follow the same path, evolving from simple to complex through uniform sequences. (400)
    a. Cyclical
    b. Uniformity
    c. Unilinear evolution
    d. Multilinear evolution

TRUE-FALSE QUESTIONS

T F   1.   Collective behaviour is characterized by a group of people becoming emotionally aroused and engaging in extraordinary behaviour. (383)

T F   2.   Gustave LeBon's central idea was, the individual is transformed by the crowd. (383)

T F   3.   Herbert Blumer identified five stages of collective behaviour. (383-384)

T F   4.   The term acting crowd is applied only to violent activities such as lynch mobs or people engaged in riots. (383)

T F   5.   Emergent norms is the development of new norms to cope with a new situation, especially among crowds. (385)

T F   6.   Thriving in conditions of ambiguity, rumours function to fill in missing information. (387)

T F   7.   Most rumours are long-lived. (387)

T F   8.   Urban legends are stories with an ironic twist that sounds realistic but are false. (388)

T F   9.   For some people, a current condition of society is intolerable and their goal is to promote social change—sociologist call this a reactive social movement. (388)

T F   10.   All social movements seek to change society. (388)

T F   11.   The advocates and the detractors of the trade union movement in Canada are not likely to give up their struggle in the foreseeable future.(389)

T F   12.   Propaganda and advertising are defined quite differently from one another. (391)

T F   13.   Deprivation theory and relative deprivation theory are identical perspectives. (393)

T F   14.   Moral shock is of little importance in motivating people to join a social movement. (393)

T F   15.   The role of the agent provocateur as a spy on the leadership of a social movement, and perhaps trying to sabotage their activities, is generally unsuccessful. (393)

T F   16.   The crucial factor that enables social movements to make it past the first stage of initial unrest and agitation is resource mobilization.(394)

T F   17.   In the final stage of a social movement, decline is certain. (394)

T F   18.   Technology is not a very powerful force for social change. (394)

T F   19.   Invention, discovery, and diffusion are Ogburn's three processes of social change. (395-396)

T F   20.   Technology carries a double meaning; it refers to both tools and the shells or procedures to make and use the tools. (394)

T F   21.   Marx believed that the change to the factory system was a source of alienation. (397)

T F   22.   While technology may produce ideological changes, it has little impact on underlying social values. (397)

T F   23.   Automobiles altered the architecture of North American homes. (397)

T F   24.   The use of computers in education will significantly reduce existing social inequalities between school districts. (399)

T F   25.   Computers create the possibility for increased surveillance of workers and depersonalization. (399)

T F   26.   Today's information revolution will perpetuate global stratification. (399)

T F   27.   Unilinear theories of social change have been replaced by multilinear theories, which assume that different paths can lead to the same stage.(400)

T F   28.   Postmodernists see no progress or purpose or continuity of values, beliefs, and disbeliefs, since the confidence in the association between science and morality has been broken.(400)

FILL-IN QUESTIONS

1. At the root of collective behaviour is a background condition of _____ and _____. (383)
2. In Blumer's model, the stage at which a sense of collective agreement about what should be done emerges is called _____. (384)
3. Ralph Turner and Lewis Killian's term for the development of new norms to cope with a new situation, especially among crowds is _____. (385)
4. A(n) _____ is violent crowd behaviour aimed against people and property. (385)
5. A fear that grips large numbers of people that some evil group or behaviour threatens the well-being of society, followed by intense hostility, and sometimes violence, towards those thought responsible is _____. (387)
6. _____ are unfounded information spread among people. (387)
7. When a fad lasts, it is called a _____. (388)
8. A(n) _____ is a story with an ironic twist that sounds realistic but is false. (388)
9. A religious social movement that stresses conversion, which will produce a change in the entire person, is an example of _____. (389)
10. Social movements that span the globe, emphasizing changing conditions throughout the world rather than in just one country, are referred to as _____. (390)
11. _____, in the sense of organized attempts to manipulate public opinion, is a regular part of modern life. (391)
12. _____ is an industrialized, highly bureaucratized, impersonal society. (392)
13. _____ states that people who are deprived of things deemed valuable in society join social movements with the hope of redressing their grievances. (393)
14. _____ is the alteration of culture and societies over time. (395)
15. The combination of existing elements and materials to form new ones is _____. (395)
16. _____ is a new way of seeing reality. (396)
17. According to Ogburn, because of travel, trade, or conquest, _____ of an invention or discovery occurs. (396)
18. The situation in which some elements of a culture adapt to an invention or discovery more rapidly than others is _____. (396)
19. _____ is Marx's term for workers' lack of connection to the product of their labour caused by their being assigned repetitive tasks on a small part of a product. (397)
20. The assumption that all societies follow the same path, from the same starting point to the same end point, is central to _____. (400)

MATCH THESE SOCIAL SCIENTISTS WITH THEIR CONTRIBUTIONS

___1.	Charles Mackay	a.	*emergent norm*
___2.	William Kornhauser	b.	*herd mentality*
___3.	Robert Park	c.	*minimax strategy*
___4.	Turner and Killian	d.	*social movements classified by type and amount of social change*
___5.	Gustave LeBon	e.	*mass society theory*
___6.	David Aberle	f.	*social unrest and circular reaction*
___7.	Herbert Blumer	g.	*the acting crowd*
___8.	Richard Berk	h.	*collective mind*
___9.	James Flink	i.	*changes to factory system produced worker alienation*
___10.	William Ogburn	j.	*studied the impact of the auto on U.S. society*
___11.	Karl Marx	k.	*three processes of social change*

ESSAY QUESTIONS

1. Compare and contrast the early explanations of collective behaviour, as advanced by Charles Mackay, Gustave LeBon, Robert Park, and Herbert Blumer, with more contemporary explanations developed by Richard Berk, Ralph Turner, and Lewis Killian.
2. Discuss the different theories about why people join social movements and consider how they could all be accurate.
3. Consider why the author combined the topics of collective behaviour and social movements in one chapter.
4. Choose a particular technology—you can use the automobile or the computer—and discuss the impact that it has had on Canadian society.
5. Discuss Ogburn's three processes of social change and provide examples to illustrate each.

"DOWN-TO-EARTH SOCIOLOGY"

1. Read "Which Side of the Barricades? The Pros and Cons of Trade Unions in Canada" on page 389. In thinking about this social movement, where would you place yourself in relationship to memberships and/or publics? What kind of tactics does each side use in order to promote its cause without alienating sympathetic publics? How does each side try to influence public opinion by making use of some of the "tricks of the trade"?
2. After considering the contemporary theories of social change, (table 18.2) indicate which two theories you find the most useful explanations for social change in Canada, why? (400)
3. Before reading the article about the movement against the MAI (395), were you aware of this movement? What stages did this social movement go through? What kinds of tactics did the movement use? Has this movement gone into decline or has it been able to keep itself alive in the years since 1997?
4. Why do you think there is a tendency to view new technologies so negatively? (Refer to "When Old Technology was New: Miss-guessing the Future" on page397.) Can you think of some new technology today, whose introduction has been met with mostly negative responses?

CHAPTER-BY-CHAPTER ANSWER KEY

ANSWERS FOR CHAPTER 1

ANSWERS FOR THE MULTIPLE-CHOICE QUESTIONS

1. b The sociological perspective is an approach to understanding human behaviour by placing it within its broader social context. (3)
2. b Using systematic methods to study and explain the social and natural worlds is the intent of scientists. (3)
3. c Sociology is the study of society and human behaviour. (3)
4. d Positivism is the application of the scientific approach to the social world. (7)
5. a Auguste Comte was interested in the twin problems of social order and social change and was the individual responsible for giving the name "sociology" to the new social science. (7)
6. b The proletariat is the large group of workers who are exploited by the controlling class of capitalists, according to Karl Marx. (8)
7. a Durkheim believed that social factors—patterns of behaviour that characterize a social group—explain many types of behaviour, including suicide rates. (8)
8. a The knowledge gained by social research belongs to the scientific community and to the world. (10)
9. c Max Weber's research identified Protestantism as the key to the development of capitalism. (10)
10. d All are correct. Replication helps researchers overcome distortions that values can cause, results can be compared when a study is repeated, and replication involves the repetition of a study by other researchers. (10)
11. c Social facts and *Verstehen* go hand-in-hand. Social facts are patterns of behaviour that characterize a social group. By applying *Verstehen*—your understanding of what it means to be human and to face various situations in life—you gain an understanding of people's behaviour (11)
12. b In the nineteenth century, it was unlikely that women would become sociology professors at the universities because of sexism. (11)
13. d All of the above (12)
14. d All of the above (12)
15. a Was particularly useful when studying the development of Canada as a distinct economy and society (12)
16. d All of the above (13)
17. c W.E.B. Du Bois was an African American sociologist who wrote extensively on race relations. In both his personal and professional life he experienced prejudice and discrimination. His commitment to racial equality led him to establish the NAACP. (13-14)
18. b Symbolic interactionism is the theoretical perspective which views society as composed of symbols that people use to establish meaning, develop their views of the world, and communicate with one another. (16-17)
19. c The symbolic interaction perspective focuses on the symbolic meaning attached to social relationships to understand the social world. (16-17)

20. a   According to Robert Merton, an action intended to help some part of the system is a manifest function. (16)
21. a   Conflict theory was first asserted by Karl Marx. (17)
22. b   Conflict theorists such as Dahrendorf attribute conflict in society to relations of authority in all layers of society. (17)
23. c   Liberal feminist theories claim that legal restraints and customs are the root of subservience of women in society. (17)
24. b.   Postmodernism emphasizes the cultural and sexual diversity of contemporary societies. (18)
25. a   The symbolic interactionist perspective does not focus on macro-level analysis but rather on the micro-level. It emphasizes social interaction and communication. (16)
26. b   In studying the homeless, functionalists would focus on how changes in parts of the society are related to homelessness. Symbolic interactionists would emphasize what the homeless say and what they do. Conflict theorists tend to focus on macro-level inequalities in society—such as how the policies of the wealthy push certain groups into unemployment. (19)
27. d   Since each theoretical perspective provides a different, often sharply contrasting picture of our world, no theory or level of analysis encompasses all of reality. By putting the contributions of each perspective and level of analysis together, we gain a more comprehensive picture of social life. (20)
28. a   The purpose of pure or basic sociological research is to make discoveries about life in human groups, not to make changes in those groups. On the other hand, applied and clinical sociology are more involved in suggesting or bringing about social change. (20-21)
29. c   Applied sociology is the effort to blend sociological knowledge with practical results. (21)
30. d   In recent years sociology departments are again applying their knowledge to practical issues like gender in the workplace, criminology and family violence, co-ops and internships. (21)

ANSWERS FOR TRUE-FALSE QUESTIONS

1. *True* (3)
2. *True* (3)
3. *False* Sociologists focus on external influences (people's experiences) instead of internal mechanisms, such as instincts. (3)
4. *True* (4)
5. *True* (4)
6. *True* (5)
7. *True* (5)
8. *True* (6)
9. *True* (7)
10. *True* (7)
11. *True* (8)
12. *True* (8)
13. *True* (8)

14. *False* Weber agreed with much of what Marx wrote, but he strongly disagreed that economics is the central force in social change. Weber saw religion as playing that role. (8,10)
15. *True* (9)
16. *True* (11)
17. *True* (11)
18. *True* (12)
19. *False* Du Bois moved to Ghana at the age of 93 and was buried there. (14)
20. *.False* Besides the five major theoretical perspectives within the discipline of sociology, there are two emerging theories, queer theory and critical race theory. (15)
21. *True* (16)
22. *False* The conflict theorists point out that conflict is especially likely to develop among people who are in close relationships. (17)
23. *True* (17)
24. *False* The three feminist theories have a number of things in common: they recognize that gender differences are not simply derived from biology; that the gender division of labour is hierarchical; that gender relations are intertwined in many areas of social life; that knowledge is largely derived from men's experiences because of their position of authority within the social order. (18)
25. *True* (18)
26. *True* (19)
27. *True* (14)

ANSWERS FOR THE FILL-IN QUESTIONS

1. People's group memberships because of their location in history and society are known as SOCIAL LOCATION. (3)
2. The NATURAL SCIENCES are the intellectual and academic disciplines designed to comprehend, explain, and predict the events in our natural environment. On the other hand. the SOCIAL SCIENCES examine human relationships. (4)
3. The use of objective systematic observation to test theories is SCIENTIFIC METHOD. (7)
4. CLASS CONFLICT was Karl Marx's term for the struggle between the proletariat and the bourgeoisie. (8)
5. Durkheim used the term SOCIAL INTEGRATION to refer to the degree to which people feel a part of social groups. (8)
6. VALUE FREE is the view that a sociologist's personal values or biases should not influence social research, while OBJECTIVITY is total neutrality. (10)
7. The meanings that people attach to their own behaviour are called SUBJECTIVE MEANINGS. (11)
8. Durkheim used the term SOCIAL FACT to refer to patterns of behaviour that characterize a social group. (11)
9. A THEORY is a general statement about how some parts of the world fit together and how they work. (15)
10. The theoretical perspective in which society is viewed as composed of symbols that people use to establish meaning, develop their views of the world, and communicate with one another is SYMBOLIC INTERACTIONISM. (16)

11. FUNCTIONAL analysis is a theoretical framework in which society is viewed as composed of various parts, each with a function that contributes to society's equilibrium. (16)
12. Power that people consider legitimate is known as AUTHORITY. (17)
13. MARXIST FEMINIST THEORIES stress that the exploitation of women includes their objectification into roles that serve men's interests. (17)
14. MACRO-LEVEL analysis examines large-scale patterns of society, while MICRO-LEVEL analysis examines small-scale patterns of society. (19)
15. PURE (OR) BASIC sociology makes discoveries about life in human groups, not to make changes in those groups; APPLIED sociology is the use of sociology to solve problems. (21)
16. QUEER THEORY and CRITICAL RACE THEORY are two emerging theories. The former owes much to developments in feminist and post-modern scholarship while the latter is a more distinctly U.S.-based multidisciplinary theory. (22)

ANSWERS TO MATCH THESE SOCIAL SCIENTISTS WITH THEIR CONTRIBUTIONS

1.   b   Auguste Comte: *proposed the use of positivism*
2.   e   Karl Marx: *believed the key to human history was class struggle*
3.   f   C. Wright Mills: *encouraged the use of the sociological perspective*
4.   c   Emile Durkheim: *stressed social facts*
5.   g   Harriet Martineau: *published Society in America and translated Comte's work into English*
6.   h   Robert K. Merton: *stressed the need for middle-range theories*
7.   a   W.E.B. Du Bois: *was an early African American sociologist*
8.   d   Max Weber: *believed religion was a central force in social change*
9.   i   Ralf Dahrendorf: *was a conflict theorist*
10. j   Carl Dawson: *is credited with introducing sociology to English speaking Canada*

GUIDELINES FOR ANSWERING THE ESSAY QUESTIONS

1. *Explain what the sociological perspective encompasses and then, using that perspective, discuss the forces that shaped the discipline of sociology.*

There are two parts to this question. First, you are asked to define the sociological perspective. This involves the logical definition of the unit of analysis; sociology is the study of human behaviour ranging from social interaction to the analysis of global social processes. In your analysis, you would want to mention the idea of social location, perhaps by bringing into your essay C. Wright Mills' observations on the connection between biography and history.

Another way to get at what the perspective is would be to contrast sociology with other disciplines, talking about what sociology is and what it isn't. The second part of the essay is to discuss the forces that shaped sociology and its early followers. What you are being asked is to think about what was going on in the social world in the early 19th century that might have led to the birth of this new discipline. Referring back to the book, you would want to identify three: (1) the Industrial Revolution; (2) imperialism; and (3) the emergence of the scientific method. You would conclude by discussing how each of the early sociologists—Auguste Comte, Karl Marx, Emile Durkheim, Max Weber—was influenced by these broader forces in making a contribution to sociology. You could also bring into the discussion some of the material on sexism in early sociology, noting that the ideas about the appropriate role for women in society functioned to exclude women like Harriet Martineau and Jane Addams from the discipline, or you could talk about the emergence of sociology in North America.

2. *The textbook notes that Verstehen and social facts go hand in hand, explain how this is so. Assume that you have been asked to carry out research to find out more about why growing numbers of women and children are homeless and what particular problems they face. Discuss how you could you use both Verstehen and social facts in your study.*

First, you would want to define what Verstehen and social facts are and how they are compatible in terms of arriving at a complete picture of a social pattern. Then you can argue that social facts would be most appropriate in trying to explain why growing numbers of women and children are homeless—you might suggest that you would look at the changing economic status of women in society, the increase in the number of female-headed households, and the decline in the amount of affordable housing. On the other hand, by applying Verstehen, you would be able to discover what particular problems they face—through face-to-face interviews at shelter sites you would be able to experience firsthand some of what they are experiencing.

3. *Explain each of the theoretical perspectives used in sociology and describe how a sociologist affiliated with one or another of the perspectives might research a social phenomenon, for example gangs. Discuss how the various perspectives can be used in such research.*

Using the major sociological perspectives, symbolic interactionism, functional analysis, conflict theory, feminist theories, postmodernism, the emergent queer theory or critical race theory, analyze a sociological phenomenon of your choice. Your first step is to explain the essential nature of each perspective and then to propose a research topic that would be consistent with the perspective. Using the example of gangs, symbolic interactionism focuses on the symbols that people use to establish meaning, develop their views of the world, and communicate with one another; a symbolic interactionist would want to find out what meaning gangs and gang membership have for individuals who belong to them as well as those who live in communities in which gangs operate. Functional analysis, which tries to identify the functions of a particular social pattern, would choose to study what contributions gangs make within the fabric of social life as well as the dysfunctions of gangs. A conflict theorist would study the competition for scarce resources among gangs and between gangs and the larger society because he or she is interested in struggles over power and control within social groups. A feminist theorist would study the gender dynamics of gangs, while a postmodernist would focus on the social and cultural diversity of gangs in contemporary society, queer theory would focus on gay an lesbian issues in gangs, and critical race theory would address the social construction of race and race identities and the reality of discrimination as it relates to gangs. You would conclude by noting that each perspective provides an answer to an important question about the social order and by combining perspectives you arrive at a more complete picture.

4. *Explain what is meant by levels of analysis and give examples of theoretical perspectives on both levels.*

Theoretical perspectives in sociology utilize different levels of analysis. Macro-level deals with large-scale patterns of society and micro-level focuses on social interaction. Table 1.1 gives an overview of the major theoretical perspectives and their usual levels of analysis, followed by more detailed explanations of the content of each perspective.

ANSWERS FOR CHAPTER 2

ANSWERS FOR MULTIPLE CHOICE QUESTIONS

1. b   A researcher interested in doing a macro-level study could choose multinational corporations as a topic. (25)

2. d   "All of the above" is correct. Sociologists believe that research is necessary because common sense ideas may or may not be true; they want to move beyond guesswork; and researchers want to know what really is going on. (25)

3. a   Ethnocentrism is the use of one's own culture as a yardstick for judging other cultures and is not a research method. Surveys, unobtrusive measures, and secondary analysis are research methods for gathering data. (26-30)

4. c   In a random sample, everyone in the population has the same chance of being included in the study. (26)

5. d   "Loading the dice" involves biased samples, biased questions, discarding undesirable results.(27)

6. b   Self-administered questionnaires allow a large number of people to be sampled at a relatively low cost. (27)

7. c   The primary disadvantage of structured interviews is that they may not include all the respondent's opinions. (27)

8. d   In doing participant observation, sex, age, and race can affect the researchers' findings. (28)

9. b   A researcher might "load the dice" in designing a research project because of a vested interest in the outcome of the research. He or she may be hired by business firms and is thus motivated to find results that are consistent with the interests of the firm. (27)

10. d   A qualitative interview, commonly referred to as a structured conversation, is a research method, in which the interviewer asks most of the questions, and interviewer and interviewee are part of the conversation, which could also be taperecorded. (29)

11. c   The analysis of data already collected by other researchers is secondary analysis. (29)

12. d   Sources such as newspapers, diaries, bank records, police reports, household accounts and immigration files are documents that provide useful information for investigating social life. (29-30)

13. c   In order to study patterns of alcohol consumption in different neighbourhoods, you decide to go through the recycling bins in your town and count the number of beer cans, and wine and hard liquor bottles. This study would be using unobtrusive

methods because you are making observations on people without their knowledge that they are being studied. (30)

14.   d   When deciding which method to use, sociologists consider the purpose of the research, sources of potential funding, and access to subjects. (30)

15.   a   Sociologists trained in quantitative research methods emphasize measurement, numbers, and statistics. (30)

16.   c   Eight basic steps are involved in sociological research. (33)

17.   a   The change behaviour that occurs when subjects know they are being studied is referred to as the Hawthorne effect. (31)

18.   c   Surveys are more likely to be used by researchers trained in quantitative research methods. (30)

19.   d   Marketing researchers attempt to find out what customers think they want, how they select and use products, also the images they hold of a product or a service. (30)

20.   c   Researchers review the literature in order to help them to narrow down the problem by pinpointing particular areas to examine; to get ideas about how to do their own research; and to determine whether or not the problem has been answered already. They are not concerned about whether or not the topic is controversial. (33)

21.   a   A relationship between or among variables is predicted by a hypothesis. (34)

22.   b   Reliability refers to the extent to which data produce consistent results. (34)

23.   c   In analyzing data gathered by participant observation, a researcher is likely to choose qualitative analysis. (35)

24.   c   Replication is the repetition of research in order to test its findings. (35)

25.   d   All of the above is correct. Research ethics require openness; that a researcher not falsify results or plagiarize someone else's work; and that research subjects should not be harmed by the research. (35)

ANSWERS FOR TRUE-FALSE QUESTIONS

1. *True.* (25)
2. *False.* Research often does not confirm common sense. The application of research methods takes us beyond common sense and allows us to penetrate surface realities so we can better understand social life. (25-26)
3. *True.* (26)
4. *False.* In survey research, it is always desirable for respondents to express their own ideas. (25)
5. *True.* (27)
6. *True.* (27)
7. *True.* (28)
8. *False.* Many feminist methodologists reject the impersonal nature of scientific research and are drawn to qualitative techniques, particularly interviewing. (29)
9. *False.* Secondary analysis and use of documents are not the same thing. The data used in secondary analysis are gathered by other researchers, while documents may be anything from diaries to police records. (29)
10. *True.* (35)
11. *True.* (35)
12. *False.* The term reliability refers to the extent to which different studies come up with similar results. (35)
13. *True.* (30)

14. *True.* (33)
15. *True.* (34)
16. *False.* Sociologists do not place one above the other. Rather, they take great care to assure that both are achieved. (34)
17. *True.* (35)
18. *False.* Computers are valuable to researchers not because they store information efficiently, but because they reduce large amounts of data to basic patterns, they take the drudgery out of analyzing data, they can do different statistical tests easily, and they free the researcher up to do more interpretation of the data. (35)
19. *True.* (35)
20. *True.*(33)

ANSWERS FOR FILL-IN QUESTIONS

1. The six research methods are: (I) SURVEYS, (2) SECONDARY ANALYSIS, (3) DOCUMENTS, (4) PARTICIPANT OBSERVATION, (5) QUALITATIVE INTERVIEWS, (6) UNOBTRUSIVE MEASURES. (26)
2. A SELF-ADMINISTERED QUESTIONNAIRE allows a large number of people to be sampled at a relatively low cost. (27)
3. Closed-ended questions are used in STRUCTURED INTERVIEWS. (27)
4. RAPPORT is a feeling of trust between researchers and subjects. (28)
5. PARTICIPANT OBSERVATION is a form of research where the researcher spends a great deal of time with the people he or she is studying. (28)
6. Generalizability is one of the major problems in PARTICIPANT OBSERVATION. (28)
7. A hypothesis predicts a relationship between or among VARIABLES. (34)
8. VALIDITY is the extent to which operational definitions measure what they are intended to measure. (34)
9. Research in which the emphasis is placed on precise measurement, the use of statistics and numbers is QUANTITATIVE TECHNIQUES. (30)
10. Research in which the emphasis is placed on describing and interpreting people's behaviour is QUALITATIVE TECHNIQUES. (30)
11. A factor or concept thought to be significant for human behaviour, which varies from one case to another, is a(n) VARIABLE. (34)
12. Hypotheses need OPERATIONAL DEFINITIONS, which are precise ways to measure variables. (34)
13. RELIABILITY is the extent to which data produce consistent results. (35)
14. Research ETHICS require openness, honesty, and truth. (35)
15. Research and THEORY are interdependent, and sociologists combine them in their work. (35)
16. Hypothesis need OPERATIONAL DEFINITIONS to measure their variables. (34)

ANSWERS TO THE MATCHING QUESTIONS

1. b Hawthorne effect: *behaviour change due to subject's awareness of being studied*
2. f Population: *the target group to be studied*
3. h Sample: *the individuals intended to represent the population to be studied*
4. c Interview bias: *the effect that interviewers have on respondents that leads to biased answers*

5. g Secondary analysis: *the analysis of data already collected by other researchers*
6. e Documents: *written sources of data*
7. i Independent variable: *a factor that causes a change in another variable*
8. d Dependent variable: *a factor that is changed by an independent variable*
9   a Unobtrusive measures: *the observation of people who do not know that they are being studied*
10. j Research methods: *together with the application of social theory take us beyond common sense*

GUIDELINES FOR ANSWERING THE ESSAY QUESTIONS

1. *Choose a topic and explain how you would go through the different steps in the research model.*

   In order to answer this question, you must select a topic and then develop this from the beginning to the end of the research process, identifying all eight steps and explaining what tasks are carried out each step of the way. Your answer should make reference to variables, hypothesis, operational definitions, the different research methods, validity and reliability, different ways of analyzing the data, and replication.

2. *Discuss some of the things that can go wrong in the process of doing research and provide suggestions on how to overcome such problems.*

   There are a number of problems that can arise if the researcher is not careful. Included would be: (1) deriving invalid and unreliable results because of inadequate operational definitions and inaccurate sampling procedures; (2) obtaining biased answers because biased questions were asked; (3) failing to establish rapport with research subjects because of personal qualities or characteristics; and (4) failing to gain access to necessary documents because those who control the documents are unwilling to cooperate. Each of these potential problems can be overcome if the researcher follows the steps in the research process carefully.

3. *Explain why ethical guidelines are necessary in social science research.*

   Ethical guidelines are necessary for several reasons. First and foremost, the researcher is working with human subjects; there must be guidelines to protect these subjects from any undue physical or psychological harm. Second, the research is only valid and reliable if the subjects have honestly and accurately provided information to the researcher. For this reason, they must have confidence in the researcher and the research process; guidelines assure subjects that their identities will remain anonymous and their information will be confidential. Finally, an essential aspect of research is that it be shared with others in the research community as well as members of the wider society. Guidelines regarding falsification and plagiarism guarantee that all research will be carefully scrutinized, thereby assuring its validity and reliability.

4. *Describe the Hawthorne effect—what did it reveal about the research process itself?*

   The Hawthorne research is important for what it revealed about the research process itself.

Today, researchers carefully monitor the Hawthorne effect—the change in behaviour that occurs when people know they are being studied.

ANSWERS FOR CHAPTER 3

ANSWERS FOR MULTIPLE CHOICE QUESTIONS

1. d The following characteristics are indicative of culture:.language; beliefs and values; norms and behaviours (42)
2. d Material culture includes weapons and machines, eating utensils, jewelry, hairstyles, and clothing: language is part of the nonmaterial, rather than the material, culture. (42)
3. d The disorientation that James Henslin experienced when he came into contact with the fundamentally different culture of Morocco is known as cultural shock. (43)
4. c The following statement regarding culture is not true: The effects of our own culture are always clear to us. (42-43)
5. c A Canadian who thinks citizens of another country are barbarians if they like to attend bullfights is demonstrating ethnocentrism. (43)
6. d Symbols are the basis of culture and include gestures, language, values and norms. (44)
7. c Language provides transmission of a social or shared past and planning for a future. (46-47)
8. c The example of the Inuit children and their perceptions about different types of snow illustrates the Sapir-Whorf hypothesis, which suggests that language not only reflects a culture's way of thinking and perceiving the work, but also helps to shape thought and perception. (47)
9. c You have violated folkways, norms related to everyday behaviour that are not strictly enforced. (48)
10. a Mores are essential to our core values and require conformity. (48)
11. a Subcultures are a world within the larger world of the dominant culture. (48-49)
12. c Sociologically speaking, heavy metal adherents who glorify Satanism, cruelty, and sexism are examples of countercultures. (49)
13. b A sociologist would describe Canada as a pluralistic society because it is made up of many different groups. (49-50)
14. d The incorrect statement is: "A lack of endorsement for a woman's right to legal abortion if her health is in danger." (51)
15. d The Native People's present status as Canadians has been enshrined in the Indian Act of 1876. Their adverse social, psychological, and economic conditions heighten susceptibility to illness and poor health. In 1973 Native leaders reclaimed their right to educate their children through their culture. (51)
16. d Leisure, self-fulfillment, physical fitness and youth appear to be emerging as core values in a value cluster in Canada and the United States. (51)
17. a The Maclean's (2004) survey shows that 8% in 1999, 7% in 2002, and 12% of Canadians in 2004 described Canadians and Americans as essentially the same. (53)

18. c Studies of animal culture, such as those conducted by Goodall, have led to the conclusion that animal culture exists but researchers are still studying to learn more about it. (54-55)

19. d Continuing to visit physicians and to rely on the judgment about diagnosis and treatment of illness, even when computer tests do a better job, is an example of cultural lag. (55)

20. c The adoption of bagels, woks and hammocks in Canada illustrates the process of cultural diffusion. (56)

ANSWERS FOR TRUE-FALSE QUESTIONS

1. *True.* (42)
2. *True.* (43)
3. *True.* (43)
4. *True.* (44)
5. *False.* On line communication has actually developed ways to communicate humour, disappointment, and mood indicators through symbols. (45)
6. *True.* (45)
7. *True.* (48)
8. *True.* (54)
9. *False.* Motorcycle enthusiasts who emphasize personal freedom and speed, while maintaining values of success, form part of a subculture, not a counterculture. Motorcycle gangs who commit crimes and use illegal drugs are an example of a counterculture. (49)
10. *False.* Figure 3.2 shows the differences between Quebec and the rest of Canada on matters of parenting, sex, and teens. (46)
11. *False.* See table 3.2 (51)
12. *True.* (53)
13. *True.* (53)
14. *False.* Concern for the environment has not always been a core value in Canadian society. It is one of the emergent values that is now increasing in importance. (52-53)
15. *True.* (53)
16. *True.* (55)
17. *True.* (55)
18. *True.* (55)
19. *False.* Cultural leveling, occurring rapidly around the world, is apparent to any traveller. (57)
20. *False.* According to Ogburn, it is the material culture that changes first, with the nonmaterial culture lagging behind. (55)

ANSWERS FOR FILL-IN QUESTIONS

1. Objects such as art, buildings, weapons, utensils, machines, hairstyles, clothing, and jewelry that distinguish a group of people are known as MATERIAL CULTURE; their ways of thinking and doing are NONMATERIAL CULTURE. (42)
2. A SYMBOL is something to which people attach meaning and then use to communicate with others. (44)
3. LANGUAGE is a system of symbols that can be combined in an infinite number of ways and can represent not only objects but also abstract thought. (45)

4. VALUES are ideas of what is desirable in life. (48)
5. The expectations or rules of behaviour that develop out of values are referred to as NORMS. (48)
6. A TABOO is a norm so strongly ingrained that even the thought of its violation is greeted with revulsion. (48)
7. VALUE CLUSTERS are a series of interrelated values that together form a larger whole. (51)
8. CULTURAL UNIVERSALS may not exist because even though there are universal human activities, there is no universally accepted way of doing any of them. (53-54)
9. Studies of chimpanzees indicate that they were able to make and use TOOLS; they actually modified objects and used them for specific purposes. (54)
10. In its broader sense, TECHNOLOGY includes the skills or procedures necessary to make and use tools. (55)
11. Both the printing press and the computer represent NEW TECHNOLOGIES because they had a significant impact on society following their introduction. (55)
12. The idea that technology is the single greatest force in shaping our lives is central to the point of view called TECHNOLOGICAL DETERMINISM. (56)
13. William Ogburn used the term CULTURAL LAG to reflect the condition in which not all parts of a culture change at the same pace. (55)
14. The spread of cultural characteristics from one group to another is CULTURAL DIFFUSION. (56)
15. When Western industrial culture is imported and diffused into developing nations, the process is called CULTURAL LEVELLING. (57)

ANSWERS TO MATCH THESE SOCIAL SCIENTISTS WITH THEIR CONTRIBUTIONS

1. f Edward Sapir and Benjamin Whorf: *stated that language shapes reality*
2. d John Porter: *remarked that Canadians lack a unifying ideology*
3. c George Murdock: *looked for cultural universals*
4. a Jane Goodall: *studied animal culture*
5. h Robert Edgerton: *criticized aspects of cultural relativism*
6. g William Sumner: *developed the concept of ethnocentrism*
7. b William Ogburn: *introduced the concept of cultural lag*
8. e Marshall McLuhan: *coined the term "global village"*

GUIDELINES FOR ANSWERING THE ESSAY QUESTIONS

1. *Explain cultural relativism and discuss both the advantages and disadvantages of practicing it.*

   You would begin your essay by defining cultural relativism and explaining that it developed in reaction to ethnocentrism. The primary advantage of this approach to looking at other cultures is that we are able to appreciate another way of life without making judgments, thereby reducing the possibilities for conflict between cultures. The primary disadvantage is that it can be used to justify any cultural practice and especially those that endanger people's health, happiness, and survival. You could conclude with a reference to Robert Edgerton's proposed "quality of life" scale.

2. *Consider the differences between Quebec and the rest of Canada on matters of parenting, sex, and teens.*

Figure 3.2 shows the difference between Quebec and the rest of the country on matters of parenting, sex, and teens. Quebec is much more accepting of teenagers, whether gay or straight, having sex at home with a steady partner than any other province or region of the country.

3. *Evaluate what is gained and what is lost as technology advances in society.*

One way to frame a response to this would be to identify a specific technology that has had a significant impact on our society and then to discuss both the gains and losses. For example, the automobile provided us with new opportunities for mobility, freeing us from the constraints of public transportation. The automobile created economic opportunities as new industries and services opened up—car dealerships, gas stations, fast food restaurants, and malls are just a few examples. At the same time, automobiles have contributed to urban sprawl and the decline of downtown shopping areas. We have become more isolated as we travel around in our cars rather than meeting and travelling with others on public transportation. The use of automobiles has contributed to increased congestion and air pollution. Finally, you could make the argument that the automobile has contributed to cultural levelling within Canada, as regional differences have disappeared under the spread of national businesses in malls and food chains.

ANSWERS FOR CHAPTER 4

ANSWERS FOR MULTIPLE CHOICE QUESTIONS

1. d Regarding the relationship between social experience and genetic predisposition, people in nineteenth and early twentieth century believed human behaviour was innate. The debate is still with us. (61)
2. d The experience of Helen Keller shows that without language people have no mechanism for developing thought and self-awareness. (61)
3. c The study of Genie leads to the conclusion that if bonding and learning to communicate with others do not occur prior to age 13, the biological window of opportunity may close. (61)
4. b This statement "we move beyond the looking-glass self as we mature" is incorrect. All of the other statements about the development of self are correct: the development of self is an ongoing, lifelong process; the process of the looking-glass self applies to old age; and the self is always in process. (62)
5. c According to Mead's theory, children pretend to take the roles of specific people during the play stage. (62-63)
6. a To George Mead, the 'I' is the self as subject. (80)
7. d Childhood socialization may have long-term influence on educational aspirations, self-esteem, and personality traits. (70)
8 a Researchers in the U. K. report smokers are seen by their peers as fun-loving and nonconformist. (64)

9.   c   Freud's term for a balancing force between the inborn drives for self-gratification and the demands of society is the ego. (63)

10.   d   In Freuds scheme, the super ego represents culture within us, internalized norms and values and is the moral component of personality. (64)

11.   b   The significance of the example of smoking is that it illustrates that the pressures from our social environment influence our behaviour. (64-65)

12.   c   According to this chapter, the significance of socialization is that it shapes our fundamental sense of self. (62)

13.   b   The ways in which society sets children onto different courses for life purely because they are male or female are called gender socialization. (65)

14.   a   Everyone recognizes that sports teach not only physical skills but also values. (73)

15.   a   Research by Melissa Milkie indicates that young males actively used media images to help them understand what was expected of them as males in our society. (72)

16.   c   Erving Goffman defines the family as a socialization depot. (70)

17.   d   "All of the above" is the correct response. Religion plays a significant role in the socialization of many Canadians by influencing reality, deciding right from wrong, and belonging to a church family. (70)

18.   c   Summarizing the findings of studies on the impact that day care has on preschool children, we can say that children from stable families receive no clear benefits or harm from day care, but children from poor and dysfunctional families benefit from quality day care. (71)

19.   b   When school teachers use stories and examples to teach math and English grammar that contain lessons in gender inequality, conflict theorists refer to this as the hidden curriculum. (71)

20.   d   Peer groups encourage success at school, "girl gangs," and female adolescent dress code. (72)

21.   d   Resocialization occurs when a person takes a new job, joins Alchoholics Anonymous, or goes to boot camp. (74)

22.   b   The statement that is *incorrect* is: "They are not very effective in stripping away people's personal freedom." In fact, total institutions are very effective in stripping away individuals' personal freedom because they are isolated from the public, they suppress preexisting statuses. they suppress cultural norms, and they closely supervise the entire lives of their residents. (74)

23.   c   Historians have concluded that childhood—as we know it—did not exist in the past: children were considered miniature adults, dressing like adults and treated like adults, expected to work from a very young age. (75)

24.   d   The "sandwich generation" refers to people in their later middle years who are caught between caring for their own children and their aging parents. (79)

ANSWERS FOR TRUE-FALSE QUESTIONS

1. *True.* (61)
2. *True.* (60)
3. *True.* (60)
4. *True.* (62)
5. *True.* (60)
6. *True.* (63)

7. *False.* Socialization has a great deal to do with smoking, as it is a learned behaviour. Peer groups play a particularly important role. (64)
8. *True.* (65)
9. *False.* Because social groups expect boys and girls to be different, they nurture the "natural" differences they find. (65)
10. *True.* (66)
11. *True* (72)
12. *True.* (71)
13. *False.* It is a manifest function of education, not a latent function, to transmit skills and values appropriate for a role in the world beyond the family. (71)
14. *True.* (72)
15. *False.* Resocialization does not always require learning a radically different perspective; it usually only modifies existing orientations to life. (74)
16. *True.* (74)
17. *True.* (77-78)
18. True.(79)
19. *True.* (79)
20. *False.* Sociologists study the ways in which historical location and social location create different experiences within the stages of life. (75-79)

ANSWERS FOR FILL-IN QUESTIONS

1. Sociologists are interested in studying how the SOCIAL ENVIRONMENT influences the development of human characteristics. (61)
2. SOCIALIZATION is the process by which people learn the characteristics of their group—the attitudes, values, and actions thought appropriate for them. (61)
3. Charles H. Cooley coined the term LOOKING-GLASS SELF to describe the process by which a sense of self develops. (62)
4. SIGNIFICANT OTHER is the term used to describe someone, such as a parent and/or a sibling, who plays a major role in our social development. (62)
5. According to George Herbert Mead, the development of the self through role-taking goes through three stages: (1) IMITATION; (2) PLAY; and (3) GAMES. (62-63)
6. The idea that personality consists of the id, ego, and superego was developed by SIGMUND FREUD. (63-64)
7. We refer to the behaviours and attitudes which are considered appropriate for females and males as GENDER ROLES. (65)
8. Television, music, and advertising are all types of MASS MEDIA which reinforce society's expectations of gender. (66-69)
9. AGENTS OF SOCIALIZATION include the family, school, religion, peers, mass media, and workplace. (69)
10. Reading, writing, and arithmetic are all part of the MANIFEST FUNCTIONS of education. (71)
11. The HIDDEN CURRICULUM refers to values that may not be taught explicitly, but nevertheless form an inherent part of a school's "message." (71)
12. PEER GROUPS are made up of individuals the same age linked by common interests. (72)
13. The mental rehearsal for some future activity, or learning to play a role before actually entering it, is referred to as ANTICIPATORY SOCIALIZATION. (73)

14. Resocialization often takes place in TOTAL INSTITUTIONS such as boot camps, prisons, and concentration camps. (74)
15. DEGRADATION CEREMONY refers to the attempt to remake the self by stripping away an individual's self-identity and stamping a new identity in its place. (74)

ANSWERS TO MATCH THESE SOCIAL SCIENTISTS WITH THEIR CONTRIBUTIONS

1.   d   Erving Goffman: *studied total institutions*
2.   c   George Herbert Mead: *coined the term "generalized other"*
3.   a   Charles H. Cooley: *coined the term "looking-glass self"*
4.   e   Sigmund Freud: *asserted that human behaviour is based on unconscious drives*
5.   b   Melissa Milkie: *studied the impact of media messages on adolescent males*

GUIDELINES FOR ANSWERING THE ESSAY QUESTIONS

1. *Explain what is necessary in order for us to develop into full human beings.*

   You might want to begin by stating that in order for us to become full human beings we need language and intimate social connections to others. You could draw on the information presented in the previous chapter as to what language enables us to do—grasp relationships to others, think in terms of a shared past and future, and make shared plans. Our knowledge of language, and our ability to use it, develop out of social interaction, as the evidence of those children raised in isolation demonstrates. Furthermore, we learn how to get along with others only through close personal experiences with others. The experience of Genie and the children raised in institutionalized settings confirms this.

2. *Why do sociologists argue that socialization is a process and not a product?*

   Sociologists would argue that socialization is a process rather than a product because there is no end to socialization. It begins at birth and continues throughout one's life, whenever you take on a new role. Cooley was the first to note that we are continually modifying our sense of self, depending on our reading of others' reactions to us. Researchers have identified a series of stages through which we pass as we age; at each stage we are confronted by new demands and new challenges that need to be mastered.

3. *How do ads play a role in creating and sustaining our societal views of gender?*

   As a part of our "taken-for-granted" reality, ads play an important part in creating and sustaining our societal views of gender.

ANSWERS FOR CHAPTER 5

ANSWERS FOR MULTIPLE CHOICE QUESTIONS

1. a Microsociology focuses on social interaction. (83)
2. c Sociologists who study social class and how groups are related to one another are using macrosociology. (83-84)
3. b As a budding sociologist who is interested in homeless women's parenting strategies, you would use a microsociological approach. (83)
4. d The term social structure refers to "all of the above": the framework of society; the patterns of society; and relationships between individuals or groups within a society. (83-84)
5. c Religion, politics, education, and the military are examples of social institutions. (85)
6. b Sociologists would use the term "functional requisites" to describe such activities as replacing members and socializing new members of a society. (86)
7. b The conflict perspective states that social institutions are controlled by an elite that uses them to its own advantage. (86)
8. d All of the above is correct. Organic solidarity refers to a society with a highly specialized division of labour; whose members are interdependent on one another: and with a high degree of impersonal relationships. (87-88)
9. a *Gemeinschaft* is the type of society in which everyone knows everyone else, people conform because they are very sensitive to the opinions of others and want to avoid being gossiped about, and people draw comfort from being part of an intimate group. (88)
10. b Social status is the term referring to the position that an individual occupies within a society or social group; social class reflects income, education and occupation, social role refers to the social expectations about the behaviour appropriate to a social status, and social location refers to an individual's place in the social structure. (89)
11. d Being a daughter, a lawyer, a wife, and a mother represents a person's status set. (89)
12. a A sociologist would use the term "ascribed status" to describe race, sex, and the social class of his or her parents. (90)
13. c Wedding rings, military uniforms, and clerical collars are all examples of status symbols. (90)
14. c The incorrect statement is: "Status symbols are always positive signs or people would not wear them." Some social statuses are negative, and therefore, so are their status symbols (e.g., prison clothing issued to inmates). (90)
15. b A master status is one that cuts across the other statuses that a person holds. (90)
16. a Status inconsistency is most likely to occur when a contradiction or mismatch between statuses exists. (90)
17. d The behaviours, obligations, and privileges attached to statuses are called roles. (91)
18. d Thinking of a high school hockey team gives a clearer picture of social structure because of the status, positions and roles of the game. (89)
19. d The essential feature of a group is that its members have something in common and they believe that it makes a difference. (91)
20. c People who have similar characteristics are a category. (91)

21. c   Emile Durkheim believed that small groups help to prevent anomie, because, through their intimate relationships, they provide a sense of meaning and purpose to life. (91)

22. a   Cooley saw that primary groups are essential to an individual's psychological well-being. (92)

23. d   "All of the above" is correct. Secondary groups have members who are likely to interact on the basis of specific roles; are characteristic of industrial societies; and are essential to the functioning of contemporary societies. (92)

24. d   Attacks against immigrants or a national anti-immigration policy is an example of xenophobia, or the fear of strangers. (93)

25. c   Reference groups are important because they provide us with a standard to evaluate ourselves. Your reference group may include family and friends, with whom you engage in face-to-face interaction, or groups to which you belong and feel a sense of loyalty, but they do not have to be. A reference group can provide you with standards even when you are not actually a member of the group. (93)

26. a   Sociologically speaking, the social ties radiating outward from the self that link people together are social networks. (93)

27. a   The conscious use or cultivation of networks for some gain is referred to as networking. (93)

28. d   "All of the above" is correct. Dyads are the most intense or intimate of human groups; require continuing active participation and commitment of both members, and are the most unstable of social groups. (95)

29. c   Personal space might be a research topic for a sociologist using symbolic interactionism. (98)

30. b   Goffman suggests that we go to back stages to be ourselves. (100)

31. a   A fourteen year old is usually not a university student, therefore it is a case of status inconsistency. (90)

32. a   The largest and most complex group that sociologists study is society. (91)

33. b   The three types of sign-vehicles are: social setting, appearance, and manner. (102)

34. a   When a performance does not come off quite right, it may require face-saving behaviour. (102)

35. c   The Thomas theorem would fall within symbolic interactionism. (104)

ANSWERS FOR TRUE-FALSE QUESTIONS

1. *False.* Social structure has a large impact on the typical individual because it gives direction to and establishes limits on a person's behaviour. (83)

2. *False.* Sociologists have identified at least nine basic social institutions in contemporary societies. (84)

3. *True.* (86)

4. *True.* (87-88)

5. *False.* It is *Gesellschaft* society, not *Gemeinschaft* society, that is characterized by impersonal, short-term relationships. (88)

6. *True.* (84)

7. *False.* Social class is a large number of people with similar amounts of income and education who work at jobs that are roughly comparable in prestige. Social status refers to the social position that a person occupies (mother, teacher, daughter, or wife). Thus, sociologists use the two terms quite differently. (89)

8. *True.* (90)
9. *True.*(90)
10. *False.* Being male or female is considered a master status. (90)
11. *True.* (91)
12. *False.* The groups to which we belong help to determine our goals and values, and how we feel about ourselves. (91)
13. *True.*(91)
14. *True.*(91)
15. *False.* Members of secondary, not primary, groups are likely to interact on the basis of specific roles. (92)
16. *True.* (92)
17. *True.*(93)
18. *True.* (93)
19. *True.* (93)
20. *False.* Dyads are more intimate than triads because there are only two members of a dyad, as opposed to three members in a triad, but their smaller size also makes them less stable than a triad, rather than more stable. (95)
21. *True.* (95)
22. *False.* To study conformity the Asch experiment used cards with lines on them. To study obedience to authority the Milgram experiment used fake electrical shocks. (96)
23. *True.* (98)
24. *True.* (98)
25. *False.* Researchers have found that higher-status individuals tend to touch more, because they have more social power. (99)
26. *True.* (100)
27. *True.* (100)
28. *True.* (101)
29. *False.* Studied nonobservance, not impression management, is a face-saving technique in which people give the impression that they are unaware of a flaw in someone's performance. Impression management describes people's efforts to control the impressions that others receive of them. (102)
30. *True.* (104)

ANSWERS FOR FILL-IN QUESTIONS

1. MACROSOCIOLOGY investigates such things as social class and how groups are related to one another. (83)
2. The level of sociological analysis used by symbolic interactionists is MICROSOCIOLOGY (83)
3. The FUNCTIONALIST perspective states that societies must replace their members, teach new members, produce and distribute goods and services, preserve order, and provide a sense of purpose. (86)
4. A society's basic needs, that are required in order to guarantee survival, are called FUNCTIONAL REQUISITES (86).
5. Durkheim referred to a collective consciousness that people experience due to performing the same or similar tasks as MECHANICAL SOLIDARITY. (87)
6. STATUS SET is all of the statuses or positions that an individual occupies. (89)
7. A social position that a person assumes voluntarily is ACHIEVED STATUS. (90)

8. STATUS SYMBOLS are signs used to identify a status. (90)
9. Groups in which people are assigned membership rather than choose to join are INVOLUNTARY MEMBERSHIPS (OR INVOLUNTARY ASSOCIATIONS). (91)
10. The term AGGREGATE is used to describe individuals who temporarily share the same physical space but do not see themselves as belonging together. (91)
11. A SECONDARY group is characterized by relatively temporary, more anonymous, formal, and impersonal relationships. (92)
12. IN-GROUPS provide a sense of identification or belonging while producing feelings of antagonisms towards OUT-GROUPS. (92)
13. The groups we use as standards to evaluate ourselves are REFERENCE GROUPS. (93)
14. Individuals who interact with one another on the Internet, whether on a regular basis or not, are known as a(n) ELECTRONIC COMMUNITY. (94)
15. The smallest possible group is a(n) DYAD. (95)
16. Someone who influences the behaviour of others is a(n) LEADER. (95)
17. An individual who tries to keep the group moving toward its goals is a(n) INSTRUMENTAL leader. An individual who increases harmony and minimizes conflict is a(n) EXPRESSIVE leader. (95)
18. The events in the United States called 9/11 are an example of GLOBAL TERRORISM. (96)
19. GROUPTHINK is a narrowing of thought by a group of people, which results in overconfidence and tunnel vision. (96)
20. SYMBOLIC INTERACTIONISM focuses on face-to-face social interactions. (98)
21. Erving Goffman believed that in order to communicate information about the self, individuals use three types of SIGN-VEHICLES. (102)
22. Goffman called the sign-vehicle that refers to the attitudes that we demonstrate as we play our roles MANNER. (102)
23. For POSTMODERNISATION, television and electronic media are the two primary "socializing" agents. (103)
24. What people define as real because of their background assumptions and life experiences is the SOCIAL CONSTRUCTION OF REALITY. (103)
25. The THOMAS THEOREM states, "If people define situations as real, they are real in their consequences." (104)

ANSWERS TO MATCH THESE SOCIAL SCIENTISTS WITH THEIR CONTRIBUTIONS

1. b Emile Durkheim: *wrote about mechanical/organic solidarity*
2. a Ferdinand Tönnies: *described Gemeinschaft and Gesellschaft societies*
3. d Edward Hall: *studied the concept of personal space*
4. c Erving Goffman: *analyzed everyday life in terms of dramaturgy*
5. e W.I. Thomas: *wrote the theorem about the nature of social reality*
6. k Irving Janis: *groupthink*
7. h Georg Simmel: *dyads*
8. j Emile Durkheim: *small groups and strain*
9. g Stanley Milgram: *obedience to authority*
10. l Solomon Asch: *conformity to peer pressure*
11. f Charles H. Cooley: *primary group*
12. m Robert K. Merton: *in-group prejudice leads to a double standard*
13. i Mark Snyder: *studied how stereotypes influence behaviour*

GUIDELINES FOR ANSWERING THE ESSAY QUESTIONS

1. *Choose a research topic and discuss how you approach this topic using both macrosociological and microsociological approaches.*

   The way to answer this question is to first think of a topic—I've chosen the topic of labour unions. Remember that the macrosociological level focuses on the broad features of society. From this level, I might research the role that unions play within the economy of the political system, what types of workers are organized into unions, the level of union organization among workers, or the level of union activity. Shifting to a microsociological level of analysis, I would want to look at what happens within unions or between unions and management in terms of social interaction. From this perspective, I might want to investigate the behaviour of union members and leaders at a union meeting, or the behaviour of union and management negotiators at a bargaining session. By combining both perspectives, I have achieved a much broader understanding of the role of unions within society.

2. *Describe Tönnies's term Gemeinschaft as an ideal type of construct. Then, describe the community you have experienced that most closely resembles this type.*

   Gemeinschaft is an intimate community that describes the traditional type of society in which everyone toes the line because they are acutely sensitive to the opinions of others and know that if they deviate, others will gossip and damage their reputation.

3. *Discuss the benefits and drawbacks to in-groups and out-groups.*

   What are the benefits of such an arrangement? You could mention feelings of loyalty and a sense of belonging, and the control that in-groups have over our behaviour. Feeling a part of an in-group, set against an out-group, may also build self-esteem and contribute to social solidarity. While this is good, there are also drawbacks. Attachments to an in-group can quickly get out of hand if such feelings develop into ethnocentrism and rivalries between in-groups and out-groups. In the most extreme cases, such ethnocentrism can be the basis for very destructive actions directed against out-groups.

4. *Assume that you have been asked to give a presentation to your sociology class on Goffman's dramaturgy approach. Describe what information you would want to include in such a presentation.*

   You could begin by explaining how Goffman saw life as a drama that was acted out on a stage. This would lead you to making a distinction between front stage and back stage. You might even want to provide some examples—for instance, you are presenting on a front stage, but you practiced for this presentation in your bedroom without any audience. An important contribution of Goffman's was his insights into impression management, so you would want to explain what that is and how it involves the use of three different types of sign-vehicles—social setting, appearance, and manner. Finally, you could conclude with his concept of teamwork, especially as it relates to face-saving behaviour. And remember to include examples of all of these concepts as you proceed.

ANSWERS FOR CHAPTER 6

ANSWERS FOR MULTIPLE CHOICE QUESTIONS

1. b   The division of large numbers of people into layers according to their relative power, property, and prestige is social stratification. (109)
2. b   Slavery is a form of social stratification in which some people own other people. (110)
3. a   A clan system is one in which each individual is linked to a large network of relatives; membership is determined by birth and is lifelong. (111)
4. a   Class systems are characterized by social mobility—either upward or downward. (111)
5. b   Marx concluded that social class depends on the means of production. (111)
6. a   According to Max Weber, social class is determined by one's property, prestige, and power. (112)
7. c   The subjective method of measuring social class asks people to identify their own social class. (114)
8. b   The vast majority of Canadians identify themselves as middle class. (114)
9. b   The objective method of measuring social class is based on ranking people according to objective criteria such as wealth, power, and prestige. (114)
10. c   According to economist Paul Samuelson, if an income pyramid were made out of a child's blocks, most people would be near the bottom of the pyramid. (115)
11. c   All of the following are true regarding jobs that have the most prestige—they pay more, require more education, and offer greater autonomy, making less abstract thought the wrong answer. (118)
12. b   Mills used the term "power elite" to refer to those at the top of society who make the important decisions. (117)
13. d   According to the functionalist view, social stratification is not dysfunctional, but is an inevitable feature of social organization. (119-120)
14. d   Melvin Tumin's criticisms included the measurement problems (a), the reality that family background matters (b), and the dysfunctional aspects of stratification (c). The one statement that does not reflect his criticisms is "d"—in fact, what Tumin noted was that functionalists place too great an emphasis on income and ignore the fact that some people are motivated to take jobs for reasons of status or power. (120)
15. a   A form of social stratification in which all positions are awarded on the basis of merit is called a meritocratic system. (120)
16. b   According to conflict theorists, the basis of social stratification is conflict over limited resources. (120)
17. c   The majority of the world's population lives in the Least Industrialized nations. (122)
18. d   "All of the above" is the correct answer. (122-124)
19. d   In Brazil children swarm garbage dumps in search of food, owners hire armed guards to keep people out, and Brazilian police and death squads murder children. (123)
20. c   Western European nations are not on the periphery, Eastern European nations are. (125)
21. c   The culture of poverty theory was used to analyze global stratification by John Kenneth Galbraith. (126)

22.   b   Neocolonialism refers to the economic policies of the Most Industrialized Nations that are designed to control the markets of the Least Industrialized nations; they are able to set the prices they will charge for their manufactured goods and control the international markets where they purchase raw materials from the Least Industrialized nations. (126)

23.   a   Multinational corporations are companies that operate across many national boundaries. According to the text, they do not always exploit the Least Industrialized Nations directly, but they do not benefit these nations as much as they do the Most Industrialized Nations. (126)

24.   d   Wright responded to the criticism that Marx's categories were so broad that they did not accurately reflect the realities of people's lives by creating the concept of contradictory class location, which recognizes that some people can be members of more than one class simultaneously. (127)

25.   b   The super-rich who occupy the top rung is so wealthy that its members are worth more than the entire bottom 90 percent of the nation. (128)

26.   d   Working class is ill prepared for new technology. The higher one goes up the social ladder the more people benefit from technology. Technology also transforms the work place eliminating jobs and out dated skills. (130)

27.   c   According to Melvin Kohn lower-class parents are concerned that their children be conformists; they want them to obey conventional norms and authority figures while middle class parents encourage their children to be creative and independent. (131-132)

28.   a   Members of the capitalist class tend to bypass public schools entirely, in favour of exclusive private schools. (132)

29.   c   Members of the lower classes are more likely to be robbed, burglarized, or murdered. (132)

30.   d   A homeless person whose father was a physician has experienced downward mobility. (132-133)

31.   a   Sociologists used to focus only on the social mobility of men. (133)

32.   a   Currently, the wealthiest 50 percent of the Canadian population own 94 percent of all national wealth. (134)

33.   c.   It is not true that the majority of poor Canadians are living of welfare. (135)

34.   d.   "All of the above." Race/ethnicity, education, and sex of the person who heads the family are all predictors of poverty. (136-137)

35.   d   Canadians acquiring disability are likely to experience economic difficulties, discrimination in hiring, and get inadequate disability benefits. (137)

ANSWERS FOR TRUE-FALSE QUESTIONS

1. *False.* Your text notes that social stratification does not simply refer to individuals but rather to a way of ranking large groups of people into a hierarchy that shows their relative privileges. (109)

2. *False.* Historically, slavery was based on defeat in battle, a criminal act, or a debt, but not some supposedly inherently inferior status such as race. (110)

3. *True.* (110)

4. *True.* (110)

5. *True.* (111)

6. *True.* (111)

7. *True.* (112)
8. *False.* The reputational method of measuring social class involves asking people who are familiar with the reputations of others to judge those people's social class. (114)
9. *True.* (129)
10. *True.* (114)
11. *True.* (130)
12. *True.* (117)
13. *True.* (121)
14. *True.* (121)
15. *True.* (122)
16. *True.* (125)
17. *False.* Beginning more than 200 years ago, most industrialized nations pursued policies of imperialism in order to expand their economic markets and gain access to cheap raw materials: as a result of this strategy, many acquired colonies in the Middle East, Africa, Asia, and Central/South America. (125)
18. *True.* (125)
19. *True.* (125)
20. *True.* (125)
21. *True.* (129)
22. *True.* (129)
23. *True.* (130)
24. *True.* (131)
25. True. (131)
26. *True.* (132)
27. *True.* (133)
28. *True.* (133)
29. *True.* (141)
30. *True.* (142)

ANSWERS FOR FILL-IN QUESTIONS

1. SOCIAL STRATIFICATION is a system in which people are divided into layers according to their relative power, property, and prestige. (109)
2. A form of social stratification in which some people own other people is SLAVERY. (110)
3. A CASTE system is a form of social stratification in which individual status is determined by birth and is lifelong. (110)
4. Sociologists refer to movement up or down the social class ladder as SOCIAL MOBILITY. (132)
5. According to Marx, the tools, factories, land, and investment capital used to produce wealth is THE MEANS OF PRODUCTION. (111)
6. According to Marx, the awareness of a common identity based on one's position in the means of production is CLASS CONSCIOUSNESS. (112)
7. According to Max Weber, the three dimensions of social class are (1) WEALTH; (2) POWER; and (3) PRESTIGE. (114-118)
8. Most sociologists use the OBJECTIVE method of measuring social class in which people are ranked according to objective criteria such as wealth, power, and prestige. (114)
9. Property and income together make up an individual's WEALTH. (114)

10. According to C. Wright Mills, the POWER ELITE makes the big decisions in society. (117)
11. A MERITOCRACY is a form of social stratification in which all positions are awarded on the basis of merit. (120)
12. The DIVINE RIGHT OF KINGS is the idea that the king's authority comes directly from God. (121)
13. COLONIZATION is the process in which one nation takes over another nation, usually for the purpose of exploiting its labour and natural resources. (125)
14. GLOBALIZATION is the extensive interconnections among world nations resulting from the expansion of capitalism. (125)
15. CULTURE OF POVERTY is a way of life that perpetuates poverty from one generation to the next. (126)
16. NEOCOLONIALISM refers to the economic and political dominance of the Least Industrialized Nations by the Most Industrialized Nations. (126)
17. Companies that operate across many national boundaries are MULTINATIONAL CORPORATIONS. (126)
18. Erik Wright referred to a position in the class structure that generates inconsistent interests as CONTRADICTORY CLASS LOCATION. (127)
19. According to Gilbert and Kahl, the capitalist class can be divided into two groups: (1) OLD MONEY and (2) NEW MONEY. (128-129)
20. UPWARD MOBILITY is movement up the social class ladder. (132)
21. The official measure of poverty is referred to as the LOW-INCOME CUT-OFF. It is a calculation based on a ratio of gross income to family spending on food, clothing, and shelter. (134)
22. THE FEMINIZATION OF POVERTY is a trend whereby most poor families in Canada are headed by women. (137)
23. Sociologists focus on SOCIAL STRUCTURE as the source of poverty. (140-141)
24. The greatest predictor of whether Canadians are poor is not geography, but race/ethnicity, EDUCATION, age, and the SEX of the head of the household. (136)
25. Forgoing something in the present in hope of achieving greater gains in the future is DEFERRED GRATIFICATION. (141)

ANSWERS TO MATCH THESE SOCIAL SCIENTISTS WITH THEIR CONTRIBUTIONS

1. d Karl Marx: *false consciousness*
2. e Kingsley Davis and Wilbert Moore: *the functionalist view on stratification*
3. a Immanuel Wallerstein: *world system theory*
4. f Michael Harrington: *neocolonialism*
5. c John Kenneth Galbraith: *stressed the culture of poverty*
6. g Max Weber: *class based on property, prestige and power*
7. b Melvin Tumin: *criticism of the functionalist view on stratification*
8. j Gerhard Lenski: *status inconsistency*
9. h C. Wright Mills: *power elite*
10. k Erik Wright: *updated Marx's model*
11. m Gilbert and Kahl: *updated Weber's model*
12. l W. Lloyd Warner: *pioneered the reputational method*
13. i Melvin Kohn: *social class patterns of child rearing*

GUIDELINES FOR ANSWERING THE ESSAY QUESTIONS

1. *Compare and contrast Marx's theory of stratification with Weber's theory.*

   Your task is to summarize these two perspectives, pointing out the similarities as well as the differences between the two.

2. *Assume that you carry out a study of social class. Review the different ways that social class can be measured and select the one that would be most appropriate for your study. Explain your selection.*

   You would want to begin by describing what kind of study of social class you would like to do and on what scale. Then you would want to review the three different ways of measuring social class—subjective, reputational, and objective—and point out the advantages and/or disadvantages of each. Finally, you would indicate which method you are choosing and why. Your choice might be based on the scale; perhaps you are going to study a small community or a neighbourhood within a city and the reputational approach would work well. On the other hand, this would not work in a large city or on a national scale.

3. *Consider why ideology is a more effective way of maintaining stratification than brute force.*

   You should begin by considering why it is even necessary to "maintain stratification." On the surface, the idea that some people get more than other people should produce widespread instability—after all, isn't it natural for those without to want to do whatever they can to take some away from those with? However, this doesn't often happen because the elites have a number of methods for maintaining stratification, ranging from ideology to force. Without question, the most effective is ideology. Once a system of beliefs develops and people accept the idea in their minds that a particular system of stratification is right or just, then they will go along the status quo.

4. *Of what use is a division of the poor into deserving and undeserving? Would we let some people starve because they "brought poverty upon themselves"? Would we let the children go hungry because their parents are unmarried, uneducated and unskilled?*

   Try to go beyond such simplistic division and use the sociological perspective to explain poverty without blaming the victim. What social conditions create poverty? What social conditions produce the life styles of which the middle class so vehemently disapproves?

5. *Describe which groups are at greatest risk of poverty and then suggest ways in which poverty can be reduced by targeting these populations.*

   You would want to begin by identifying those groups that are at greater risk—the rural poor, minorities, the undereducated, female heads of household, and children. You would then discuss specific ideas you have for overcoming some of the conditions that place these groups at greater risk: some possible programs would be improvements in education, including more funding for postsecondary and technical training, increases in minimum wage, increased number of jobs that pay a living wage, and more aggressive enforcement of anti-discrimination laws.

ANSWERS FOR CHAPTER 7

ANSWERS FOR MULTIPLE CHOICE QUESTIONS

1. d Gender stratification cuts across all aspects of social life and all social classes and it refers to men's and women's unequal access to power, prestige, and property on the basis of their sex. It is *incorrect* to think that it is not a structured feature of society. (146)

2. b The term "sex" refers to the biological characteristics that distinguish females and males. (146)

3. c According to sociologists, if biology were the principal factor in human behaviour, around the world we would find women to be one sort of person and men another. (148)

4. d "All of the above" is correct. Patriarchy is a society in which men dominate women, it has existed throughout history, and it is universal. (147)

5. a The association of behaviours with one sex or the other is called sex-typing. (149)

6. c What Murdock found was that there was nothing about biology that required men and women to be assigned different work; rather it was social attitudes. (149)

7. c In regard to the prestige of work, greater prestige is given to male activities regardless of what those activities are. (149)

8. b The incorrect statement is the one that claims that Canada leads the world in the number of women who hold public office. In fact, it is Norway, where 40 percent of the legislators are women. (150)

9. b Worldwide, 85 percent of men compared with 76 percent of women are literate. (149)

10. a In 2004 worldwide, women held only 16 percent of seats in parliament or congresses. (149)

11. c Historically in Canada, women could not serve on juries or hold property in their own names. (152)

12. d All of the answers are correct. A "second wave" of protest and struggle against gender inequalities began in the 1960s when women began to compare their working conditions with those of men; it had as its goals everything from changing work roles to changing policies on violence against women. (153)

13. c Gender inequality in education is perpetuated by the use of sex to sort students into different academic disciplines. (154)

14. c Researchers who have studied conversation patterns between men and women conclude that even in everyday conversation, the talk between a man and a woman reflects social inequality. (155)

15. c The pay gap between men and women is found at all educational levels. (156)

16. c The glass ceiling refers to the invisible barrier that keeps women from reaching the executive suite. Men who go into fields that are traditionally associated with women often encounter a glass escalator—they advance quickly—rather than a glass ceiling. (157)

17. d Another form of violence against women is "honour killings," found in such societies as Pakistan, Jordan, and India. (150)

18. d Felice Schwartz suggested that corporations create two parallel career paths. These are the "mommy track" and the "fast track." (158)

19. c When it comes to sexual harassment, male victims are less likely than female victims to receive a sympathetic ear. (160)

20. d Date rape is not an isolated event; it is more likely to happen after a couple has dated for a period of time rather than on the first few dates; and it is difficult to prosecute because of the preexisting relationship. (162)

21. a Rather than higher testosterone levels in males, feminists would point to video games in which barely clad women are hunted down and killed, the association of strength and virility with violence, and cultural traditions that are patriarchal as sources for gender violence. (163)

22. c Women are reluctant to get involved in politics because the demands of political life are in conflict with the demands of their roles as wives and mothers. (164)

23. b In many parts of Canada today, the primary concern of voters is whether the candidate can win; gender is of less concern than winning. (164)

24. c Increased female participation in decision-making processes of social institutions is most likely going to result in breaking down the stereotypes that lock both males and females into traditional gender activities. (166)

25. d "All of the above" is correct. (166)

ANSWERS FOR TRUE-FALSE QUESTIONS

1. *False.* Sex refers to biological characteristics that distinguish females and males. Gender refers to social characteristics that a society considers proper for its males and females. (146)

2. *False.* The study supports the view that biological factors play a role in structuring behaviour, but that social factors are also important. (148)

3. *False.* Universally, greater prestige is given to male activities, regardless of what the activities are. (149)

4. *False.* Female circumcision is still quite common in parts of Africa and southeast Asia. (150)

5. *False.* As China has begun the cautious transition to capitalism, the situation of women within that country has actually deteriorated. (151)

6. *True.* (152)

7. *True.* (164)

8. *True.* (156)

9. *True.* (162)

10. *True.* (154)

11. *True.* (154)

12. *True.* (155)

13. *False.* Men are more likely to interrupt a conversation and to control changes in topics than are women. (155)

14. *False.* Fuller and Schoenberger found that the 11 percent difference between men and women business majors in starting pay had grown to 14 percent after five years in the workplace. (156)

15. *True.* (156)

16. *False.* The "glass escalator" refers to the opportunities that men have to advance quickly in traditional female occupations. (157)

17. *True.* (160)

18. *True* (160)

19. *True.* (164)
20. *False.* There are several other factors that also contribute to women not holding public office: they are underrepresented in law and business, traditional recruiting grounds for public office, the demands of running for and holding public office often conflict with a woman's other role responsibilities, they do not see themselves as a class in need of special representation. (164)

ANSWERS FOR FILL-IN QUESTIONS

1. Males' and females' unequal access to power, prestige, and property on the basis of sex reflects GENDER INEQUALITY. (146)
2. SEX refers to biological characteristics that distinguish females and males, consisting of primary and secondary sex characteristics. (146)
3. The social characteristics that a society considers proper for its males and females make up an individual's GENDER. (146)
4. You inherit your SEX, but you learn your GENDER as you are socialized into specific behaviours and attitudes. (146)
5. A society in which women dominate men is called a MATRIARCHY. (147)
6. When activities become associated with one sex or the other they are said to be SEX-TYPED. (149)
7. Violence against women has taken many forms, such as FOOT BINDING in China. (150)
8. FEMALE CIRCUMCISION is a particular form of violence directed exclusively against women. (150)
9. A MINORITY is a group that is discriminated against on the basis of its members' physical characteristics. (150)
10. FEMINISM is the philosophy that men and women should be politically, economically, and socially equal. (152-153)
11. The GLASS CEILING prevents women from advancing to top executive positions. (157)
12. Men who move into traditionally female occupations are likely to climb onto a GLASS ESCALATOR, moving very quickly into more desirable work assignments, higher level positions, and larger salaries. (157)
13. The proposed MOMMY TRACK would address the stresses that many working women experience when they attempt to combine careers and families. (157-158)
14. The abuse of one's position of authority to force unwanted sexual demands on someone is referred to as SEXUAL HARASSMENT. (160)
15. DATE RAPE most commonly occurs between couples who have known each other about a year. (162)
16. The number of women in INFORMATION TECHNOLOGY and high-tech occupations doubled between 1991 and 2001. (157)
17. On the eve of International Women's Day in 2002 the Norwegian government announced a plan whereby it would force companies to guarantee that least 40 PERCENT of board room seats are held by women. This proposal also called for at least 40 PERCENT male board members.

ANSWERS TO MATCH THESE SOCIAL SCIENTISTS WITH THEIR CONTRIBUTIONS

1. l   Janet Chafetz: *studied the second wave of feminism in the 1960s*
2. g   Alice Rossi: *women are better prepared biologically for "mothering" than are men*
3. e   Felice Schwartz: *associated with the notion of the mommy track and the fast track*
4. b   Christine Williams: *men in non-traditional occupations often experience a glass escalator*
5. i   Gerda Lerner: *patriarchy may have had different origins around the globe*
6. h   Catharine McKinnon: *identified sexual harassment as a structural problem in work places*
7. a   George Murdock: *surveyed 324 societies and found evidence of sex-typed activities*
8. k   Samuel Stouffer: *noted the devaluation of things associated with women among soldiers*
9. c   Marvin Harris: *male dominance grew out of the greater strength that men had*
10. f   Steven Goldberg: *differences between males and females are due to inborn differences*
11. j   Frederick Engels: *male dominance developed with the origin of private property*
12. d   Douglas Foley: *study supports the view that things feminine are generally devalued*

GUIDELINES FOR ANSWERING THE ESSAY QUESTIONS

1. *Before examining inequalities of gender, consider why men and women act differently—Is it due to biology or culture? What is the dominant sociological position?*

    To answer this question you need to assess the importance of the biological nature of men and women. Why are males more aggressive and females more nurturing? Are they just born that way? Study page 146. The dominant sociological position is represented by symbolic interactionists. People learn contrasting expectations of life on the basis of their sex and access to society's privileges.

2. *Compare and contrast the two waves of the feminist movement in Canada by identifying the forces that contributed to both waves.*

    You could begin by noting that both waves of the feminist movement were committed to ending gender stratification and both met with strong opposition from both males and females. The first wave was characterized by rather narrow goals—the movement focused on winning the vote for women—while the second wave was broader and wanted to address issues ranging from changing work roles to changing policies on violence against women.

3. *Evaluate the pros and cons of the two parallel career paths available to women; the "fast track" and the "mommy track."*

    The "fast track" consists of the high-powered, demanding positions that may require 60-70 hours of work per week—regular responsibilities, emergencies, out of town meetings, and a brief case jammed at night and on weekends.
    The "mommy track" allows a lower commitment to the firm, and free time for higher commitment to the family

4. *Why was rape renamed as "sexual assault" under the Reformed Criminal Code?*

    Emphasis is now placed on the violence of the act, including the power and intimidation it entails. Women are no longer exempt as perpetrators under this new definition.

ANSWERS FOR CHAPTER 8

ANSWERS FOR MULTIPLE CHOICE QUESTIONS

1. b Race is inherited physical characteristics that distinguish one group from another. (169)
2. b People often confuse race and ethnicity because of the cultural differences people see and the way they define race. (170)
3. d "All of the above" is correct. Characteristics shared by minorities world wide are: ascribed status, distinguishing physical or cultural traits, and unequal treatment. (171)
4. d "All of the above" is correct. Minority groups are singled out for unequal treatment, regard themselves as objects of discrimination but are not necessarily a numerical minority. (170)
5. c Prejudice and discrimination appear to characterize every society. (171)
6. d "All of the above" is correct. Prejudice is an attitude, it may be positive or negative, and it often is the basis for discrimination. (171)
7. d Racism is discrimination based on race. (171)
8. a The negative treatment of one person by another on the basis of that person's characteristics is referred to as individual discrimination. (171)
9. d "All of the above" is correct. Hartley's research shows that prejudice does not depend on negative experiences with others. People can be prejudiced against groups they have never met and even groups that do not exist. (171)
10. c Discrimination is woven into the fabric of society so it becomes routine and even social policy. (171)
11. a Muzafer and Sherif study shows that the social environment can be deliberately arranged to generate either positive or negative feelings about people. (172)
12. d "All of the above" is correct. According to conflict theorists, prejudice benefits capitalists by splitting workers along racial or ethnic lines; contributes to the exploitation of workers, thus producing a split-labour market; and is a factor in keeping workers from demanding higher wages and better working conditions. (172)
13. c Symbolic interactionists stress that prejudiced people learn their prejudices in interaction with others. (173)
14. b The Swiss provide an outstanding example of multiculturalism. (176)
15. d "All of the above" is correct. Genocide occurred when Hitler attempted to destroy all Jews, it is the systematic annihilation of a race or ethnic group, and it often requires the cooperation of ordinary citizens. (169,174)
16. b When a minority is expelled from a country or from a particular area of a country, the process is called direct population transfer. (174)
17. c A society's policy of exploiting a minority group, using social institutions to deny the minority access to the society's full benefits, is referred to as internal colonialism. (174-175)
18. b The process of being absorbed into the mainstream culture is assimilation. (175)
19. d Multiculturalism is another term for pluralism. (176)
20. b The French and English white settlers are referred to as the "Charter Groups." (177)

21. d "All of the above" is correct. The federal government has made efforts to gain Native Canadians' support for the Charter of Rights and Freedoms. The territory of Nunavut was created, nearly one fifth of the size of Canada. (176)

22. d "All of the above" is correct. Quebec has better record than the rest of Canada in its dealings with Native people, there is evidence of Native language retention and lower rate of imprisonment of Native peoples. (177)

23. a Porter termed Canadian society as a "vertical mosaic"   because it is structured like a pyramid with the English at the top. (177-180)

24. c The English charter group part of even the trade union elites. (179)

25. d Spencer found that unemployment and discrimination lead some immigrants to return to their native countries. (180)

ANSWERS FOR TRUE-FALSE QUESTIONS

1. *True.* (169)
2. *True.* (170)
3. *True.* (171)
4. *True.* (171)
5. *True.* (171)
6. *True* (172)
7. *False.* Discrimination is unfair treatment directed against someone. When the basis of discrimination is race, it is known as racism, but discrimination can be based on many other characteristics. (171)
8. *True.* (171)
9. *True.* (171)
10. *False.* In order to understand discrimination, it is necessary to explain the patterns of institutional discrimination. (171)
11. *True.* (171)
12. *True.* (172)
13. *True* (172)
14. *False.* Conflict theorists, not functionalists, focus on the role of the capitalist class in exploiting racism and ethnic inequalities. (198-199)
15. *True.* (172)
16. *True.* (174)
17. *True.* (175)
18. *True.* (176)
19. *True.* (179)
20. *True.* (180)

ANSWERS FOR FILL-IN QUESTIONS

1. RACE is inherited physical characteristics that distinguish one group from another. (169)
2. Membership in a minority group is a(n) ASCRIBED status; that is, it is not voluntary, but comes through birth. (171)
3. RACISM is discrimination on the basis of race. (171)
4. INSTITUTIONAL discrimination is the negative treatment of a minority group that is built into a society's institutions. (171)

5. Theodor Adorno's term for people who are prejudiced and rank high on scales of conformity, intolerance, insecurity, respect for authority, and submissiveness to superiors is THE AUTHORITARIAN PERSONALITY. (172)
6. FUNCTIONAL theorists believe that prejudice can be both functional and dysfunctional. (172)
7. Dual-labour market is used by CONFLICT theorists to explain how racial and ethnic strife can be used to pit workers against one another. (172)
8. The term used to describe the unemployed who can be put to work during times of high production and then discarded when no longer needed is THE RESERVE LABOUR FORCE. (172)
9. SELECTIVE PERCEPTION is the ability to see certain points but remain blind to others. (173)
10. The systematic annihilation or attempted annihilation of a race or ethnic group is GENOCIDE. (174)
11. The types of population transfer are: (1) DIRECT and (2) INDIRECT. (174)
12. GENOCIDE is facilitated by labeling the target group as lee than fully human. (174)
13. ASSIMILATION is the process of being absorbed into the mainstream culture. (175)
14. MULTICULTURALISM is a philosophy or political policy that permits or even encourages ethnic variation. (176)
15. VERTICAL MOSAIC is Porter's term to describe the economic and political dominance of Canada by the English charter group. (177)
16. The system of reserves for Canada's Native peoples is an example of INTERNAL COLONIALISM. (175)
17. Derived from the greek language, ETHNICITY and ETHNIC are terms that refer to people who identify with one another on the basis of common ancestry and cultural heritage. (170)

ANSWERS TO MATCH THESE SOCIAL SCIENTISTS WITH THEIR CONTRIBUTIONS

1. d Theodor Adorno: *identified the authoritarian personality type*
2. c W.I. Thomas: *observed that defining a situation as real makes it real in its consequences*
3. a John Dollard: *suggested that prejudice is the result of frustration*
4. e John Porter: *In The Vertical Mosaic used the term Charter Groups*
5. b Louis Wirth: *offered a sociological definition of minority group*
6. f Eugene Hartley: *prejudice does not depend on negative experience*
7. g Munzafer and Sherif: *prejudice is functional and shaped by the social environment*

GUIDELINES FOR ANSWERING THE ESSAY QUESTIONS

1. *Explain what the author means when he says that race is both a myth and a reality.*

   You would begin by defining the concept of race. Then you would move on to talking about the myth of race—how there is no universal agreement as to how many races there are and how a system of racial classification is more a reflection of the society in which one lives than any underlying biological bases. At the same time, race is a reality—in terms of people's subjective feelings about race and the superiority of some, and the inferiority of other, races. You should bring Thomas's observations into the essay—if people believe something is real, then it is real in its consequences.

2. *Which of the six patterns of inter group relations in Figure 8.1 have been or are part of the Canadian experience?*

On page 175, the book identifies six different types of intergroup relations—genocide, population transfer, internal colonialism, segregation, assimilation, and multiculturalism. You could begin by mentioning how these are arranged along a continuum from rejection and inhumanity to acceptance and humanity. Then, as you define each pattern, bring into your discussion an example, or examples, from Canadian history. For example, in discussing population transfer you could mention the treatment of Native peoples by the Canadian government; in discussing assimilation and multiculturalism you could examine the experiences of European and non-European immigrants.

3. *Explore how both psychological and sociological theories can be used together to gain a deeper understanding of prejudice and discrimination.*

Your essay should discuss how psychological theories provide us with a deeper understanding of individual behaviour, while sociological theories provide insights into the societal framework of prejudice and discrimination. You could discuss the work of Theodor Adorno on the authoritarian personality or Dollard's work on individual frustration and the role of scapegoats. But without an understanding of the social environment, this work is incomplete. Bridging the two perspectives is symbolic interactionism and the analysis of the role of labels, selective perception, and the self-fulfilling prophecy in maintaining prejudice. But you should also include in your essay some reference to the functionalist analysis and the work of Muzafer and Carolyn Sherif as well as the conflict theorists and how the capitalist class exploits racial and ethnic strife to retain power and control in society.

ANSWERS FOR CHAPTER 9

ANSWERS FOR MULTIPLE CHOICE QUESTIONS

1. d "All of the above" is correct. By 1999, the federal government had established a National Advisory Council on Aging. Canadian Association of Gerontology and aging study programs at Canadian universities had been established. (185)
2. d It is the process of industrialization that contributes to an increase in the number of people who reach older ages. (185)
3. b The process by which older persons make up an increasing proportion of the Canadian population is referred to as the greying of Canada. (188)
4. d Native Canadians have a lower life expectancy due to higher rates of impoverishment and social marginalization. (191-192)
5. d "All of the above" is correct. Atlantic Provinces and Quebec have older populations than the Canadian average and due to low fertility and out-migration is expected to continue aging more rapidly than the rest of Canada, with regional differences in pressure on health care. (189)
6. d "All of the above" is correct. Factors that may spur people to apply the label of old to themselves include personal history or biography, cultural signals about when a person is old, and biological factors. (192)

7. d   "All of the above" is correct. All are related to the feminist view of the aging process. (192)

8. d   "All of the above" is correct. Biology, personal history, and societal timetables are involved. (192)

9. d   "All of the above" is correct. The contradictory perspectives on aging are reflected in stereotypes about elderly; yet, the elderly are not seen as synonymous with frailty or dependency; positive notions do appear. (194)

10. d   "All of the above" is correct. Older women's economic situation is related to their traditional role in the economy, dedication to home and family, and often just part-time work. (196)

11. d   "All of the above" is correct. Aboriginal women, women of colour, and those having disabilities experience extra hardships. (196-197)

12. d   "All of the above" is correct. Retirement of the Baby Boomers, rising life expectancies, and falling birth rates could rupture our retirement and health care system. (197-198)

13. a   Currently only Manitoba bans mandatory retirement. (198)

14. d   "All of the above" is correct. Traditional gerontological approaches have been challenges for the tendency to view aging as an "ailment" to be cured, for homogenizing seniors and lack of awareness of the diversity of the aging populations. (199)

15. d   "All of the above" is correct. Caregivers find it hard to balance work and family, lack free time. and wish for relief. (200)

16. b   Researchers have found that elder abuse is fairly extensive. (200)

17. a   Canadian seniors derive between 91 and 95 percent of their total income from government transfer payments. (198)

18. d   Both a and c are correct, being a woman and recent immigrant increases becoming a victim. (202)

19. d   "All of the above" is correct. Isolation, disability and illness, and dependency increases the risk for suicide of elder men over age 75. (201)

ANSWERS FOR TRUE-FALSE QUESTIONS

1. *True.* (191)
2. *True.* (185)
3. *True.* (188)
4. *True.* (192)
5. *True.* (196)
6. *False.* There has never been a "golden era" when societies elderly were uniformly respected and valued. (193)
7. *True.* (196)
8. *True.* (202)
9. *True.* (202)
10. *True.* (197)
11. *True.* (197-198)
12. *True.* (201)
13. *True.* (202)
14. *False.* The income level of Canada's seniors has increased since 1980, largely due to government income support. (190)

15. *True.*(201)

ANSWERS FOR FILL-IN QUESTIONS

1. The process by which older persons make up an increasing proportion of Canada's population is called THE GREYING OF CANADA. (188)
2. The LIFE EXPECTANCY of an average newborn is the number of years he or she can expect to live. (188)
3. The impact of this aging population has not been felt UNIFORMLY ACROSS Canada. (188)
4. While aging is seen as EMPOWERING for many men, it is not seen to be so for women. (196)
5. Women's lack of ECONOMIC RESOURCES is related to women's traditional role in the economy. (196)
6. AGEISM is the discrimination against the elderly because of their age. (193)
7. The MASS MEDIA send the explicit message that most seniors, except the rich, famous, and powerful, do not count. (197)
8. Hundred years ago the CLEAR MAJORITY of Canadians would not live to see age 65. (188)
9. Having enough money improves your prospects for HEALTH and LONGEVITY. (190)
10. Not only how many years you will spend as a senior but the QUALITY of that life appear to be affected by ETHNICITY. (191)
11. The number of workers required to support the portion of the population aged 64 and older and 15 and under is the DEPENDENCY RATIO. (197)
12. Founded in the 1960s by Margaret Kuhn, the GRAY PANTHERS encourages people of all ages to work for the welfare of both the old and the young. (189)
13. Resistance to government efforts to DE-INDEX PENSIONS provides a telling example of the ability of seniors to mobilize effectively. (189)
14. The CANADIAN ASSOCIATION OF RETIRED PERSONS (CARP) with local chapters across Canada has launched a vigorous Canada wide campaign against AGE DISCRIMINATION. (189-190)
15. TIMETABLES are the signals societies use to inform their members they are old. (192)

ANSWERS TO MATCH THESE SOCIAL SCIENTISTS WITH THEIR CONTRIBUTIONS

1. c   Robert Butler: *coined "ageism" to refer to prejudice or discrimination based on age*
2. d   Susan McDaniel: *developed the concept of intergenerational interlinkages*
3. e   Marcel Danesi: *argues that contemporary Western culture has embraced the view that age is bad and youth good*
4. a   Ann McMullin and John Cairney: *explored the relationship between self-esteem, age, class, and gender*
5. b   Joseph Tindale et.al.: *suggested the use of "lasagna" rather than "sandwhich" generation for intergenerational support structure*

GUIDELINES FOR ANSWERING THE ESSAY QUESTIONS

1. *Choose one of the theoretical perspectives on aging and discuss how that perspective approaches the subject of aging. Consider both the strengths as well as the weaknesses of the perspective you chose.*

In this question you have the option of writing about symbolic interactionism, functionalism, or conflict theory. If you choose symbolic interactionism, you would want to talk about the process of labelling—both the cultural labels and factors that affect the individual's adoption of those labels. You would also want to bring up the concept of "ageism," the role of the media in defining images, and how the labels change over time. In particular, you could discuss how these labels changed with industrialization and how they are once again changing with the advent of a postindustrial society. The strength of this perspective is that it provides us with insights into the social nature of a biological process; a weakness would be that it does not consider the conflict that may surround the labelling process.

If you choose to write about functionalism, remember that this perspective focuses on how the different parts of society work together. The two theories associated with this perspective are disengagement theory and activity theory. Strengths might be the focus on adjustment and the smooth transitioning from one generation to the next. Weaknesses are tied to the theories; disengagement theory overlooks the possibility that the elderly disengage from one set of roles (work-related) but may engage in another set of roles (friendship), while activity theory does not identify the key variables that underlie people's activities.

Finally, if you choose conflict theory, you would want to focus on the conflict that is generated between different age groups in society as they compete for scarce resources. As an example you would want to discuss the controversy over social security—from its birth to the present time. A strength of this perspective is that it provides us with an understanding of why the elderly have reduced the level of poverty over time; a weakness might be that it tends to emphasize conflict to the extent that cooperation between generations is overlooked.

2. *Explain why aging is as much a socially constructed process as a biological process.*

Symbolic Interactionists study how aging is socially constructed. There is no single point at which people automatically cross a magical line and become "old." It involves several factors, the first of which is our biological make up; our experience with and our perception of biological changes. Second factor is our personal history and the third relates to societal timetables, the signals societies use to inform their members they are "old."

ANSWERS FOR CHAPTER 10

ANSWERS FOR MULTIPLE CHOICE QUESTIONS

1. c   Rationality is the acceptance of rules, efficiency, and practical results as the right way to approach human affairs. (206)

2. a   The idea that the past is the best guide for the present is the traditional orientation. (206)

3. b   One of the major obstacles to industrialization was a traditional orientation to life that led people to resist change. (206)

4. d   "All of the above" is correct. According to Max Weber, capitalism is the investment of capital in the hopes of producing profits. It became an outlet for the excess money of Calvinists, as well as producing success for many that was then interpreted as a sign of God's approval. (206)

5. d   Because sociologists have not been able to determine whose views are most accurate, the two views still remain side by side. (207)

6. d   "All of the above" is correct. Today, secondary groups have become common. We take them for granted and spend a good deal of time in them. (208)

7. b   In a bureaucracy assignments flow downward—not upward—and accountability flows upward—not downward. (208-209)

8. a   Ideal types are composites of characteristics based on many specific examples. (210)

9. c   George Ritzer used the term "the McDonaldization of society" to refer to the increasing rationalization of daily living. (209)

10. d   "McDonaldization of society" refers to shopping malls as controlled environments, prepackaged tours by travel agents and packaged news. (209)

11. d   "All of the above" is correct because alienation, goal displacement, and red tape are dysfunctions of bureaucracies. (210-213)

12. b   What Linda is feeling is referred to as alienation by sociologists. (212)

13. d   "All of the above" is correct because workers resist alienation by forming primary groups, praising each other and expressing sympathy when something goes wrong, and putting pictures and personal items in their work areas. (212)

14. c   According to your text, the alienated bureaucrat is not likely to do anything for the organization beyond what he or she is required to do. (212)

15. d   b. and c. are correct. War Amps turned its attention to child amputees since war amputees declined.(213)

16. b   The Peter Principle states that each employee of a bureaucracy is promoted to his or her level of incompetence. (213)

17. d   "All of the above" is correct. There was evidence of voluntary associations when Tocqueville visited the U.S. in 1830s. (213)

18. d   "All of the above" is correct. People aged 35 to 44 have highest rate of volunteerism, but seniors spend more hours per week volunteering. (213-214)

19. c   The tendency for organizations to be dominated by a small, self-perpetuating elite is called the iron law of oligarchy. (216)

20. a   According to Rosabeth Moss Kanter, in a large corporation the corporate culture determines an individual's corporate fate. (217)

21. d   "All of the above" is correct. Humanizing a work setting refers to organizing a workplace in such a way that human potential is developed rather than impeded.

Among the characteristics of more humane bureaucracies are the availability of opportunities on the basis of ability and contributions, a more equal distribution of power, and less rigid rules and more open decision making. (219)

22. d Research on the costs and benefits of employer-financed day care demonstrates that such a benefit can save the employer money in terms of reducing employee turnover and absenteeism. (220-221)

23. b The cooperative is the type of organization that attempts to provide a high level of personal satisfaction for members at the same time that they are working towards their goals. (221)

24. c According to conflict theorists the interests of workers and owners are fundamentally opposed and, in the final analysis, workers are always exploited. (221)

25. d "All of the above" is correct. Computers in the workplace have the potential of improving the quality of work life, could lead to more surveillance of workers by managers, may be the first step towards a society in which every move a citizen makes is recorded. (222)

ANSWERS FOR TRUE-FALSE QUESTIONS

1. *True.* (206)
2. *True.* (206)
3. *False.* Max Weber did not believe that the growth of capitalism contributed to the rise of the Protestant ethic but, rather, that the rise of the Protestant ethic as a result of Calvinism contributed to the growth of capitalism. (206)
4. *True.* (206)
5. *True.* (207)
6. *False.* By definition, only secondary groups can be formal organizations. The text defines a formal organization as "a secondary group designed to achieve explicit objectives." (207)
7. *True.* (208-209)
8. *False.* Most colleges and universities do have written systems of accountability for faculty members. (208-209)
9. *True.* (209)
10. *True.* (210)
11. *True.* (207)
12. *False.* It is difficult for workers to resist becoming alienated because of the nature of the organizational environment in which they work. According to Marx, alienation occurs because workers are cut off from the product of their own labour, which results in estrangement not only from the products but from their whole work environment. (212)
13. *False.* The Peter Principle has not been proven to be true. If it were generally true, bureaucracies would be staffed entirely be incompetents, and none of these organizations could succeed. In reality, bureaucracies are remarkably successful. (213)
14. *True.* (213-215)
15. *True.* (215)
16. *True.* (216)
17. *False.* Bureaucracies are not likely to disappear as our dominant form of social organization in the near future because they generally are effective in getting the job done. Most people spend their working lives in such organizational environments. (224)
18. True. (218-220)
19. *True.* (220)

20. *True.* (223)

ANSWERS FOR FILL-IN QUESTIONS

1. In a HIERARCHICAL ORGANIZATION assignments flow downward and accountability flows upward. (208)
2. The idea that the past is the best guide for the present is known as TRADITIONAL ORIENTATION. (206)
3. THE PROTESTANT ETHIC AND THE SPIRIT OF CAPITALISM was written by Max Weber and emphasizes that religion holds the key to understanding the development of certain types of economic systems. (206)
4. The investment of capital in the hope of producing profits is called CAPITALISM. (206)
5. CO-OPERATIVES are organizations owned by members who collectively make decisions, determine goals, evaluate resources, set salaries, and assign work tasks. (221)
6. George Ritzer has coined the term "McDONALDIZATION OF SOCIETY" to refer to the increasing rationalization of life's routine tasks. (209)
7. ALIENATION is a feeling of powerlessness and normlessness; the experience of being cut off from the product of one's labour. (207)
8. GOAL DISPLACEMENT occurs when new goals are adopted by an organization to replace previous goals that may have been fulfilled. (213)
9. A group made up of volunteers who have organized on the basis of some mutual interest is called a(n) VOLUNTARY ASSOCIATION. (213)
10. THE IRON LAW OF OLIGARCHY refers to the tendency of formal organizations to be dominated by a small, self-perpetuating elite. (216)
11. The orientation that characterizes corporate work settings is referred to as CORPORATE CULTURE. (216-217)
12. Women and minorities are often SHOWCASED, which means that they are placed in highly visible positions with little power in order to demonstrate to the public and affirmative action officials how progressive the company is. (217)
13. QUALITY CIRCLES consist of perhaps a dozen workers and a manager or two who meet regularly to try to improve the quality of the work setting and of the company's products. (220)
14. Professor Ursula Huws has studied the revolution in MICROTECHNOLOGY and the ways in which it has transformed WORK. (222)
15. Lean production, almost total involvement, broad training, and collective decision making are characteristics of the JAPANESE CORPORATE model. (223-24)

ANSWERS TO MATCH THESE SOCIAL SCIENTISTS WITH THEIR CONTRIBUTIONS

1. e Max Weber: *the rationalization of society*
2. a Robert Michels: *the iron law of oligarchy*
3. f William Ouchi: *the Japanese corporate model*
4. d Karl Marx: *the exploitation of workers by capitalists*
5. c Rosabeth Moss Kanter: *the hidden values in the corporate culture*
6. b George Ritzer: *the McDonaldization of society*

GUIDELINES FOR ANSWERING THE ESSAY QUESTIONS

1. *Explain what an ideal type is and why such constructs are useful.*

   You would begin by explaining how Weber studied several different bureaucracies and used these real entities to construct composite characteristics that he thought were typical of bureaucratic structures. The result was a list of characteristics that a bureaucratic organization would ideally have. This constructed list of characteristics can then be used to measure the degree to which any organization is bureaucratized.

2. *Discuss the differences between the Japanese and North American corporate models.*

   The Japanese practice just-in-time, lean production unlike Fordist production, which relies on enormous inventories of parts and massive warehouse space. The Japanese model incorporates kaizen which means—continuous improvement. The Japanese have a commitment to lifetime security of work which is unusual in North America.

3. *Discuss the impact of "Macdonaldization" of society.*

   See the Down-to-Earth box p.209. Ritzer stresses that "Macdonaldization" does not refer to just the robotlike assembly of food. Rather, this process occurring throughout society, is transforming our lives. Shopping malls are controlled environments of approved design, logo, colours, and opening and closing doors and so forth.

ANSWERS FOR CHAPTER 11

ANSWERS FOR MULTIPLE CHOICE QUESTIONS

1. d "All of the above" is correct. Market is any process of buying and selling. It is the mechanism that establishes values for the exchange of goods and services. It also means the movement of vast amounts of goods across international borders. (228)
2. c Hunting and gathering societies are characterized by a subsistence economy. (228)
3. c The primary sociological significance of surplus and trade was fostering social inequality. (228)
4. d Industrial economies are based on machines powered by fuels. Industrial economies also created a surplus unlike anything the world had seen, and these economies were based on the invention of the steam engine. Therefore, the incorrect answer is "A service sector developed and employed the majority of workers"; this is actually a characteristic of a *postindustrial society*. (228)
5. d Thorstein Veblen used the term conspicuous consumption to describe the lavishly wasteful spending of goods in order to enhance social prestige. (228)
6. a Postindustrial economies are characterized by a large surplus of goods; extensive trade among nations; and a "global village." While machines may still be powered by fuel, this is *not* a defining characteristic of this type of economy. (229)
7. a Money was first used extensively in agricultural societies. (230)
8. a The gross national product is total goods and services produced by a nation. (230)
9. c The debit card came into existence in the postindustrial economy. (230)
10. d Private ownership, pursuit of profit, and market competition are features of capitalism. (231)

11. c "Pure" capitalism is a system where market forces operate without interference from government. (231)

12. d "All of the above" is correct. In the few socialist/communist economies that remain in the world, government owns the factories, land and railroads, oil wells and gold mines. (232)

13. b Some Western nations have developed systems of democratic socialism as a response to dissatisfaction with both capitalism and socialism. (232)

14. d "All of the above" is correct. The following are criticisms of capitalism: it produces a tiny top layer of wealthy and powerful people with political power that exploits a vast bottom layer of poorly paid workers. (233)

15. d "All of the above" is correct. Primary criticism against socialism is that it does not respect individual rights and does not produce enough consumer goods and central planning is inefficient. (233)

16. a Oligopoly is the control of an entire industry by several large companies. (235)

17. a Neoliberalism refers to a new expansion in time and space of the free market. (234)

18. c The elite who sit on the boards of directors of not just one but several companies are referred to as interlocking directorates. (235)

19. d Rigorous educational training, authority over clients based on the specialized training, and service to society rather than to the self are all characteristics that describe a profession. (238)

20. a Work binds us together, according to the functionalist perspective. (239)

21. b As societies industrialize, they become based on organic solidarity. (239)

22. c According to conflict theory, low-level workers bear the brunt of technological change. (239)

23. b Workers who package fish, process copper into electrical wire, and turn trees into lumber and paper are in the secondary sector. (240)

24. c The fundamental changes in society that follow the movement of vast numbers of women from the home to the work force is referred to as the quiet revolution. (242)

25. d "All of the above" is correct. The underground economy is an exchange of goods and services that is not reported to the government; it helps many Canadians avoid what they consider exorbitant taxes; and it includes illegal activities such as drug dealing. (242)

ANSWERS FOR TRUE-FALSE QUESTIONS

1. *False.* Pastoral and horticultural societies, not hunting and gathering societies, were the first economies to have a surplus. (228)
2. *True.* (228)
3. *True.* (229)
4. *False.* Gold standard of U.S. money was changed to fiat money. (230)
5. *True.* (230)
6. *True.* (230)
7. *False.* Credit cards and debit cards are not the same thing. A credit card allows its owner to purchase goods but to be billed later. A debit card allows its owner to purchase against his or her bank account. (230)
8. *True.* (231)
9. *True.* (231)
10. *True.* (232)

11. *True.* (234)
12. *True.* (235)
13. *True.* (236)
14. *True.* (238)
15. *True.* (239)
16. *True.* (239)
17. *False.* Researchers have found that women workers are more likely than male workers to be concerned with maintaining a balance between their work and family lives. (242)
18. *True.* (242)
19. *True.* (242)
20. *False.* In recent decades, workers in Canada have actually experienced an increase in work hours and a decrease in leisure, which is contrary to the pattern found in other western industrialized nations. (244)

ANSWERS FOR FILL-IN QUESTIONS

1. ECONOMY is the term for a system of distribution of goods and services. (228)
2. Toward the end of the agricultural period CURRENCY or paper money, came into use. (230)
3. A CREDIT CARD allows its owners to purchase goods but to be billed later. A DEBIT CARD allows its owners to charge purchases against his or her bank account. (230)
4. The economic system where market forces operate without interference from government is called LAISSEZ-FAIRE CAPITALISM. (231)
5. UNDEREMPLOYMENT is the condition of having to work at a job beneath one's level of training and abilities, or of being able to find only part-time work. (233)
6. A CORPORATION is a business that is treated in law as a person. (235)
7. One way in which the wealthy use corporations to wield power is by means of INTERLOCKING DIRECTORSHIPS, or serving as directors of several companies simultaneously. (235)
8. Durkheim's term for the unity that comes from being involved in similar occupations or activities is MECHANICAL SOLIDARITY. (239)
9. Members of the INNER CIRCLE may compete with one another, but they are united by a mutual interest in preserving capitalism. (239)
10. That part of the economy in which raw materials are turned into manufactured goods is the SECONDARY SECTOR. (240)
11. In the TERTIARY sector, workers are primarily involved in providing services. (240)
12. The QUIET REVOLUTION has contributed to a transformation of consumer patterns, relations at work, self-concepts, and relationships with family and friends. (242)
13. The UNDERGROUND ECONOMY consists of economic activities, whether legal or illegal, that people don't report to the government. (242)
14. LEISURE is time not taken up by work or required activities such as eating and sleeping. (243)

ANSWERS TO MATCH THESE SOCIAL SCIENTISTS WITH THEIR CONTRIBUTIONS

1. c Daniel Bell: *identified six characteristics of postindustrial society*
2. e Emile Durkheim: *contributed the concepts of mechanical and organic solidarity*
3. a Michael Useem: *studied the activities of the "inner circle"*
4. b Wallace Clement: *studied the concentration of corporate power in Canada*
5. d Thorstein Veblen: *created the term "conspicuous consumption"*

GUIDELINES FOR ANSWERING THE ESSAY QUESTIONS

1. *Discuss the advantages and disadvantages of both capitalism and socialism as ideologies and as economic systems.*

   This is a difficult question to answer because it is laden with social values. In this country we have been taught that capitalism is good and socialism is bad. Nevertheless, you should try to approach this from as objective a position as possible. You would want to begin by discussing the advantages and disadvantages of capitalism. For advantages you could mention the idea of private ownership and the pursuit of profits, the motivation among workers to work hard, and the vast array of goods that are available in the marketplace. Among the disadvantages you could note the possibility for monopoly, the creation of constant discontent through advertising, and the violation of certain basic human right like freedom from poverty. Turning to socialism, you could note that advantages include production for the general welfare rather than individual enrichment and the distribution of goods and services according to need rather than ability to pay. Critics point out that socialism violates basic human rights such as individual freedom of decision and opportunity.

2. *Identify the defining characteristics of professions and discuss the usefulness of this framework for understanding work.*

   Your first task is to discuss the five characteristics that symbolic interactionists have identified as the defining characteristics of professions. You would then want to discuss how these create a kind of "ideal type" of professions against which real professions can be measured. Rather than seeing this as an "either/or" situation—work is either a profession or a job—these characteristics should be used to measure the degree to which specific work reflects one or more of them.

3. *Discuss the sociological significance of global capitalism, the underground economy, and shrinking paychecks of Canadian households.*

   This question asks you to draw information from throughout this and other chapters in order to think about what impact globalization of capital has had on our lives, our society, and our economy. The first development is the global corporation; you could refer back to Chapter 6, and the discussion of the growth of multinational corporations and their use of technology to create a globally integrated system of production. The underground economy is also known as *informal* and *off-the-books economy*; these are economic activities—legal or illegal, that people don't report to the government. The size of this informal economy is probably about 15 to 20 percent of the regular economy, although no-one knows exactly what it is. The shrinking of workers' paychecks is also connected to technology—as employers introduce new technologies to increase productivity and profits, workers are working harder but not necessarily being paid more, and many are laid off because technology has reduced the number of jobs in the workforce. Finally, technology has contributed to increased leisure for workers because machines can take over much of the work that was previously done by humans, and because in an industrial economy, workers have organized and demanded greater leisure. Is there a link between the shrinking paychecks and the informal economy?

4. *In what way is neoliberalism different from classical market liberalism?*

Neoliberalism is not the same as classical market liberalism even though they share a belief in the centrality of private property, its inheritance, and the pursuit of profit. What is the difference between these two philosophies? Market liberalism or classical liberalism has its origins in the Enlightenment ideas of human rights or an individual's rights to life, liberty, and the pursuit of property. According to classical liberalism, it was the goal of the state to protect these rights. Neoliberalism, on the other hand refers to a new expansion in time and space of the free market: Nothing less than a 24-hour global economy will satisfy neoliberals. This type of economy is made possible by the rapid expansion of global information and telecommunications technologies. In contrast to classical liberalism, instead of property, neoliberalism emphasizes the contract, especially the labour contract.

ANSWERS FOR CHAPTER 12

ANSWERS FOR MULTIPLE CHOICE QUESTIONS

1. d   "All of the above" is correct. Power was defined by Max Weber; is the ability to carry out one's will in spite of resistance from others; is an inevitable part of everyday life, and we perceive power as either legitimate or illegitimate. (250)
2. b   Governments, whether dictatorships or the elected forms, are examples of macropolitics. (250)
3. c   The government claims the exclusive right to use violence and the right to punish everyone else who does. (250)
4. d   "All of the above" is correct. Good examples are kings and queens, widows wearing black, and parents having authority over their children. (250-251)
5. a   Pierre Elliott Trudeau combined rational-legal and charismatic authority, and is an example of a leader who is difficult to classify in terms of ideal types. (252)
6. d   "All of the above" is correct. Ayatollah Khomeini of Iran shows that charismatic and traditional authority can also overlap. He was a charismatic leader, and he was holder of the traditional position of Ayatollah Khomeini. (252-253)
7. b   A government run by a single person who has seized power is a dictatorship. (255)
8. c   A form of government that exerts almost total control is a totalitarian regime. (255)
9. a   Canada's political system is a parliamentary democracy. (255)
10. b   The history of the political party system in Canada demonstrates that a multi-party system developed during the twentieth century. (256-257)

11. c The Quiet Revolution and the rise of the sovereignty movement (both in Quebec) have transformed Canadian politics. (258-259)
12. d Most European countries base their elections on a system of proportional representation. (260)
13. b Functionalists believe that pluralism prevents any one group from gaining control of the government. (260)
14. a Functionalists suggest that political conflict is minimized as special-interest groups negotiate with one another and reach compromise. (260)
15. d Members of Canada's corporate elite are drawn from banking and insurance, not from industrial-military complex like in the US. (261)
16. c According to conflict theorists, the ruling class is made up of people whose backgrounds and orientations to life are so similar that they automatically share the same goals. (261)
17. a War is armed conflict between nations or politically distinct groups. It is not necessarily universal nor is it chosen for dealing with disagreements by all societies at one time or another. (262)
18. a A cultural tradition of war, an antagonistic situation in which two or more states confront incompatible objectives, and the presence of a "fuel" that heats the antagonistic situation to a boiling point are the three essential conditions of war identified by Nicholas Timasheff. The existence of a strong, well-armed military force was not one of the factors he identified as essential. (262)
19. d "All of the above" is correct. If the leaders see the situation as an opportunity to exact revenge, dictate their will on weaker nations or save the nation's "honour" a war is likely. (262)
20. d "All of the above" is correct. The following are characteristics of a "nation": shared language and culture, shared political organization and a shared territory. (264)

ANSWERS FOR TRUE-FALSE QUESTIONS

1. *True.* (250)
2. *False.* Authority, not coercion, refers to legitimate power. (250)
3. *True.* (250)
4. *True.* (251)
5. *True.* (251)
6. *False.* It is because the authority of charismatic leaders is based on their personal ability to attract followers that they pose a threat to the established political system. They work outside the political structure and owe allegiance to nothing. (252)
7. *True.* (252)
8. *True.* (253)
9. *True.* (253)
10. *True.* (253)
11. *True.* (253)
12. *False.* The idea of universal citizenship caught on very slowly in Canada. (254)
13. *True.* (258)
14. *True.* (258)
15. *False.* Europeans are different. Most European countries base their elections on a system of proportional representation; that is, the seats in the national legislature are divided according to the proportion of votes received by each political party. (260)

16. *True.* (260)
17. *False.* Conflict theorists point out that we should not think that the behaviour of the ruling class stems from some grand conspiracy to control the country. Rather, it is grounded in mutual interests in solving problems that face large businesses. (261)
18. *True.* (262)
19. *False.* Sociologists attribute the causes of war to social causes—conditions in a society that encourage or discourage combat between nations. (262)
20. *True.* (263)

ANSWERS FOR FILL-IN QUESTIONS

1. The exercise of power in everyday life, such as deciding who is going to do the housework is referred to as MICROPOLITICS. (250)
2. STATE is synonymous with government; the source of legitimate violence in society. (250)
3. A REVOLUTION is armed resistance designed to overthrow a government. (250)
4. TRADITIONAL AUTHORITY is authority based on custom. (250)
5. Bureaucratic authority is also called RATIONAL-LEGAL AUTHORITY. (251)
6. TRUDEAU may have had mass appeal in English Canada, but he was far from a hero in his home province of QUEBEC. (252)
7. DIRECT DEMOCRACY is a form of democracy in which the eligible voters meet together to discuss issues and make their decisions. (253)
8. The concept that birth and residence in a country impart basic rights is known as CITIZENSHIP. (254)
9. A form of government that exerts almost total control over the people is TOTALITARIANISM. (255)
10. An electoral system in which seats in a legislature are divided according to the proportion of votes each political party receives is called PROPORTIONAL REPRESENTATION. (260)
11. A COALITION GOVERNMENT is a government where the party with the most seats aligns itself with one or more of the smaller parties to maintain power. (260)
12. CITY-STATES were the first type of government. (253)
13. Canada has a FEDERAL system of government, but the PROVINCES have evolved a number of separate and significant powers of their own. (255)
14. The act or process of reducing people to objects that do not deserve the treatment accorded humans is DEHUMANIZATION. (263)
15. Today NATIONALISM, a strong identity with a nation, accompanied by the desire for that nation to be dominant, challenges efforts to forge a new world order. (264)

ANSWERS TO MATCH THESE SOCIAL SCIENTISTS WITH THEIR CONTRIBUTIONS

1. b Peter Berger: *violence is the foundation of the political order*
2. d John Porter: *identified Canadian elite*
3. a C. Wright Mills: *power elite*
4. c Max Weber: *three types of authority*
5. f Nicholas Timasheff: *essential conditions of war*
6. e Wallace Clement : *classified three components of Canada's corporate elite*

GUIDELINES FOR ANSWERING THE ESSAY QUESTIONS

1. *Distinguish between macropolitics and micropolitics, explaining what each is and which perspectives are associated with each, and provide your own examples to illustrate each.*

You would begin by defining what each of these is—micropolitics is the exercise of power in everyday life, while macropolitics is the exercise of large-scale power over a large group. In general, symbolic interactionists focus more on micropolitics, because it is rooted in the social interactions that take place within social groups, although some conflict theorists could also take a micropolitical approach by focusing on the conflict that is generated by power inequalities. On the other hand, functionalists and conflict theorists are concerned with macropolitics, because they are concerned with the large-scale structures and patterns of a society. (Note: You could refer to the differences between macro and micro sociology.) Finally, you would include some of your own examples of micropolitics (struggles between husbands and wives, parents and children) and macropolitics (struggles between political parties, between unions and elected officials, between nations).

2. *Compare and contrast the systems of democracy found in Canada and Europe.*

For this essay you would want to point out that both systems are democratic, which means that the ultimate power resides in the people. Both are representative rather than direct democracies, which means that citizens vote for representatives who actually make the decisions rather than the citizens themselves voting on each decision. Despite these similarities, the two systems have differences. You would want to mention the proportional representation of the European system vs. the parliamentary democratic system in Canada; the encouragement of minority parties in the European system vs. the multi-party system in Canada; and the implications of systems of coalition governments in Europe vs. single-party governments in Canada.

3. *Discuss the impact of voter turnout at federal elections in Canada. How different would the distribution of seats in the parliament be, if voter turnout would be 90 percent?*

Look at Table 12.2 p. 255, and see the highest and lowest voter turnout. What could account for the increasingly lower turnout? What is the sociological impact of the non-voters on Canadian politics?

ANSWERS FOR CHAPTER 13

ANSWERS FOR MULTIPLE CHOICE QUESTIONS

1. a Polyandry is a marriage in which a woman has more than one husband. (268)
2. b Endogamy is the practice of marrying within one's own group. (270)
3. a In a matrilineal system descent is figured only on the mother's side. (270)
4. d "None of the above" is correct; family of orientation is the one in which a person grows up. (270)
5. b According to functionalists, the family serves certain essential functions in all societies. (271)

6. d   "All of the above" is correct. The incest taboo is rules specifying the degrees of kinship that prohibit sex or marriage; helps families avoid role confusion; and facilitates the socialization of children. (271)

7. c   According to research findings, men who earn less money than their wives feel most threatened by doing housework and consequently do the least. (274)

8. a   Meg Luxton and June Corman wrote the book, Getting by in Hard Times. (275)

9. b   Researchers conclude that the reason men and women give different answers to the same question is because they have different perspectives on the motivation for love-making. Jessie Bernard has concluded that in general husbands and wives see their marriage differently, resulting in two marriages within one union. (276)

10. c   The tendency of people with similar characteristics to marry one another is homogamy. (277)

11. b   When the last child left home was once thought to be a difficult time of adjustment, but contrary to the stereotype, Lillian Rubin found that this picture is largely a myth; satisfaction generally increases when that happens. (278)

12. a   53 percent is correct. (278)

13. a   The name is Boomerang kids. (278)

14. d   "All of the above" is correct. According to your text, language, cultural beliefs, and cultural values all contribute to family diversity in Canada. (279)

15. d   "All of the above" is correct. Simply by being a Native Canadian you are more likely to be low income, less educated and more likely to commit suicide. (280)

16. d   "All of the above" is correct. Poor children are penalized in terms of physical, social, and mental health. (280)

17. a   41 percent of married couples have no children at home. (281)

18. c   Sociologist Kathleen Gerson found that couples choose not to have children because children would limit their options in life, be too expensive, and would diminish their career opportunities. (281)

19. c   A family whose members were once part of other families is known as a blended family. (281)

20. d   "All of the above" is correct. With a few exceptions people tend to pick a marriage partner who is similar to themselves in education, ethnicity and age. (277)

21. d   The "sandwich generation" refers to people who find themselves caught between two generations, simultaneously responsible for the care of their children and their aging parents. (285)

22. d   48 % of custody is awarded to mothers and 10 percent to fathers, while 42 percent is joint custody. (286)

23. d   "All of the above" is correct. Children growing up in lone-parent families tend to have poorer scores of academic achievement, worse health, and poorer relationships. (287)

24. d   "All of the above" is correct. The victims of incest who suffer the most are victimized longest, most often, and more "intrusively." (290)

25. d   "All of the above" is correct. The continuing trends are likely to be increased in cohabitation, increased in mother-headed families, and increased in blended families. (290)

ANSWERS FOR TRUE-FALSE QUESTIONS

1. *True.* (268)

2. *True.* (270)
3. *False.* Households are people who live together in the same housing unit; families consist of two or more people who consider themselves related by blood, marriage or adoption. (270)
4. *True.* (270)
5. *True.* (271)
6. *True.* (274)
7. *True.* (277)
8. *False.* Hochschild, like Luxton, found considerable evidence of resistance to household duties. (273)
9. *False.* Symbolic interactionists have found that husbands and wives have vastly different perceptions about their marriages. For instance, when asked how much housework each does, wives and husbands give very different answers; they even disagree about whether or not they fight over doing housework! Jessie Bernard has suggested that their experiences are in such contrast that every marriage actually contains two separate marriages—his and hers. (276)
10. *True.* (277)
11. *True.* (274)
12. *True.* (274)
13. *False.* Researchers have found that most husbands and wives do not experience the empty nest when their last child leaves home. Often just the opposite occurs because the couple now have more time and money to use at their own discretion. (278)
14. *False.* Women are more likely than men to face the problem of widowhood, not only because they live longer, but also because they are likely to have married older men. (278)
15. *False.* Recent research has found that 7 percent of women and 8 percent of men aged 20-34 intend to remain childless. (281)
16. *True.* (281)
17. *False.* Marriage between same-sex couples is not legal in most countries. However Denmark, Sweden, Norway and the Netherlands have legalized gay marriages. (282)
18. *True.* (290)
19. *True.* (285)
20. *True.* (288)

ANSWERS FOR FILL-IN QUESTIONS

1. A marriage in which a man has more than one wife is POLYGYNY. (268)
2. EXOGAMY is the practice of marrying outside one's group. (270)
3. Female control of a society or group is a(n) MATRIARCHY. (270)
4. A FAMILY is a group who consider themselves related by blood, marriage, or adoption. (270)
5. A(n) NUCLEAR FAMILY is a family consisting of a husband, wife, and child(ren). (271)
6. Rules specifying the degrees of kinship that prohibit sex or marriage are INCEST TABOOS. (289-290)
7. HOMOGAMY is the tendency of people with similar characteristics to get married. (277)
8. A married couple's domestic situation after the last child has left home is sometimes referred to as the EMPTY NEST. (278)
9. A HOUSEHOLD may or may not be also a family. (270)

10. Historically, IMMIGRATION POLICIES have intentionally blocked family formation among working-class Chinese, South Asian, and Japanese men and women, and more recently black Caribbean women. (280)
11. In 1998, British Columbia became the first jurisdiction in North America to grant custody, access and child support rights to SAME-SEX COUPLES. (282)
12. To overcome such problems as loneliness, some have started INTENTIONAL families. (283)
13. The term SANDWICH GENERATION refers to people who find themselves caught between two generations and responsible for the care of both. (285)
14. From the time of Confederation until 1968 ADULTERY was the only grounds for divorce in most of Canada. (286)
15. Sexual relations between specified relatives, such as brothers and sisters, or parents and children, is INCEST. (289)

ANSWERS TO MATCH THESE SOCIAL SCIENTISTS WITH THEIR CONTRIBUTIONS

1. a Jessie Bernard: *noted the existence of two marriages within one union*
2. f Meg Luxton: *studied the gendered division of household labour*
3. d Kathleen Gerson: *identified reasons why couples choose to be child-free*
4. e Margrit Eichler: *suggested that the definition of the nuclear family supports a very limited view of family life*
5. b Lillian Rubin: *found that women's satisfaction increased after last child moved out*
6. c Diana Russell: *studied incest victims*

GUIDELINES FOR ANSWERING THE ESSAY QUESTIONS

1. *Consider the impact on families of the reform of divorce laws in Canada in 1968 and later in 1985.*

   In the past, divorce was a distinctly uncommon phenomenon. From the time of confederation until 1968, adultery was the only grounds of divorce in most of Canada. Formal divorces were uncommon but informal separations and desertions existed. Finally in 1968, under growing pressure, the Divorce Act was changed, the grounds for divorce were expanded and a number of "no-fault," "no-blame" grounds were added. In 1985 the Divorce Act was amended again: A couple living separately for a period of not less than one year, as well as adultery or mental or physical cruelty were viewed as indications of marriage breakdown and legitimate grounds for divorce.

2. *Explain the social forces that have contributed to the emergence of intentional families.*

   For this answer you will need to use some of the knowledge you gained in previous chapters. Specifically, you would want to refer to the shift from Gemeinschaft to Gesellschaft societies and the transformation of relationships. In a Gemeinschaft society, relationships are based on personal relationships; family is a vital social institution. As societies are transformed to Gesellschaft societies because of industrialization, personal ties, family connections, and lifelong friendships are less important. The consequence is that we feel disconnected from others. To overcome this problem, some people have turned to intentional families and consciously created relationships that mirror those of families.

3. *Discuss the impact that divorce has on family members—men, women, and children.*

You would want to discuss each family role separately—children, wives and husbands. In your response, be sure to talk about the research on the impact on children, both short-term and long-term. In the short-term, this includes hostility, anxiety, nightmares, and poor school performance. In the long-term, it includes a loss of connection to parents, and difficulties forming intimate relations. For spouses, there is anger, depression and anxiety following a divorce, but each also experiences unique problems related to gender. For women, there is often a decrease in the standard of living, although the impact varies by social class. For men, there is a loss of connection to their children and the possible development of a series of families.

ANSWERS FOR CHAPTER 14

ANSWERS FOR MULTIPLE CHOICE QUESTIONS

1. a The use of diplomas and degrees to determine who is eligible for jobs, even though the diploma or degree may be irrelevant to the actual work, is known as a credential society. (294)
2. d "All of the above" is correct. In earlier societies there was no separate social institution called education; education was synonymous with acculturation; and persons who already possessed certain skills taught them to others. (294)
3. a Education is a formal system of teaching knowledge, values, and skills. (294-295)
4. a All of the following are manifest functions of education: transmitting cultural values; helping to mould students into a more or less cohesive unit; and teaching patriotism. Helping to maintain social inequality is *not* one of the functions, according to the functionalists. (296, 297, 298)
5. b The function of education that sorts people into a society's various positions is social placement. (300)
6. c The hidden curriculum refers to the unwritten rules of behaviour and attitudes that are taught in school. (301)
7. c Public schools are largely supported by local property taxes. (303)
8. b The correspondence principle is the ways in which schools correspond to, or reflect, the social structure of society. (304)
9. a From a conflict perspective, the real purpose of education is to perpetuate existing social inequalities. (304)
10. c Teacher expectations and the self-fulfilling prophecy are of interest to symbolic interaction theorists. (304-305)
11. c Ray Rist found that social class was the underlying basis for assigning children to different tables in a kindergarten classroom. (305)
12. a A self-fulfilling prophecy is an originally false assertion that becomes true simply because it was predicted. (305)
13. b When compared to grades forty years ago, today's grades are higher. (306)
14. c High school graduates who have difficulty with basic reading and writing are known as functional illiterates. (307)
15. d Durkheim wrote *The Elementary Forms of the Religious Life* in order to identify elements common to all religions. (309)

16.   c   Durkheim used the term moral community to refer to a group of people united by their religious practices. (310)
17.   a   All of the following are functions of religion: support for the government, social change, and social control. Encouraging wars for holy causes is a dysfunction of religion. (310)
18.   c   War and religious persecution are dysfunctions of religion. (310)
19.   c   Religion is the opium of the people according to some conflict theorists. (312)
20.   a   Weber believed that religion held the key to modernization. (314)
21.   c   The spirit of capitalism is the desire to accumulate capital as a duty—not to spend it, but as an end in itself. It is not the desire to accumulate capital in order to spend it and show others how one "has it made." Nor is it Marx's term for the driving force in the exploitation of workers or the ideal of a highly moral life, hard work, industriousness, and frugality (which is the Protestant ethic). (314)
22.   c   Polytheism is the belief that there are many gods. (315)
23.   d   "All of the above" is correct. The essence of female/feminist religiosity is commitment to diversity, recognition that the spiritual is deeply personal and women have been neglected in religious studies. (313)
24.   b   The religion with no specific founder is Hinduism. (315)
25.   b   Islam, whose followers are known as Muslims, began in the same part of the world as Judaism and Christianity. (315)
26.   d   "All of the above" is correct. A cult is a new religion with few followers; has teachings and practices which put it at odds with the dominant culture; and often is at odds with other religions. (317)
27.   c   Although larger than a cult, a sect still feels substantial hostility from society. (317)
28.   a   Eastern non-Christian religions, such as Islam, Hinduism, and Buddhism, were the only religious groups that grew in any significant degree between 1986 and 1996 in Canada. (319)

ANSWERS FOR TRUE-FALSE QUESTIONS

1. *True.* (294)
2. *False.* In earlier societies there was no separate social institution called education. (294)
3. *True.* (295)
4. *False.* Rates of high school are not evenly distributed across the provinces. (296)
5. *True.* (296)
6. *False.* Canadian schools encourage, rather than discourage, individualism and although teamwork is encouraged, individuals are singled out for praise when the team does well. (297)
7. *True.* (297)
8. *False.* Parental influence is generally not strong enough to challenge the influence of peer culture when it comes to molding students' appearance, ideas, speech patterns, and interactions with the opposite sex. (299)
9. *False.* Functional theorists believe that social placement is helpful, not harmful, to society because the process helps insure that the "best" people will acquire a good education and subsequently perform the most needed tasks of society. (300)
10. *True.* (299)
11. *True.* (303)
12. *True.* (303)

13. *True.* (304)
14. *False.* Research by Ray Rist concluded that the child's journey through school was preordained by the eighth day, not the end of the first year, of kindergarten. (305)
15. *False.* Teacher expectations are shaped by their class background. For example, teachers with a middle-class background have been observed to encourage middle-class students and react negatively to working-class students. (305)
16. *False.* The goal of the sociological study of religion is to analyze the relationship between society and religion and to gain insight into the role that religion plays in people's lives. It is not to determine which religions are most effective in people's lives. (309)
17. *True.* (309)
18. *True.* (310)
19. *True.* (310)
20. *True.* (312)
21. *False.* Conflict theorists believe that religion mirrors and legitimates existing social inequalities. (312)
22. False. Max Weber wrote The Protestant Ethic and the Spirit of Capitalism. (314)
23. *False.* Contemporary Judaism comprises three main branches: Orthodox, Reform, and Conservative. (314)
24. *True.* (315)
25. *True.* (303)
26. *True.* (313)
27. *False.* Both cults and sects stress evangelism, or the active recruitment of new members. (317)
28. *True.* (318)
29. *False.* Survey research indicates that the incidence of those in Canada reporting "no religion" has grown significantly over the past four decades. (319)
30. *False.* Feminist approaches to spirituality have attempted to challenge sexist practices and create more space for women within different religious traditions. (313)

ANSWERS FQR FILL-IN QUESTIONS

1. Using diplomas and degrees to determine eligibility for jobs occurs in a CREDENTIAL SOCIETY. (294)
2. ACCULTURATION is the transmission of culture from one generation to the next. (294)
3. A formal system of teaching knowledge, values, and skills is the definition for EDUCATION. (294-295)
4. Tracking and social placement both contribute to the GATEKEEPING function of education. (300)
5. A new function of education today is MAINSTREAMING, incorporating people with disabilities into regular social activities. (300)
6. The unwritten rules of behaviour and attitude, such as obedience to authority and conformity to cultural norms, is referred to as the HIDDEN CURRICULUM. (301)
7. CONFLICT theorists believe that culturally biased IQ tests favour the middle classes and discriminate against minorities and students from lower-class backgrounds. (302)
8. The idea that schools reflect the social structure of society is the CORRESPONDENCE PRINCIPLE. (304)
9. SYMBOLIC INTERACTION theorists found that the expectations of teachers are especially significant for determining what students learn. (305)

10. GRADE INFLATION refers to the trend of giving higher grades for the same work, so that there is a general rise in student grades despite the fact that neither learning nor test scores have increased. (306-307)
11. It is not uncommon today for schools to practice SOCIAL PROMOTION, which involves passing students to the next grade even though they have not mastered basic material. (306)
12. Someone who has graduated from high school but still has difficulties with reading and writing is considered FUNCTIONAL ILLITERATE. (307)
13. Durkheim's term for common elements of everyday life was PROFANE.(309)
14. Answering questions about ultimate meaning, providing emotional comfort, and uniting believers into a community are FUNCTIONS of religion. (310)
15. Ceremonies or repetitive practices that help unite people into a moral community are RITUALS.(311-312)
16. COSMOLOGY is teachings or ideas that provide a unified picture of the world. (312)
17. According to conflict theorists, religion is the OPIUM OF THE PEOPLE. (312)
18. THE PROTESTANT ETHIC is Weber's term to describe the ideal of a highly moral life, hard work, industriousness, and frugality. (314)
19. The belief that there is only one God is MONOTHEISM. (314)
20. Hindus are POLYTHEISTS, believing there are many gods (315)
21. FUNDAMENTALISM is the belief that true religion is threatened by modernism and that the faith as it originally was practiced should be restored. (315)
22. A(n) CHARISMATIC LEADER is someone who exerts extraordinary appeal to a group of followers. (316)
23. A group larger than a cult that still feels substantial hostility from and toward society is a(n) SECT. (317)
24. A(n) ECCLESIA is a religious group so integrated into the dominant culture that it is difficult to tell where the one begins and the other leaves off. (318)
25. Within the categories of feminist spirituality, REVOLUTIONARIES seek to change the established orthodoxy by importing language, images, and rituals from other traditions.(313)

ANSWERS TO MATCH THESE SOCIAL SCIENTISTS WITH THEIR CONTRIBUTIONS

1. b Randall Collins: *credential society*
2. c Bowles and Gintis: *correspondence principle*
3. d Ray Rist: *tracking and expectations of kindergarten teachers*
4. i Karl Marx: *"religion is the opium of the people"*
5. e Harry Gracey: *kindergarten as boot camp*
6. a Davis and Moore: *gatekeeping sorts people on the basis of merit*
7. g George Farkas: *students are rewarded for the signals they send teachers*
8. j Emile Durkheim: *The Elementary Forms of the Religious Life*
9. k Johanna Stuckey: *outlined four categories of feminist spirituality*
10. h Max Weber: *The Protestant Ethic and the Spirit of Capitalism*
11. l John Hostetler: *studied "shunning"*
12. f Ernst Troeltsch: *cult-sect-church-ecclesia typology*

GUIDELINES FOR ANSWERING THE ESSAY QUESTIONS

1. *Explain the link between democracy, industrialization and universal education.*

For this question there are two strains of thought that need to be developed. The first is the link between democracy and universal education. Here you will want to talk about the need for voters who are knowledgeable about the issues and are capable of making sound decisions; it is necessary that they read and understand news that is published in newspapers. In addition, the political culture is maintained through the educational system, as children learn patriotism and the facts of the political process. The second strain is to connect industrialization and universal education. Here you would want to talk about the need for an educated work force that is able to read instructions and learn how to use increasingly complex machines. The work force must also be able to move from job to job, learning new skills as the work requires. The most efficient way in which to train workers, both to have the specific skills needed for a particular job and the general skills needed to survive in a constantly changing workplace, is through universal education. For these two reasons, universal education developed in Canada, as well as other industrialized nations.

2. *Select one of the three perspectives and design a research project to test the claims of that perspective about the nature of education.*

In order to answer this question you must first choose one of the three perspectives. For example, you might choose the conflict perspective and decide to do a research project on the relationship between ethnicity and individual educational achievement and goals. Your research will involve an analysis of student choices of curricula, their grades, retention rates, and graduation from a large racially/ethnically diverse high school. You have access to student records and you collect data on students in one class as this class moves through the high school. You will compare students' records in order to test whether the conflict theorists are correct in their assertion that the educational system reproduces the students' class background.

3. *Assume that you have been asked to make a presentation about religion to a group of people who have absolutely no idea what religion is. Prepare a speech in which you define religion and explain why it exists.*

For this question, your first task is to explain what religion is. To do this you might want to refer to Durkheim's work on the elementary forms of religious life, talking about the differences between the sacred and profane, the presence of beliefs, practices, and a moral community. Once you've done this you next task is to discuss why religion exists. Here you could talk about either the functionalist perspective or the conflict perspective or both. If you choose to focus only on the functionalist view, you would want to talk about how religion meets basic human needs; you might also want to refer to the symbolic interactionist views on community. If you want to focus only on conflict theory, or add that to your discussion of functionalism, you would want to talk about how, for Marx, religion is like a drug that helps the oppressed forget about their exploitation at the hands of the capitalists. Furthermore, conflict theorists point out that capitalists use religion legitimate social inequalities and maintain the status quo.

4. *Discuss which elements define religion.*

Emile Durkheim published an influential book, *The Elementary Forms of the Religious Life,* in which he tried to identify the elements common to all religions. He found that all religions, regardless of their name or teaching separate the *sacred* from the *profane.*

To Durkheim, religion is a unified system of beliefs and practices relative to sacred things. Thus, religion is defined by three elements: beliefs, practices, and a moral community.

ANSWERS FOR CHAPTER 15

ANSWERS FOR MULTIPLE CHOICE QUESTIONS

1. d   Sociologists focus on medicine as a profession, a bureaucracy, and a business; therefore, "all of the above" would be the correct answer. (325)
2. c   The healing specialist of a preliterate tribe who attempts to control the spirits thought to cause a disease or injury is a shaman. (325)
3. d   "All of the above" is correct. Doctors and parents are gatekeepers of the "sick role." (326)
4. b   When a person is unable to fulfill her or his normal obligations because sick or injured, the person is said to be in the sick role. (325-326)
5. d   "All of the above" is correct. People are not responsible for being sick; they are exempt from normal responsibilities and try to get help so they can return to normal life according to Talcott Parsons, a functionalist. (326)
6. d   "All of the above" is correct. Life expectancy in the Least Developed Nations is lower than in the Developed Industrial Nations in part because of lack of access to affordable medical technology; malnutrition; and higher risk of catching life-threatening diseases. (326)
7. c   The field of epidemiology is the study of how medical disorders are distributed throughout a population. (329)
8. a   The top causes of death for Canadians are cancer, heart diseases, and cerebrovascular diseases. (329)
9. d   The criteria of the Canada Health Act are comprehensive scope, universal coverage and public administration, portability, and accessibility. (330)
10. c   The most significant findings of the National Population Health Survey point to the fact that social factors such as class, gender, age, and ethnicity influence health. (331-332)
11. a   Depersonalization is the practice of dealing with people as though they were objects; means treating patients as though they were merely cases and diseases; and occurs when an individual is treated as if he or she was not a person. The one statement that is incorrect is that "It is less common today because of all the development of the Canada Health Act." (332)
12. a   Doctor recommendations for total hysterectomies even when no cancer is present is are an example of sexism in medicine. (327)
13. d   The demands of the "double day," and role accumulation place excessive demands on women's time and energy, and illustrate that there are gender differences in experiences of health and illness. (328)
14. c   The term medicalization refers to the process of turning something that was not previously medical into a medical matter. (332)
15. b   AIDS is known to be transmitted by exchange of blood and/or semen. (334)
16. c   A cure for AIDS has not been found. (334-335)

17.   d   "All of the above" is correct. Older diseases have mutated and created "super bugs," antibiotics are ineffective against 28 new diseases and modern travel has wiped out frontiers that used to contain diseases. (335)
18.   a   Of all of the drugs, nicotine is the most harmful to health. (336)
19.   a   An environment that is harmful to health is referred to as a disabling environment. (336)
20.   d   "All of the above" is correct. If prevention is the goal, doing exercise, eliminating disabling environments and practising preventive medicine all help. (337-338)

ANSWERS FOR TRUE-FALSE QUESTIONS

1. *True.* (325)
2. *False.* People who don't seek competent help when they are sick are not behaving according to the expectations of the sick role; in the sick role an individual is expected to seek help in order to get better and return to his/her normal routine. Someone who doesn't do this is denied the right to claim sympathy from others; they get the cold shoulder for wrongfully claiming the sick role. (326)
3. *True.* (325)
4. *True.* (326)
5. *False.* Epidemiology is the study of the distribution of medical disorders throughout a population. (329)
6. *False.* There is the suggestion that men are socialized to take more risks than women while women are socialized to be cautious—women tend to smoke and drink less alcohol than men. (329)
7. *True.* (329)
8. *True.* (329)
9. *False.* Universal, government-funded health care has only been available since 1971. (330)
10. *True.* (330)
11. *False.* The Canada Health Act sets out national standards for health care that must be complied with by the provinces. (330)
12. *True.* (332)
13. *True.* (327)
14. True. (327)
15. *True.* (333)
16. *True.* (335)
17. *False.* The number of deaths due to AIDS in Canada began to decline in 1996. (335)
18. *False.* While alcohol consumption (in moderation) has some positive effects, it increases the risk of a variety of diseases, from cancer to stroke. It also increases possibilities of birth defects. (336)
19. *False.* While the health risks of some occupations is evident, in many occupations people do not become aware of the risks until years after they were exposed. (336)
20. *True.* (337)

ANSWERS FOR FILL-IN QUESTIONS

1. The healing specialist of a preliterate tribe who attempts to control the spirits thought to cause a disease or injury is a SHAMAN. (325)

2. HEALTH is a human condition measured by four components: physical, mental, social, and spiritual. (325)
3. The SICK ROLE is a social role that excuses people from normal obligations because they are sick or injured. (325-326)
4. Parents and physicians are the primary GATEKEEPERS to the sick role. (326)
5. One consequence of the inequitable distribution of economic and military power between nations is the GLOBAL STRATIFICATION of medical care.(326)
6. The study of disease and disability patterns in a population is EPIDEMIOLOGY. (329)
7. In 1984, the CANADA HEALTH ACT was enacted to ensure that health services would be available to all Canadians.(330)
8. The practice of dealing with people as though they are cases, not individuals, is termed DEPERSONALIZATION. (332)
9. The percentage of Canadian medical degrees earned by women has risen from only 24.3 PERCENT in 1975 to 40.5 PERCENT today. (327)
10. The theory of SOCIAL ACCEPTABILITY suggests that due to socialization, women are more likely to accept help in dealing with their health problems than are men. (328)
11. The term MEDICALIZATION refers to the process whereby what was not previously considered medical is transformed into a medical matter. (332)
12. A(n) LIVING WILL is a statement people in good health sign that clearly expresses their feelings about being kept alive on artificial life-support systems. (333)
13. One of the most significant sociological aspects of AIDS is its STIGMA. (334)
14. The origin of AIDS is unknown. (334)
15. Lumberjacking, mining, and the construction industry are all examples of DISABLING ENVIRONMENTS. (336)

ANSWERS TO MATCH THESE SOCIAL SCIENTISTS WITH THEIR CONTRIBUTIONS

1. b Talcott Parsons: *sick role*
2. a Erich Goode: *compared health of smokers and nonsmokers*
3. c Haas and Shaffir: *transformation of medical students*
4. d Leonard Stein: *interaction games played by doctors and nurses*

GUIDELINES FOR ANSWERING THE ESSAY QUESTIONS

1. *Describe the elements of the sick role and identify variations in the pattern of claiming this role.*

   In order to answer this question you should acknowledge Talcott Parsons' contribution to our understanding of the sick role and his work in identifying the elements in that role. In terms of variations in claiming that role, the text talks about gender differences, but you could expand beyond this to talk about other variations within our society. For instance, children and old people have an easier time claiming this role because they are seen as more vulnerable and more dependent than are adults.

2. *Explain the pattern of the worldwide AIDS epidemic and suggest reasons why this threat to the health of the world's population has not be addressed more aggressively.*

   You could immediately point out that the distribution of AIDS cases is not evenly balanced around the globe, but heavily concentrated in Sub-Saharan Africa and South and Southeast

Asia. What is even more interesting is the percentage change in cases between 1992 and 1996; among the Most Industrialized Nations the percentage change has been relatively small—and in some cases in the negative column—while the change among the Least Industrialized Nations has been great. Looking at AIDS globally, you would want to point out this maldistribution and note that those countries most directly affected have the least amount of money to spend. Looking at AIDS within Canada, you would want to point out that the number of deaths due to AIDS began to decline in 1996. Furthermore, the most common way in which to contract the disease is through behaviours that are stigmatized in our society—homosexual sex, promiscuous heterosexual sex, and I.V. drug use. You could point out that policy makers may have been slow to respond because of the character of those most directly affected by the epidemic.

3. *Discuss the obstacles to developing preventive medicine and suggest ways in which these obstacles can be overcome.*

To answer this question you should note the obstacles—resistance from the medical community, the public, businesses, and other nations. In your essay remember to outline the nature of each of these obstacles. Then you should suggest ways around each of these. For example, overcome public resistance could be accomplished through educational programs or through initiatives like lower health insurance costs for people who can demonstrate they have adopted preventive measures, e.g., regular exercise programs, altered diet, and no drug use. You would need to do this for each of the obstacles listed.

ANSWERS FOR CHAPTER 16

ANSWERS FOR MULTIPLE CHOICE QUESTIONS

1. b   In sociology, the term deviance refers to all violations of social rules. (342)
2. d   "All of the above" is correct. Goffman used the term stigma to denote attributes that discredit people, violations of norms of ability and certain norms of appearance. (343)
3. d   The pluralistic theory of social control takes the view that different groups mediate and balance their competing interests with the result that social stability is achieved. Conflict theorists see law as an instrument of oppression in the hands of the ruling elite. (347)
4. b   According to conflict theory, social control represents the interests of the wealthy and powerful. (350)
5. c   Differential association theory is based on the symbolic interactionist perspective. (343)
6. d   "All of the above" is correct. Merton's typology of deviance: innovators, ritualists, and retreatists. (348)
7. d   "All of the above" is correct. All of the following are ways of neutralizing deviance: denial of responsibility, denial of injury and of a victim, and condemnation of the condemners. (344-345)
8. a   The term for acts of deviance that have little effect on the self-concept is primary deviance. (345)

9. c   Tertiary deviance is stage of deviant behaviour at which most people simply reject the judgment that the behaviour is wrong. (345)
10. b   William Chambliss's study of the Saints and the Roughnecks suggests that people often live up to the labels that a community gives them. (346)
11. d   "All of the above" is correct. Teachers expected good, law-abiding behaviour from the "Saints" and saw "Roughnecks" heading for trouble even though both groups were involved in deviant behaviour. The community's "double vision" was due to the social class background of the boys. (346)
12. d   "All of the above" is correct. Durkheim was a functionalist and argued that crime and social deviance clarifies moral boundaries and promotes unity and social change. (346-347)
13. d   Recidivism is not one of the responses to anomie identified by Merton. (348)
14. b   According to Merton, revolutionaries are the most committed type of rebels. (348)
15. d   "All of the above" is correct. Gambling, hustling and glamorous "easy money" are all part of the illegitimate opportunity structure (349)
16. c   Crimes committed by people of respectable and high social status in the course of their occupations are called white-collar crime. (349)
17. b   Conflict theorists see the law as an instrument of oppression because it is used by the powerful to maintain their privileged position. (350)
18. d   "All of the above" is correct. The police use a symbolic system as they enforce the law. They deal with ideas of "the typical good citizen" and "typical criminals." (351)
19. c   Feminist theorists relate male violence against women to patriarchal ideologies which promote male superiority. (351)
20. d   "All of the above" is correct. Job creation programs, expanded social services, and anti-sexist self-help groups for men are all examples of public policy strategies to address male violence against women. (352)
21. c   Frowns, gossip, and crossing people off guest lists are examples of negative sanctions. (355)
22. a   A court martial in which the insignia of rank are publicly ripped off the uniforms of the officers found guilty is an example of degradation ceremonies. (355-356)
23. b   Imprisonment follows a public pronouncement that a person is "unfit to live among decent, law-abiding people." (356)
24. c   The medicalization of deviance refers to viewing deviance as a medical matter. (357)
25. d   "All of the above" is correct. A more humane approach to dealing with social deviance is needed because social deviance is inevitable; it is often the result of systems of inequality; and a measure of a society is how it treats deviant behaviour. (358)

ANSWERS FOR TRUE-FALSE QUESTIONS

1. *True.* (341)
2. *False.* This is incorrect. Sociologists use the label deviance for an infraction as minor as jay walking or as serious as murder.(342)
3. *True.* (341)
4. *True.* (347)
5. *True.* (350)
6. *True.* (341)
7. *True.* (343)

8. *True* (345)
9. *False.* Some people and groups do embrace deviance and want to be labelled with a deviant identity. Examples include: teenagers who make certain that their clothing, music, and hairstyles are outside adult norms; and outlaw bikers. (346)
10. *True.* (343)
11. *True.* (346)
12. *True.* (346-347)
13. *False.* According to strain theory, everyone does not have an equal chance to get ahead in society because of structural factors in the society (e.g., racism, sexism, and social class) which may deny them access to the approved ways of achieving cultural goals. (347-348)
14. *True.* (348-349)
15. *True.* (349)
16. *False.* White-collar crime often is more costly than street crime. (349)
17. *False.* Conflict theorists believe that the criminal justice system functions for the well-being of the capitalist class. (351)
18. *False.* Official statistics are not always accurate counts of the crimes committed in our society. Both conflict theorists and symbolic interactionists believe that these statistics have bias built into them because of police discretion in arresting people, as well as many other factors. (351)
19. *True.* (351)
20. *False.* The purpose of positive sanctions is to reward people for conforming to social norms. (355)

ANSWERS FOR FILL-IN QUESTIONS

1. DEVIANCE is the violation of rules or norms. (342)
2. Erving Goffman used the term STIGMA to refer to attributes that discredit people. (343)
3. Formal and informal means of enforcing norms constitute a system of SOCIAL CONTROL. (341)
4. According to the CONFLICT perspective, society is made up of competing groups, and the group that holds power uses social control to maintain its position of privilege. (350)
5. NORMS make social life possible by making behaviour predictable. (341)
6. SOCIAL ORDER is a group's usual and customary social arrangements, on which its members depend and on which they base their lives. (341)
7. Labelling theory is used to show what strategies people use to neutralize SOCIAL DEVIANCE. (344)
8. PRIMARY social deviance refers to fleeting acts that do not become part of the self-concept.(345)
9. Strain theory is based on the idea that large numbers of people are socialized into desiring CULTURAL GOALS (the legitimate objects held out to everyone) but many do not have access to INSTITUTIONALIZED MEANS in order to achieve those goals. (347)
10. CONFORMISTS are the ones in Merton's typology of deviance who accept both cultural goals and the institutionalized means to reach those goals (348)
11. Edwin Sutherland used the term WHITE-COLLAR CRIME to refer to crimes that people of respectable and high social status commit in the course of their occupations. (349)
12. In combination the policy, courts, and prisons that deal with people who are accused of having committed crimes make up the CRIMINAL JUSTICE SYSTEM. (350)

13. Steps to strip an individual of his or her identity as a group member occur during DEGRADATION CEREMONIES. (355-356)
14. The view that deviance, including crime, is the product of mental illness is referred to as MEDICALIZATION OF DEVIANCE. (357)

ANSWERS TO MATCH THESE SOCIAL SCIENTISTS WITH THEIR CONTRIBUTIONS

1.   d   Edwin Sutherland: *white-collar crime*
2.   a   Robert Merton: *strain theory*
3.   g   Erving Goffman: *importance of stigma*
4.   b   Thomas Szasz: *myth of mental illness*
5.   e   Emile Durkheim: *functions of deviance*
6.   f   William Chambliss: *effects of labelling*
7.   h   Gresham Sykes and David Matza: *techniques of neutralization*
8.   c   Harold Garfinkel: *degradation ceremonies*

GUIDELINES FOR ANSWERING THE ESSAY QUESTIONS

1. *Discuss how the different sociological perspectives could be combined in order to provide a more complete picture of deviance.*

   You would begin by identifying the strengths of each perspective—symbolic interactionism focuses on group membership and interaction within and between groups, functionalism focuses on how deviance is a part of the social order, and conflict theory focuses on how social inequality impacts on definitions of and reactions to acts of deviance. An example of combining perspectives is reflected in the work of William Chambliss on the Saints and the Roughnecks; he looked at patterns of inequality and different interaction styles to explain the different treatment the two groups received. Another example would be Cloward and Ohlin's work on illegitimate opportunity structures; they added the concept of social class inequality to the notion of the strain between institutionalized means and cultural goals to explain patterns of lower class deviance.

2. *Explain how forms of deviance such as street gangs can be both functional and dysfunctional at the same time.*

   Jankowski studied street gangs and discovered that gangs functioned within low-income neighbourhoods as sources of employment (often the only source), recreation, and protection. In a few cases the gangs were involved in legitimate activities such as running small groceries and renovating and renting abandoned apartment buildings. All of these demonstrate the functional nature of gangs. At the same time, gangs generate most of their income through illegal activities—a dysfunctional aspect. Another dysfunctional aspect is the violence that accompanies gangs—violence that is not confined to gangs but often spills over into the neighbourhood as a whole.

3. *Compare the societal harm caused by white-collar and street crime*

   The more privileged social classes are not crime-free, but they find different types of illegitimate opportunities than people who commit street crimes. Only, street crimes are more visible and the victims more obvious to the beholder. Although white-collar crime is not as dramatic as a street killing or an abduction and rape—and therefore usually considered less newsworthy—it too, can involve physical harm, and sometimes death. Unsafe working conditions, for example, may be the result of executive decisions to put profits ahead of workers' safety.

ANSWERS FOR CHAPTER 17

ANSWERS FOR MULTIPLE CHOICE QUESTIONS

1. c   The specialists who study the size, composition, growth, and distribution of human population are referred to as demographers. (362)
2. b   The proposition that the population grows geometrically while food supply increases arithmetically is known as the Malthus theorem. (362)
3. d   Anti-Malthusians believe that the demographic transition, an explanation of the shift from high birth and death rates to low ones that occurred previously in Europe, is an accurate picture of what will happen in the future in the Least Industrialized Nations of the world. (363)
4. b   The three-stage historical process of population growth is the demographic transition. (363)
5. c   The process by which a country's population becomes smaller because its birth rate and immigration are too low to replace those who die and emigrate is population shrinkage. (364)
6. d   "All of the above" is correct. Starvation occurs not because there is not enough fertile land, or there are too many people, or there are natural disasters. Rather, experts argue that it occurs because some parts of the world lack food while other parts of the world produce more than they can consume. (364-366)
7. d   "All of the above" is correct. People in the Least Industrialized Nations have so many children because parenthood provides status, children are considered to be an economic asset, and the community encourages people to have children. (366)
8. a   Factors that influence population growth (fertility, mortality, and net migration) are demographic variables. (367)
9. d   "All of the above" is correct. Economic booms and busts, wars, plagues and famines have an impact on the population growth rate. (367)
10. a   The annual number of deaths per 1,000 population is the crude death rate. (367)
11. d   The factors pushing someone to emigrate include poverty, lack of religious and political freedoms, and political persecution. (367)
12. a   Fertility, mortality, and net migration are demographic variables used in population projections, poverty is not. (367)
13. d   Urbanization is when an increasing proportion of a population lives in cities. (370)
14. a   In 1800 only 3 percent of the world's population lived in cities. (370)
15. b   The concentric-zone model was proposed by Ernest Burgess. (371)
16. d   The pattern of a growing number of immigrants sealing an area, with the consequence that those already living in the area move out because they are threatened by their presence is referred to invasion-succession cycle. (371)

17. c   The model which is based on the idea that land use in cities is based on several centres, such as a clustering of restaurants or automobile dealerships, is the multiple-nuclei model. (371)

18. d   "All of the above" is correct. Urban dwellers counteract alienation by personalizing their shopping, frequenting taverns, restaurants and laundromats, as well as attending sports events. (374)

19. d   "All of the above" is correct. According to Gans' typology, the trapped includes downwardly mobile persons, elderly persons, and alcoholics and drug addicts. (374)

20. b   Suburbanization is the movement from the city to the suburbs. (374)

21. d   "All of the above" is correct. According to Gans's typology the following are considered Cosmopolitans: city-students, the city's intellectuals, professionals, musicians, artists, and entertainers. (374)

22. c   Conflict theorists note that there is no energy shortage. Rather, they argue that multinational corporations are unwilling to develop alternative energy sources, because it would threaten their monopoly over existing fossil fuels and cut into their profits. (376)

23. c   The disappearance of the world's rain forests presents the greatest threat to the survival of numerous plant and animal species. (376)

24. d   "All of the above" is correct. Environmental sociology examines how the physical environment affects human activities; how human activities affect the physical environment; and the unintended consequences of human actions. (377-378)

25. b   The goal of environmental sociologists is to do research on the mutual impact that individuals and environments have on one another. (378)

ANSWERS FOR TRUE-FALSE QUESTIONS

1. *False.* Thomas Malthus was not a sociologist at the University of Chicago in the 1920s. He was an English Protestant theologian who lived from 1766 to 1834. (362)
2. *True.* (363)
3. *True.* (364)
4. *True.* (363)
5. *False.* The opposite is true. The amount of food produced per person today is more than it was in 1950. (364)
6. *False.* The major reason why people in poor countries have so many children is not necessarily because they do not know how to prevent conception. The reason is more sociological in nature, including the status which is conferred on women for producing children, as well as the need for children to take care of a person when she or he is old. (366)
7. *True.* (367)
8. *True.* (364)
9. *True.* (367)
10. *True.* (368)
11. *True.* (370)
12. *True.* (371)
13. *False.* No one model is considered to be the most accurate because different cities develop and grow in different ways, especially if there are certain kinds of natural barriers such as rivers or mountains. (371)
14. *True.* (374)

15. *True.* (374)
16. *False.* There is evidence that past civilizations—Mesopotamia, the Anasazi, the Mayans—were destroyed because of environmental abuse. (375)
17. *False.* Rain containing sulfuric and nitric acid, released into the air with the burning of fossil fuels, is acid rain. While the burning of fossil fuels contributes to the greenhouse effect, acid rain itself does not. (375)
18. *False.* Scientists are not in agreement that the problems of acid rain and the greenhouse effect must be solved quickly. Some even doubt that the greenhouse effect exists. (375)
19. *True.* (377)
20. *False.* The goal of environmental sociology is to study the relationships between humans and the physical environment. (378)

ANSWERS FOR FILL-IN QUESTIONS

1. From demographers' point of view, we will be at ZERO population growth with every 1000 women giving birth to 2100 children. (368)
2. A pattern of growth in which numbers double during approximately equal intervals, thus accelerating in the latter stages, is the EXPONENTIAL GROWTH CURVE. (362)
3. The Anti-Malthusians believe that Europe's DEMOGRAPHIC TRANSITION, a three-stage historical process of population growth, provides an accurate picture of the future. (363)
4. When the people in a society do not produce enough children to replace the people who die, there is concern about POPULATION SHRINKAGE. (364)
5. The FERTILITY RATE refers to the number of children that the average woman bears. (367)
6. The basic demographic equation is growth = BIRTHS – DEATHS + MIGRATION. (367)
7. When women bear only enough children to replace the population, ZERO POPULATION GROWTH has been achieved. (368)
8. A CITY is a place in which a large number of people are permanently based and do not produce their own food. (370)
9. URBANIZATION is the process by which an increasing number of people live in cities. (370)
10. A central city, surrounding smaller cities and their suburbs, forming an interconnected urban area, is a METROPOLIS. (370)
11. The SUN, for example, produces more energy than humanity could ever use. (375)
12. The displacement of the poor by the relatively affluent, who renovate the former's homes, is GENTRIFICATION. (371)
13. COMMUNITY exists when people identify with an area and with one another. (372)
14. The greenhouse effect is believed to produce GLOBAL WARMING. (375)
15. Two of the worst polluters, INDIA and CHINA have not, and are not required to sign on the Koyto because they are industrializing nations. (376)

ANSWERS TO MATCH THESE SOCIAL SCIENTISTS WITH THEIR CONTRIBUTIONS

1. a Thomas Malthus: *theorem on population growth*
2. c Ernest Burgess: *concentric-zone model*
3. d Herbert Gans: *urban villagers*
4. e Homer Hoyt: *sector model*

5.   b   Robert Park: *human ecology*

GUIDELINES FOR ANSWERING THE ESSAY QUESTIONS

1. *State the positions of the New Malthusians and the Anti-Malthusians and discuss which view you think is more accurate, based on the information provided about each position.*

   You should begin this essay by summarizing each side's arguments. For the New Malthusians you would want to include the idea of the exponential growth curve, while for the Anti-Malthusians you would want to refer to the concepts of the demographic transition and population shrinkage. For both you would want to include some of the facts—that world population growth does seem to reflect the exponential growth curve (New Malthusians), while the Least Industrialized Nations reflect the second stage of the demographic transition and the population of European countries is shrinking (Anti-Malthusians). Finally, you need to draw conclusions about which view you think is more accurate.

2. *Identify the problems that are associated with forecasting population growth.*

   Your first step is to define the basic demographic equation, that calculation which is used to project population growth. Then you need to identify problems that make the demographer's job more difficult. These would include natural phenomena (famines and plagues), economic factors (short-term booms and busts as well as longer-term industrialization), political factors (wars and government policy), and social factors (educational levels). In your essay you need to not only identify these, but discuss the ways in which they make forecasting a challenge.

3. *Describe the dilemma of China's and India's unwanted baby girls and what happens to them.*

   See Perspectives Box (369). Around the globe, for every 100 baby girls, about 105 boys are born. In China, however, there are 111 baby boys. The reason is female infanticide. At the root of China's sexist infanticide is economics. The modern technology also has an impact on these practices. Discuss what you see as the solution.

4. *Will cities of the least industrialized nations satisfy the people's longing for a better life?*

See Perspectives Box (372). Images of the least industrialized nations that portray serene pastoral scenes distort today's reality. In these nations, poor rural people have flocked to the cities in such numbers that the nations now contain most of the world's largest cities. What is their quality of life, compared with when North American rural migrants and immigrants move to the cities? Are the cities in the least industrialized nations heading for a total break down? Why are people flocking to the cities? Would they not be better off to return to the rural area? Discuss what you see as the solution

ANSWERS FOR CHAPTER 18

ANSWERS FOR MULTIPLE CHOICE QUESTIONS

1. c It was Gustave LeBon, not Charles Mackay, who suggested that the crowd develops a collective mind. (383)
2. d Gustave LeBon's term for the tendency of people in a crowd to feel, think, and act in extraordinary ways is collective mind. (383)
3. a Social calm is incorrect. Social unrest is the condition most conductive to the emergence of collective behaviour. (384)
4. d "All of the above" is correct. Acting crowd, a term coined by Herbert Blumer; is an excited group that collectively moves toward a goal; and is the end result of the five stages of collective behaviour. (383)
5. b Richard Berk used the term "minimax strategy" to describe the tendency for humans to minimize costs and maximize rewards. This is true whether an individual is deciding what card(s) to discard in a poker game or what store to loot in an urban riot. (384)
6. c The agitators were not a category of participants in the model of emergent norms by Turner and Killian. (385)
7. d "All of the above" is correct. Urban riots are usually caused by feelings of frustration and anger at being deprived of the same opportunities as others. Frustration builds up to such a level that it takes only a precipitating event to erupt in collective violence. (385)
8. b A behaviour that results when people become so fearful that they cannot function normally and may even flee is a panic. (386)
9. a Not everyone panics. In disturbances many people continue to act responsibly. Sociologists us the term role extension to describe these actions. (387)
10. b Moral panics are generally fed by rumour, information for which there is no discernible source and which is usually unfounded. (387)
11. c Sociologists refer to unfounded information spread among people as rumour. (387)
12. d A temporary pattern of behaviour that catches people's attention is a fad. (388)
13. c Eating goldfish and bungee jumping are both examples of activity fads. Fads are novel forms of behaviour that briefly catch people's attention. (388)
14. b Social movements that seek to change people totally are redemptive social movements. (389)
15. d A social movement that seeks to change society totally is a transformative social movement. (390)

16. d   "All of the above" is correct. Levels of membership in social movements include the inner core, the committed, and a wider circle of members. (390)

17. d   The public that social movements face can really be divided into sympathetic public, hostile public, and disinterested people. (391)

18. b   How people think about some issue is public opinion. (391)

19. b   Although the term is often used to refer to a one-sided presentation of information that distorts reality, it is actually a neutral word. (391).

20. d   "All of the above" is correct. Advertising is a type of propaganda, an organized attempt to manipulate public opinion, and a one-sided presentation of information that distorts reality. (391)

21. d   All of the answers are correct. The mass media are the gatekeepers to social movements; they engage in biased reporting, controlled and influenced by people who have an agenda to get across; and they are sympathetic to some social movements, while ignoring others; it all depends on their individual biases. (391-392)

22. c   According to mass society theory, as societies become more industrialized, bureaucratized, and impersonal, members of such mass societies experience feelings of isolation. For them, social movements fill a void because they offer them a sense of belonging. (392)

23. b   In order to turn a group of people who are upset about a social condition into a social movement, there must be resource mobilization. The resources that must be mobilized include time, money, people's skills, technologies such as direct mailings and fax machines, attention by the mass media, and even legitimacy among the public and authorities. (394)

24. d   The shift in the characteristics of culture and society over time is social change. (394)

25. d   All of the choices refer to technology; it includes items that people use to accomplish a wide range of tasks; the skills and procedures that are employed in the development and utilization of tools; and tools ranging from combs or hairbrushes to computers and the Internet. (394)

26. b   Ogburn called the process of change that involves new ways of seeing reality discovery. The other two processes he identified were invention and diffusion. (395-396)

27. b   The situation in which some elements of a culture adapt to an invention or discovery more rapidly than others is cultural lag. (396)

28. b   According to Karl Marx, the change-over to the factory system produced alienation. (397)

29. d   "All of the above" is correct. The automobile has changed the shape of cities; has stimulated mass suburbanization; and changed dating and courtship rituals. (397-398)

30. c   With the latest developments in medical technology, it is now possible for a doctor at one site to check the heart condition of a patient at another site; this new arrangement is referred to as telemedicine. (399)

31. b   One concern about the expansion of the information superhighway is social inequalities will become greater, both on a national and global basis. (399)

32. a   Dependency theory argues that the least industrialized nations became dependent on countries that have already industrialized. (400)

33.   c   Unilinear evolution theories assume that all societies follow the same path, evolving from simple to complex through uniform sequences. (400)

ANSWERS FOR TRUE-FALSE QUESTIONS

1. *True.* (383)
2. *True.* (383)
3. *True.* (383-384)
4. *False.* The term acting crowd is not applied just to violent activities such as lynch mobs or people engaged in riots. It includes such diverse activities as food fights! (383)
5. *True.* (385)
6. *True.* (387)
7. *False.* This is incorrect. They are short-lived and arise in situations of ambiguity, only to dissipate when replaced by factual information or a new rumour. (387)
8. *True.* (388)
9. *False.* This is called proactive social movement. (388)
10. *False.* Not all social movements seek to change society; some seek to change people. (388)
11. *True.* (389)
12. *False.* Propaganda and advertising are not quite different from one another. In essence, advertising is a type of propaganda because it fits both the broad and the narrow definition of propaganda perfectly. (391)
13. *False.* Deprivation theory and relative deprivation theory are not identical perspectives. Deprivation theory is based on the idea that people who are deprived of things deemed valuable in society join social movements with the hope of redressing their grievances. Relative deprivation theory asserts that it is not people's actual negative conditions that matter but, rather, it is what people think they should have relative to what others have, or even compared with their own past or perceived future. (393)
14. *False.* For some, moral shock, a sense of outrage at finding out what is really going on, is the motivating factor in deciding to join a social movement. (393)
15. *False.* There is evidence that at times the agent provocateur has been able to push the social movement into illegal activity. (393)
16. *True.* (394)
17. *False.* In the final stage of a social movement, decline is not always certain. Sometimes an emerging group with the same goals and new leadership will take over the "cause." (394)
18. *False.* Technology is a very powerful force for social change because it alters the ways in which those tools are used. (394)
19. *True.* (395-396)
20. *True.* (394)
21. *True.* (397)
22. *False.* Technology not only produces ideological changes, it can also transform social values. For example, today's emphasis on materialism depends on a certain state of technology. (397)
23. *True.* (397)
24. *False.* The use of computers in education is likely to increase, rather than decrease, the social inequality between school districts, because poor districts will not be able to afford the hardware. (399)
25. *True.* (399)
26. *True.* (399)

27. *True.* (400)
28. *True.* (446)

ANSWERS FOR FILL-IN QUESTIONS

1. At the root of collective behaviour is a background condition of TENSION and UNREST. (383)
2. In Blumer's model, the stage at which a sense of collective agreement about what should be done emerges is COMMON IMPULSES. (384)
3. Ralph Turner and Lewis Killian's term for the development of new norms to cope with a new situation, especially among crowds, is EMERGENT NORMS. (385)
4. A(n) RIOT is violent crowd behaviour aimed against people and property. (385)
5. A fear that grips large numbers of people that some evil group or behaviour threatens the well- being of society, followed by intense hostility, and sometimes violence, towards those thought responsible is MORAL PANIC. (387)
6. RUMOURS are unfounded information spread among people. (387)
7. When a fad lasts, it is called a FASHION. (388)
8. A(n) URBAN LEGEND is a story with an ironic twist that sounds realistic but is false. (388)
9. A religious social movement that stresses conversion, which will produce a change in the entire person, is an example of REDEMPTIVE SOCIAL MOVEMENTS. (389)
10. Social movements that span the globe, emphasizing changing conditions throughout the world rather than in just one country, are referred to as NEW SOCIAL MOVEMENTS. (390)
11. PROPAGANDA, in the sense of organized attempts to manipulate public opinion, is a regular part of modern life. (391)
12. MASS SOCIETY is an industrialized, highly bureaucratized, impersonal society. (392)
13. DEPRIVATION THEORY states that people who are deprived of things deemed valuable in society join social movements with the hope of redressing their grievances. (393)
14. SOCIAL CHANGE is the alteration of culture and societies over time. (395)
15. The combination of existing elements and materials to form new ones is INVENTION. (395)
16. DISCOVERY is a new way of seeing reality. (396)
17. According to Ogburn, because of travel, trade, or conquest, DIFFUSION of an invention or discovery occurs. (396)
18. The situation in which some elements of a culture adapt to an invention or discovery more rapidly than others is CULTURAL LAG. (396)
19. ALIENATION is Marx's term for workers' lack of connection to the product of their labour caused by their being assigned repetitive tasks on a small part of a product. (397)
20. The assumption that all societies follow the same path, evolving from the simple to complex, is central to UNILINEAR EVOLUTIONARY THEORY. (400)

ANSWERS TO MATCH THESE SOCIAL SCIENTISTS WITH THEIR CONTRIBUTIONS

1. b Charles Mackay: *herd mentality*
2. e William Kornhauser: *mass society theory*
3. f Robert Park: *social unrest and circular reaction*
4. a Ralph Turner and Lewis Killian: *emergent norms*

5. h Gustave LeBon: *collective mind*
6. d David Aberle: *classified social movements by type and amount of social change*
7. g Herbert Blumer: *the acting crowd*
8. c Richard Berk: *minimax strategy*
9. j James Flink: *studied the impact of the auto on U.S. society*
10. k William Ogburn: *three processes of social change*
11. i Karl Marx: *changes to factory system produced worker alienation*

GUIDELINES FOR ANSWERING THE ESSAY QUESTIONS

1. *Compare and contrast the early explanations of collective behaviour, as advanced by Charles Mackay, Gustave LeBon, Robert Park and Herbert Blumer, with more contemporary explanations developed by Richard Berk, Ralph Turner and Lewis Killian.*

    You must first discuss the elements that these different theories have in common and then move on to the elements that separate them. First, they are all trying to explain why people act differently when they are swept up into a crowd of people. That is probably the single point on which there is agreement. The early explanations focused on the individual and how he or she was affected by forces outside the self. Mackay talked about the herd, LeBon the collective mind, and Park the collective impulse. While Blumer developed a more systematic explanation, his also focused on events outside of the individual that impacted on his or her behaviour. In contrast, the more contemporary explanations focus on the individual as a rational actor. Berk depicts humans as calculating, weighing the costs against the benefits before taking any action. Turner and Killian also see humans as rational; in their work they argue that people develop new norms when confronted with new and unfamiliar situations. They also suggest that there are different kinds of participants, with different motives for being involved.

2. *Discuss the different theories about why people join social movements and consider how they could all be accurate.*

    The text presents three different theories about why people get involved in social movements—mass society theory, deprivation theory, and ideological commitment theory. Each provides us with an understanding of why some people get involved, but no one theory explains why all people get involved in social movements. One theory may be more appropriate at explaining why some people get involved in some social movements but not others. By using all three, we come away with a better understanding of the process by which individuals are drawn into social movements. You might also want to tie this discussion to that of the different types of members. For example, those people at the core of the movement may be connected for moral or ideological reasons, while those further out—the committed or less committed—may be involved because they feel isolated or alienated by modern society.

3. *Consider why the author combined the topics of collective behaviour and social movements in one chapter.*

    Different types of collective behaviour—riots, panics, rumors, fads, and urban legends—that are largely unorganized and temporary seem to be incompatible with social movements, which are generally well-organized and more long-lasting. So why did the author include these two within the same chapter? One point you might want to make is that both involve large numbers of people. Both emerge out of circumstances of situations of uncertainty, change, or ambiguity. And although one is fleeting while the other hangs around for a while, neither is institutionalized and lasts across generations.

4. *Choose a particular technology—you can use the automobile or the computer—and discuss the impact that it has had on Canadian society.*

The author presents five different ways in which technology can transform society—transformation of existing technologies; changes in social organization; changes in ideology; transformation of values; and transformation of social relationships. The first part of your essay should include some discussion of these five. Then you would want to discuss how one particular technology impacts these five different aspects of social life. The book provides information on automobiles and computers, but you could choose another one—television, airplanes, the telephone but to name a few significant ones. Remember to provide examples to illustrate each aspect.

5. *Discuss Ogburn's three processes of social change and provide examples to illustrate each.*

This is a fairly straightforward essay question. What you need to do is to discuss each of Ogburn's processes—invention, discovery, and diffusion—and provide examples for each.